CORPORATE LAW AND GOVERNANCE

(As Per the Syllabus of M.G. University, Kottayam, for B.Com., IInd Semester)

Prof. P. SARAVANAVEL,
M.Com., M.L.
Member, Bar Council of Tamil Nadu,
Chennai.

S. BALAKUMAR,
M.Com.
Consultant.

Himalaya Publishing House

MUMBAI • NEW DELHI • NAGPUR • BENGALURU • HYDERABAD • CHENNAI • PUNE • LUCKNOW • AHMEDABAD • ERNAKULAM • BHUBANESWAR • INDORE

First Edition : 2010

Published by : Mrs. Meena Pandey
for **HIMALAYA PUBLISHING HOUSE PVT. LTD.,**
"Ramdoot", Dr. Bhalerao Marg, Girgaon, **Mumbai - 400 004.**
Phones: 2386 01 70/2386 38 63, Fax: 022-2387 71 78
Email: himpub@vsnl.com
Website: www.himpub.com

Branch Offices:

New Delhi : "Pooja Apartments", 4-B, Murari Lal Street, Ansari Road, Darya Ganj, **New Delhi - 110 002.** Phone: 23270392, 23278631
Fax: 011-23256286

Nagpur : Kundanlal Chandak Industrial Estate, Ghat Road, **Nagpur - 440 018.**
Phone: 2738731, 3296733 Telefax : 0712-2721215

Bengaluru : No. 16/1 (Old 12/1), 1st Floor, Next to Hotel Highlands, Madhava Nagar, Race Course Road, **Bengaluru - 560 001.**
Phone : 22281541, 22385461, Telefax: 080-22286611

Hyderabad : No. 3-4-184, Lingampally, Besides Raghavendra Swamy Matham,Kachiguda, **Hyderabad - 500 027.** Phone: 040-27560041, 27550139, Mobile:- 09848130433

Chennai : No. 85/50, Bazullah Road, T. Nagar, **Chennai - 600 017.**
Phone: 044-28144004/28144005

Pune : First Floor, "Laksha" Apartment, No. 527, Mehunpura, Shaniwarpeth, (Near Prabhat Theatre), **Pune - 411 030.** Phone: 020-24496323/ 24496333

Lucknow : C-43, Sector - C, Ali Gunj, **Lucknow - 226 024.**
Phone: 0522-2339329

Ahmedabad : 114, "SHAIL", 1st Floor, Opp. Madhu Sudan House, C.G.Road, Navrang Pura, **Ahmedabad – 380 009.**
Phone: 079-26560126, Mobiles: 09327324149,09314679413

Ernakulam : 39/104 A, Lakshmi Apartment, Karikkamuri Cross Rd., Ernakulam, **Cochin – 622011**, Kerala.
Phone: 0484-2378012, 2378016, Mob.: 09344199799

Bhubaneswar : 5 Station Square, **Bhubaneswar (Orissa) - 751 001.**
Mobile: 9861046007, E-mail:- orissa@himpub.com

Indore : Kesardeep Avenue Extension, 73, Narayan Bagh.Flat No. 302, IIIrd Floor, Near Humpty Dumpty School, Narayan Bagh, **Indore (M.P.) 452 007** Mobile: 09301386468

DTP by : HPH Editorial Office, Bhandup (Kishori)

Printed by : Bengaluru

PREFACE

Legal framework is an important constituent of the business and corporate environment. No corporate entity can effectively work and survive without meeting legal obligations. The law relating to companies is perhaps the most significant and all pervasive amongst the various corporate legislations.

The Companies Act, 1956 which governs companies in India, is not only the longest piece of legislation which the country has produced so far but it is also a very complicated one. Following the British jurisprudence successive enactments and amendments on company law have been passed from time-to-time and the latest being the Companies (Amendment) Act of 2006.

Since the book is meant for students of Law, Commerce and Management Institutes, the authors have dealt with the provisions of the Act topic-wise for facilitating better understanding of the subject. Examples, case laws, etc., have been given to illustrate the provisions of the Act. Section numbers have been given at appropriate places to enable the readers to make reference to the Companies Act for further details. Suitable headings and subheadings have been given to focus the attention of the reader on important aspects of company law.

We acknowledge with gratitude our thanks to the learned authors whose writings have helped us to write this book. We also sincerely thank Shri Niraj Pandey of Himalaya Publishing House for his interest in this edition and for constant encouragement.

Any suggestions for the improvement of the book from the teachers and students will be accepted and incorporated in subsequent edition of the book.

Kumaran Illam
20 Parisutham Nagar,
First Cross Street,
THANJAVUR – 613007

P. SARAVANAVEL
S. BALAKUMAR

SYLLABUS

Module – 1 Company – Definition – Characteristics – Advantages and Disadvantages – Illegal Association – Corporate Veil – Lifting the Corporate Veil –Promotion – Promoter – Position – Incorporation – Procedure – Documents to be Filed – Certificate of Incorporation – Procedure – Effect of Registration – Pre-Incorporation Contract – Memorandum of Association – Articles of Association – Doctrine of Ultravires – Doctrine of Indoor Management – Doctrine of Constructive Notice – Prospectus – Registration – Contents – Statement in Lieu of Prospectus – Deemed Prospectus – Liability for Misstatement in Prospectus – Commencement of Business.

Module – 2 Management and Administration – Directors – Appointment – Qualification and Disqualification – Qualification Shares – Position of Directors –Powers and Duties – Retirement – Vacation of Office – Liabilities of Directors – Removal of Directors.

Module – 3 Corporate Governance – Meaning – Background – Importance – CG in India – Statutory Measures – SEBI Regulation – Clause 49 of Listing Agreement – Constitution of Board of Directors – Audit Committee – Provisions Under Section 292A of Companies Act – Remuneration of Directors – Board Procedure – CEO/CFO Certification – Role of Management – Information to Shareholders – CG Report – Non-mandatory Requirements, i.e., Chairman of Board – Remuneration Committee – Shareholders' Rights – Postal Ballet – Whistle-blower Policy – Benefits of Corporate Governance.

Module – 4 Company Meetings – Kinds of Companies – Essentials of Valid Meeting – Chairman – Agenda – Minutes – Quorum – Motion – Types of Motion – Interruption of Debate – Proxy – Poll – Modes of Poll – Resolution – Types of Resolution – Motion vs. Resolution.

Module – 5 Winding Up of Companies – Modes – Compulsory Winding Up – Grounds and Procedure – Liquidator – Duties and Functions – Contributories – Voluntary Winding Up – Types – Winding Up Under the Supervision of the Court – Effects of Winding Up – Defunct Companies.

CONTENTS

DETAIL CONTENTS

CHAPTER

1

Nature of a Company

The Company Legislation in India has developed on the lines almost parallel to the English Company Law. The Companies Act, passed from time-to-time in India have been following the English Companies Act with certain modifications to suit Indian conditions. The English Companies Act of 1844 is treated to be the first enactment on modern system of joint stock enterprises. On that very line, the first Indian Companies Act providing for the registration of joint stock companies was passed in the year 1850.

THE COMPANIES ACT, 1956

The Indian Companies Act, 1913 was repealed by the present Companies Act of 1956 which came into force on 1st April, 1956. The present Companies Act is based largely on the recommendations of the Company Law Committee (Bhabha Committee) which submitted its report in March, 1952. This Act is the largest statute ever passed by our Parliament. It consists of 658 Sections and 12 Schedules. The Act was amended several times since 1956. The latest amendments were effected in 2003 and 2006.

Applicability of the Act

The Act applies to the following companies:

1. The Companies formed or registered under the Act;
2. Companies formed or registered under previous companies laws, *i.e.*, existing Companies (Sec. 561);
3. Companies formed or registered under any previous companies laws to the extent and the manner declared in part IX of the Act (Sec. 562);
4. Unlimited Companies registered as limited companies in pursuance of any previous Companies laws (Sec. 563);

5. Unregistered Companies for the purpose of winding up under Part X of the Act (Secs. 582, 592 and 589);
6. Foreign Companies (Sec. 592 and 602);
7. Insurance Companies except in sofaras the provisions of the Companies Act 1956 are inconsistent with the provisions of Insurance Act, 1938 (IV of the 1938);
8. Banking Companies except in sofaras the provisions of the Companies Act, 1956 are inconsistent with the provisions of the Banking Companies Act, 1959 (X of 1949);
9. Companies engaged in the generating or supply of electricity except in sofaras the provisions of the Companies Act 1956 are inconsistent with the provisions of the Indian Electricity Act, 1910 or the Electricity Supply Act, 1948;
10. Such body corporate incorporated by any Act for the time-being in force, as the Central Government may, by notification in Official Gazette.
11. Government Companies (Section 617);
12. Nidhis or mutual benefit societies delcared as such by the Central Government by notification in the Official Gazette (Sec. 620-A(2)(b)).

The Act does not apply to

1. Companies established under the special Acts of Parliament such as the Reserve Bank of India, Life Insurance Corporation of India, State Transport Corporation, etc.
2. Partnership firms.
3. Cooperative societies.
4. Societies which are governed by the Societies Registration Act, 1860.
5. Trusts which are governed by the Indian Trust Act, 1882.

Definition of Company

The word 'company' ordinarily means an association of a number of individuals formed for some common object. According to Section 3(1)(i) of the **Companies Act, 1956** a company means, "A company formed and registered under this Act or existing company. An existing company means a company formed and registered under any of the previous Company Laws."

This definition is not exhautive and does not reveal the true characteristics of a company. **Lord Justice Lindley** has given a comprehensive definition of a company. According to him a company is, *"An association of many persons who contribute money or money's worth to a common stock and employed for a common purpose. The* *common stock so contributed is denoted in money and is capital of the company. The persons who contribute it or to whom it belongs are members. The proportion of capital to which each member is entitled is his share. Shares are always transferable although the right to transfer them is often more or less restricted."*

A company, thus, may be defined as *an incorporated association, which is an artificial person, having an independent legal entity, with a perpetual succession, a common seal, a common capital comprised of transferable shares and carrying limited liability.*

CORPORATION OR BODY CORPORATE

The term '**corporation**' (a word derived from the Latin word **'corpus'** which means 'body' or a **'body corporate'** is used for a company in the Companies Act, 1956.

"Body corporate" or "corporation" includes a company incorporated outside India but does not include (a) a corporation sole, (b) a registered cooperative society, and (c) any other body corporate (not being a company as defined in the Act) which the Central Government may specify in this behalf [Sec. 2(7)].

A body which has been or is incorporated under some statute and which has a perpetual succession, a common seal and a legal entity apart from the members constituting it, will come within the definition of the term 'body corporate'.

The use of the word "includes" in the definition must be understood as comprising something more than is defined. The term "body corporate' or "corporation" is thus wider in scope than the term "company" and is used in several Sections of the Act to denote not only a company incorporated in India but also a foreign company. It induces (a) public financial institutions as defined in Sec. 4-a, (b) nationalised banks, and (c) corporations formed under Acts of Parliament.

A *society registered* under the Societies Registration Act, 1860 does not fall within the definition of the term "body corporate" though it is a legal person capable of holding property and becoming member of a company ***(Board of Trustees vs. State of Delhi, A.I.R. (1962 S.C. 458).***

A ***corporation sole*** is a corporation constituted in a single person who, in right of some office or function, has corporate status. Examples of corporate sole are to be found in perpetual offices such as the President, Governors, Crown, Ministers, a public trustee. A corporation sole is not a "body corporate" for the purposes of the Companies Act, 1956. It is still a legal person and as such can member of a company ***(Star Tile Works Ltd. vs. Govindan, A.I.R. (1959) Ker.254).***

A ***corporation aggregate*** consists of a group of persons contemporaneously associated so that they form a single person, e.g., a limited company, a municipality, or a municipal corporation.

Characteristics of a Company

A company enjoys certain advantages over other forms of associations. Such advantages are termed as the characteristics of a company and are discussed as under.

1. Incorporated Association: A company must be incorporated or registered under the Companies Act. Minimum number of persons required for the purpose is seven, in case of a public company, and two, in case of a private company (Sec. 12). It may also be mentioned that as per Section 11, an association of more than ten persons, in case of banking business, and twenty in case of any other business, if not registered as a company under the Companies Act, or under any other law for the time-being in force, becomes an *illegal association.*

2. Artificial Person: The law divides persons into two kinds., (i) natural (human) persons, and (ii) legal persons. Legal or artificial persons are created by law (legal process). It can act only through natural persons. A company is created with the sanction of law and is not itself a human being, it is, therefore, called **artificial**; and since it is clothed with certain rights and obligations, it is called a **person**. A company is accordingly an *artificial person.*

3. Separate Legal Entity: A company formed and registered under the Companies Act is a distinct legal entity. It is a creation of law and is sometimes called artificial person being *invisible* and *intangible*. It is a fiction of law with legal, but *no natural or physical existence*. Though devoid of natural existence, it enjoys certain attributes of a natural person. It has individuality, has the power and be used in its own name, has the right to hold and alienate its own property and has the right to enter into contracts with third parties in its own name.

A company is not, like a partnership, a mere collection or aggregation of individuals. The company is, at law, of different person altogether from the subscribers to the memorandum of association. Its personality is separate and distinct from the personality of those who compose it. The property of the company is not the property of the shareholders. A company may contract with its own members.

The principle that a company is a legal entity separate from the individuals who compose it is very clearly illustrated in the leading case of ***Saloman vs. Saloman & Co. Ltd., ((1897)A.C.22).***

Saloman had a boot business. He sold the business to a company named Saloman & Company Ltd., which he formed. There were seven members–his wife, daughter and four sons who took one share each and Saloman himself who took 20,000 shares. The price paid by the company to Saloman was £ 30,000; but instead of paying him cash, the company gave him 20,000 fully paid share of one £ each and £ 10,000 in debentures. Owing to strike in the boot trade the company was wound up. The assets of the company amounted to £ 6,000 only. Debts amounted to £10,000 due to Saloman and secured by debentures and a further £ 7,000 due to unsecured creditors. The unsecured creditors claimed that as Saloman & Company Ltd., was really the same person as Saloman, he could not own money to himself and that they should be paid their £ 7,000 first. It was held by the House of Lords that Saloman was entitled to £ 6,000 as the company was an entirely separate person from Saloman. The unsecured creditors got nothing.

Thus, the Saloman's case established beyond doubt that in law a registered company is an entity distinct from its members, even if one person holds all the shares in the company. There is no differences in principle between a company consisting of only two shareholders and a company consisting of two hundred members. In each the company is a separate legal entity.

Lee vs. Lee's Air Farming Co.Ltd. (1960)3.All.E.R.420P.C.

Of the 3,000 shares in a company L held 2,999. He voted himself as the governing director and chief pilot at a salary. L was killed in an air crash while working for the company. His widow claimed compensation for personal injuries to her husband while in the course of his employment. It was argued that no compensation was due because L and Lee's Air Farming Co. Ltd. were the same person.

The Privy Council applied Saloman's case and said that L was a separate person from the company he formed and compensation was payable.

In Bacha F. Guzdar vs. The Commissioner of Income-Tax, Bombay (AIR (1955) SC. 74), the facts of the case were as follows:

The plaintiff (Mrs. Guzdar) received certain amounts as dividend in respect of shares held by her in a tea company. Under the Indian Income-tax Act, agricultural income is exempted from payment of income-tax. As income of a tea company is partly agricultural, only 40 per cent of the company's income is treated as income from manufacture and sale and, therefore, liable to tax. The plaintiff claimed that the dividend income in her hands should be treated as agricultural income up to 60 per cent, as in the case of a tea company, on the ground that dividends received by shareholders represented the income of the company.

Held by the Supreme Court, that though the income in the hands of the company was partly agricultural yet the same income when received by Mrs. Guzdar as dividend could not be regarded as agricultural income.

In Rajendra Nath Dutta vs. Shibendar Nath Mukherjee (1982) 52 Comp. Cas. 293 Cal.), a lease deed was executed by the directors of the company without the seal of the company and later a suit was filed by the directors and not the company to avoid the lease on the ground that a new term had been fraudulently included in the lease deed by the defendants, it was held that a director of the board of directors or managing director could not file a suit, unless it was by the company in order to avoid anytime which admittedly was executed by one of the directors and admittedly also the company accepted the rent. The case as made out in the plaint was not made on by the company but by some of the directors of the company and the company was not even a plaintiff. If the company was aggrieved, it was the company which was to file the suit and not the directors. Therefore the suit was not maintained.

4. Perpetual Succession: Unlike a natural person a company never dies. It is an entity with a perpetual succession. Its existence is not affected by the death, lunacy and insolvency of its members. A company is an immortal person. Members may come and members may go, but the company continues its operations unless it is wound up. The existence of the company is not affected by the death of all shareholders even. Thus, where all the members of a company were killed by a bomb, the company was deemed to survive.

Gower, L.C.B. in his book entitled ***'The Principles of Modern Company Law'*** gives an interesting example. He says, 'During the war all the members of one private company, while in general meeting, were killed by a hydrogen bomb. But the company survived, not even a hydrogen bomb could have destroyed it.

Section 34(2) of the Companies Act, 1956 gives the effect of registration of a company under the Companies Act by identifying the features it acquires as a consequence thereof. The section provides that:

From the date of incorporation mentioned in the certificate of incorporation, such of the subscribers of the memorandum and other persons, as may from time-to-time be members of the company, shall be a body corporate by the name contained in the memorandum, capable forthwith of exercising all the functions of an incorporated company and having perpetual succession and a common seal, but with such liability on the part of the members to contribute to the assets of the company in the event of its being wound up as is mentioned in the Act.

5. Limited Liability: Limited liability of members is another most important characteristic of a company. It is the reason why many people invest their money in limited companies. The liability of a members is limited. His liability is limited to the face value of shares subscribed to by him. If the shares are fully paid-up, his liability is nil. Where the assets of the company are insufficient to meet the claims of the creditors of the company, the members cannot be asked to pay anything more than what is due on the shares of the company held by them.

Unlimited Liability of a Member of a Limited Liability Company: In the following cases, a shareholder or member shall lose the privilege of limited liability:

(i) Where members of the company are reduced below the statutory minimum, viz., seven in case of a public company and two in case of a private company, and the company carries on the business for more than 6 months while the members are so reduced, every person who is a member during the time that it so carries on business after those 6 months and is aware of the fact that it is operating with fewer than the requisite number shall be personally liable for the whole of the debts contracted during the time (*Sec. 45*).

(ii) Where in the course of winding up, it appears that any business of the company has been carried on with intent to defraud creditors, the Court may declare the persons who were knowingly parties to the transaction personally liable without limitation of liability for all or any of the debts or other liabilities of the company (*Sec. 542*).

6. Common Seal: As a company is an artificial person it cannot sign its name on a contract. So it functions with the help of a seal. Common seal is used as a substitute for its signature. Every company must have a seal with its name engraved on it. A mere rubber stamp does not serve the purpose. Anything done under an agreement between the company and the third party requires recognition of the company in the form of an official seal unless exempted by the commit.

Seal of Company when to be used: The Articles of association of the company provide for putting the seal of the company on documents. Apart from those documents, the company seal is to be put on power of attorney, deed of lease, share certificates, debentures, debenture trust deed, deed of mortgage, promissory notes, negotiable instruments (except cheques), agreement of hypothecation, loan agreements with banks and financial institutions, contract of employment, guarantees issued by the company and all formal documents and documents executed on stamp papers:

Use of Seal-Outside India (Sec. 50): Where a company has any business or transaction in a place outside India a facsimile (exact-reproduction) of the common seal may be kept there. The seal should also contain the name of the place where the seal would be used. For such use these must be power in the Articles. A person must be properly authorised to use the seal, who shall sign his name, and also put the name of the place and the fact that he has been authorised to do so by the specified resolution.

As per Section 48, a company may, by writing under its common seal, empower any person, either generally or in respect of any specified matters, as its attorney, to execute deeds on its behalf in any place either in or outside India (Sec. 48(1)).

It further provides that a deed signed by such an attorney on behalf of the company and under his seal where sealing required, shall bind the company and have the same effect as if it were under its common seal (Sec. 48(2)).

7. Transferability of Shares: The shares of a company are freely transferable and can be sold or purchased in the share market. This is one of the reason and why people prefer to form companies than partnerships. A member by transferring the shares can get back his investment without withdrawing his money from the company. Section 82 of the Companies Act recognises the right of transferability of shares and provides that, "the shares or other interest of any member shall be *movable property* transferable in the manner provided for in the Articles of the company." However, in the case of private companies certain restictions are placed on the right of a shreholder to transfer his shares.

8. Capacity to Sue and be Sued: On incorporation a company acquires a separate and independent legal personality. As a legal person it can sue and be sued in its own name. A company may be sued for contempt of Court. It may be sued for malicious prosecution, infringement of copyrights and negligence. It may sue for injury done to its business reputation by deformation.

9. Right to acquire, possess and dispose of property in its own name. (The principle of separate property): Shareholders are not, in the eyes of the law, part owners of the undertaking. In India, this *principle of separate property* was best laid down by the Supreme Court in ***Bacha F. Guzdar vs. The Commissioner of Income Tax, Bombay*** *(Supra).* The Supreme Court held that a shareholder is not the part owner of the company or its property, he is only given certain rights by law, e.g., to vote or attend meetings, to receive dividends. Similarly, in ***R.F. Perumal vs. H. John,*** it was observed that no member can claim himself to be owner of the company's property during its existence or on its winding up. In another case, it was observed that even where a shareholder held almost entire share capital, he did not even have an insurable interest in the property of the company. It was the case of ***Macaure vs. Northern Assurance Co. Ltd. (1925) A.C. 619*** and the facts were as follows:

'**Macaure'** held all except one share of timber company. He had also advanced substantial amount to the company. He insured the company's timber in his personal name. On timber being destroyed by fire his claim was rejected for want of insurable interest. The court applying principle of separate legal entity held, the insurance company was not liable.

10. Not a Citizen: Although a company is a legal person having nationality, domicile and residence, but it is not a citizen. The nationality of a company is the country in which the company is incorporated. Its domicile refers to the place in which is registered and its residence refers to the place where the control and management of its business is exercised. The residential status has particular reference and importance in matters connected with taxation. A company can have only one nationality and one domicile but may have several residences at the same time. A company incorporated in India will be an Indian company even though its members may be foreigners. On this point, Justice Hidyatulla in ***State Trading Corporation of India Ltd. vs. C.T.O. and others (1963) AIR S.C. 1811*** very lucidly stated in the following words:

The members who form the incorporated company do not pool their status or personality. If all of them are citizens of India (according to the Citizen Act, 1955) the company does not become a citizen of India any more than, if all are married the company would be a married person.

As such, a company cannot, therefore, claim the protection of those *fundamental rights* which are explicitly guaranteed to citizens only, namely, the right of franchise. But, still they are sufficiently protected under the Constitution, for instances—their freedom of trade or commerce or right to equality, etc., cannot be curtailed, and no unjust discrimination in any matter whatsoever can be done against them. It is, thus, to be remembered that the company has a right to challenge the law if the law happens to violate fundamental rights of citizens.

11. Company's Actions Limited: A company cannot go beyond the powers of its charter–the memorandum of association. Its action is, therefore, limited. In order to enable it to carry out its actions without such restrictions and limitations, in most cases, sufficient powers are granted in the memorandum of association. But once the power have been laid down, it cannot go beyond unless the memorandum of associations is itself altered prior to doing so.

LIFTING THE CORPORATE VEIL

The general rule is that a company is a legal person and is distinct from its members. The principle is regarded as a curtain, a veil, or shield between the company and its members, thus, protecting the latter from the liability of the former. The veil is impassable as an iron curtain. But when the notion of legal entity is used to defeat public convenience, justify wrong, protect fraud or defend crime the law will regard the company as an association of persons. In these cases the law disregards the corporate entity and pays regard to the economic realities behind the legal facade. Here the court may look behind the artificial person – the company and take account of the personalities of natural persons – the cooperators.

Exceptions to the Principle of Separate Legal Entry in Saloman vs. Saloman & Co. Ltd.

The circumstances under which the controls may lift the corporate veil may be discussed under the following two heads:

(i) Exceptions under Common Law (Judicial Interpretations)

(ii) Statutory Exceptions.

Exceptions Under Comon Law

In these exceptional cases the law either goes behind the corporate personality to the individual members or ignores the separate personality of each company in favour of the economic reality constituted by a group of associated concerns. When this protection is taken away, the veil is said to have been lifted or pierced. The corporate veil is lifted in the following cases:

1. Determination of the Character: In times of war the court will lift the veil to see whether a company is controlled by enemy/aliens. Consequently, a company registered in England may be 'alien enemy' if its agents or the persons in fact control of its affairs, are alien enemies. ***(Daimler Company Ltd. vs. Continental Tyre & Rubber Ltd. (1916)2.A.C.3O7).***

2. Where Company is a Sham: The court will lift the veil where the company is a mere cloak or sham, i.e., where the device of incorporation is used for some illegal or improper purpose. Thus, where a seller of land sought to avoid an action for specific performance by transferring the land in breach of contract to a company he had formed for the purpose, the court treated the company as a mere sham and made the order applied for by the purchaser ***(Jones vs. Lipman (1962) I.W.L.R. 483).***

Where a company has been formed for some fraudulent purpose or is a "sham", the court will lift the corporate veil to identify the perpetrator of the fraud.

In ***Delhi Development Authority vs. Skipper Construction Company (P) Ltd. (1996) 4 SCALE 202,*** the skipper construction company failed to pay the full purchase price of a plot to Delhi Development Authority. Instead construction was started and space sold to various persons. The two sons of the directors who had businesses in their own names that they had separated from the father and the companies they were running had nothing to do with the properties of their parents. But no satisfactory proof in support of their claim could be produced. Held that the transfer of shareholding between the father and the sons must also be treated as a sham. The fact that the director and members of his family had created several corporate bodies did not prevent the court from treating all of them as one entity belonging to and controlled by the director and his family.

3. Where the Company is acting as the agent of the Shareholders: Where a company is acting as an agent for its shareholders, they will be liable for its acts. Whether it is acting as an agent is a question of fact in each case.

4. Protection of Revenue: The courts may disregard the corporate entity of a company where it is used for tax evasion or to circumvent tax obligation. Further, where it is desired to establish the residential status/character of a company for tax purposes the court will lift the veil and find out where its central management is, and the place determines its residence.

D was a rich man having dividend and interest income. He wanted to avoid surtax. For this purpose, he formed four private companies, in all of which he was the majority shareholders. The companies made investments and whenever interest and dividend incomes were received by the companies. D applied to the companies for loans which were immediately granted and never repaid. In a legal proceeding the corporate veils of all the companies were lifted, and the incomes of the companies treated as if they were of "D" **(In Re Dinshaw Maneckjee Petit (1927) Bom. 371)**.

5. Prevention of Fraud or Improper Conduct: Where a company has been formed by certain persons to avoid their own valid contractual and statutory obligation, the court may proceed on the assumption as if no company existed.

Example: A sold his business to B and agreed not to compete with him for a given number of years within reasonable local limits. A, desirous of re-entering business, in violation of the contractual obligation, formed a private company with majority shareholdings. B filed a suit against A and the private company and the court granted an injunction restraining A and his company with going ahead in the competing business *(Gilford Motor Co. vs. Horne (1933) I Ch. 935).*

Statutory Exceptions

1. Number of members below Statutory Minimum: If at anytime the number of members of a company is reduced below two in the case of private company or below seven in the case of a public company and it carries on business for more than six months while the number is so reduced, every member, who knows of this fact, will become liable to an unlimited extent for the payment of the whole debts of the company contracted during that time. *(Section 45)*

2. Where Prospectus includes a Fraudulent Misrepresentation. In case of a prospectus containing fraudulent misreperesentation as to a material fact, Sections 62 and 63 make the promoters, directors, etc., personally liable not only in damages but they may even be prosecuted in terms of fine up to Rs. 50,000 or imprisonment up to 2 years or both.

3. Failure to refund application money: Where the minimum subscription from applicants for shares shall be returned, if the amount is not refunded within 130 days of the opening of the issue, the directors shall be jointly and severally liable to repay that money with interest.

4. Company's name not mentioned on a Bill of Exchange, etc.: Where an officer of the company or any person signs on behalf of the company, a bill of exchange, promissory note, cheque or order for money or goods, wherein the name of the company is not mentioned, he is personally liable unless the amount is paid by the company. *(Section 147)*

5. Group Accounts: The principle of separate legal entity may be disregarded where a company has subsidiaries and group accounts must laid before the company in General Meeting when the company's own Profit and Loss Account and Balance Sheet is so laid. *(Section 212)*

6. Fraudulent Trading: If in the course of the winding up of a company it appears that any business of the company has been carried on with intent of defraud creditors, the court may declare that any persons who were knowingly parties to the carrying on of such business are to be personally liable for the debts and other liabilities of the company. *(Section 542)*

7. Investigation into related Companies: An inspector appointed under Section 239 by the Central Government may lift the veil of incorporation if he thinks it necessary for the purpose of investigation into the affairs of its subsidiary or holding company.

8. For investigation of ownership of a company: The separate legal entity may be disregarded under Section 247 of the Companies Act, 1956. This section authorises the Central Government to appoint one or more inspectors to investigate and report on the membership of any company for the purpose of determining the true persons who are financially interested in the company and who control or materially influence its policy.

9. Where in the course of winding up of a company, it appears that any business of the company has been carried on, with intent to defraud creditors of the company, or any other persons, or for any fraudulent purpose, the court on the application of the liquidator, or any creditor or contributory of the company, may, if it thinks proper, declare that any person, who are knowingly parties to the carrying on of the business in the manner aforesaid shall be personally responsible, without any limitation of liability, for all of any of the debts or other liabilities of the company as the court may direct (Section 542).

10. Where breach of Economic Offence is involved. In ***Santanu Ray vs. Union of India (1989) 65 Comp. Cas. 196 (Delhi)***, the Delhi High Court held that where a company had failed to pay proper excise duty, the individual directors could well be served notices to showcause so that the adjudicating authorities could determine as to which of the directors was concerned with the evasion of the excise duty by reason of fraud, concealment or wilful misstatement or suppression of facts, or contravention by the provisions of the Act and the Rules made thereunder.

11. Where company is used as a medium Avoid Welfare Legislation: A Ltd. had purchased shares of B Ltd. by investing a sum of Rs. 4,50,000. It was getting annual dividends in respect of these shares and the amount so received was shown in the profit and loss account of the company year after year. It was taken into account for the purpose of calculating the bonus payable to the workman of the company. Sometime in the course of the year 1968, the company transferred the shares of B Ltd. to C Ltd., a subsidiary company wholly-owned by it. C Ltd., had no other capital except the shares of B Ltd. transferred to it by A Ltd. It had no other business or source of income whatsoever except receiving the dividend on the shares of B Ltd. The dividend income from the shares of B Ltd. was not transferred to A Ltd. and therefore, it did not find place in the profit and loss account of the company with the result that the available surplus for the purposes of bonus to the workmen of the company became reduced.

Held that, it was true that in law the A Ltd. and C Ltd. were distinct legal entities having separate existence. But, that was not an end of the matter. Here new company was created wholly-owned by the principal company, with no assets of its own except those transferred to it by the principal company, with no business or income of its own except receiving dividends from shares transferred to it by the principal company and serving no purpose whatsoever except to reduce the gross profits of the principal company. These facts spoke for themselves. There could not be direct evidence that the second company was formed as a device to reduce the amount to be paid by way of bonus to workmen. The amount of dividend received by C Ltd. was, therefore, to be taken into account while computing A's profits available for bonus ***(Workmen of Associated Rubber Industry Ltd. vs. Associated Rubber Industry Ltd. (1986) 59 Comp. Cas. 134 SC).***

12. Where device of incorporation is used for some Illegal or Improper Purpose ***(PNB Finance Ltd. v. Shital Prasad Jain (1983) 54 Comp. Cas 66 (Delhi)).*** S, the financial adviser of a financing public limited company was given a loan of Rs. 15 lakh by the company to purchase immovable properties in Delhi. A pronote with regard to the same was also executed by S. S diverted the amount of the loan to three public limited companies floated by him and his son. These companies, in turn, applied the amount in purchasing immovable properties at New Delhi. The Delhi High Court refrained the defendants from in any manner alienating, transferring, disposing of or encumbering the properties in question.

13. To punish for contempt of Court ***(Jyoti Ltd. vs. Knawaljit Kaur Bhasin (1987) 62 Comp. Cas. 626 (Delhi)).***

14. For determination of technical competence of a Company ***(New Horzons Ltd. vs. Union of India (1995) I Comp. L.J. 100 (S.C.)).*** The Supreme Court in this case held that the experience of the promoters could well be considered as the experience of the company in determinating its technical competence.

Advantages of a Comopany

The company form of business organisation offers the following benefits:

1. Limited liability: The liability of the members of a company is limited to the extent of the unpaid amount on the shares held by them. The personal assets of a member are safe and he knows well in advance the extent of his liability. This encourages people to invest money in the shares and debentures of a company.

2. Stability: A joint stock company enjoys *perpetual existence*. Changes in its ownership and management do not affect the continuity of business. Therefore, company organisation is most suitable for businesses which take a long period of time to establish and become profitable.

3. Transferability of interest: Shares of a public limited company are freely transferable. This provides liquidity to investment encouraging even cautious and conservative investors to buy shares. Promotion of investment habit facilitates capital formation and industrial development of the country. Shares of a company are quoted in the stock exchange so that investors always know the value of their holdings.

4. Financial strength: A public limited company can accumulate huge financial resources. Its capital is divided into shares of small denomination so that people with limited means can be attracted to buy them. There is no limit on the number of members.

Different types of securities can be issued to mobilise funds from different kinds of investors. It enjoys high credit standing.

5. Economies of Scale: The company form of ownership offers infinite scope for expansion and growth. With continuous expansion and large financial resources at its command, a joint stock company can fully obtain the economies of large scale operations.

6. Efficient management: A company can employ specialists in different areas of business. Combined experience and judgement of the directors results in balanced and rational decisions. Centralisation of management helps in ensuring unity of action and continuity of policy. The expert professional managers can adopt a bold and adventurous approach to the problems of business.

7. Diffused risk: In a company, the risk of loss is spread over a large number of shareholders. Ownership is also diffused.

8. Tax relief: A company is required to pay income-tax at a flat rate. At higher levels of income, the tax liability is comparatively low. Several tax incentives are available for export promotion, development of backward areas, etc.

9. Goodwill: Due to strict statutory control and wide publicity of affairs, a joint stock company enjoys reputation and prestige in the society. Shareholders exercise voting right making for a democratic set up.

Disdavantages of a Company

1. Legal formalities: Formation of a company is a difficult, time consuming and expensive process. Several legal formalities are to be complied with. A large number of documents have to be prepared and filed with the registrar.

2. Lack of personal interest: A company is managed by directors and paid officials who cannot be expected to take personal interest in business. There is no direct link between effort and reward. There is lack of pesonal touch with shareholders, customers and employees.

3. Corrupt management: There is scope for fraudulent management in a company. Dishonest persons may indulge in several malpractices to deprive the investors of their hard earned money. The frequent 'securities scams' are glaring examples of how corrupt officials can exploit a company for selfish gains.

4. Oligarchy: In theory, management of a company appears to be democratic as directors are the elected representatives of shareholders. But in practice, company management is the worst example of oligarchy, i.e., rule by a few. Shreholders of a company are scattered and disunited. They do not take much interest in company meetings. Therefore, a small groupf of directors may misuse their powers and work against the interests of shareholders.

5. Excessive statutory control: The day-to-day working of a company is bound by elaborate rules and regulations. At every step, there is some formality to be observed and a penalty for infringement of the prescribed legal provisions. A lot of precious time and effort is wasted in complying with the statutory requirements.

6. Delay in decisions: There appears a lack of flexibility and prompt decisions in a joint stock company. All important decisions require the convening of meetings and passing of resolutions. As a result decisions may be delayed. Due to redtapism and bureaucratic procedures, there is little scope for individual initiative. Due to excessive redtape and top heavy administration, there is a tendancy to shift responsibility and play safe.

7. Conflict of interest: There are chances of conflicts between the various interest groups, e.g., equity shareholders, preference shareholders, debentureholders, financial institutions, directors, etc. Continuous conflict may affect the efficiency of management and the moral of employees. There is lack of unified approach of management due to changes in board of directors.

8. Unhealthy speculation: The share of a public company are dealt on stock exchange. Directors and officials are tempted to manipulate share prices to make easy personal gains. They may show artificial profits or losses. Reckless speculation reduces the goodwill of the company.

9. Social evils: A giant company may result in monopoly and concentration of economic power which is against public interest. The officials of the company may indulge in political corruption. They may misue their financial powers to seek undue favours for the company. They may spoil democratic institutions by making underhand payments to political parties and the bureaucrats.

The foregoing description reveals that the advantages of a company organisation are greater than its disadvantages. The company form of business organisation is best suited to those business which require huge capital investment, specialized management, long gestation periods and heavy risks.

Partnership and Company Distinguished

1. Registration: Registration of a firm is not compulsory even under the Partnership Act, 1932, whereas incorporation/registration of a company is compulsory under the Companies Act, 1956.

2. No. of members: Minimum two persons may constitute a partnership. Maximum membership in case of partnership doing banking business is ten persons and for other business is twenty persons, while minimum two and maximum fifty constitute private limited company and minimum seven and maximum, *i.e.*, unlimited constitute public limited company.

3. Legal Status: A firm has no individual legal status while a company has a separate legal existence of its own, and is considered a separate person from its members.

4. Property: Property of the firm is the property of the partners. On the contrary, in case of company property always belongs to the company, not to the shareholders.

5. Contracts: A partner cannot contract with the firm, whereas a shareholder can contract with the company.

6. Management: Management in case of partnership vests in the hands of the active or managing, partners, whereas in case of company, management vests in the board of directors elected by the shareholders.

7. Life: Partnership has no perpetual existence, whereas a company has a long and continued perpetual existence.

8. Liability: Partners of the firm are liable to an unlimited extent, (*i.e.*, in partnership there is an unlimited liability), whereas the liability of shareholders is usually limited.

9. Creditors: Creditors of the firm are also creditors of the partners individually, whereas in case of company creditors are only the creditors of company and not of the individual shareholders. Death of a partner may mean dissolution of partnership while the death of a shareholder or even of a director does not affect the existence of a company. Every partner is an agent of the other partner, whereas shareholder of a company is not an agent of the company.

10. Transfer of Interest: A partner cannot transfer his interest in the firm without the consent of the other partners. A transferee becomes a partner of the firm only with the consent of the other partners, whereas in case of a company's shares are easily and freely transferable and the transferee of a share becomes a member of the company, without any difficulty, on registration of transfer dead.

11. Statutory Obligations: Partnership has less statutory obligations under the Partnership Act, 1932, whereas a company is regulated strictly under the Companies Act, 1956.

QUESTIONS

Objective Type Questions

I. Fill in the Blanks

1. A company comes into existence only by the issue of___________.
2. Unlike a partnership firm, a company has ___________.
3. Formation of a Public Company requires minimum _________ number of members.

4. Solomon vs. Solomon case gives an example of __________ company.
5. Corporate veil reveals __________, __________, __________ of the company.
6. Corporate veil ensures ____________________ to the company.
7. Shares of Public limited company represent not less than ________ % of contribution from the public.
8. A company has perpetual __________.
9. Company approves all its transactions by using __________ of the company.
10. A Public Limited Company must have minimum of __________ number of directors.

[*Answers:* (1) Certificate of Incorporation; (2) an independent existence quite apart from the members; (3) Seven; (4) One man; (5) identity, composition and constitution; (6) legal immunity; (7) 25; (8) existence; (9) Common Seal; (10) Not less than 3]

II. State Whether the following Statements are True or False

1. A company has no personality of its own.
2. Association of persons is known as Body Corporate.
3. When there is disorder with regard to the functioning of a company, corporate veil has to be lifted.
4. A holding company has no control over its subsidiary.
5. When a Partnership firm does business other than banking with more than 20 persons, it becomes a company.
6. Certificate of Incorporation signifies the birth certificate of the company.
7. In order to know the status of a signatory belonging to a company, the corporate veil cannot be lifted.
8. The liability of members of a company become unlimited when the minimum number of membership gets reduced to less than 7 for a period of more than 6 months.
9. Certificate of Incorporation is a conclusive evidence for the legal personality of the company.
10. A company can file a writ petition in the High Court as a citizen of this nation.

[*Answers:* True : (3), (6), (8), (9); False : (1), (2), (4), (5), (7), (10)]

III. Multiple Choice Questions

1. Which of the following are not characteristics of a company?
   (a) It exists only in contemplation of law.
   (b) The members of the company can not be sued for the debts of the company.
   (c) It comes to an end on the death of all its members.
2. A company is a juristic person with a perpetual succession.
   (a) As such it acquires fundamental rights.
   (b) Its life depends on the life of its members.
   (c) It is created by a process of law and can be put to an end only by a process of law.
3. Since a company is regarded as an legal entity separate from its members,
   (a) the property of the company is the property of its shareholders.
   (b) the debts of the company are the debts of its shareholders.
   (c) the shareholders can enter into contracts with the company.
4. On a share of Rs. 100 of a company, a shareholder has already paid Rs. 70. His liability is now limited to
   (a) Rs. 100.
   (b) Rs. 30.
   (c) Rs. 70.
5. 5 of the 7 shareholders of a public company die. The company
   (a) comes to an end.
   (b) belongs to the 2 living members along with the legal representatives of the deceased members.
   (c) becomes a private company.

[*Answers:* 1 (c); 2 (c); 3 (c); 4 (b); 5 (b)]

Review Questions

1. Define the term "*Company*".
2. Is the company a citizen?
3. What is meant by perpetual succession and common seal ?
4. Discuss the principles of law laid down by the House of Lords in a case ***Salomon vs. Salomon & Company Ltd.***
5. What is corporate veil ?

6. *"Members of a limited company may nevertheless have unlimited liability".* Comment.

7. What do you mean by company? What are its characteristics?

8. What do you mean by lifting the corporate veil?

9. What are the circumstances under which the corporate veil can be lifted?

10. Briefly describe the statutory provisions as to the lifting of corporate veil.

11. Distinguish between company and partnership.

12. ".A *joint slack company is described as an artificial person created bv law, endowed with perpetual succession and common seal. But it does not differ from an ordinary individual in having a backbone and limbs".* Comment citing relevant case law.

13. *"The fundamental attribute of corporate personality is that the company is a legal entity distinct from the members".* Elucidate the above statement.

14. What is meant by corporate veil? State the circumstances under which it can be lifted. Refer to decided cases and provisions of the Companies Act. 1956.

15. What are the advantages of an incorporated company compared to partnership firms and unincorporated companies?

16. Write short notes on:
    (a) Perpetual Succession
    (b) Transferability of Shares
    (c) Limited Liability
    (d) Corporate Personality.

◈◈◈

CHAPTER 2

Kinds of a Company

The companies may be classified into several groups or kinds as discussed below:

1. From the point of view of *incorporation* [Chartered Companies, Statutory Companies and Registered Companies].
2. From the point of view of *liability* [Comapny with unlimited liability, Companies with limited liability - limited by shares and limited by guarantee].
3. From the point of view of *public interest* and *functions* [Private Companies, Public Companies, Government Companies and Associations not for Profit].

On the basis of incorporation companies are classified into two kinds, viz., Incorporated Companies and Unincorporated Companies. Then the Incorporated Comapnies are classified into Chartered Companies, Statutory Companies and Registered Companies. Secondly, the Registered Companies are classified into Companies Limited by Shares, Companies Limited by Guarantee and Unlimited Companies. All the three kinds of registered companies have two basic kinds, viz., Private Companies and Public Companies. Under certain circumstances, a Regitered Company may be either a Holding Company or a Subsidiary Company. A Registered Company may also be either a Government Company or a Foreign Company or an Association not for Profit.

Now let us discuss the different kinds of companies as shown in the chart given in the next page in detail.

I. Unincorporated Companies

The companies which are not incorporated under the Companies Act or Special Act or Charter are called "Unincorporated Companies". They are nothing but large partnerships. According to Sec. 11 of the Companies Act, 1956, if the number of members exceeds 10 in the case of banking companies and 20 in the case of other business companies, such companies cannot be legally formed without registration under the Companies Act and so they will be treated as *illegal associations*.

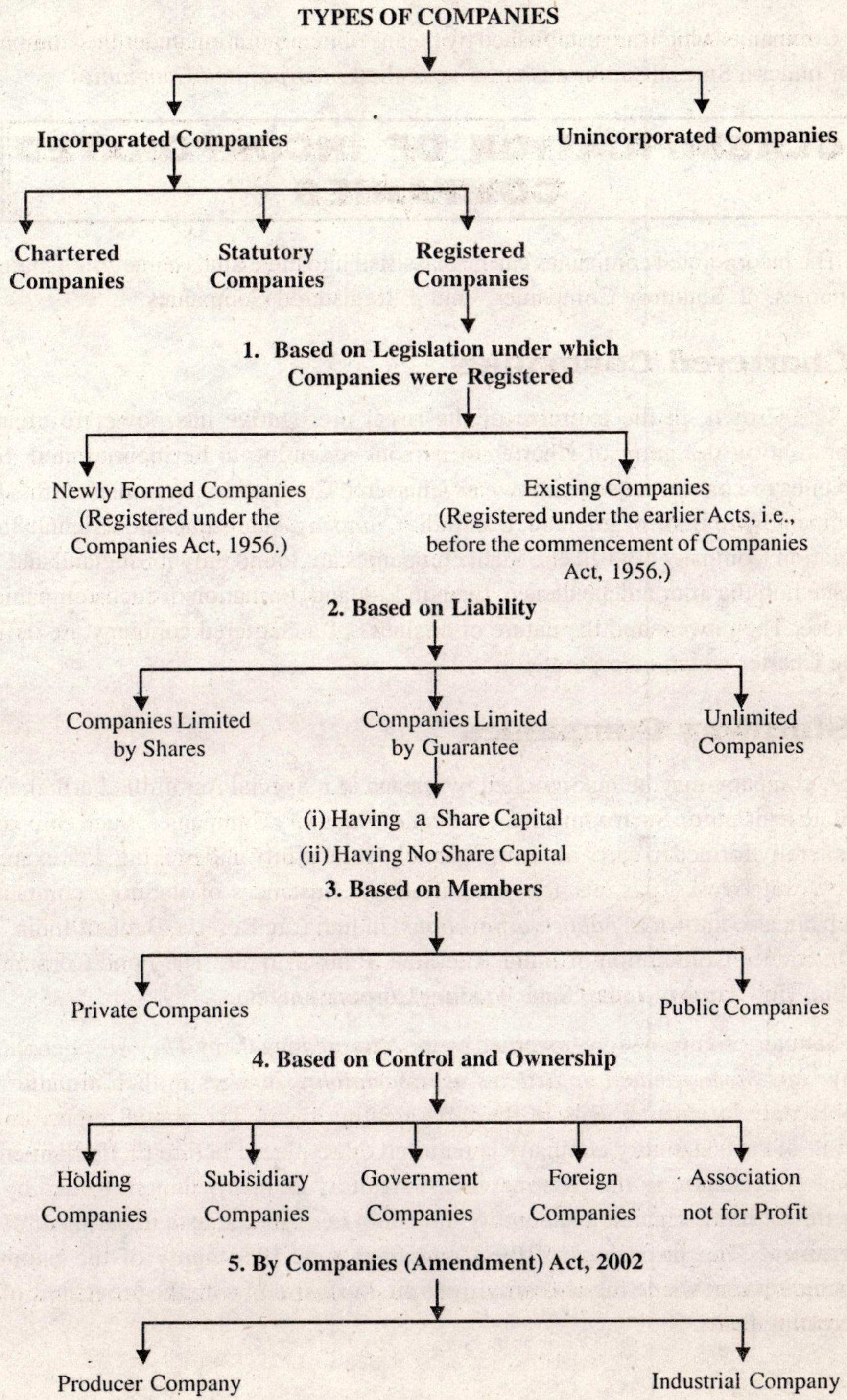
TYPES OF COMPANIES
Incorporated Companies
Unincorporated Companies
Chartered Companies
Statutory Companies
Registered Companies
1. Based on Legislation under which Companies were Registered
Newly Formed Companies (Registered under the Companies Act, 1956.)
Existing Companies (Registered under the earlier Acts, i.e., before the commencement of Companies Act, 1956.)
2. Based on Liability
Companies Limited by Shares
Companies Limited by Guarantee
Unlimited Companies
(i) Having a Share Capital
(ii) Having No Share Capital
3. Based on Members
Private Companies
Public Companies
4. Based on Control and Ownership
Holding Companies
Subisidiary Companies
Government Companies
Foreign Companies
Association not for Profit
5. By Companies (Amendment) Act, 2002
Producer Company
Industrial Company

II. Incorporated Companies

Companies which are established by means of incorporation under the Companies Act or under a Special Act or a Charter are called *Incorporated Companies*.

CLASSIFICATION OF INCORPORATED COMPANIES

The incorporated companies can be classified into three kinds namely: 1. Chartered Companies, 2. Statutory Companies, and 3. Registered Companies.

1. Chartered Companies

The Crown, in the exercise of the royal prerogative has power to create a corporation by the grant of Charter to persons assenting to be incorporated. Such companies or corporations are known as Chartered Companies. Examples of this type of companies are Bank of England, East India Company, Peninsular and Oriental Steam Navigation Company (1840), etc. Such companies are found only in England and find no place in India after independence. Even in England, formation of such companies is now rare. The powers and the nature of business of a chartered company are defined by the Charter which incorporated it.

2. Statutory Companies

A company may be incorporated by means of a Special Act of the Parliament or any State legislature. Such companies .are called Statutory Companies. Such companies are generally formed to carry out some special public utility undertaking. For example, railway, waterworks, gas, electric generation, etc. Instances of statutory companies, (which are also known as *public corporations*) in India are Reserve Bank of India. The Life Insurance Corporation of India, The State Bank of India, The Food Corporation of India, Unit Trust of India, State Trading Corporation, etc.

Statutory companies are governed by the Acts creating them. *They are not required to have any Memorandum or Articles of Association*. Changes in their structure are possible only by amendments in the Acts creating them. The annual report on the working of each statutory company is required to be placed before the Parliament or the State Legislature as the case may be. A statutory company though owned by the Government has a separate legal entity. It cannot be regarded as a department of the Government. The provisions of the Companies Act, 1956 apply of the Statutory companies except where the said provisions are inconsistent with the provisions of the Act creating them.

3. Registered Companies

Companies registered under the Companies Act, 1956, or the earlier Companies Acts are called *registered companies.* Such companies came into existence when they are registered under the Companies Act and a certificate of incorporation is granted to them by the Registrar. Section 12(2) provides that a company registered under the Act may be (i) a company limited by shares, (ii) a company limited by guarantee, and (iii) an unlimited company.

(i) Companies Limited by Shares: Companies limited by shares are the most common types of companies. This is a company where the liability of its members is limited by the amount, if any, unpaid on the shares respectively held by them. The liability can be enforced during the existence of the company as well as during the winding up. When the shares are fully paid-up, normally no further liability rests on them.

(ii) Companies Limited by Guarantee: This is a company where the liability of its members is limited to such amounts as they may respectively undertaken by the subscribers to the memorandum to contribute to the assets of the company in the event of its being wound up. In such companies, as in the case of companies limited by shares, the liability of its members is limited, but it is limited to the amount of guarantee undertaken by them. For example, the Madras Stock Exchange. A company limited by guarantee may or may not have a share capital. If it has a share capital, the liability of the members is two-fold; (i) Liability to pay the share amount, and (ii) the amount guaranteed. A guarantee company may not be suitable for ordinary business purposes. Clubs, trade associations, research associations and societies for promoting various objects are the examples of guarantee companies. Many of such companies obtain permission of the Central Government to dispense with the word 'limited'.

(iii) Unlimited Companies: It is a company where the liability of its members is not limited at all. In such a company the liability of each member extends to the whole amount of the company's debts and liabilities, but he will be entitled to claim contribution from other member or members . The Articles shall state the number of members with which the company is to be registered and if the company has a share capital, the amount of share capital with which the company is to be registered. Such companies are rarely formed/found.

Unlimited company shall not incorporate 'limited' as the last word. It need not have a capital, but it must file the Articles and the Memorandum. An unlimited company may be converted into a limited company either limited by shares or limited by guarantee.

PRIVATE AND PUBLIC COMPANIES

There are two varieties of each of these kinds of companies. A company may either a public company or a private company.

Public Company

A public company means a company which is not a private company. There must be at least seven persons to form a public company; however there is no maximum limit as to its number of shareholders or members. It is of the essence of a public company that its Articles do not contain provisions restricting the number of its members or excluding generally the transfer of its shares to the public or prohibiting any invitation to the public to subscribes for its shares or debentures. Generally, any member of the public may acquire shares in a public company on payment of the share money. The Articles of a public company may, however, contain restrictions on the issue or transfer of shares. The company remains a public company despite such restrictions. Only the shares of a public company are capable of being dealt in on a stock exchange. A company is a public company unless it is clear from its constitution that it is a private company.

Private Company

A private company means a company which by its Articles.

(i) restricts the rights to transfer its shares,

(ii) limits the number of its members to fifty (excluding members who are or were in the employment of the company), and

(iii) prohibits any invitation to the public to subscribe for any shares or debentures of the company. [Section 3(l)(iii)]

(iv) prohibits an invitation or acceptance of deposits from persons other than its members, directors or their relatives. (The Amendment Act, 2000)

Where two or more persons hold one or more shares in a company jointly, they shall be treated as a single member. There should be at least two persons to forms a private company and the maximum number of members in a private company cannot exceed 50. A private limited company is required to add the words "Private Limited" at end of its name. The Companies Act does not specify in what manner the right to transfer shares must be restricted. It is probably sufficient if the right is so restricted in the Articles. The restriction as to transfer of shares must be made applicable in respect of all shareholders. There cannot be any discrimination. If a private company fails to comply with any of the restrictions contained in the Articles, it ceases to be entitled to some of the privileges of a private company.

Special Privileges and Exemptions available to a Private Company

A private company enjoys certain special privileges which are not available to a public company. It is so because a private company the money is raised from few people and generally they belong to the same family or group or are close friends. Therefore, not much public interest is involved therein. But in case of public companies where the money is raised from general public and the number is quite large, it is necessary to safeguard their interests, hence several restrictions are imposed on public companies.

Following are the Special Privileges available to a private company:

1. A private company may consist of *two members only.*
2. A private company is *entitled to commence business* immediately on incorporation.
3. A private company may *allot shares without issuing a prospectus* or delivering to the registrar a statement in lieu of prospectus.
4. A private company can *give financial assistance for purchase of its shares* or its holding company's shares.
5. A private company is *not required to hold a statutory meeting* or file a statutory report with the registrar. [Sec. 165(10]
6. The provisions of Section 81 as regards *further issue of capital* do not apply to a private company.
7. A private company may issue not only equity and preference shares but also *deferred shares* or any other kind of *shares with disproportionate voting rights* as it may think fit.
8. Copies of *Balance Sheet and Profit and Loss Account* filed with the registrar cannot be inspected by the public.
9. A private company can have a *minimum of two directors.*
10. A director of a private company need not hold the *share qualification.*
11. Restrictions in regard to *overall managerial remuneration* imposed by Section 309 do not apply to a private company.
12. An *interested director* can participate in the board meeting and proceedings and exercise his vote.
13. All the directors may be appointed by a *single resolution.*
14. The directors of a private company need not file their *written consent* to act as directors or to take up their qualification share (Sec. 264 and 266).

15. The directors of a private company need not *retire by rotation* (Sec. 255).
16. Section 266 dealing with restrictions on *appointment or advertisement* of directors is not applicable to a private company [Sec. 266 (5) (b)].
17. Where a new director is to be appointed, a *special notice of fourteen days is* required. This provision is not applicable to a private company, unless it is a subsidiary of a public company [Sec. 257 (2)].
18. It need not have an *index of members* [Sec. 151 (1)]
19. Only two members, who are personally present at the *meeting,* shall form the quorum unless the Articles provide for a larger number [Sec. 174 (1)]
20. In case of a private company, *poll can be demanded* by one person present in person or by proxy, if not more than seven persons are present; if the number of members present is more than seven, two members present in person or by proxy can demand a poll [Sec. 179 (1) (b)].

Loss of Privileges by a Private Company

Section 43 provides that if a private company contravenes any of the conditions included in its Articles as per Section 3(1) (iii), then it will be treated as if it is a public company and it will then result in loss of privileges and exemptions to which it is normally entitled to.

The proviso to Section 43 states that if the contravention of any of the restrictions contained in the Articles was accidental, or if the Company Law Board is satisfied that it is just and equitable to grant relief, it may relieve the company from these consequences on the application by the company or any other interested person.

The privileges mentioned above are not available to a private company which is a subsidiary of public company. It also applies to a private company which become a public company by virtue of Section 43-A. Further, a private company ceases to be entitled to privileges above mentioned if, having made provisions required of a private company in its Articles, the company makes a default in complying with any one of those provisions.

DISTINCTION BETWEEN A PUBLIC COMPANY AND A PRIVATE COMPANY

1. Minimum Number of Members: The minimum number of persons required to form a public company is seven, whereas in a private company it is only two.

2. Maximum Number of Members: There is no limit as to maximum number of members of a public company, but a private company cannot have more than fifty members excluding past and present employees.

3. Commencement of Business: A private company can commence its business as soon as it is incorporated. But a public company shall not commence its business immediately unless it has been granted the certificate of commencement of business.

4. Invitation to public: A public company by issuing a prospectus may invite public to subscribe to its share/debentures to deposit money (public deposits), whereas a private company cannot extend such invitation to the public.

5. Transferability of Shares: There is no restriction on the transfer of shares in the case of a public company, whereas a private company by its Articles must restrict the rights of members to transfer the shares.

6. Number of Directors: A public company must have at least three directors whereas a private company may have two directors.

7. Statutory Meeting: A public company must hold a statutory meeting and file with the registrar a statutory report. But in a private company there are no such obligations.

8. Restrictions on Appointment of Directors: A director of a public company shall file with the registrar a consent to act as such. He shall sign the memorandum and enter into a contract for qualification shares. He cannot vote or take part in the discussion on a contract in which he is interested. Two-thirds of the directors of a public company must retire by rotation. These restrictions do not apply to a private company.

9. Managerial Remuneration: Total managerial remuneration in the case of a public company cannot exceed 11% of net profit, but in the case of inadequacy of profits a minimum of Rs. 50,000 can be paid. These restrictions do no apply to a private company.

10. Further Issue of Capital: A public company proposing further issue of shares must offer them to the existing members. A private company is free to allot new issues to outsiders.

In addition to the above, a private company enjoys some additional or special privileges. A public company enjoys no such privileges.

CONVERSION OF PRIVATE COMPANY INTO A PUBLIC COMPANY

Conversion by Resolution

A private company may deliberately choose to become a public company. If a private company deletes from its Articles the requirements of Section 3(i)(iii) by passing a *special resolution,* the company will cease to be a private company from the date of the alteration of the Articles.

When a private company chooses to become a public company it will have to comply with all the provisions of the Companies Act applicable to a public company. Within 30 days of its becoming a public company, it shall file with the Registrar a Prospectus or a Statement in lieu of prospectus.

Increase in Members/Directors: If the number of members is below seven, steps should be taken to increase it to at least seven, whilst the number of directors should be increased to at least three, if there are only two directors.

The word *"Private"* is to be deleted before the word *"Limited"* in the name.

Within thirty days of the passing of the special resolution altering the Articles, the company shall file with the registrar (i) a printed or typewritten copy of the special resolution, and (ii) a prospectus or a statement in lieu of prospectus.

If default is made in filing the resolution and the Prospectus or the Statement in lieu of prospectus, the company and every officer in default shall be liable to a fine up to Rs. 500 for every day of default.

Conversion by Default

A private company is entitled to certain privileges and exemptions. It can enjoy those privileges as long as it complies with the requirements of its definition as given in Section 3(i)(iii). Where any default is made in complying with these provisions (*viz.*, restriction on transfer of shares, limitation of the number of members to 50 and prohibition of invitation to public to buy shares and debentures), the company loses the privileges and the exemptions and the provisions of the Act apply to the company as if it was not a private company. However, the company may be relieved of the consequences on an application made to the court, and the court is satisfied that the failure to comply with the conditions is not wilful or that it is just and equitable to grant relief. [Sec.43]

Conversion by the Operation of Law

Private companies are exempted from the operation of several sections of the Act and enjoy certain privileges on the ground that they are family concerns in which the public is not directly interested. As public money is invested in such companies, there is no reasons for treating such companies as private companies. The law tries to tackle the problem by creating another type of company, *viz.*, *Deemed Public Company*, Actually it is a private company which, under certain circumstances, can be treated by the laws as the public company.

Firstly, where a private company is a subsidiary of a public company, it is dealt with as a public company for all purposes of the Act.

Companies Deemed to be Public

Secondly, the Companies Amendment Act, 1960, has introduced a new Section 43-A which provides that private companies which employ public money to an appreciable extent should be subject to the same restrictions and limitations as to disclosure and otherwise—as applied to public companies.

Share Capital Holding Criteria: According to Section 43-A, a private company will become a public company if 25% or more of its paid-up share capital is held by one or more bodies corporate. In calculating the above percentage the shares held by a Bank as trustees or executor of a deceased shareholder shall not be taken into account. In the following cases a private company will not be treated as a public company.

(a) If the entire paid-up share capital is held by another single private company or by one or more bodies corporate incorporated outside India.

(b) If the shares are held by one or more of the body corporates incorporated outside India, which is incorporated in India would have been private companies provided that the Central Government by order so directs.

(c) Where the shareholding of the company is itself a private company or all the shareholding companies are private companies and no other company holds shares in any such company and the total number of shareholders in all these companies including the private company does not exceed fifty.

Turnover Criterion: Section 43-A has been further amended by the Companies Amendment Act, 1974, by adding Sub-Sections (IA) and (IB). Section 43-A (IA) provides the *turnover criterion,* that is where the *average annual turnover is not less than rupees 25 crore,* or more for three consecutive financial years, the private company will become a public company after the expiry of three months form the period at the close of which the accounts show that amount of turnover.

According to Section 43-A (1B) where a private company holds not less than 25 per cent of the paid-up share capital of a public company it will become a public company from the date it holds such shares.

Where a private company has become a public company by reasons of the foregoing provisions, it may include in its Articles provisions relating to the matters specified in Section 3(i)(iii). Such a private company shall within three months from the date on which it has become a public company inform the registrar that it has become a public company. On such informations the registrar shall delete the word 'Private' before the word 'Limited' and shall also make necessary amendments in the documents of the company. In case of non-compliance, the company and every officer who is in default, shall be liable to a fine up to Rs. 500 for each day of default.

Acceptance of Deposits criterion

Sub-Section 1C of Section 43 has been added by the Amendment Act, 1988. This sub-section provides that if a private company invites deposits from public by advertisement or renews deposits from public, other than its members, directors or their relatives, it shall become a public company.

Thus, the position under Sec. 43-A, may be summarised as follows:

A private company shall be deemed as a public company in the following cases:

(a) where it invites public deposits through an advertisement;

(b) it holds 25% or more of the paid-up share capital of a public company;

(c) it has public company(ies) or deemed public company(ies) as its shareholders holding in aggregate 25% or more of its paid-up share capital;

(d) its average annual turnover for the last three consecutive financial years is Rs.25 crore or more.

A private company which has become a public company by virtue of these provisions shall continue to be so until it has with the approval of the Central Government and in accordance with the provisions of the Act again become a private company.

Privileges of Section 43-A Companies: The Articles of Association of a private company which has become a public company by virtue of Section 43A may continue to have the restrictions relating to the matters specified in Section 3(1) (ii) and the number of its members may be or may at anytime be reduced below seven. Again, such a company may have two directors as minimum.

The category of a company deemed to be public has been eliminated by the Companies (Amendment) Act, 2000 w..e.f. 13.12.2000. It has now been provided that any such deemed to be public company which becomes private company on or after the commencemtn of the Companies (Amendment) Act, 2000. On such information been received, the Registrar shall institute the words "Private Company" for the words "Public Company" in the name of the company in the companies register and shall also make necessary alternations in the Certificate of Incorporation issued to the company and its Memorandum of Association within 4 weeks from the date of application made by the company.

Conversion of Public Company into Private Company

A public company may be converted into a private company be altering the Articles incorporating the three restrictions mentioned in Sections 3(i)(iii). Such alteration of Articles will be made by a *special resolution* and the *approval of the Central Government* is necessary, for such alteration. A copy of the special resolution has to be *filed with the registrar* within 30 days and when the approval of the Central Government for conversion of a public company into private company is obtained a copy of such approval shall also be filed within one month. A printed copy of the Articles as altered shall be filed by the company with the registrar within one month of the date of receipt of the order of approval.

The word "Private" should be added before "Limited".

HOLDING COMPANY AND SUBSIDIARY COMPANY

A company which controls another company is known as the *'holding company'* and the company so controlled is termed as *'subsidiary company'*.

Section 4 of the Companies Act, 1956 provides that a holding company is one if it —

(i) controls the composition of board of directors of another company; or

(ii) holds more than half of the nominal value of equity share capital of another company; or

(iii) is a subsidiary of any company which is in turn a subsidiary of another company.

Example: Company B is a subsidiary of company A, and company C is a subsidiary of company B. Company C will be a subsidiary of company A.

(iv) controls more than 1/2 of the total voting power of the other company.

The requirement as to be the control of the composition of the board of directors is satisfied if the member company has independent power to appoint or remove all or a majority of the directors. Such power is deemed to exist where.

(a) a persons cannot be appointed to a directorship without the exercise in his favour of the power of appointment held by the company.

(b) a person's appointment to directorship follows necessarily from his appointment as director or manager.

(c) the directorship is held by an individual nominated by the company or by any of its subsidiaries.

A subsidiary company cannot hold shares or be a member of its holding company except as a legal representative of a deceased member of the holding company or any trustee.

Thus, in order to be a holding company, a company must either control the composition of the board of directors or hold more than half of the nominal value of the equity share capital of another company.

GOVERNMENT COMPANY

Section 617 of the Companies Act defines a government company as a company in which not less than 51 per cent of the paid-up share capital is held by the Central Government, or by any State Government, or Governments, or partly by the Central Government and partly by one or more State Governments. It also includes a company which is a subsidiary of a government company.

Certain special provisions have been laid down in the Act regarding a government company. They are discussed below:

1. The auditor of a government company shall be appointed or re-appointed by the Central Government on the advice of the Comptroller and Auditor General of India. The Comptroller and Auditor General of India will have the power to direct the manner in which the company's accounts shall be audited by the auditor. He shall also have the power to conduct a supplementary or test audit of the company's accounts by such person as he may authorise in this behalf.

2. The Auditor will submit a copy of the audit report to the Comptroller and Auditor General of India who may comment upon or supplement the audit report in such manner as he may think fit. Such comments or supplementary report shall be placed before the Annual General Meeting along with the audit report. [Section 619]

3. Where the Central Government is a member of the government company it shall cause an annual report on the working and affairs of the company to be prepared and laid before both Houses of Parliament along with the audit report and the comments, if any, of the Comptroller and Auditor General of India. The report shall be prepared within 3 months of the Annual General Meeting. Where the State Government is also a member, the report shall also be laid before the State Legislature. But where the Central Government is not a member of the government company, the State Government concerned shall cause the above documents prepared and laid before the State Legislature. [Section 619-A]

4. The Companies Amendment Act, 1974 has enlarged the concept of government company for the purpose of audit. Section 619-B has been inserted and it provides that the provisions of Section 619 for the purposes of audit shall apply to a company in which at least 15% of the paid-up share capital is held by the one or more the following or any combination thereof:

(a) the Central Government and one or more government companies;

(b) any State Government or governments and one or more Government Companies;

(c) the Central Government, one or more State Governments and one or more government companies;

(d) the Central Government and one or more corporation owned or controlled by the Central Government;

(e) the Central Government, one or more State Governments and one or more corporations owned or controlled by the Central Government;

(f) one or more corporations owned or controlled by the Central Government or any State Government;

(g) more than one government company. [Section 619-B]

5. The Central Government may by notification in the Official Gazette direct that any of the provisions of the Act (except the above noted provisions) shall not apply to any government company or shall apply with such exceptions, modification and adaptations as may be specified in the notification. A copy of every such notification shall be laid down before both Houses of the Parliament for a period of not less than 30 days while they are in session. Since the said period of 30 days cannot, sometimes be completed in one session, Section 620 has been amended by the Companies Amendment, Act, 1977 to permit the period of 30 days to be completed in one session or in two or more successive sessions.

FOREIGN COMPANIES

It means a company incorporated outside India having a place of business in India. The Companies Amendment Act, 1974 provides that where not less than 50% of the share capital is held by Indian citizens and/or companies incorporated in India it shall have comply with such of the provisions of the Act as may be prescribed as if it were a company incorporated in India.

1. Documents: Every foreign company shall, within 30 days of the establishment of the business in India, furnish with the registrar for registration the following documents:

(i) A certified copy of the Charter, Statute, Memorandum and Articles of the company, containing the constitution of the company and if the instrument is not in English language a certified translation thereof.

(ii) The full address of the registered or principal office of the company.

(iii) A list of the directors and secretary of the company with particular as to name, nationality, etc.

(iv) The names and addresses of any person or persons resident, in India, authorised to accept service of legal processes and notices on behalf of the company.

(v) The full address of the principal place of business in India. [Section 592]

Where any change occurs in the above particulars, the company shall file with the registrar a return of such alterations within the prescribed time. [Section 593]

2. Accounts: Every foreign company, unless exempted by the Central Government, shall file with the registrar every year three copies of its Balance Sheet and Profit and Loss Account and other documents required under the Act. Such documents must be in English language. Apart from these documents, it shall also send to the registrar, three copies of a list in the prescribed form of all places of business established by the company in India. [Section 594]

3. Name: Every foreign company shall exhibit on the outside of every office or place of business its name and the country of incorporation in English and in one of the local language. It shall also have the name of the company and the country of incorporation stated in English on business letters, bill heads, and letter papers and on all notices and other official publications of the company. It shall also state the name of the country in which it is incorporated on every prospectus. If the liability of the members is limited it must be stated in every prospectus and in all official publications and must be exhibited outside every office or place of business. [Section 595]

4. Service on Foreign Company: Any notice or other document may be served on a foreign company by addressing the same to the authorised person of the company and either left at his address or sent to the addressed by post. [Section 596]

5. Delivery of Documents: All documents required to be filed by the foreign company shall be delivered to the Registrar at New Delhi and also to the registrar of the state in which the principal place of the business of the company is situated [Section 597]

6. Registration of Charges: The provisions of Sections 124 to 145 relating to registration of charges apply to the foreign company in respect of charges created on property in India. Further the provisions relating to annual returns [Section 159], inspection of books of account [Sections 209 and 209-A], special audit [Section 233-A], audit of cost accounts [Section 233-A], investigations [Sections 234 to 246] shall apply to a foreign company in respect of its Indian business, [Section 600]

7. Requirements as to the Prospectus: Section 603 provides that the prospectus of a foreign company to be circulated or distributed in India shall contain the following particulars.

(a) The instrument constituting or defining the constitution of the company.

(b) The statute under which the company was incorporated.

(c) An address in India where the said instrument, enactment, etc., can be inspected.

(d) The date on which and the country in which it is incorporated.

(e) The address of its principal office, if any, in India.

The above particulars are in addition to those required to be specified in a prospectus to be issued by any company incorporated under the Act. [Section 603].

8. Winding up: All foreign companies carrying on business in India may be wound up by an order of the court as unregistered companies. It can also be wound up even if it has been dissolved or cease to exit according to its own law of incorporation [Section 584]

MULTINATIONAL COMPANIES

Multinational corporation refers to an organisation which is having its headquarters in one country and have business operations in other countries. This means, this type of organisation will have business across many countries. Some suggest that a multinational organisation should be at least operating in six countries with minimum of 20% of its business in those countries. For our purpose we will consider a company with business in more than one country as a multinational company. For example, Sandoz India Limited, Hindustan Levers, Richardson Hindustan, Ranbaxy, etc., can be called as multinational organisations.

ONE-MAN COMPANY (FAMILY COMPANY)

These are the companies in which one man holds virtually the whole of the share capital with a few extra members holding the remainder, who may be his relations or nominees. Being the largest holder such a person is generally the sole or the managing director and enjoys complete control over the company. This is done with a view to fulfil the statutory requirement of at least seven members in the case of a public company and at least two members in the case of a private company. He is, thus, in a position to enjoy the profits of the business with limited liability. Such types of companies are perfectly valid and not illegal. As already established in ***Saloman vs. Saloman & Co. Ltd.*** such companies are legal entities distinct from the members.

Non-Trading Companies or Licensed Companies or Companies not for Profit

Section 25 of the Companies Act relates to licensed company. These licensed companies are formed for a non-trading object or for a noble cause, like the promotion of art, education, commerce, etc. Charitable associations, sports clubs, trade associations, chambers of commerce, etc., are examples of companies not for profit. Organised markets for commodities or securities also can be formed as companies not for profit. The object of such a company is not to make profits and distribute dividends. Such companies may or may not have share capital. Membership fees, entrance fees, donations, grants and subsidies from the government are enough to finance their establishment expenses and routine management.

Such companies can be formed only on obtaining the licence from the Central Government or State Government, i.e., they can be registered only after such licence.

Main Features of Licensed Companies

1. On registration, it enjoys certain exemptions and privileges as compared to an ordinary limited company.
2. Such companies are allowed to exclude the words 'Limited' or 'Private Limited' from their names.
3. They are registered without paying any stamp duty in connection with their Memorandum and Articles of Association,
4. A licensed company must apply its profits, if any, or other income in promoting its object and must prohibit payment of any dividend to its members.
5. As soon as it obtains a licence and is registered accordingly, it will have the same privileges and obligations that a limited company has under the Companies Act, 1956.
6. This licence is revocable by the Central Government, and on revocation, the Registrar of Companies will put "Limited" or "Private Ltd." against the company's name in the Register of Companies maintained by him. But before taking such a step, the Central Government has to give a written notice of its intention to revoke the licence and also an opportunity to be heard in the matter.

Note: *Even a patnership firm can be a member of such a company, in its own name. But on the dissoluation of partnership, its membership of the company will come to an end [Sec. 25 (4)].*

PRODUCER COMPANIES

Till recently, the Companies Act, 1956 recognised only three types of companies, namely, companies limited by shares (subdivided into public limited and private limited companies), companies limited by guarantees and unlimited companies. With the coming into force on February 6 of the **Companies (Amendment) Act, 2002,** a fourth category, *'producer companies,'* finds a place in the Act.

The new concept of producer companies is based on the recommendations of an expert committee led by noted economist, Y. K. Alagh. The committee was asked (a) to frame a legislation that would enable incorporation of cooperatives as companies and conversion of existing cooperatives into companies and (b) to ensure that the proposed legislation accommodated the unique elements of cooperative business with a regulatory framework similar to that of companies.

The new type is termed as *'producer company'*, to indicate that only certain categories of persons can participate in the ownership of such companies. The members have necessarily to be 'primary producers,' that is, persons engaged in an activity connected with, or related to, primary produce.

Meaning of Primary Produce

In terms of the Act it is a produce of farmers arising from agriculture including animal husbandry, horticulture, floriculture, pisciculture, viticulture, forestry, forest products, revegetation, bee raising and farming plantation products, produce of persons engaged in handloom, handicraft and other cottage industries, byproducts of such products, and products arising out of ancillary industries.

Formation: Any ten or more individuals, each of them being a producer, that is, any person engaged in any activity connected with primary produce, any two or more producer institutions, that is, producer companies or any other institution having only producers or producer companies as its members or a combination of ten or more individuals and producer institutions, can get a producer company incorporated under the Companies Act.

The companies shall be termed as limited and the liability of the members will be limited to the amount, if any, unpaid on the shares.On registration, the producer company shall become as if it is a private limited company with the significant difference that a minimum of two persons cannot get them registered, the provision relating to a minimum pail-up capital of Rs.1 lakh will not apply and the maximum number of members can also exceed 50.

Members' equity cannot be publicly traded but be only transferred. As such, "producer companies would not be vulnerable to takeover by other companies or by MNCs."

Objects: The objects of producer companies shall include one or more of the eleven items specified in the Act, the more important being:

(i) Production, harvesting, procurement, grading, pooling, handling, marketing, selling, export of primary produce of members or import of goods or services for their benefit;

(ii) Processing including preserving, drying, distilling, brewing, venting, canning and packaging of produce of its members; and

(iii) Manufacture, sale or supply of machinery, equipment or consumables mainly to its members.

The other objects include rendering technical or consultancy services, insurance, generation, transmission and distribution of power and revitalisation of land and water resources; promoting techniques of mutuality and mutual assistance, welfare measures and providing education on mutual assistance principles.

It is to be noted that private limited or public limited companies are not hamstrung by such restrictions as to their objectives, provided they are legal.

INDUSTRIAL COMPANY

Induastrial company is a new kind of company inserted by the companies (Second Amendment) Act, 2002, with effect from 01-04-2003. **"Industrial Company"** means a company, which owns one or more industrial undertakings [Sec. 2(19AA)].

"Industrial undertaking" means any undertaking, pertaining to any industry carried on in one or more factories or units by any company, as defined in Clause (aa) of Section 3 of the Industries (Development and Regulation) Act, 1951 (65 of 1951) but does not include a small-scale industrial undertaking as defined in Clause (j) of that Section [Sec. 2(19AB)].

Sick Industrial Company

The Companies Amendment Act, 2000 has incorporated several provisions regarding sick industrial companies. A sick industrial company means an industrial company which has:

(i) the accumuleted losses in any financial year equal to fifty per cent, or more of its average net worth during four years immediately proceeding such financial year; or

(ii) failed to repay its debts within any three consecutive quarters on demand made in writing for its repayment by a creditor or creditors of such company.

ILLEGAL ASSOCIATIONS

Unincorporated Associations/Companies

Prohibition of Large Perternships: The aim of Companies Act is to prevent the mischief arising from large trading undertakings being carried on by large fluctuating and unincorporated bodies making it difficult for persons dealing with them to know with whom they are contracting. The law requires these association to be compulsorily registered under the Companies Act, before they can function as legal associations.

Section 11 provides that no company, association or partnership consisting of more than 10 persons in case of banking business and of more than 20 persons in the case of any other business which has for its objects the acquisition of gain can be legally formed unless it is registered under the Companies Act or is formed in pursuance of some other Indian law. If they are not so registered they would be considered as illegal associations. The law does not recognise them being illegal.

In order to come within the operation of Section 11 the following conditions are necessary.

1. There must be an association.
2. The association must be formed for the purpose of carrying on a business.
3. The business must have for its object the acquisition of gain
4. The number of persons composing such association should exceed 10 in case of banking business and 20 in the case of any other business.

All the above conditions must be fulfilled before an unregistered association can be called an illegal association. An association once illegal retains its illegal character until registration or dissolution.

Associations with more than 20 persons as members and which carry on business but whose object is not the earning of profit are not compulsorily registerable. Associations formed for the purpose of promoting art, science religion or charity are excluded from the scope of this section. This section does not also apply to a joint Hindu family carrying on business, even though the number of members may be more than twenty. But if two or more joint families carry on business with more than 20 adult persons the association will be unlawful. In computing the number of persons of two or more joint Hindu families, minor members of such families are excluded.

Effect of Illegal Association

An association or partnership which is not registered under Section 11 can have no legal recognition as a separate legal entity. "Such association" in the words of **Sir, Palmer** " is a phantom. It has no legal existence." The result of this is —

1. Such an association cannot enter into any binding contract.
2. It cannot sue or be used. But such an association may get itself registered and enforce its claims. Such an association cannot sue any of its members or any outsider, not even if the association is subsequently registered as a company. It cannot be used by a member or an outsider for any debts due to it because it cannot contract any debt.
3. Such an association cannot be dissolved under the Act either at the instance of a creditor, member, or the association itself.
4. Every member of such an association shall be personally liable for all liabilities incurred in such business and shall also be liable to a fine which may extend up to Rs. 1,000.
5. Can a member ask for partition of dissolution of accounts of an illegal association? The question was brought before the High Court of Allahabad in ***Mewa Ram vs. Ram Gopal***. It was held that where an association was illegal and the business had been carried for some years, none of its members could sue for partition because partition would involve realisation of the assets of the company and payment of its debts, the very things which would be done in a suit for dissolution of partnership or winding up of a company.

It should be noted that while an unregistered firm can be dissolved, an illegal association cannot be dissolved, because law does not recognise its very existence.

6. The illegality of an illegal association cannot be cured by subsequent reduction in the number of its member ***Kumara swami Chettiar vs. M.S.M. Chinnathambi Chettiar.***

7. The profits made by an illegal association are, however, liable to assessment to income-tax ***(Gopalji Co.vs. C.I.T.A.)***

QUESTIONS

Objective Type Questions

I. Fill up the Blanks

1. According to the Companies Amendment Act, 2000, a public limited company must have not less than __________ paid up capital and a private company not less than __________ as paid-up capital.
2. A public limited company must have capital contributed by the public which must not be less than __________ per cent of the paid-up capital.
3. A Government company is one in which not less than __________ % of the shares must be held by the State or Central Government.
4. For converting a public limited company into a private limited company, sanction must be given by _______.
5. Restriction on transfer of shares is imposed by __________ company.
6. Obtaining Certificate to commence business is a must for __________ company.
7. An illegal association is one which does banking business with more than __________ members.
8. Example for Licensed company is __________ .
9. A private company can have a maximum __________ members which excludes ________.

[*Answers* : (1) (i) Rs. 50,0000: (ii) Rs. 1,00,000; (2) Not less than 25 per cent; (3) 51%; (4) Central Government; (5) Private; (6) Public Limited Company; (7) 10 members or partners; (8) Board of Control of Cricket in India; (9) (i) 50; (ii) employees]

II. Multiple Choice Questions

1. The Reserve Bank of India is an example of a
   (a) registered company.
   (b) statutory company.
   (c) chartered company.
2. A company limited by guarantee and having a share capital
   (a) can be only a public company.
   (b) can be only private company.
   (c) may be both a public company or a private company.
3. A private company becomes a public company by process of law
   (a) where not less than 25 per cent of its paid-up share capital is held by one or more bodies corporate.
   (b) where not less than 10 per cent of its paid-up share capital is held by another single private company.
   (c) where not less than 50 per cent of the paid-up share capital of a public company is held by it.
4. A public company can be converted into a private company by passing
   (a) a special resolution to alter the Articles to include the restrictions on private companies.
   (b) an ordinary resolution.
   (c) a special resolution to alter the Articles and obtaining the approval of the Central Government.
5. The liability of a shareholder in a company limited by shares is
   (a) unlimited.
   (b) limited by guarantee.
   (c) limited to the unpaid value of shares subscribed by him.

[*Answers:* 1 (b); 2 (c); 3 (a); 4 (c); 5 (c)]

III. Match the Following

1. Partnership firm	1. Report to be approved by Controller
2. Government undertaking	2. Investment for Reinvestment
3. Deemed company	3. More than 50% foreign capital involved.
4. Subsidiary company	4. Shareholders belong to the same family

5. Government company	5. Company limited by shares
6. Portfolio Investment	6. Company limited by guarantee without capital
7. FERA company	7. Public sector unit
8. One man company	8. Control of the Board of Directors
9. Table B	9. Cannot exist under 2000 Act
10. Table C	10. Joint and several liability

[*Answers:* (1) 10; (2) 7; (3) 9; (4) 8; (5) 1; (6) 2; (7) 3; (8) 4; (9) 5; (10) 6.]

Review Questions

1. What is chartered company? Give two examples.
2. What is a statutory company? Give two examples.
3. Define a government company.
4. What is meant by holding companies?
5. What is a subsidiary company?
6. Explain the kinds of companies limited by guarantee.
7. What are private companies?
8. What do you mean by a producer company?
9. What is an industrial company?
10. What is a licensed company?
11. State the different types of companies under the Companies Act, 1956.
12. What are registered companies?
13. What are the points of distinction between a private company and a public company?
14. What are the features of producer company?
15. What are holding companies?
16. Write a short note on association not for profit.
17. What are the circumstances under which a private company is converted into a public company?
18. What do you mean by one man company?
19. What are illegal associations?
20. Briefly explain the legal effects and consequences of illegal associations.
21. State in brief the various kinds of companies which can be registered under the Companies Act, 1956.

22. Define a private company and state the special privileges which it enjoys; under the Companies Act, 1956.

23. Under what circumstances does a private company become a *"Deemed Public Company"?*

24. What is a public company? Distinguish it from a private company.

25. Define a government company. Summarise the special provisions of the Companies Act relating to government companies.

26. What is a foreign company? Summarise the provisions of the Companies Act relating to foreign companies.

27. Write short notes on:

    (a) Holding and subsidiary companies.

    (b) Producer companies.

    (c) Industrial companies.

    (d) Unlimited companies.

    (e) One man companies.

    (f) Illegal associations.

CHAPTER 3

Incorporation of a Company

The whole process of formation of a company may be roughly divided, for convenience, into three parts.These are;

(i) Promotion

(ii) Registration or Incorporation

(iii) Floatation

PROMOTION OF A COMPANY

A company comes into existence when a number of persons come together with a view to exploit some business opportunity. These persons are called *promoters*. Under Section 12, any seven or more persons (2 or more in the case of private company) may form an incorporated company for a lawful purpose of subscribing their names to the memorandum of association and complying with other requirements in respect of registration. Such an incorporated company may be a company (a) limited by shares, (b) limited by guarantee, or (c) an unlimited company.

The promoter has to take the following *preliminary steps* in this connection:

(i) Ascertainment of availability of the Proposed Name of the Company: This has to be confirmed from the Registrar of Companies. Application has to be made in the prescribed form with the prescribed fee. It will be better for the promoters to select and send to the registrar three or four names in order of preference.

(ii) Application for Licence: In case the industry to be run by the proposed company falls within the category of those industries for the establishment of which licence is necessary under the Industries (Development and Regulation) Act, 1951, the application should be made to the concerned Ministry of the Central Government.

(iii) SEBI's approval to Draft Prospectus: In case a company proposes to raise capital by issue of shares or debentures to the general public, a draft prospectus has to be submitted to the Securities and Exchange Board of India (SEBI) duly certified by a merchant banker acting as a lead banker to the issue regarding compliance of all legal formalities.

(iv) Prepare and finally get printed the company's Memorandum and Articles of Association.

(v) Fixation of the Underwriters, Brokers, Solicitors, Auditors, etc.

INCORPORATION OR REGISTRATION OF A COMPANY

In addition to the above preliminary steps the promoter will have to take the following steps to get the company incorporated:

(i) Filing of the necessary documents.

(ii) Payment of the necessary fees.

(iii) Obtaining the Certificate of Incorporation.

Filing Documents with Registrar

The application for registration of a company should be presented to the registrar of the state in which the business office of the company is to be situated. The application shall be accompanied by the following documents with the required fees:

1. The Memorandum of Association.
2. This Articles of Association, if any, duly signed by the subscribers of the memorandum.
3. A statement of the nominal or authorised capital.
4. A notice of address of the registered office of the company. This may be done within 30 days of registration if it cannot be filed at the time of registration.
5. A list of directors and their consent to act as such, signed by each.
6. An undertaking in writing signed by each such director to take and pay for their qualification shares.
7. The agreement, if any, which the company proposes to enter into with any individual for appointment as its managing or whole-time director or manager.
8. A declaration that all the requirements of the Act have been complied with. Such a declaration may be signed by an advocate of the Supreme Court or High Court, an Attorney or Pleader entitled to appear before a High Court, or a Chartered Accountant practising in India who is engaged in the formation of

the company, or by a person named in the Articles as Director, Manager or Secretary of the company.

Items number 5 and 6 are not required to be filed in the case of private company.

Registration of Documents

If the registrar is satisfied that all the requisite documents delivered to him are in order, he shall register the Memorandum and the Articles, if any, provided he is satisfied on the following points:

(a) the relevant documents has been properly made.

(b) the objects of the company are lawful.

(c) the requisite number of persons required under the Act have subscribed and duly signed.

(d) The Memorandum and the Articles comply in all respects with the provisions of the Act.

(e) The name selected by the company is acceptable.

(f) The statutory declaration has been properly made.

If the registrar of companies is satisfied that all the aforesaid requirements have been complied with, he will register the company and place its name on the Register of companies. It is clear that once the statutory requirements have been complied with, the registrar has no option but to register it. On refusal to register on improper grounds, he may be compelled by a *Writ of mandamus*.

CERTIFICATE OF INCORPORATION

On registration the registrar will issue a certificate of incorporation whereby he certifies that the company is incorporated and in the case of a limited company, that the company is limited. From the date of incorporation mentioned in the certificate, the company becomes a legal person separate from its shareholders.

Legal Effects of Incorporation

1. A company becomes a body corporate distinct from its members. It becomes a legal persons and not a mere aggregate of the shareholders. Thus, where all the members of a company are killed by a bomb the company is deemed to survive.
2. A company has a perpetual succession and a common seal. It is an immortal being.
3. A company can sue and be sued in its own name.

4. A company has a right to hold and alienate its own property. The property of the company belongs to the company itself and not to the individual members.
5. Company's debts and obligations are the liabilities of the company only and cannot be enforced against the individuals shareholders.

CONCLUSIVENESS OF THE CERTIFICATE OF INCORPORATION

The certificate of incorporation shall be conclusive evidence that —

(i) all the requirements of the Act have been complied with in respect of registration;

(ii) all the preconditions of registration have been complied with;

(iii) the company is duly registered, and

(vi) that the company came into existence on the date of the certificate. Hence, it is the *Birth Certificate* of the company.

The certificate of incorporation prevents the reopening of matter prior to the registration and essential to it. It places the existence of the company as a legal person beyond doubt. Consequently, even if the seven signatures to a memorandum were written by one person or were all forged, the certificate would be conclusive that the company was duly registered. Similarly, if the signatories were all infants, the certificate would still be conclusive.

***(Moosa Goolam Ariff vs. Ebrahim Goolam Ariff. 40. Cal.1. (1913) (PC))*:** The memorandum of a company was signed by two adult persons and by a guardian of the other five, who were minor at that time, the guardian making a separate signature for each of the minors. The registrar registered the company and issued under his hand a certificate of incorporation. The plaintiff contended that this certificate of incorporation should be declared void. The Privy Council held that the certificate of incorporation was conclusive. The memorandum shall be deemed to have been properly signed, registered and presented to the registrar and no evidence can be admitted to the contrary, even a plea of fraud would also be shut out.

In another case of ***Jubilee Cotton Mills Ltd. vs. Lewis*,** the registrar issued a certificate of incorporation on January 8th, but dated it January 6th, which was the date he received the documents. On January 6th the company made an allotment of shares to Lewis. Held that the certificate was conclusive evidence of incorporation on January 6th and that the allotment was not void on the ground that it was made before the company was incorporated.

However, if a company has been incorporated with illegal objects, the illegal objects would not become legal by the issue of the certificate.

Section 36 states that, on registration, Memorandum and Articles of the company bind the company and its members to the same extent as if they respectively had been signed by the company and by the members and contained covenants on its and their part to observe all the provisions contained in the Memorandum and Articles.

FLOATATION/CAPITAL SUBSCRIPTION

When a company has been registered and has received its certificate of incorporation, it is ready for "floatation", that is to say, it can go ahead with raising capital sufficient to commence business and to carry it on satisfactorily.

We have seen earlier under "classification of companies" that a private company is prohibited from inviting public to subscribe to its share capital. Therefore, when a private company is formed, the necessary capital is obtained from friends and relatives by private arrangement.

In the case of a public company also, the promoters may not invite public to subscribe to its share capital and may arrange the capital privately as in the case of a private company. In such a case, the intention of the promoters is to take advantages of incorporation not available to a private company, e.g., to have unlimited number of members, to confer unrestricted right to transfer shares on the members, etc. However, by far the largest number of public companies raise their capital in the very first instance by inviting public to subscribe to its share capital.

Section 70 makes it obligatory for every public company to take either of the following two steps:

(i) *Issue* a prospectus in case public is to be invited to subscribe to its capital, or

(ii) *Submit* a 'statement in lieu of prospectus' in case capital has been arranged privately. It must be done at least 3 days before the allotment.

SEBI Guidelines : SEBI guidelines, 2000 provides that a new company shall not be allowed to make a public issue unless:

(i) its project to be financed through the proposed issue has been appraised by a public financial institution or a scheduled commercial bank;

(ii) the appraising agency is part-financing such a project by way of loan or equity participation to the extent of a minimum of 10 per cent of the project cost (5 per cent in case of infrastructure companies);

A public sector bank or a private sector bank shall be allowed to make a public issue at a price approved by Reserve Bank of India.

COMMENCEMENT OF BUSINESS

A private company may commence its business immediately on incorporation but a public company cannot commence business immediately after incorporation unless it has obtained a Certificate of Commencement of business (also known as *Trading Certificate*) from the registrar.

Companies which issues a Prospectus

If the company has a share capital and has issued a prospectus inviting the public to subscribe for its shares or debentures it cannot commence business until —

(a) shares payable in cash have been allotted to the extent of the minimum subscription;

(b) every director has paid in cash the application and allotment money on the shares taken by him;

(c) no money is liable to be repaid to the application for failure to apply or obtain permission for the shares or debentures to be dealt in on any recognised stock exchange.

(d) a statutory declaration duly verified by one of the directors or the secretary in the prescribed form that the above conditions have been complied with has been filed with the registrar (Section 149)

Companies Which do not Issue a Prospectus

If the company has a share capital but has not issued a prospectus to the public, it shall not commence the business unless —

(a) statement in lieu of prospectus has been filed with the registrar.

(b) every director has paid in cash the application and allotment money on the shares taken by him.

(c) a statutory declaration, duly verified by one of the directors or the secretary in the prescribed form that the above conditions have been complied with, has been filed with the registrar. (Section 149 (2))

On the above requirements beings duly fulfilled, the registrar shall certify that the company is entitled to commence business. This certificate is a conclusive evidence that the company is so entitled. (Section 149(3))

Contracts made by the company before it has obtained the certificate of commencement are provisional only and do not become binding on the company until it has become entitled to commence business. (Section 149(4)). Where a company is wound up before it becomes entitled to commence business anybody who has supplied goods cannot have any claim against the company. (***Re Otto Electrical Manufacturing Company Jenkin's Claim (1906) 2 Ch.390***)

Mr. Jenk in this case bought furniture and had it put into an office which he took for the company. He paid furniture dealer and claimed payment of that from the company which never became entitled to commence business. It was held that he could not sue the company.

A company is bound to commence business within a year of its incorporation or else it is liable to be wound up by the court. (Section 433(c))

Where a company acts in contradiction to of Section 149, every person who is responsible for contravention is liable to a fine up to Rs. 500 for every day during which the contravention continues. This is in addition to any other liability. [Section 149(6)]. The provisions of this section do not apply to a private company.

PROMOTER

Before a company can be formed, there must be some persons who have an intention to form a company and who take the necessary steps to carry that intention into operation. Such persons are called '*promoters*'. The word 'promoter' has not been defined anywhere in the Companies Act. Although the term is used expressly in Sections 62, 69, 76, 478 and 519. Section 62 of the Companies Act only refers to the liabilities of a promoter. The term '*promotion*' is a term not of law but of business, usefully summing up in a single word a number of business operations familiar to the commercial world by which a company is generally brought into existence.

Even in English law, no general statutory definition of a promoter is available. In Section 38(1) of the English Companies Act, a promoter is indirectly described as a person engaged or interested in the formation of a company and Section 43(5) gives a definition for the purpose of that section only, stating: the expression 'promoter' means a promoter who was a party to the preparation of the prospectus, but does not include any person by reason of his acting in a professional capacity or persons engaged in procuring the formation of the company.

Thus, *the persons assisting the promoters by acting in a professional capacity do not thereby become promoters themselves.* The solicitor who drafts the Articles, or the accountant who values assets of a business to be purchased, are merely giving professional assistance to the promoters. If, however, he goes further than this, e.g., by introducing his client to a person who may be interested in purchasing shares in the proposed company, he would be regarded as promoter. Thus, "anyone who assists in the promotion, e.g., by obtained a director, or agreeing to place shares or negotiating an agreement or merely by putting a vendor in touch with persons who may form a company to exploit or purchase his goods may find himself a promoter of a company which is consequently formed" (*Palmer*)

An attempt to define exactly who a promoter is was made by Cockburns, C.J., in **Twycross vs. Grant** who described a promoter as 'one who undertakes to form a company with reference to a given project, and to set it going, and who takes the necessary steps to accomplish that purpose. Another attempt was made by ***Bowen, L.J., in Whaley Bridge Printing Co. vs. Green***. He observed that the term promoter is a term not of law but of business, usefully summing up, in a single word a number of business operations familiar to the commercial world by which a company is brought into existence.

Perhaps, *the true test* of whether a person is a promoter is whether he has a desire that the company be formed, and is prepared to take some steps, which may or may not involve other persons, to implement it.

The promoter is a person who conceives the idea of starting a business, plans the formation of a company and actually brings a company into existence. A promoter is a convenient way of designating those who set in motion the machinery by which the Act enables them to create an incorporated company. A promoter is one "who undertakes to form a company with reference to a given object and to set it going and who takes the necessary steps to accomplish that purpose". The promoters of a company decide the scope of its business activities. They negotiate, if necessary, for the purchase of an existing business. They instruct the solicitors to prepare the necessary documents and secure the services of directors. They provide the registration fees and carry out other duties involved in the formation of a company. They also make arrangement for advertising and circulating the prospectus, and placing the capital.

Palmer has defined company promoter as "a person who originates a scheme for the formation of the company, have the Memorandum and the Articles prepared, executed and registered, and finds the first directors, settles the terms of preliminary contracts and prospectus (if any) and makes arrangements for advertising and circulation of the prospectus and placing the capital".

Thus, the company may have several promoters. A person may be a promoter though he has taken a comparatively minor part in the promotion proceedings. But everyone who is connected with the formation of a company may not be a promoter. A person who merely acts in a professional capacity on behalf of a promoter such as a solicitor, engineer, accountant, or a valuer is not a promoter in the eye of law. Whether a person is a promoter or not is question of fact in each case. Much depends upon the role played by him in the promotion business.

Kinds of Promoters

(i) *Professional promoters*: A person who specialises in the job of promotion of companies is termed as a professional promoter. Such a promoter after bringing the company into existence hands it over to a buyer who may be interested in running the company. Such type of promoters are rarely found in India.

(ii) *Occasional promoters*: A person who promotes a company once a while but not on regular basis, is termed as an occasional promoter. Such a promoter, having promoted the company and handling it over to the new owners, goes back to his business or occupation.

(iii) *Financial promoters*: Financial institutions like Industrial Development Bank of India, ICICI Ltd., Commercial Banks, etc., also promote companies. Such promoters are termed as Financial Promoters. Mutual Funds and Insurance companies promoted by certain commercial banks are a recent example of establishment of companies by financial institutions.

(iv) *Entrepreneurial promoters*: Such a promoter conceives of a business idea, takes all necessary steps for bringing a company into existence. He later on continues to manage and control such a company promoted by him. A large category of promoters in India come in this category.

Functions of Promoters

The chief functions of a promoter can be put as follows:

(i) To conceive an idea of starting a business and explore its possibilities.

(ii) To conduct the negotiation for the purchase of a business in case it is intended to purchase an existing business. The help of experts may be taken in this context, if considered necessary.

(iii) To collect the requisite number of persons *i.e.,* two in the case of a private company and seven in the case of a public company, who can sign the Memorandum and Articles of the company and also agree to act as the first directors of the company.

(iv) To decide about the following: (a) the suitable name of the company, (b) the location of its registered office, (c) the amount and form of its capital, (d) the underwriters or brokers for capital issue, if necessary, (e) the bankers, (f) the auditors, (g) the legal advisors.

(v) To get the Memorandum, Articles of Association drafted and printed.

(vi) To enter into preliminary contracts with vendors, underwriters, etc.

(vii) To arrange for the preparation of prospectus, its filing, advertisement and issue of capital.

(viii) To pay for preliminary expenses.

(ix) To arrange for loans and other type of financial assistance from the various financial institutions.

A person cannot be held as promoter because he has signed at the foot of the memorandum or that he has provided money for the payment of formation expenses. A signatory of the memorandum, if he has not performed the functions of a promoter of the company may not be liable as a promoter.

Legal Position of a Promoter: Fiduciary Relationship

A promoter is not an *agent* for the company which he is forming because a company cannot have an agent before it comes into existence. For the same reason he cannot be the *trustee* of the company. However, from the moment he acts with the company in mind, a promoter stands in a fiduciary position towards the company. Lord Cairns has correctly stated the position of a promoter in ***"Erlanger vs. New Sombrero Phosphate Co."*** the promoters of a company stand undoubtedly in a fiduciary position. They have in their hands the creation and moulding of the company. They have the power of defining how, and when, and in what shape and under whose supervision, it shall start into existence and begin to act as a trading corporation.

Duties and Liabilities of a Promoter

The importance of the rule which creates a fiduciary relationship between the promoter and the company he brings into existence, can be seen when we consider its consequences as discussed below:

1. Duty not to make Secret Profit at the Cost of the Company

A promoter cannot make either directly or indirectly any profit at the expense of the company he promotes, without the knowledge and consent of the company and that if he does so , in disregard of this rule, company can compel him to account for it.

A promoter is not forbidden to make profit but to make secret profit. In ***Gluckstein vs. Barnes***, a Syndicate of persons was formed to buy a property called 'Olympia' and resell this Olympia to a company to be formed for the purpose. The Syndicate first bought the debentures of the old Olympia company at a discount. Then they bought the company itself for £1,40,000. Out of this money provided by themselves the debentures were repaid in full and a profit of £20,000 made thereon. They promoted a new company and sold Olympia to it for £1,80,000. The profit of £40,000 was revealed in the prospectus but not the profit of £20,000.

Held, profit of £20,000 was a secret profit and the promoters of the company were bound to pay it to the company because the disclosure of this profit by themselves in the capacity of directors of the purchasing company was not sufficient.

2. Duty to Disclose all Materials Facts

A promoters is not allowed to derive a profit from the sale of his own property to the company unless all material facts are disclosed. If a promoter contracts to sell his own property to the company without making a full disclosure, the company may either repudiate the sale or affirm the contract and recover the profit made out of it by the promoter. Either way the dishonest promoter is deprived of his advantage.

Disclosure to be made to whom?

A promoter who wishes to sell his own property to the company must make a full disclosure of his interest in the transaction. The disclosure may be made (a) to an independent board of directors, or (b) in the articles of association of the company or (c) in the prospectus or (d) to the existing and intended shareholders directly. Lord Cairns observed in this regard as follows:

"I do not say that an owner of property may not promote and form a joint stock company and then sell his property to it but I do say that if he does he is bound to take care that he sells it to the company through the medium of a board of directors who can and do exercise an independent and intelligent judgement on the transaction" **Erlanger vs. New Sombrero Phosphate Co. (1878) 3 A.C. 1218.**

Secret profits on the sale of property can be recovered from a promoter only where the property was bought and sold to the company while he was acting as a promoter. A promoters can be compelled by the company to hand over any secret profit which he has made without full disclosures to the company. The company can also sue for the recision of the contract of sale by the promoter where the promoter has not disclosed his interest therein.

3. Liable for False Statement, Omission of Facts, etc.

A promoter is subject to the following liabilities under the various provisions of the Companies Act, 1956

(i) Section 56 lays down matter to be stated and reports to be set out in the prospectus. He may be held liable for the non-compliance of the provisions of this section.

(ii) Under Section 62, a promoter is liable for any untrue statement in the prospectus to a person who has subscribed for any shares or debentures on the faith of the prospectus. Such a person may sue the promoter for compensation for any loss or damage sustained by him.

(iii) Besides civil liability, the promoters are criminally liable under Section 63 for the issue of prospectus containing untrue statements. Section 68 imposes severe penalty on promoters who make untrue and deceptive statements in a prospectus with a view to obtaining capital.

(iv) A promoter may be liable to public examination like any other director or officer of the company if the court so directs on a liquidators report alleging fraud in promotion or formation of the company. [*Section 478*].

(v) A company may proceed against a promoter on action for deceit or breach of duty under Section 543, where the promoter has misapplied or retained any property of the company or is guilty of misfeasance or breach of trust in relation to the company.

Where there are more than one promoters, they are *jointly and severally liable* and if one of them is sued and pays damages, he is entitled to claim *contribution* from other or others.

The death of a promoter does not relieve his estate from liability arising out of abuse of his fiduciary position.

Liability of Promoters for Preliminary Contracts

Preliminary contracts are contracts entered into by the promoters on behalf of the company, before its incorporation, with third parties.

It is very usual that the promoters enter into some contracts as agents or trustees of the company, which has not yet come into existence. Such contracts are legally not binding upon the company even after it comes into existence. The company can neither ratify those contracts nor sue the vendors on them after its incorporation because ratification requires existence of the principal at the time when the contract was entered into.

Examples: (i) *N & Co.* entered into an agreement with one *C*, who acted on behalf of a proposed syndicate. Under the agreement *N & Co.* was to give the syndicate lease of coal mining rights. The syndicate was then registered and asked *N & Co.* to give these rights, which *N & Co.* refused. An action by the syndicate for specific performance of the agreement or in the alternative for damages. Held that it was not maintainable as "a company cannot by adoption or ratification obtain the benefit of a contract purported to have been made on its behalf before the company came into existence." ***(Natal Land and Colonisation Co. Ltd. vs. Pauline Colliery & Development Syndicate Ltd. (1904) A.C. 120.)***

(ii) On the request of the promoters of a company, a solicitor prepared the Memorandum and Articles of Association of a company, paid the registration fees and got the company registered. Held that the company was not bound to pay for the services and expenses of the solicitor. "The company could not be sued in law for those expenses in as much as it was not in existence at the time when the expenses were incurred... and ratification was impossible." ***(Re. English and Colonial Produce Co. Ltd., (1906) 2 Ch. 435 C.A.)***

A company cannot adopt contracts entered into before its incorporation even by passing a special resolution or by making adoption of such contracts as one of the objects of the company in its memorandum of association. ***(North Sydney Investment and Tramway Co. vs. Higgins (1899) A.C. 263.)***

Example: The memorandum of association of a proposed company provided that a particular firm would be appointed as its managing agent. The firm was appointed as the company's managing agent after the company's incorporation but soon afterward the directors resolved to dismiss them. The firm field a suit against the company for restraining the company from committing a breach of the contract. It was held that the contract was in the nature of a preliminary contract made by the promoters with the third parties before the company's formation. The company could not be held liable for such a contract even if a clause to that effect had been entered in the company's memorandum. ***(Raj Kumar Potdar vs. Sholaput Spinning & Weaving Co. A.I.R. 1935 Bom. L.R. 907.)***

Thus, preliminary contracts will either have to be left as mere 'gentlemen's agreement' or the promoters will have to undertake personal liability, which of these courses will be adopted depends largely on demands of the other party. ***(Gower L.C.B. "The Principles of Modern Company Law", third Ed., p. 280.)***

The nature of the liability of promoter may be expressly stated in the memorandum or otherwise it may have to be ascertained taking into account the terminology employed in the contract. He can be held personally liable if he has purported to act as an agent and the non-existence of the company was known to both the parties. But if the contract is purported to be made by the company itself, which is not in existence, the director or promoter signing on behalf of such non-existent company does not incur any liability, since there in no contract at all.

In case of personal liability the promoters will continue to be liable until the company adopts the contracts. This personal liability will continue, even after the incorporation of the company for those things which they had started doing before the incorporation of the company. The company will adopt these contracts by entering into new contracts with the third parties on the same terms as were embodied in the original contracts. Such a new agreement of adoption may not be implied by the acts of the company. In order to avoid their liability, the promoters usually insert a clause in the original contract to the effect that if the contract is not adopted by the company after its incorporation within a limited time, both the promoters and the third party will be exonerated from liability. Some of the promoters simply agree to the draft contract to be entered into by the vendor and the company after incorporation.

However, the principles enunciated above have no application in our country on account of the provisions of Sections 15(h) and 19(e) of the *Specific Relief Act, 1963*. These sections provide that a contract entered into by the promoters on behalf of the company before its incorporation can be enforced by or against the company, if the following two conditions are satisfied:

(a) If the contract is entered into, for the purpose of the company and such contract is warranted by the terms of incorporation. The term "for the purpose of the company" implies that the contract should be for the working purpose of the company.

(b) The company accepts the contract after its incorporation and communicates such acceptance to the other party to the contract.

Remuneration of Promoters

The nature of the promoters work in the formation of a company calls for considerable skill for which he should be adequately remunerated. A promoter has no right against the company for his remuneration unless there is a contract to that effect. In the absence of such a contract, he cannot even recover from the company payments he has made in connection with the formation of the company.

Clinton's Claim (1908) 2.Ch.515: A syndicate promoted a company and paid £ 416.2 s, in respect of registration fees and stamp duty. The company shortly afterwards went into liquidation. It was held that syndicate could not recover the payments it had made.

The Articles generally give the directors power to pay the preliminary expenses out of the company's funds. Even in such a case it does not amount in law to a binding contract between the promoters and the company. However, the promoters are usually the first directors, so that in practice the promoters will receive their remuneration.

Methods of Remunerating Promoters

Remuneration may be paid to a promoter in any of the following ways:

1. The promoter may purchase the business or other property and sell the same to the company at a higher price or he may sell his own business to the company at a profit.
2. Commission may be paid to the promoter on the purchase price of the business or property acquired by the company through him.
3. The company may pay him a certain lump sum as remuneration for the services.
4. Promoters may be given fully or partly paid-up shares in consideration of the services.
5. He may be given a commission on the shares sold.
6. The promoters may be given the option to subscribe within a fixed period for a certain portion of the company's unissued shares at par.

Whatever be the nature of remuneration it must be disclosed in the prospectus if paid within the preceding two years or intended to be paid at anytime.

PRELIMINARY OR PRE-INCORPORATION CONTRACTS

We have mentioned earlier that a company is an artificial person and is capable of entering into contracts. The promoters may enter into contracts with third parties on behalf of the proposed company before obtaining the certificate of incorporation or after obtaining the certificate of incorporation but before obtaining the certificate to commence business. Thus, in the case of a public company following are the three situations when contracts may be entered into: (i) contracts before incorporation, (ii) contracts after incorporation but before obtaining the certificate to commence business, and (iii) contracts after obtaining the certificate to commence business.

However, in the case of a private company, as it is not required to obtain the certificate to commence business, there are only two situations, i.e., (i) contracts before incorporation, and (ii) contracts after incorporation.

Preliminary contracts are purported to be made on behalf of a company before its incorporation. Such contracts may relate to property which the promoters wish to purchase for the company or they may be made with persons whose know-how is vital to the success of the company and whose services it is essential to secure. The promoters may perhaps have arranged for the company to takeover an existing business, and therefore, need to make a contract with vendor for its sale or purchase.

Legal Position of Pre-Incorporation Contracts

Legal position about validity of pre-incorporation contracts may be discussed under the following two heads:

Position Before 1963 (i.e., Before Passing of the Specific Relief Act, 1963)

Before its incorporation, a company has no capacity to contract. A contract entered into by promoters on behalf of a proposed company is void so far as the company is concerned. The promoters cannot be the agents for a principal which has not yet come into existence. In such a case the company cannot sue or be sued on it. The company has no legal existence until it is incorporated. It therefore follows:

1. That when the company is registered, it is not bound by the preliminary contract.

Re English & Colonical Produce Co. Ltd. (1906)2 Ch.435 (C.A.): A solicitor prepared the Memorandum and Articles of Association and paid the necessary registration fees on the instruction of persons who later became directors. He claimed his fees and expenses on the liquidation of the company. The Court of Appeal held that the company was not liable to pay the solicitors costs though it had taken the benefit of his work.

2. That the company when registered cannot ratify the agreement. The company was not a principal with contractual capacity at the time when the contract was made. A contract can be ratified only when it is made by an agent for a principal who is in existence and who is competent to contract at the time when the contract is made.
3. That if the agent undertook any liability under the agreement, he would be personally liable notwithstanding that he is described in the agreement as an agent and that the company may have attempted to ratify the agreement.

***Kelner vs. Baxter (1866) L.R. 2 C.P. 174*:** An agreement was made between K and B, B was acting on behalf of the proposed hotel company. Wine supplied under the contract was used by the company which had 'ratified' the agreement after incorporation. The company went into liquidation before paying the debt. It was held that B was personally liable and no ratification could release him from his liability.

4. The company cannot enforce the preliminary agreement.

***Natal Land and Colonisation Company Limited vs. Pauline Colliery & Development Syndicate Ltd. (1904) A.C. 120*:** N company agreed with C an agent of syndicate before its incorporation that N company would grant a mining lease to the syndicate. The syndicate was incorporated as P company. P company discovered coal where upon N company refused to grant the lease. The Privy Council held that there was no binding contract between N company and the P company as latter was not in existence when the contract was signed.

Position Since 1963 (i.e., After Passing of the Specific Relief Act, 1963)

Until the passing of the Specific Relief Act, 1963, the promoters found it very difficult to carry out the work of incorporation. Since contracts prior to incorporation were void and also could not be ratified, people hesitated to either supply any goods or work for the cause of incorporation. Promoters also felt shy of accepting personal responsibility. The Specific Relief Act, 1963 came as a sigh of relief to the promoters. Sections 15(h) and 19(e) of this Act provide that when promoters of a company have, before its incorporation entered into a contract for the purposes of the company and such a contract is warranted by the terms of its incorporation, the contract may be specifically enforced by or against the company. It is, however, necessary that the company in such a case must have accepted the contract after its incorporation and communicated such acceptance to the other party to the contract. Contracts like preparation and printing of the Memorandum, Articles, etc., renting a premises, hiring secretarial staff are envisaged under the Act.

Liability of Promoters *vis-a-vis* Pre-Incorporation Contracts

An important question that needs to be tackled is what the position of a promoter *vis-a-vis* preliminary contracts? If the company does not execute a fresh contract after incorporation and the contract is not one warranted for the purpose of incorporation of the company, what will be the legal position of the promoter who brings about such a contract.

In ***Phonogram Ltd. vs. Lane (1982) QB 938***, it was observed that although a contract made before a company's incorporation cannot bind the company, it is not wholly devoid of legal effect, even if all the persons who negotiated the contract are aware that the company has not yet been incorporated.

The contract takes effect as a personal contract with the persons who purport to contract on the company's behalf (***Kelner vs. Baxter (1866) LR 2 CP 174***). Promoters shall be liable to pay damages for failure to perform the promises made in the company's name. This shall be so even where the contract expressly provides that only the company's paid-up capital shall be answerable for performance (***Scot vs. Lord Ebury (1867) LR 2 CP 255).***

The persons who make the contract are liable as parties to it, and are not merely liable to pay damages for breach of implied warranty that they had authority to contract on the company's behalf. This distinction may be of importance when the contract is specifically enforceable (e.g., a contract for the sale of land to the unformed company), for there seems no reason why the vendor should not obtain an order for specific performance against the persons who make the contract instead of suing them for damages.

Formerly, these consequences did not ensue when a contract was *made* in the name of a company before its incorporation by a person who did not purport to the contract on its behalf or as its agent, but simply described himself in the offer or acceptance as an officer of the company or as being in some other way connected with it (***Newborne vs. Sensolid (Great Britain) Ltd. (1954) 1 QB 45***). Such contracts were declared void both against the company and the person authenticating the same by adding his name.

However, now, besides the judicial decisions on the subject, Section 36(4) of the English Companies Act, 1985 specifically provides that such contracts take effect as contracts entered into personally by the persons who make them. Even the knowledge or ignorance of those persons of the fact that the company has not yet been incorporated is immaterial.

Form of Contracts made by Companies

Section 46 provides that a company can in general contract in the same form as an individual. Thus, a contract which, if made between private persons, is required to be in writing, may be made on behalf of the company also in *writing*. It should be *signed by a person acting under the express or implied authority of the company.* Such contracts may also be varied or discharged in the same manner. Also a contract which would be valid if made between private persons although made orally or by parol could also be made orally or by parol on behalf of the company by any person acting under express or implied authority. Such contracts could also be varied or discharged in the same manner.

Some *contracts are required to be under seal* and therefore, Section 147 requires every company incorporated under the Act to have a common seal upon which its name should be engraved in legible characters.

Under Section 50, a company may obtain power through its Articles to have an official seal, for use outside India. This is in addition to a common seal.

The preliminary contracts made by promoters generally provide that if the company adopts the agreement the promoter's liability shall cease and if the company does not adopt the agreement within a certain time either party may rescind the contract. In such a case the promoter's liability would cease after the lapse of the fixed time.

A company is not bound by the preliminary contracts is subject to an important exception which is laid down in Sections 15 and 19 of the Specific Relief Act, 1963. These provide that "where the promoters of a company have before its incorporation, entered into contracts for the purposes of the company and such contracts are warranted by terms of incorporation, specific performance may be obtained by or against the company if the company has accepted the contract after its incorporation and has communicated such acceptance to the other party."

PROVISIONAL CONTRACTS

Pre-incorporation contracts must be distinguished from provisional contracts which are entered into by a company after incorporation, but before it is entitled to commerce business.

Contracts entered into by a company after its incorporation and before it is entitled to commence business are provisional only and are not binding on the company until the *trading certificate* is issued [*Section 149(4)*]. The expression "provisional" denotes that the contract should be read subject to an implied term that it shall not be binding until the company becomes entitled to commence business. Consequently, should the company go into liquidation, without commencing business, such contracts cannot be enforced at all (***Re Otto Electrical Co. (1906) 2 Ch. 390***). This rule is applicable to :

- allotment whether first or subsequent (***Mutual Bank of India vs. Suban Singh (1936) Lah. 790***).
- moneys for goods supplied ***(Re Otto Electrical Co.)***
- remuneration for service rendered (***New Drive & Co. vs. Blackiston (1908) 24 T.L.R. 563***)
- preliminary expenses incurred on behalf of the company to be incorporated (***Re National Motor Co. 908 2 Ch. 228***) cannot be recovered.

It is also not possible to invoke Section 70 of the Contract Act in such a case (***Re Ambica Textiles 54 C.W.N. 157***). Also the company cannot enter for the sale or purchase of any property (***Kishangarh Electric Co.vs. United States of Rajasthan A.I.R. 1960 Raj.40***)

Difference between Preliminary Contracts and Provisional Contracts

Pre-Incorporation Contracts	Provisional Contracts
1.Contracts which are entered into before the company comes into existence	Contracts entered into by a company after its incorporation and before commencement of business.
2. No effect so far as the company is concerned	Not binding until the company is entitled to commence business and ratified the contract.
3. Can be enforced against the company only if warranted by terms of incorporation	Cannot be enforced should the company go into liquidation without commencing business.

QUESTIONS

Objective Type Questions

I. Fill up the Blanks

1. One who works for the formation of a company is known as __________.
2. The relationship between the Promoter and the proposed company is one of __________ nature.
3. Any contract made by the company after the issue of Certificate of Incorporation but before the issue of certificate to commence business is known as _________.
4. Promoters' contracts when replaced by the company by entering into a new contract with third parties is known as __________.
5. Once the certificate of incorporation is issued, it cannot be challenged. This was established in the leading case known as __________ case.
6. Certificate to commence business must be obtained only by __________ companies.
7. Promoters are known as __________ directors.
8. Remuneration of Promoters for innovative service to the company could be rewarded by company in issuing __________ kind of shares.
9. Promoters cannot make __________ profits in their dealings with the company.
10. Obtaining Stock Exchange permission for marketing the shares in public is important for securing certificate __________.

[*Answers:* (1) Promoter; (2) Fiduciary; (3) Provisional contract; (4) Novation; (5) Peels' Case; 6. Public Limited; (7) Defacto or Founder; (8) Sweat Equity; (9) Secret; (10) To commence business]

II. State whether the following Statements are True or False

1. Promoters are agents of the company.
2. Any contract entered into by the company before obtaining the certificate to commence business is not binding upon the company.
3. Promoters need not account for the gains they have made in promoting the company.
4. A Certificate of Incorporation wrongly issued by the Registrar with mistakes can be rectified.
5. Declaration for compliance of formalities pertaining to the task of obtaining Certificate of Incorporation must be signed by all promoters.
6. A suit can be enforced against the company only when it has been registered.
7. Promoters' contracts with third party creditors are not binding on the company.
8. Primary duties of the promoters for starting a company are to arrange for finance.
9. Pre-incorporation expenses are not at all binding upon the company.
10. Promoters can be legitimately called First Directors of the company until directors are appointed.

[*Answers:* True: (2), (6), (7), (10); False: (1), (3), (4), (5), (8), (9)]

Review Questions

1. Who is a promoter?
2. What are pre-incorporation contracts?
3. What is certificate of incorporation?
4. Explain briefly the consequences of default in obtaining the certificate of commencement of business.
5. Briefly explain the functions of a promoter.
6. Distinguish between preliminary contracts and provisional contracts.

5. Who are promoters? What are their functions?
6. Describe the legal position of a promoter?
7. What are the duties of a promoter?
8. What are preliminary contracts?

9. What are the documents to be filed with the registrar while incorporating a company?
10. What is certificate of incorporation? Describe its legal effects.
11. When a newly formed company can commence its business immediately?
12. Write about the provisions of the Companies Act regarding the commencement of new business.
13. Define the term promoter. Explain his duties, functions and legal position.
14. "A *certificate of incorporation is conclusive evidence that all the requirements of the Companies Act have been complied with*". Comment.
15. Discuss the various stages in the formation a company.
16. Detail the procedure for obtaining certificate of commencement of business.
    (1) of a company which has not issued a prospectus.
    (2) of a company which has issued a prospectus.
17. Write short notes on: (a) Pre-incorporation contracts (b) Certificate of incorporation (c) Commencement of business.
18. *"A promoter is not a trustee or agent for the company but he stands in a fiduciary position towards it"*. Discuss.
19. Can a promoter be remunerated for the services rendered by him in connection with the formation of a company ? How can he realise such remuneration?

◈◈◈

CHAPTER 4

Memorandum of Association

MEANING OF MEMORANDUM OF ASSOCIATION

Memorandum of association is one of the main documents which has to be filed with the Registrar of Companies at the time of incorporation of a company. Section 2(28) defines a memorandum to mean "the memorandum of association of a company as originally framed or as altered from time-to-time in pursuance of any previous company law or of this Act." The definition, however, neither gives us any idea as to what a memorandum of association really is nor does it point out the role which it plays in the affairs of the company.

The memorandum of association is an extremely important document in relation to the affairs of the company. It is a document which sets out the *constitution of the company* and is really the foundation on which the structure of the company is based. It contains the fundamentals conditions upon which alone the company is allowed to be incorporated. A company may pursue only such objects and exercise only such powers as are conferred expressly in the memorandum or by implication therefrom, i.e., such powers as are incidental to the attainment of the objects. A company cannot depart from the provisions contained in its memorandum, however, grave the necessity may be. If it does, it would be *ultra vires* the company, and therefore wholly void. It defines its relation with the outside world and the scope of its activities. *The purpose of the memorandum is to enable shareholders, creditors and those who deal with the company to know what is the permitted range of the enterprise.*

It defines as well as confines the powers of the company; it not only shows the objects of its formation, but also the utmost possible scope of its operation beyond which its action cannot go. Lord Cairns in ***Ashbury Railway Carriage Co. vs. Riche (1875) L.R.7.H.L.653*** pointed out, "The memorandum is at where, the area beyond which the action of the company cannot go; inside that area the shareholders may make such regulations for their own government as they think fit".

A Public document: Memorandum of association is a public document, and therefore, every person who deals with the company is presumed to have sufficient knowledge of its contents. It is kept open for public inspection.

Purpose of Memorandum: The purpose of the memorandum is two fold.

1. **Spread of Risk :** The intending shareholders who contemplates the investment of his capital shall know within what field it is to be put at risk.
2. **Corporate Objectives and its Limitations:** Anyone who shall deal with the company shall know without reasonable doubt whether the contractual relation into which he contemplates entering with the company is one relating a matter within its corporate objects.

At least seven persons in the case of a public company and at least two in the case of a private company must subscribe to the memorandum (*Section 12*). The memorandum shall be printed, divided into consecutively numbered paragraphs, and shall be signed by each subscriber, with his address, description and occupation added, in the presence of at least one witness who will attest the same (*Section 15*).

CLAUSES AND CONTENTS OF MEMORANDUM

Form and Contents

Section 14 requires that the memorandum of a company shall be such one of the Forms in Tables B, C, D and E in Schedule I to the Companies Act, 1956 as may be applicable in the case of the company, or in Forms as near thereto as circumstances admit.

Section 15 requires the memorandum to be printed, divided into paragraphs, numbered consecutively, and signed by at least seven persons (two in the case of a private company) in the presence of at least one witness, who will attest the signatures. Each of the members must take at least one share and write opposite his name the number of shares he takes.

According to Section 13, the memorandum of association of every company must contain the following clauses:

1. The name of the company with 'Limited' as the last word of the name in the case of public limited company and with 'Private Limited' as the last word in the case of a private limited company.
2. The state in which the registered office of the company is to be situated.

3. The objects of the company to be classified as—(i) the main objects of the company to be pursued by the company on its incorporation and objects incidental to the attainments of the main objects, and (ii) other objects not included above.
4. The liability of members is limited if the company is limited by shares or by guarantee.
5. In the case of a company having a share capital, the amount of share capital with which the company proposes to be registered and its division into shares of a fixed amount.

An limited company need not include items 4 and 5 in its memorandum.

A brief discussion of the various clauses is as follows:

Name Clause

A company may be registered with any name it likes. But no company shall be registered by a name which in the opinion of the Central Government is undesirable and in particular which is identical or which too nearly resembles the name of an existing company (*Section 20*).

Use of the word 'Limited' (Ltd) or 'Private Limited' or (P) Ltd. : Every public company must write the word *'limited'* after its name and every private limited company must write the word *'private limited' after its name.*

When the word 'Limited' may be dropped : The use of the word 'company' is however, not compulsory. Companies, whose liabilities are not limited, are prohibited from using the word 'limited'. The words limited may be dispensed within the name of charitable companies. But companies formed to promote art, science, religion, etc., which do not propose to pay dividend but intend to apply all its profits towards the working of the company, can be registered without the word 'limited' under licence granted by the Central Government.

Prohibition on Use of Certain Names

A company cannot adopt a name which violates the provisions of the *Emblems and Names (Prevention of Improper Use) Act 1950.* This Act prohibits the use of the name and emblems of the United Nations, and the World Health Organisation, the official seal and emblems of the Central and the State Governments, the Indian National Flag, the name and pictorial representation of Mahatma Gandhi.

If a limited company makes a contract without using the word 'limited' the directors who make the contract on behalf of the company would be personally liable.

Publication of Name : Every company is required to publish or display it name outside its registered office, and outside every place where it carries to business, to have its name engraved seal and to have its name on all business letters, bill heads, notices and other official publication of the company (*Section 147*).

Registered Office Clause

This clause states the name of the state where the registered office of the company is to situate. The registered office clause is important for several reasons. *Firstly,* it ascertains the domicile and nationality of a company. This domicile clings to it throughout its existence. *Secondly*, it is the place where various registers and statutory books relating to the company must be kept and to which all communications, letters and notices must be sent. A company need not carry on its business at its registered office. *Thirdly*, the domicile of the registered office helps to determine jurisdiction of courts.

A company shall have its registered office from the date on which the company begins to carry on business or within 30 days after incorporation, whichever is earlier. Notice of situation of the registered office and every change therein must be given within 30 days from the date of incorporation of the company or after the date of the change, as the case may be (*Section 146*).

Objects Clause

The objects clause is the most important clause in the memorandum of association of a company. It is not merely a record of what is contemplated by the subscribers, but it serves a two-fold purpose –

(a) It gives an idea to the prospective shareholders the purposes for which their money will be utilised.

(b) It enables the persons dealing with the company to ascertain its powers.

In case of companies which were in existence immediately before the commencement of the Companies (Amendment) Act, 1965, the objects clause has simply to state the objects of the company. But in the case of a company registered after the amendment, the objects clause must state separately –

(i) Main Objects: This sub-clause has to state the main objects to be pursued by the company on its incorporation and objects incidental or ancillary to the attainment of the main objects.

(ii) Other Objects: This sub-clause shall state other objects which are not included in the above clause.

Further, in the case of a non-trading company, whose objects are not confined to one state, the objects clause must mention specifically the states to whose territories the objects extend. (Sec. 13)

The subscribers to the memorandum of association may choose any object or objects for their company. There are, however, certain restrictions.

1. **Not against Constitution of India:** The objects should not be against the policy of the Constitution of India. For example, the object should not be such as to encourage untouchability which has been abolished under the constitution of India.

2. **Not illegal or against Public Policy:** The objects should not include anything which is illegal or against public policy. For example, forming a company for dealing in lotteries or for trading with the alien enemies.

3. **Not Against Companies Act:** The objects must not be against the provisions of the Companies Act, as for example, authorising a company registered in India to have its registered office outside India.

On its being registered, the company has power to do whatever is necessary to do for attaining the objects stated in the memorandum, and to do whatever else is incidental to or consequential upon the attainment of the main object. It is, therefore, clear, that any act of the company outside its stated objects is *ultra-vires* and therefore void and cannot be ratified even by the whole body of shareholders.

Liability Clause

This clause states that the liability of the members of the company is limited. In the case of a company limited by shares, the shareholder is liable , only to the amount unpaid on the shares taken by him. In the case of a company limited by guarantee the members are liable to the amount undertaken to be contributed by them to the assets of the company in the event of its being wound up. *However, this clause is omitted from the memorandum of association of unlimited companies.* Any alteration in the memorandum compelling a member to take up more shares, or which increases his liability, would be null and void [*Section 38*]. *In fact,* the absence of this clause in the memorandum means that the liability of its members is unlimited.

*Specimen Liability Clause in a Memorandum of Association of Guarantee Company not having a Share Capital.**

Every member of a company undertakes to contribute to the assets of the company in the event of its being wound up while he is a member or within one year after he ceases to be a member, for the payment of the debts and liabilities of the company contracted before he ceased to be a member and the costs, charges and expenses of winding up and for the adjustment of the rights of the contributories among themselves, such amount as may be required, not exceeding one thousand rupees.

As per Section 45, under certain circumstances the liability of members of a limited company becomes unlimited."

If a company carries on business for more than six months, while the number of members of less than 7, in the case of public company and less than 2 in case of a private company, each members aware of this fact, is liable for all the debts contracts by the company after the period of six months has elapsed (*Section 45*).

Capital Clause

The memorandum of a company limited by shares must state the authorised or nominal share capital, the different kinds of shares, the nominal value of each share. The chief point to consider in regard to this clause is what funds are necessary to set the business going or, if it is proposed to by an existing concern what sum is needed to pay its price and what, in addition, is wanted to keep the business going. It is generally advisable to have a certain reasonable amount of more capital and have some shares in reserve as unissued so that further capital may be raised as and when required.

Association or Subscription Clause

This clause provides that those who have agreed to subscribe to the memorandum must signify their willingness to associate and form a company. According to Section 12 of the Act, at least seven persons are required to sign the memorandum in the case of a public company, and at least two persons in the case of a private company.

The memorandum has to be signed by each subscriber in the presence of at least one witness who must attest the signatures. Each subscriber must write opposite his name the number of shares he shall take. No subscriber of the memorandum shall take less than one share. This clause need not be numbered.

ALTERATION OF MEMORANDUM

The Memorandum of Association of a company being its charter, the right of the company to alter its contents is rigidly limited by the provisions of the Act. Section 16 of the Act provides that a company shall not alter the conditions contained in its memorandum except in the cases, in the manner and to the extent provided in the Act.

Change of Name

A company can change its name at anytime. For this purpose it must first pass a special resolution and then obtain approval of the Central Government in writing. A copy of the special resolution should be filed with the registrar within 30 days of its passing.

Addition or Repetition: However, no such approval is necessary for merely including or deleting the word 'Private' consequent on the conversion of the public company into private company and *vice versa* (*Section 21*).

Minor Mistakes: Minor mistakes to be spelling mistakes, etc., may be altered by an ordinary resolution. If through inadvertance or otherwise a company is registered by a name, which in the opinion of the Central Government, is identical, with or too nearly resembles the name of an existing company, it can change its name by passing an ordinary resolution and with the previous approval of the Central Government signified in writing.

Change of Name under the Direction of the Central Government: The Central Government may also, within twelve months of its registration direct the company to change its name. Within three months of such direction, the company must change its name by passing an ordinary resolution and with the previous approval of the Central Government signified in writing. Default in complying with the direction is punishable with the fine up to Rs. 100 for everyday during which the default continues (*Section 22*).

A copy of the ordinary resolution has to be filed with the registrar within 30 days of its date of passing. The registrar shall enter the new name of the registrar in place of former name and shall issue a fresh certificate of incorporation. Necessary alteration shall also be made in the memorandum by the Registrar. The change of name shall be complete and effective only on the issue of such a certificate. The rights and obligations of a company will not be affected on the change of its name (*Section 23*).

Change of Registered Office

A company can shift its registered office from one premise or place to another within the same city, town or village, provided a resolution is passed by the board of directors and a notice of change is given to the registrar within 30 days of such change. But, where the registered office is to be changed outside the local limits of any city, town or village in the same state, special resolutions to that effect must be passed. A notice of such change shall be given to the registrar within 30 days of the change. These two changes in the registered office do not involve alteration of memorandum.

Change of Registered Office within a State (Section 17-A)

1. No company shall change the place of its registered office from one place to another within a state unless such change is confirmed by the regional director.
2. The company shall make an application in the prescribed form to the regional director for confirmation under Sub-Section (I)
3. The confirmation referred to in Sub-Section (1), shall be communicated to the company within four weeks from the date of receipt of application for such change.

   Explanation — For the purposes of this section, it is hereby declared that the provisions of this section shall apply only to the companies which change the registered office from the jurisdiction of one registrar of companies to the jurisdiction of another registrar of companies within the same state.
4. The company shall file, with the registrar a certified copy of the confirmation by the regional director for change of its registered office under this section, within two months from the date of confirmation, together with a printed

copy of the memorandum as altered and the registrar shall register the same and certify the registration under his hand within one month from the date of filing of such document.

5. The certificate shall be conclusive evidence that all the requirements of this Act with respect to the alteration and confirmation have been complied with and henceforth the memorandum as altered shall be the memorandum of the company.

Procedure for Shifting Registered from one State to Another

A company can change its registered office from one state to another only for purpose specified in Section 17(1) of the Companies Act, 1956 and for no other purpose.

1. ***Resolution of the Board of Directors:*** The first step in changing registered office is that the board of directors must adopt a resolution to that effect.
2. ***Special Resolution:*** A special resolution must be passed by the company in the general body meeting of shareholders/members. (Sec.17(l).
3. ***Confirmation by the Central Government:*** The change shall not take effect unless and until it is confirmed by the Central Government on a petition by the Company. (Sec 17(2). Consequent to the Companies (Amendment) Act, 1996, the change of registered office requires no confirmation by Central Government.
4. ***Notice to Affected Parties:*** Before confirming the change the Central Government shall ensure that sufficient notice has been given to every person whose interest will be affected by the change and that the consent of the creditors of the company has been obtained or their debts or claims have been discharged or secured. (Sec. 17(3).
5. ***Notice to Registrar:*** The Central Government shall cause notice of the petition for confirmation of the change to be served on the registrar. The registrar shall also be given a reasonable opportunity to appear before the Central Government and state his objections and suggestions, if any, with respect to the confirmation of the alteration. (Sec. 17(4).
6. The Central Government as it may think fit impose such terms and conditions.
7. ***Copy of the Order to be Filed with ROCs:*** A certified copy of the order confirming the alteration, together with a printed copy of altered memorandum shall be filed by the company within 3 months thereof with the registrar of each of the states who shall register the same. All the records of the company shall be transferred. If it not filed within the prescribed time, then the alteration shall, at the expiry of such period, become void and inoperative.

Loss of Revenue of the States Whether Relevant Consideration

The Central Government before confirming a resolution will satisfy itself that sufficient notice has been given to every creditor and all other persons whose interests are likely to be affected by the alteration including the Registrar of Companies and the government of the state in which the registered office is situated.

In ***Orient Paper Mills Ltd. vs. State of AIR (1957)Ori. 232,*** it was observed that a state whose interests are affected by the change of the registered office to a different state has a *locus standi* to oppose shift of the registered office of a company. Accordingly, the Orissa High Court declined to confirm change of registered office from Orissa to West Bengal on the ground that the state has the right to protect its revenue and therefore the interest of the state must be taken into account.

The state government has no right to object on the ground of loss of possible future revenue, though it may do so as a creditor in respect of arrears of revenue due to it. The question of loss of revene to one state should be considered in the total prospects of revenue for the Republic of India and no parochial consideration should be allowed. That is, it is the interest of the counting as a whole should be considered **(In Re Machinnon Mackenzie & Co. (1967) 37. Com. Cas. 516)**.

Also in ***Minerva Mills Ltd, vs. Govt. of Maharashtra,*** the Bombay High Court held that the Central Government cannot refuse confirmation of the shifting of the registered office on the ground of loss of revenue to a state or would adverse effects on the general economy of the state. Similar views was expressed in ***Rank Film Distributors of India Ltd vs. Registrar of Companies, West Bengal*** **(1969) Cal. 32.**

The registrar of the state, from which such office is transferred, shall send to the registrar of the other states, all records relating to the company (Section 18). A company cannot change its registered office from India to another country and the Company Law Board or the Tribunal has no power to sanction such alteration of the memorandum.

Change of the Objects Clause

A company has no unlimited right to alter the objects clause of the memorandum, however, urgent or beneficial such alternation may be. The intention of the legislature is to prevent too easy an alteration of the conditions contained in the memorandum. Section 17 only gives a limited right to the company to alter its objects clause. The limits are *substantive* as well as *procedural*. This section provides specific purposes that the objects clause can be altered only if the change enables the company.

Substantive Limits

(a) to carry on its business more economically or more efficiently;

(b) to attain its main object by new or improved means;

(c) to enlarge or change the local area of its operation;

(d) to carry on some business which under existing circumstances may be conveniently or advantageously combined with the business of the company;

(e) to restrict or abandon any of the objects specified in the memorandum;

(f) to sell or dispose of the whole or any part of the undertaking of the company.

(g) to amalgamate with any other company or body of persons;

The company can alter its objects clause only to the above named purposes. The Central Government has no jurisdiction to confirm any alteration which is not covered by Section 17(i). The alteration must leave the business of the company substantially the same what it was before with only such changes in the mode of conducting it as will enable it to be carried on more economically or more efficiently. The additions or alterations should be a step in aid to improve efficiency.

A company is not allowed to undertake any new business having no relation to its existing business except that it must be such as can conveniently or advantageously be combined with the company's existing business. Whether one business can be conveniently combined with another is essentially a business question to be determined by the directors and shareholders. The new business must not, of course, be destructive of or inconsistent with the existing business of the company.

Re Cyclists Club, (1907) 1. Ch. 269: The company's business was to promote, assist and protect cyclists on the public roads. The company by altering the object clause desired to include among the persons to be assisted all tourists, including motorists. Held, it was impossible to combine the two business as one of the objects of the company was to protect cyclists against motorists.

The courts have sanctioned alteration permitting a marine insurance company to take up fire and life insurance business, a tyre manufacturing company to take up the business of bankers and financiers; sugar and oil manufacturing company to take up the business of steel making.

Procedural Limits

(i) Before the company can alter objects clause, it shall *pass a special resolution* sanctioning the alteration.

(ii) A copy of the special resolution shall be *filed with the Registrar* within 30 days of its passing.

(iii) But the alteration shall not take effect unless it is *confirmed by the Central Government* on petition.

Before confirming the Central Government shall see that :

(a) alteration is fair in relation to the interest of the members,

(b) sufficient notice of the petition has been given to every debentureholder and every other person whose interests are likely to be affected by the proposed alteration,

(c) Further it will see that if any creditor raises a valid objection, his consent has been procured or his claim has been satisfied.

It may confirm the alteration either wholly or in part and on such terms and conditions as it may think fit. A certified copy of the order.of the Central Government together with a printed copy of the altered memorandum must be filed with the registrar within three months of the order who shall register the same and issue a certificate of registration within one month. (*Section 18*).

Consequences of not filing: If the copy of the order is not registered within the prescribed period, the proceedings connected with the order will become void and inoperative. However, the government may revive the order on an application made within one month of its lapse. (*Section 19*).

Change Liability Clause

Ordinarily the liability clause cannot be altered so as to make liability of members unlimited. Any alteration in the memorandum will be void if the effect of the alteration is enhancement of the liability of members. This provision, however, will not apply to a case where the members agree in writing to be bound by the alteration. (*Section 38*).

The consent of the member may, however, be given either before or after the alteration. Increase in liability may be by way of subscribing for more shares than the number held by him at the date on which the alteration is made or in any other manner.

In case where the company is a club or any other similar assoication and the alteration in the memorandum requires the member to pay recurring or periodical subscription or charges at a higher rate, although he does not agree in writing to be bound by the alteration, it shall be binding on him.

In case of unlimited liability company, the liability may be made limited by re-registration of the company (Section 32). The alteration will, however, not affect any debts, liabilities, obligations or contracts entered into by or with the company before the registration of the unlimited company as a limited company [Sec. 32(3)]. Where liability of the members of a limited liability company is sought to be reduced, the procedure relating to 'reduction of share capital' as contained in Sections 100 to 103 shall be required to be followed. The procedure under said sections requires passing of a special resolution and obtaining the court's approval. A copy of the special resolution must be filed with the registrar within the specified time.

A limited company if authorised by its Articles by a special resolution may alter its memorandum to make the liability of its directors or managers unlimited. This rule applies to future appointees only. Such alteration will not affect the existing directors and managers unless they have accorded their consent. (*Section 323*).

Change of the Capital Clause

A limited company, having a share capital may alter its capital clause subject to the provisions of its Articles by a resolution in the general meeting. The confirmation of the court is not required if alteration is made for any of the following purposes:

(1) To increase its share capital.

(2) To consolidate and divide its capital into shares of larger amount.

(3) To convert its fully paid shares into stock and reconvert the stock into fully paid-up shares,

(4) To subdivide its shares into shares of smaller amount.

(5) To cancel its shares.

But for reduction of share capital, special resolution and confirmation by the Court are necessary. For detailed discussion on the above, see chapter *"Share capital"*.

DOCTRINE OF *ULTRA-VIRES*

The Company's Act requires that the memorandum of every company must state the objects of the company. The objected clause must "delimit and identify the objects in such plain unambiguous manner as that the reader can identify the field or industry within which corporate activities are to be confined." A company has power to carry out the objects set out in the memorandum and also everything which is reasonably necessary to enable it to carry out those objects. Any activities not expressly or impliedly authorised by the memorandum are *ultra-vires* the memorandum of the company. An act is said to be *ultra-vires* when it is performed which, though legal in itself, is not authorised by the objects clause in the memorandum of association or the statue. Such an act is null and void *ab initio* and cannot be ratified even by a unanimous resolution of all the shareholders.

The purpose of *ultra-vires* rule is to ensure, "that an investor in a gold mining company did not find himself holding shares in a fried fish shop and to give those who allowed credit to a limited company some assurance that its assets would not be dissipated in unauthorised enterprises" (*Gower's Modern Company Law, 2nd Edn.p.82*).

The doctrine of *ultra-vires* was put in its modern form in the famous case of ***Ashbury Railway Carriage and Iron Co. Ltd. vs. Riche*. ((1875) L.R. 7.H.L. 653).**

"The memorandum gave the company power to make, and sell, or lend on hire railway carriages and wagons and to carry on the business of mechanical engineers and general contractors. The directors contracted to purchase a concession for making a railway in Belgium. The Articles gave express power to the company to extend its business beyond the memorandum by special resolution. The company passed a special resolution to ratify the purchase. Later the company repudiated the agreement and was sued for breach of the contract. The company took the plea of *ultra-vires* as a defence. It was held by the House of Lords that the agreement was *ultra-vires*, and therefore, void and that not even the unanimous agreement of the members could validate it.

Lord Cairns observed in this case, "It is not a question whether the contract ever was ratified or was not afraid. If it was a contract void at its beginning, it was void because the company could not make the contract. If every shareholder of the company had said "That is a contract which we desire to make,..." the case would not have stood in any different position from that in which it stand now. The shareholders would thereby, by unanimous consent, have been attempting to do the very thing which, by the Act of Parliament, they were prohibited from doing." ***Ashbury Railway Carriage and Iron Co. Ltd. vs. Riche*. ((1875) L.R. 7.H.L. 653).**

There may be certain acts are *ultra-vires* the directors or *ultra-vires* the Articles but which are *intra-vires* (within the power) the company. If an act is *ultra-vires* the directors only and the shareholders have ratified it, the company would be bound by it. Where an act is *ultra-vires* the Articles, it can be ratified by altering the Articles through a special resolution. Further, if an act is within the powers of the company, any irregularities can be corrected by the consent of all the shareholders.

The doctrine was further confirmed in the case of ***Re. German Date Coffee Co. (1882) 20 Ch. D. 169***

The memorandum of this company stated that it was formed for working a German patent which would be granted for manufacturing coffee from dates; for obtaining other patents for improvements and extensions of the said invention; and to acquire and pruchase any other invention for similar purposes. The company could not get the intended German patent but purchased a Swedish patent and started making and selling coffee from dates. On a petition by the two shareholders the court held that it would be just and equitable to wind up the company since the main object for which the company was established had become impossible.

However, the doctrine of *ultra-vires* should not be unreasonably understood and applied. It does not restrain a company from doing such things which are reasonably fair and incidental to its objects or which it is authorised to do under the Companies Act.

Examples. *(i) A*, a chemical manufacturer, distributed £ 10,00,000 to universities and scientific institutions for furtherance of scientific education and research. It was held that distribution was *intra-vires* since it was conductive to the continued growth of the company as chemical manufacturers.

(*ii*) A company was authorised to keep boats for the purpose of a ferry. It used them for excursion trips to the sea when they were otherwise unemployed. The act was held to be *intra-vires*.

(*iii*) Payments to widows of ex-employees have been held to be *intra-vires* since such payments encouraged persons to enter the employment of the company.

(iv) Similarly, *exgratia* payments to workers have also been held to be *intra-vires* since they encourage the workers to work hard.

Effects of *Ultra-vires* Act

The effects of an *ultra-vires* act are as follows:

1. **Contract Void:** An act or a contract which is *ultra-vires* the company is absolutely null and void *ab initio*. A company is not bound by and cannot enforce an *ultra-vires* contract.

2. **Injunction :** The company has the capacity to do those acts which are within the scope of powers conferred on it by its memorandum. As such a company may be restrained by an injunction to do an act if it is *ultra-vires* of its objects.

   London County Council vs. Attorney General, (1902) A.C. 165: The council had power to run tramways. It ran omnibuses to feed the tramways. It was held that the running of omnibus was *ultra-vires* and the council was restrained from running the omnibus.

3. **Personal Liability of Directors:** It is the duty of directors to see that the corporate money is used only for the legitimate business of the company. If any money is unlawfully disbursed, the directors shall be personally liable to make good the amount.

4. **Breach of Warranty of Authority:** Where the officers of a company persuade a third party to enter into a transaction which is *ultra-vires* the company, an action may lie against them in breach of warranty of authority.

5. ***Ultra-vires* Contracts:** The contracts which are *ultra-vires* are a nullity and cannot be enforced against the company. If a person has supplied goods or performed services under such a contract he cannot obtain payment. The company also cannot enforce such *ultra-vires* transactions against outsiders. An *ultra-vires* contract cannot become *intra-vires* by reason of estoppel, lapse of time, ratification or delay.

6. ***Ultra-vires* Acquired Property:** A company can protect its property acquired by an *ultra-vires* expenditure; thus, in a case where the company's telephone wires were cut, and it had no power in the memorandum to put up the wires, it was held entitled to recover damages for the injury. (***National Telephone Co. vs. Vonstables of St. Peter Port (1990) A.C. 317***).

7. **Restitution and Subrogation:** If the property acquired by the company on account of an *ultra-vires* transaction exists in *specie* or if it can be traced, the person handing it over can recover it from the company. ***('Sinclair vs. Brougham (1914) A.C. 398).***

8. ***Ultra-vires*** **Lending of Money**: If the money has been lent on behalf of the company, and the lending is *ultra-vires*, the company can sue for the recovery of the money since "the only objection to this loan is that it was made without authority. But the borrower cannot set up as a defence to an action that the person who lent him the money, and to whom he had made a promise to repay that money, had no authority to lend him that money." *Re. Coltman, 19 Ch. D. 64.*

9. ***Ultra-vires*** **Torts:** A company will be liable for torts or crimes committed in the pursuit of its stated objects. But a tort or crime committed in the course of an activity which is *ultra-vires* the company, the company would not be liable in respect of it. However, the officer, agent or servant of the company who commits the act would be personally liable in such a case.

QUESTIONS

Objective Type Questions

I. Fill up the Blanks

1. Memorandum of Association is the __________ of the company.
2. Memorandum is not necessary for a __________members for a public limited company.
3. Memorandum must be signed by at least ___________ company.
4. Memorandum of a company limited by guarantee having a share capital must be in accordance with Table __________
5. Memorandum of an unlimited company must be in accordance with Table_________.
6. According to the Companies Act, when the Memorandum is registered with the Registrar of Companies it will bind the ________ and the __________.
7. The Clauses to be contained in the Memorandum are Name; Domicile; Object; Liability and _________.
8. Doctrine of Ultravires has reference to__________ clause.
9. Alteration of Memorandum requires __________ resolution.
10. The Companies Amendment Act, 1965 provides for the Object clause to be stated in two clauses as _________ object and __________ objects.

[*Answers:* (1) Constitution; (2) Statutory company; (3) Seven; (4) D; (5) E; (6) Company, members; (7) Subscription or Association clauses; (8) Object; (9) Special; (10) 1965; Main; Other]

II. State whether the following statements are True or False

1. Memorandum defines, confines and confirms the scope and limitation of the powers of the company.
2. Alteration of capital or liability clause requires special resolution.
3. A company can alter its name out of its own accord by passing a special resolution with the consent of the Government.
4. For shifting the registered office from one place to another in the same city, Board resolution is enough.
5. Doctrine of Ultravires will not be applicable when once a company has purchased immovable properties beyond its power.
6. Any contract entered into by the company with others or *vice versa* upon ultravires act is voidable.
7. For bringing an item falling under Other Clauses to the Main Clause of the Object Clause, special resolution is required.
8. Object Clause need not be amended for bifurcating the existing business.
9. In Memorandum, object clause and power to amend the object clause are one and the same.
10. Association or Subscription Clause in the Memorandum represents the undertaking of the Directors' liabilities.

[*Answers:* True: (1), (3), (4), (5), (7), (8), (10); False: (2), (6), (9)]

Review Questions

1. What do you understand by the Memorandum of Association?
2. Briefly explain the requisites of tile memorandum.
3. List out the principles to be followed for selecting the name of a company.
4. State the various clauses of memorandum of association and explain any two clauses briefly.
5. What do you understand by doctrine *of ''Ultra-vires''?*
6. Can an *Ultra-vires* act be ratified?
7. Briefly explain the types of *Ultra-vires* acts.
8. What is Memorandum of Association? State its purposes?
9. Briefly explain the contents of memorandum.

10. How will you alter the registered office clauses of the memorandum?
11. Briefly describe the alteration of the objects clause in the memorandum of Associations.
12. What do you mean by doctrine of *Ultra-vires?* Can the *Ultra-vires* act be ratified?
13. Explain the various types of *Ultra-vires* acts.
14. What is a Memorandum of Association? Describe its contents. Also discuss the importance of objects clause.
15. Discuss the doctrine of *Ultra-vires.*
16. What is the procedure for alteration of a Memorandum of Association? Can new objects be added by way of alteration?
17. What is the importance of the objects clause of the Memorandum of Association? If a company undertakes to do anything which is not either expressly or impliedly provided for by the objects clause, what would be the consequences?
18. When and how does a company alter its capital clause?

CHAPTER 5

Articles of Association

Meaning of Articles

'Articles' means the Articles of Association of a company as originally framed or as altered from time-to-time in pursuance of any previous companies law or of this Act. The Articles of Association are the rules and regulations of a company framed for the purpose of internal management of its affairs. It deals with the rights of the members of the company *inter-se.* The Articles are framed for carrying out the aims and objects of the Memorandum of Association. The Articles of Association of a company are subordinate to and are controlled by the Memorandum of Association. *Lord Cairs* observed in this regard. "The memorandum is as it were the area beyond which the action of the company cannot go; inside that area the shareholder may make such regulations for their own government as they think fit."

It is not obligatory to register Articles in the case of a public company limited by shares. In such a case Model Articles contained in 'Table A' of Schedule I will apply. However, a private company, a company limited by guarantee and an unlimited company must compulsorily register their Articles along with the memorandum. (Section 26).

In the case of an unlimited company, the Articles shall state the number of the members, with which the company is to be registered, and if it has a share capital, the amount of share capital with which it is to be registered. (Section 27(1))

In the case of a company limited by guarantee, the Articles shall state the number of member with which company is to be registered. (Section 27(2))

In the case of a private company, Articles must contain provisions which

(a) restrict the right to transfer its shares;

(b) limit the number of its members to fifty excluding past and the present employees of the company;

(c) prohibit any invitation to the public to subscribe for any shares in or debentures or public deposits of the company. (Section 27(3))

Form and Signature of Articles [Sections 29 and 30]

The Articles of Association of any company not being a company limited by shares, shall be in one such form in Tables 'C', 'D', and 'E' in Schedule I as may be applicable, or in a form as near thereto as circumstances admit. However, a company may include any additional matters in its Articles in sofaras they are not inconsistent with the provisions contained in the form in any of the Tables 'C', 'D' and 'E' adopted by the company (Section 29).

Thus, in the case of a company limited by guarantee and having no share capital such as a club or library, or society, an Article giving power to the board of directors or managing committee to expel a member is not invalid being not inconsistent with Table C *[Gaiman vs. National Association for Mental Health (1971] 41 Comp. Cas. 929 (Ch. D)]*. But, in ***P. C. Arvindhan vs. M.A. Kesavan [1973] Tax LR 1844 (Ker.)***, it was held that provision in the Articles of a guarantee company that prevented its members from participating in the annual general meeting was illegal and void, and also inconsistent with or contrary to 'Table C'. Similarly, where 'Article 2' of the Articles of company limited by guarantee without share capital provided "for the purpose of registration, the number of members is 1,500 and this may be reduced or increased from time-to-time by the general committee", the Articles was held to be void. The Articles can be altered only by a special resolution by the general body ***[Dharam Pal Bhasin vs. B.N. Khanna [1988] 64 Comp. Cas. 651]***.

Section 30 requires that Articles shall:-

1. be printed;
2. be divided into paragraph numbered consecutively;
3. be signed by each subscriber of the Memorandum of Association (who shall add his address, description and occupation, if any) in the presence of at least one witness who shall attest and shall likewise add his address, description and occupation, if any.

CONTENTS OF ARTICLES OF ASSOCIATION

The articles usually contain the following matters:

1. Exclusion wholly or in part of Table A.
2. Adoption of preliminary contracts.
3. Number and value of shares.
4. Allotment of shares.

5. Calls on shares.
6. Lien on shares.
7. Transfer and transmission of shares.
8. Forfeiture of shares.
9. Alteration of capital.
10. Share certificates.
11. Conversion of shares into stock.
12. Issue of share warrants.
13. Issue of bonus shares.
14. Voting rights and proxies.
15. Meetings.
16. Directors, their appointment, etc.
17. Borrowing powers.
18. Accounts and audit.
19. Dividends and reserves.
20. Winding up.

In framing Articles of Association, care must be taken to see that regulations framed do not go beyond the powers of the company itself as contemplated by the Memorandum of Association nor should they be such as would violate any of the requirements of the Companies Act itself. All clauses in the Articles *ultra-vires* the Memorandum or the Act shall be null and void.

ALTERATION OF ARTICLES OF ASSOCIATION

Companies have wide powers to alter their Articles. Any restriction on the exercise of their powers will be invalid. Articles of Association may be altered by a company by passing a *special resolution* to that effect. The altered Articles will bind the members in the same way as did the original Articles. *The company must file with the registrar a copy of the special resolution within one month from the date of its passing.*

Limitations: The right of alteration of Articles is subject to the following conditions:

1. Consistent with Memorandum: The alteration must not be inconsistent with or go beyond the provisions of the memorandum.

2. In Compliance with Companies Act: The alteration must not provide for anything which is opposed to the provisions of the Act; for example, Articles cannot authorise a company to issue shares at a discount of more than 10% at anytime and everytime..

3. Interests of Company as a Whole: The alteration of Articles must be made, in good faith for the benefit of the company as a whole. The alteration will not, however, be bad merely because it inflicts hardship on an individual shareholder.

Examples

(1) A company had a lien on all shares "not fully paid" for calls due to the company. There was only one shareholder. A, who owned fully paid-up shares. He also held partly-paid shares in the company. A died. The company altered its Articles by striking out the words "not fully paid-up" and thus gave itself a lien on all shares, whether fully paid-up or not. The legal representative of A challenged the alteration on the ground that the alteration had retrospective effect.

Held: The alteration was good, as it was done *bona fide* for the benefit of the company as a whole, even though the alteration had a retrospective effect ***(Allen vs. Gold Reefs of West Africa Ltd. (1900) 1 Ch. 656).***

(2) By an alteration in the Articles, a company was empowered to expropriate shares held by any member who was in business in competition with the company. At the time of alteration, there was only one member doing business in competition with the company. He challenged the alternation.

Held*:** The alteration was valid, although only one member was at that time within the ambit of alteration, as the alteration was *bona fide* and for the benefit of the company ***(Sidebottom vs. Kershaw Leese & Co. (1920) Ch. 154 (C.A.)).

4. No fraud on Minority: The alteration of Articles must not oppress or constitute a fraud on minority.

5. No Additional Liability on a Member to be Imposed: No member of a company will be bound by any alteration made in the Memorandum or the Articles after he became a member which requires him to take or subscribe for more shares or in any way increases his liability to contribute to the share capital of or otherwise to pay money to the company, unless he agrees in writing before or after the alteration is made.

6. Approval of Central Government: No alteration can be made in the Articles which has the effect of converting the public company into a private company unless such alteration has been approved by the Central Government.

7. Not Causing Breach of Contract: An alteration in the Articles which causes a breach of contract with an outsider will be inoperative.

8. Not Illegal: The alteration must not sanction anything which is illegal.

9. Public Policy: The alteration in Articles should not be against public policy or interest.

10. Consistent with the Court Orders: Alteration must not be inconsistent with the alteration ordered by the court. For instance, where the court has amended the Memorandum or Articles of Association in pursuance of its powers in cases of oppression and mismanagement under Sections 397 and 398, the company cannot make the alteration later on which is inconsistent with the court's order without the leave of the court.

11. It may be regarded as having a retrospective effect so long as it does not affect the things already done by the company ***(Allen vs. Gold Reefs of West African (1990) I ch. 656; McArthur vs. Gulf Line (1909) S.C. 732).***

12. It may further be noted that an injunction cannot be granted to prevent the adoption of new articles which constituted a breach of contract. But if the company acts on them it may be liable to damages ***(Shirtlaw vs. Southern Foundaries Ltd. 1040 A.Cc.7.1 (760))***

13. A reserve liability once created cannot be undone but may be cancelled on a reduction of capital ***(Midland Railway Carriage Wagon Co. (1907) W.N.1715; (Section 99).***

14. Any irregular alterations which have been acted upon for many years are binding.

Inspection and Copies of the Articles

A company shall, on being so required by a member, send to him within seven days of the requirement, on payment of one rupee, a copy of the articles. If a company makes default, the company and every officer of the company, who is in default, shall be punishable with fine up to Rs. 50 (Section 39).

LEGAL EFFECT OF MEMORANDUM AND ARTICLES

'The Memorandum and the Articles shall, when registered, bind the company and the members thereof to the same extent as if they respectively had been signed by the company and each member to observe all the provisions of the Memorandum and the Articles [Section 36(1)].

Binding Effects of Memorandum and Articles

The effect of these provisions is to constitute through the Memorandum and the Articles of Association of a company a contract between each member and the company.

The effect and the implications of this section may be appreciated by considering how for the Memorandum and the Articles bind.

(i) The members to the company.

(ii) The company to the members.

(iii) The members *inter-se*

(iv) The company to the outsiders.

Members Bound to the Company: As between the member and the company, each member of the company is bound to observe the various provisions of the Memorandum and Articles of Association as if he had actually signed of the same.

Each member must observe the provisions of the Articles and Memorandum. *For instance*, a company has a right of lien on members' shares, or to forefeit the shares on non-payment of calls. Every member is bound by the whatever is contained in the Memorandum and Articles.

Examples

The Articles of a company contained a clause that on the bankruptcy of a member, his shares should be sold to other person and at a price fixed by the directors. 'B', a shareholder was adjudicated bankrupt. His trustee in bankruptcy claimed that he was not bound by these provisions and should be at liberty to sell the shares at the true value.

Held: That the trustee was bound by the Articles, as shares were purchased 'B' in terms of the Articles. ***(Borland Trustees vs. Steel Bros. Co. Ltd. (1901) 1 Ch. 279).***

Each member is not only bound by the covenants of Memorandum and Articles as originally framed but as altered from time-to-time in accordance with the provisions of the Compaines Act.

The Articles of association are the regulations of the company binding on the company and on its shareholders.

Shareholders cannot among themselves enter into an agreement which is contrary to or inconsistent with the Articles of Association of the company ***(V.B. Rangaraj vs. V.B. Gopalakrsihnan (1992) 73 Comp. Cas. 201 (S.C.)).***

Bradford Banking Corporation vs. Briggs (1816) 12 A.C 29: The Articles provided that the company shall have a first and paramount lien upon each share for debt due to the company by the shareholders. One of the shareholders owing money to the company borrowed money from the bank on the security of shares. The bank gave notice of deposit of shares to the company. It was held that the shares deposited with the bank were bound by the Articles just as if the shareholders had contracted with the company, and therefore, the lien which the company acquired under the Articles on those shares precluded the bank from getting priority in respect of the debts incurred by a shareholders before the notice was given.

In ***Hickman vs. Kent or Romney Marsh Sheep Breeders Association (1915), 1. Ch. 881*** the Articles provided for the reference of disputes between a member and the company to arbitration. H, a shareholder brought an action against the company in connection with a dispute between the company and himself in his capacity as a member. It was held that the company was entitled to have the action stayed, as the Articles amounted to a contract between the company and H to refer such disputes between them to arbitration.

But a dispute between the company and a director in his capacity as director would not be within the terms of such Articles even if the directors was also a member. It is, thus, clear from the above that the company can sue its members for the enforcement of its Articles as well as for restraining their breach.

Company Bound to the Members

The company is bound to the members by the various provisions contained in the Memorandum and the Articles of Association in the same way as the members are bound to the company. The company can, therefore, exercise its rights as against any members only in pursuance of and in accordance with the Articles and the Memorandum. Any member is entitled to sue the company to prevent any breach of the Articles which would affect his right as a member of the company. Thus, where a right is conferred by the Articles on a shareholder to record his vote at a company meeting, the chairman of the meeting, cannot deprive him on this right.

Wood vs. Odessa Waterworks Co.(1989) 42. Ch D. 636: In this case, the judge granted an injunction at the instance of a member to restrain the company from contravening the Articles. The Articles of Association of defendant company provided that "the directors may, with the sanction of the company at general meeting, declare a dividend to be paid to the members." Instead of paying the dividend in cash to the shareholders, resolution was passed to give them debenture bonds. The plaintiff, a member sued the directors for acting on the resolution. The directors were restrained from acting on the resolutions on the ground that 'to be paid' mean to be paid in cash and the debenture bonds proposed to be issued, were not payment in cash.

Members *Inter-se*

The Articles and the Memorandum do not constitute express agreement between the members of the company. Yet each member of the company is bound by the Memorandum and Articles on the basis of an implied contract to the other members. The Articles regulate the rights of the members *inter-se* but such rights can be enforced only through the company.

It is well settled that the Articles of Association will have a contractual force between the company and its members as also between the members *inter-se* in relation to their rights as such members ***(Ramakrishna Industries (P) Ltd. vs. P.R. Ramakrishnan (Supra)).***

Example

The Articles of a company provided that whenever any member wished to transfer his shares under an obligation to inform the directors of his intention and the directors were under an obligation to take the said shares equally between them at a fair value. The directors refused to take the shares of a particular member on the ground that the Articles did not impose an enforceable liability upon them.

Held: The directors were under an obligation to purchase the shares, as members of the company, in terms of the provisions of the Articles. There was a personal liability of members *inter-se* ***(Rayfield vs. Hand (1960) Ch. 1).***

Company Bound to the Outsiders

Articles do not constitute any contract between the company and an outsider. This is because outsider is not a party to the contract, and therefore, cannot sue on it. An outsider is not entitled to enforce the Articles against the company for any breach of right that is conferred on him by the Articles. Thus, a provision in the Articles to pay remuneration to the promoters constitutes no contract between them and the company on which they can sue the company in damages, if the remuneration is not paid to them.

The term 'outsider' means a person who is not a member of the company. Even a member will be regarded as on outsider and he will not be in a position to enforce a right against the company if he enjoys the right in the capacity of a solicitor or a director and not in the capacity of a member.

Example

1. The Articles of a company provided that E should be solicitor for life to the company and should not be removed from office except for misconduct. Later on he also became a member of the company. But after employing him as solicitor for a number of years, the company discontinued his services. He, being a member, sued the company for damages for breach of the contract contained in the Articles of association.

Held: His suit was dismissed on the ground that, he as a solicitor, was no party to the Articles. He must prove a contract independent of the Articles. There was no infringement of his right as a member. The breach of contract was there but in this capacity as a non-member ***(Eley vs. Positive Government Security Life Assurance Co., (1876) 1 Ex. D. 88).***

2. *Major-General Shanta Shamsher Jung Bahadur Rana vs. Kamani Bros. (P) Ltd. (1959) 20 Comp.Cas. 501 (Bom).* The Articles of a company provided that the board of directors could from time-to-time appoint any one or more of them as managing director(s). Under the Articles a managing director could be removed in the same way as other directors of the company, viz., by a special resolution. S, was appointed on 24.6.1957 as managing director by a resolution of the board. The contention of S was that special resolution not having been passed, he could not be removed. The question was whether S who was not a shareholder could rely upon the Articles.

Held: That the plaintiff was not entitled to place any reliance on the Articles. It was observed that even between a member and the company the Articles of Association constitute a contract only in respect of his rights and liabilities as a shareholders, but not in respect of rights and liabilities which he has in a capacity other than that of a member. But as between the company and outside, i.e, persons who are not shareholders, the Articles do not constitute a contract which that person can take advantage.

In ***Eley vs. Positive Government Life Assurance Company (1876) 1 .Ex. E. 88:*** The Articles of Association of a company provided that E should be a solicitor of the company for life and should not be removed from his office except on account of misconduct. He was also a member of the company. E acted as a solicitor of the company for sometime but ultimately the company discontinued his services without any allegation of misconduct. He sued the company for damages for breach of the contract. It was held that the action was to maintainable because the right which he attempted to enforce was conferred upon him in a capacity other than that of a shareholder.

The rule as laid down in Eley's has proved to be rather harsh, and the courts have modified it. The courts have in some cases acted on the footing that a clause in the Articles not dealing with the rights of a member as such, but apparently intended to operate as a contract with him is to be regarded as the basis of the contract.

The Articles provided that the remuneration of the directors should be the annual sum of Rs.1,000. The directors were employed and accepted office on the footing of the Articles. For sometime the directors, who were also members acted as directors but were not paid. The company went into liquidation. It was held that they were entitled to recover the arrears of remuneration as the Articles were embodied in the contract between the company and the directors. ***[Ex.p. Beckwith (1898) l.Ch. 324].***

Whether Directors are Bound by Whatever is Contained in the Articles?

Yes, the directors of the company derive their powers from the Articles and are subjected to limitations, if any, placed on their powers by the Articles. If they contravene any provisions of Articles, two parties may be affected: (i) the company itself, and (2) then outsiders.

In case of contravention of the provisions of the Articles, the directors render themselves liable to an action at the instance of the members. However, members may ratify the act of the director, if they so desire. But if as a result of the breach of duty any loss has resulted to the company, the directors are liable to refund to the company any damage so suffered.

Further, where the directors contravene the provisions of the Articles, it may affect outsiders' interests also. This is explained below with the help of a case, viz., ***Royal British Bank vs. Turquand (1876) 619 ER 886.***

Constructive Notices of Memorandum and Articles of Association

The Memorandum and Articles of Association of every company are required to be registered with Registrar of Companies. On registration they become public documents. They are open for public inspection on payment. Everyone dealing with the company, whether, a shareholder or an outsider is presumed to have read the two documents. He will be presumed to know the contents of these documents. This deemed knowledge of the two document and their contents is known as the *constructive notice of Memorandum and Articles.* Accordingly, where a person deals with a company in manner which is inconsistent with the provisions of the Memorandum or Articles, he must take the consequences in respect of such dealing.

Kotta Venkataswamy vs. Ram Murthi AIR (1934) Mad. 579. In this case, the Articles of a company required that all deeds and other important documents should be signed by the managing director, the secretary and working director on behalf of the company. The plaintiff accepted a deed of mortgage executed by the secretary and the working director only. It was held that the plaintiff could not claim under this deed as the bond was invalid. The court applied the documents of constructive notice in favour of the company.

Moreover, the parties dealing with the company must be taken not only to have read these documents but also to have understood them according to their proper meaning. Even if the party dealing with the company does not have actual notice of the contents, it is presumed that he has "constructive notice" of them.

Examples

1. One of the Articles of a company provides that a bill of exchange to be effective must be signed by two directors. A bill of exchange is signed only by one of the director, the payee cannot claim under the bill.
2. Similarly, if a person enters into a contract which is beyond the powers of the company, he cannot acquire any rights under the contract against the company.

DOCTRINE OF INDOOR MANAGEMENT

The doctrine of indoor management is an exception to the rule of constructive notice. A person dealing with a company is deemed to have company. So, if he enters into a transaction with the company which is *ultra-vires* of the Memorandum or Articles, he cannot treat the transaction as binding on the company. On the other hand, if the transaction appears to be proper one, when compared with the Memorandum and Articles, it would be grossly unfair if the company could escape liability it by showing that there was some irregularity in the conduct of the company's affairs leading up to the transaction, when the other party did not know of the irregularity and had no means of discovering it.

This rule has been described by *Lord Hatherley* as the doctrine of indoor management. It means that outsiders dealing with the company is entitled to assume that everything has been regularly done sofaras its internal proceeding are concerned. The doctrine had its origin in the famous case of ***Royal British Bank vs. Turquand (1856, 6 E & B.327*** whose facts are asunder.

The directors of the bank issued a bond to Mr. Turquand. The Articles provided that the directors had the power to issue bond if authorised by a proper resolution of the company. No such resolution was passed. It was held that Turquand could sue on the bond as he was entitled to assume that the resolution must have been passed. It was observed that persons dealing with the company are bound to read the registered documents and to see that the proposed dealing is not inconsistent therewith. But they are not bound to do more, they need not inquire into the regularity of internal proceedings.

The doctrine of indoor management is eminently practical and is based on business convenience, for business could not be carried smoothly if a person dealing with the company was compelled to call for evidence that all internal regulations have been duly observed. The doctrine is not only convenient, it is also just. The lot of creditors of a company is not a particularly happy one; it would be unhappier still if the company could escape liability by denying the authority of the officials to act on its behalf.

The Memorandum and the Articles of a company are public documents and accessible to all who are to consult them; but the details of the internal procedure are not registered and not accessible to all.

Exceptions to the Doctrine of Indoor Management: The doctrine is however, subject to the following exceptions:

1. Knowledge of Irregularity: A person, who deal with the company and who has knowledge of the irregularity in its internal management in connection with the subject-matter of his dealings, cannot claim the benefit of the rule in Turquand's case.

Howard vs. Patent Ivory Manufacturing Co. (1888) 38. Ch.D. 156: Under the Articles the directors were empowered to borrow up to £1,000 on behalf of the company without the consent of the general meeting and to borrow further money with such consent. The directors themselves lent £3,500 to the company and took debentures. No resolution in any general meeting was passed to authorise such borrowings. The company went into liquidation. It was held that the company was liable to the extent of £1,000 and directors were not entitled to the further amount because they had the knowledge of the irregularity.

This exception is not confined to a person dealing with the company. Even a company may have notice of irregularity in the internal management of another company with which it had been dealing.

Pratt Ltd. vs. Sasson & Co. Ltd. (1938) 40 Bom. L. R.1109 P.C.: Company A lent money to company B on the mortgage of its assets. The procedure laid down in the Articles for such a transaction was not complied with. The directors of the two companies were same. It was held that the mortage is not binding as company A who had the knowledge of the irregularity through its directors.

2. Negligence: A person cannot claim the benefit of the rule in Turquand's case in circumstances under which he would have discovered the irregularity if he had made proper inquires. Further, where the circumstance surrounding the transaction are suspicious, and therefore invite inquiry, the outsider cannot claim the benefit of this rule.

Underwood vs. Bank of Liverpool (1924) 1 K.B.: The Articles of a company provided that the business of the company was to be managed by the directors. The sole director and the principal shareholder of the company paid cheques in favour of the company into his own account. The bank collected the cheques and credited him with the proceeds. An action was brought against the bank by the company on behalf of the debentureholders. The bank sought to rely on the rule in ***Royal British Bank vs. Turquand.*** It was held that the bank was not entitled to do so because the fact that the director has paid the cheques into his own account was an unusual one, and the bank should have enquired as to whether the company had a separate banking account.

3. Void or Illegal e.g., Forgery: The rule in Turquand's case will not apply where a document on which the person seeks to rely is a forgery. The doctrine of indoor management applies to irregularities which otherwise might affect genuine transactions. It cannot apply to a forgery.

Ruben vs. Great Fingall Consolidated Co. (1906) A.C. 439 H.L.: Ruben lent from a company a sum of money on the security of a share certificate. The secretary had forged the signatures of the two directors and had affixed the seal on the certificate without authority. The company refused to register the share certificate. Rubben claimed damages relying on the Turquand's rule. It was held that he could not do so because the rule did not apply where the document was forged.

4. Acts Outside the Apparent Authority: The rule in Turquand's case does not apply where a person acting on behalf of the company exceeds any actual or ostensible authority given to him. A person, who enters into a transaction with an official of the company, who has acted beyond his powers, such a person will not be protected by the rule of indoor management. ***Anand Bihari Lal vs. Dinshaw & Co.: AIR 1942 Oudh 417***. P accepted a transfer of a company's property from its accountant. Since such a transaction is apparently beyond the scope of accountant's authority, it was void.

Kredit Bank Cassel vs. Schenkers Ltd. (1927) I.K.B. 826.: The branch manager of a bank drew, and endorsed bills on behalf of his company without having any authority from the company to do so. The court held that the company was not liable for the bills because the drawing of bills was not within the usual or apparent authority of the branch manager and nor the company had given him actual authority.

5. No Knowledge of the Contents of the Articles: A person who has not actually read the Memorandum and Articles of a company and who was seek to the time, he entered into the contract, aware of their contents, cannot seek to rely on statement contained therein. *The doctrine of indoor management is based on the principle of estoppel*, and therefore, it cannot be invoked in favour of a person who has not consulted the company's Memorandum and Articles of Association. No one can rely and act upon something with he was in fact completely ignorant.

In ***Rama Corporation vs. Proved Tin and General Investment Co. (1952) 1 All ER 554,*** T was a director in the investment company. He purporting to act on behalf of the company, entered into a contract with the Rama Corporation and took a cheque from the latter. The Articles of the company did provide that the directors could delegate their powers to one of them. But Rama Corporation never read the Articles. Later, it was found that the directors of the company did not delegate their powers to T. Plaintiffs relied on the rule of indoor management.

Held: They could not, because they did not know the existence of the power to delegate.

6. Doctrine does not apply where question is in regard to very existence of agency. In ***Varkey Souriar vs. Keraleeya Banking Co. Ltd. (1957) 27 Comp. Cas. 591 (Ker.)***, the Kerala High Court held that the doctrine of indoor management cannot apply where the question is not one as to the scope of the power exercised by an apparent agent of the company, but is in regard to the very existence of the agency.

7. Doctrine is not applicable where a *precondition is to be fulfilled* before the *company itself* can exercise a particular power ***(Pacific Coast Coal Mines vs. Arbuthnot (1917) AC 607).***

MEMORANDUM AND ARTICLES DISTINGUISHED

Memorandum and Articles are public documents. They are interlinked and require to be registered for the formation of a company. Where there is any ambiguity or where the memorandum is silent on any point, the Articles may serve to explain or supplement the memorandum. Beyond this, the two documents have nothing in common and differ from one another in the following aspects:

1. Contents and Scope: Memorandum of Association is the charter of the company and defines the scope of its activities. Articles of Association of the company is a document which regulates the internal management of the company. These are the rules made by the company for carrying out the objects of the company as set out in the memorandum.

2. Relationship between Company, Members and Outsiders: Memorandum of Association defines the relation of the company with the outside world, whereas, Articles of Association deals with the rights of the members of the company *inter-se* and also establishes the relationship of the company with the members.

3. Alteration: Memorandum of Association cannot be altered except in the maner and to the extent provided by the Act, whereas the Articles being only the bye-laws of the company, can be altered by a special resolution.

4. Supremacy: Memorandum is a supreme document of the company, whereas Articles are subordinate to the memorandum. They cannot alter or control the memorandum.

5. Adoption: Every company must have its own memorandum. But a company limited by shares need not register its Articles. In such a case Table A applies.

6. *Ultra-vires* Acts: A company cannot depart from the provision contained in its memorandum, and if it does, it would be *ultra-vires* the company. Anything done against the provisions of Articles, but which is *intra-vires* the memorandum, can be ratified.

QUESTIONS

Objective Type Questions

I. Fill up the Blanks

1. Articles of Association is a contract between __________ and __________.
2. Public Limited Company need not file Articles because Table __________ will apply.

3. Articles can be amended only by passing a ______ resolution.
4. Articles are not contracts as among ______________.
5. Royal British Bank vs. Turquand explains the Doctrine of ______________.
6. First and foremost exception to the doctrine of Indoor Management is doctrine of ______________.
7. Typographical and clerical mistakes found in the Articles have to be amended only by passing ____________ Resolution.
8. Doctrine of Indoor Management is a protection to __________ dealing with the company.
9. Doctrine of Constructive notice is a protection to __________ from being penalised by __________.
10. Articles are generally known as __________ laws of a Company

[*Answers:* (1) Members and the Company; (2) A; (3) Special; (4) Members; (5) Indoor Management; (6) Constructive Notice; (7) Special; (8) Outsiders; (9) Company; third parties, i.e., outsiders; (10) Bye]

II. State whether following statements are True or False

1. Articles can substitute the Memorandum on matters where Memorandum is silent.
2. Copies of laser printed Articles of Association can be accepted by the Registrar.
3. In the case of a Public Limited Company, if any clause is found missing in its Articles, the appropriate clauses as found in Table A will not apply.
4. Unless Articles authorise for borrowing funds by directors they cannot borrow.
5. *Ultravires* of Articles of Association are *Intravires* the Company law.
6. Articles can be amended by the Board of Directors.
7. Persons directly appointed under the Articles of Association are subjected to alteration of the relevant clauses under which they are employed.
8. Articles can provide for quorum of meetings which may he a larger one than that are prescribed under Companies Act.
9. Articles may provide that a member of a company cannot do competing business against the company.
10. Any provision contained in the Article cannot he amended in a retrospective manner.

[*Answers:* True: (2), (4), (5), (7), (8), (9); False: (1), (3), (6), (10)]

III. Multiple Choice Questions

1. Which of the following companies need not have their own Articles of Association?
   (a) unlimited companies.
   (b) companies limited by guarantee.
   (c) public companies limited by shares.
2. If a public company limited by shares does not have its own Articles, it may adopt
   (a) Table A in Schedule I to the Act.
   (b) Table B in Schedule I to the Act.
   (c) Table C in Schedule I to the Act.
3. If the Articles of a company conflict with the Memorandum,
   (a) the Articles shall prevail.
   (b) the directors will resolve the conflict.
   (c) the Court will resolve the conflict.
4. The Memorandum and Articles of a company are open to inspection by
   (a) the members of the company.
   (b) the members and creditors of the company.
   (c) everybody.
5. Doctrine of constructive notice means:
   (a) Notice of alteration of objects clause to the Registrar.
   (b) Notice of change of name to members.
   (c) Notice to outsiders dealing with the company as to contents of Memorandum and Articles.

[*Answers:* 1 (c); 2 (a); 3 (a); 4 (c); 5 (c)]

Review Questions

1. Define articles of association of a company.
2. List out the contents of articles of association.
3. Describe the doctrine of constructive notice.
4. What do you understand by doctrine of indoor management?
5. What is the legal effect of articles of association between the members and the company?

6. Is it necessary for every company to have articles of association of its own?
7. What are the articles of association? State its contents.
8. How can you alter the articles? State the points to be observed while altering the articles?
9. Distinguish between Memorandum of Association and Articles of Association.
10. Briefly describe the legal effects of the memorandum and articles.
11. What do you mean by doctrine of constructive notice?
12. What do you mean by doctrine of indoor management? What are its exceptions?
13. *"The power of altering the articles is wide, yet it is subject to a large number of limitation"*. Explain.
14. Discuss the extent to which Articles of Association of a company binds:
    (a) the members to the company,
    (b) the company to the members,
    (c) the members among themselves, and
    (d) the company to the outsiders.
15. Distinguish Articles of Association from memorandum.
16. What is the meaning and significance of the doctrine of *"Indoor Management"?* Discuss with reference to decided case, ***"Royal British Bank vs. Turquand"***.
17. How can the Articles of association of a company be altered? Discuss the limits on the powers of a company to alter or to add to the Articles.
18. *"Articles of Association constitute a contract between the company and its members and between the members intre-se"*. Elucidate this statement and state whether an outsider can enforce the Articles against the company.
19. *"Memorandum of Association and Articles of Association are public documents."* Explain this statement and discuss the *"doctrine of indoor management"* in this connection.

◈◈◈

CHAPTER 6

Prospectus

A public company may raise its capital by issuing shares or debentures. The public is invited to subscribe for its shares or debentures. The invitation containing the offer states the prospects of the company and the purposes for which the capital is required. The document inviting the public to purchase the shares or debentures of the company is called a *prospectus*.

Definition of a Prospectus

Section 2(36) defines a prospectus as "any document described or issued as a prospectus and includes any notice, circular, advertisement or other document inviting deposits from the public or inviting offer from the public for the subscription or purchase of any shares in, or debentures of, a body corporate."

A prospectus is usually a circular or newspaper advertisement published by the promoters after the formation of the company to induce the public to take share in the company. The invitation must be to the public if the document is to be a prospectus. Thus, a prospectus is not merely an advertisement; it may be a circular or even a notice to the public.

Conditions for a Prospectus

Any document which satisfies the conditions laid down in the Companies Act shall be taken as a prospectus within the meaning of the Act. The following are the requirements to consider a document as a prospectus:

1. **Invitation to the Public:** The prospectus is an invitation to offer to the public to subscribe for the shares and debentures of the company. If the invitation is not made to the public at large but made only to a small section of it, it is not a prospectus.

2. **Issued to the Public:** The prospectus should be considered as such only when it is issued to the public. Therefore, a document which is for private circulation or confidential shall not be considered as a prospectus even though it contains the particulars to be set out in the prospectus.

3. **Issued as a Prospectus:** The prospectus should be issued or described as a prospectus. Otherwise, it is not a prospectus within the meaning of this Act.

Objects of Issuing a Prospectus

The prospectus is issued for the following purposes:

1. To attract the investors.
2. To make enough disclosure to the investors to enable them to decide whether or not to purchase shares or debentures of the company.
3. To secure that the directors of the company accepted responsibility for the statement in the prospectus. A prospectus is thus only a window through which a prospective investor can look the soundness of a company's venture.

What Constitutes an Offer to the Public?

The word 'public' is a general word. No particular numbers are prescribed. Anything from two to infinity may serve. Where the invitation or offer of shares made to a section of the public do not entitle other than those who received the invitation or offer it will not be an invitation to the public. The offering of shares to the kith and kin of a director is not an invitation to the public to buy shares. ***(Rattan Singh vs. Moga Transport Co. Ltd. (1959)).*** Further, the learned judge in this case held that in all cases the determination of the question of an offer begin made to the public depends upon the facts and language of the notice and the particular circumstances of each case.

***Nash vs. Lynde. (1929) A.C. 158*:** The director of a company prepared a document which was in the form of a prospectus and was marked "strictly private and confidential." The document did not contain all the material facts required by the Act to be disclosed. It was circulated among the directors and their friends. The plaintiff has purchased shares on the footing of these documents which he obtained from a friend of a director. *It was held that the document received by him was not a prospectus as private communication between business friends does not constitute a prospectus.*

Lord Summer in the above case observed, "The test is whether the offer is such as to be open to any one who brings his money and applies in due form whether the prospectus was addressed to him on behalf of the company or not."

The 'public' is not restricted to the public at large but includes any section of the public whether selected as members or debentureholders or as clients of the person issuing the prospectus or in any other manner.

In the case, South of England Natural Gas and Petroleum Company Ltd. (1911) 1. Ch .573. 3000 copies of a prospectus headed 'for private circulation only' were distributed to shareholders of gas companies. It was not publicly advertised. It was held that the prospectus was an offer of shares 'to the public'.

Is the issue of prospectus compulsory? When prospectus is not required to be issued?

No, issue of prospectus by a company is not compulsory in the following cases:

(i) A private company is not required to issue a prospectus.

(ii) Even a public company need not issue a prospectus if the promoters or directors feel that they can mobilise resources through personal relationship and contacts. In such cases, the company is required to file a statement called *'statement in lieu of prospectus'* with the registrar of companies.

(iii) As per the Amendment Act, 1988, a company may issue any forms of application for shares or debentures accompanied by a *memorandum* containing the prescribed salient features of a prospectus (instead of prospectus). However, in such a case, a copy of the prospectus must be made available to any person on request [Sec. 56(3)].

(iv) Where the application form is issued in connection with a bonafied invitation to a person to enter into an underwriting agreement with respect to the shares or debentures [Sec. 56(3)].

(v) Where the application form is issued in relation to shares or debentures not offered to the public [Sec. 56(3)].

(vi) Where the shares or debentures are offered to existing holders of shares or debentures (*i.e.*, rights issue) with or without the right of renunciation in favour or other persons [Sec. 56(5)].

(vii) Where the issue relates to shares or debentures which are, or to be uniform in all respects with shares or debentures previsouly issued and dealt in and quoted on a recognised stock exchange [Sec.56(5)].

(viii) Where invitation to the public for subscription to the shares or debentures of a company is from of an advertisement, ordinarily called as "prospectus announcement."

REQUIREMENTS AND FORMALITIES IN ISSUING A PROSPECTUS

Issue of prospectus in order to be valid, must satisfy the following legal requirements:

1. **Issued after Incorporation:** A prospectus is generally issued after incorporation of the company. However, the Companies Act permits the issue of prospectus in relation to an intended company.

2. ***SEBI's* approval to the draft prospectus:** In case the company proposes to raise capital by issue of shares or debentures to the general public, a draft prospectus has to be submitted to the Securities Exchange Board of India (*SEBI*) through an eligible merchant banker at least 21 days prior to the filing of prospectus with the registrar of companies. In case *SEBI* suggests certain changes in the draft prospectus, such changes should be made by the companies before filing the prospectus with the registrar.

3. **Dating of Prospectus:** Every prospectus issued by or on behalf of a company must be dated and that date shall unless the contrary is proved, be regarded as the date of its publication. (Section 55)

4. **Registration of Prospectus (Section 60):** A copy of the prospectus signed by every director or prospect directors or by his agent must be delivered to the registrar on or before the date of publication. The prospectus issued to the public should mention on the face it that a copy of the prospectus along with the specified documents have been filed with the registrar. Where a person is named therein as auditor, legal adviser, attorney, solicitor, banker or broker of the company, it must be accompanied by a consent in writing of such persons to act as such. Where a prospectus is issued without a copy thereof being delivered to the registrar, as above, or without the required documents and consent attached thereto, the company and every person knowingly party to the issue of the prospectus, is liable to fine up to Rs.5,000.

5. **Time Limit to Issue Prospectus:** A prospectus must not be issued more than 90 days after the date on which a copy thereof is delivered for registration. If a prospectus is so issued it will be deemed to be prospectus a copy of which has not been delivered to the registrar.

6. **Approval of Prospectus by Various Agencies:** The draft prospectus has to be approved by various agencies before it is filed with the Registrar of Companies of the concerned state. The various authorities who approve the prospectus are the following:

   (i) All the *lead managers* to the issue.

   (ii) Each of the *stock exchanges* where the shares of the company are listed and where the shares/debentures are proposed to be listed.

   (iii) The lead financial institution underwriting the issue, if applicable.

   The draft prospectus is vetted by SEBI to ensure adequacy of disclosures. However, vetting by SEBI does not amount to approval of prospectus. SEBI does not take any responsibility for the correctness of the statements made or opinions expressed in the prospectus.

   The Department of Company Affairs, also advised the Registrar of Companies to ensure that in respect of every prospectus of public issues which comes up for filing with them the merchant bankers to the issue, whether as lead managers, co-managers, advisers or consultants are only those authorised by SEBI. Each merchant bankers has been given a code number.

It was also decided that Registrar of Companies shall not register a prospectus where prior to registration of the prospectus, the Registrar of Companies before whom the prospectus is filed for registration is informed by SEBI that the contents of prospectus filed are in contravention of any law or statutory rules and regulations.

7. **Draft Prospectus to be Made Public:** SEBI has provided for making public the draft prospectus filed with SEBI. The lead merchant bankers shall simultaneously file copies of the draft document with the stock exchanges where the issue is proposed to be listed. Lead merchant bankers shall also make copies available to the public. Lead managers/stock exchanges can charge an appropriate sum to the person requesting such a copy.

8. **Applications Form to be Accompanied With Prospectus:** According to Section 56, every form of application for subscribing the shares or debentures of a company shall not be issued unless it is accompanied by a copy of the prospectus. However, there are certain exceptions to this *viz*:

   (a) When it is issued in connection with a bonafide invitation to a person to enter into an underwriting agreement with regard to shares or debentures;

   (b) Where shares or debentures are not offered to the public;

   (c) Where offers is made only to existing members or debentureholders of the company;

   (d) Where the shares or debentures are uniform in all respects with those previously issued and quoted on a stock exchange.

   The rationale behind above exception is in regard to exceptions (a) and (b), since the public is not involved thus no need of protection, while exceptions (c) and (d), the offered being already a member must have adequate information about the company to protect himself.

9. **Experts to be Unconnected With the Formation or Management of the Company:** A prospectus shall not include statement purporting to be made by experts if they are connected either with the formation or with the management of the company. (Section 57). The expression *expert* includes an 'engineer, a valuer, an accountant and any other person whose profession gives authority to a statement made by him.

10. **Expert's Consent to be Obtained:** Where a prospectus includes a statement by an expert, it must not be issued unless the expert has given his written consent to the issue of the prospectus with the statement included in the form

and context in which it is included. A statement that he has given and not withdrawn, his consent must also appear in the prospectus. [Section 58]. This is intended to protect the prospective shareholders by making the expert a party to the issue of the prospectus and making him liable for untrue statements.

11. **Terms of the Contracts Mentioned in the Prospectus not to be Varied:** A company cannot, at anytime, vary the terms of a contract referred to in the prospectus or statement in lieu of prospectus. Any alteration can be made only by a resolution passed at a general meeting of the shareholders, or on authority given by the company. (Section 61). In the case of ***Rajagopal Iyer vs. South India Rubber Works Ltd (1943) I.L.R. Mad. 133*** it was observed that even a properly authorised alteration in the prospectus before the date of allotment of shares will give valid ground to an applicant for shares to revoke his application.

12. **Share Application Form to be a Part of Memorandum Containing Salient Features of the Prospectus:** As per the recently revised rules the share application form should be a part of the memorandum containing salient features of the prospectus being attached to it along a perforated line. Such memorandum is also termed as *"abridged prospectus"*. The investor may detach the share application form along the perforated line after he had an opportunity to study the contents of the abridged prospectus, before submitting the same to the company or its designated bankers. There can be two application forms against one memorandum of prospectus.

13. **Consequences of Applying for Shares in Fictitious Names to be Prominently Displayed:** The following provision of the Companies Act must be prominently reproduced in every prospectus and every application form issued by the company to any person.

    "Any person who:

    (a) makes in a fictitious name an application to a company for acquiring or subscribing for, any shares therein, or

    (b) otherwise induces a company to allot, or register any transfer of shares therein to him or any other person in fictitious name shall be punishable with imprisonment for a term which may extend to five years."

14. The prospectus must be issued within 90 days after the date on which a copy thereof has been delivered for registration. If a prospectus is issued subsequently after the expiry of this period, it shall be deemed to be a prospectus a copy of which has not been delivered to registrar for registration.

    The registration of the prospectus with the registrar serves as an authority record of the terms and conditions of the capital issue.

15. **Contents as per Schedule II:** Every prospectus must disclose the matter as required in Schedule II of the Act.

CONTENTS OF PROSPECTUS

In order to protect the interests of the investing public against the fraud of the promoters, etc., Companies Act has provided for a large number of regulations seeking the fullest disclosure of all material and essential particulars in the prospectus. Every prospectus issued by a company must state the matters specified in Part I of the Second schedule to the Act and contain information and reports specified in Part II of the Schedule, and that the said Parts I and II shall have effect subject to the provisions contained in Part III of the Schedule.

The main contents are given below:

Part I of Schedule II

1. **General Information**

(a) Name the address of registered office of the company.

(b) Names of Regional Stock Exchanges and other stock exchanges where application has been made for listing of present issue.

(c) Statement/Declaration about refund of the issue if minimum subscription of 90%, is not received within 90 days from closure of the issue.

(d) Declaration about the issue of allotment letters/refunds within a period of 10 weeks and interest in case of any delay in refund at the prescribed rate.

(e) Date of opening of the issue.

Date of closing of the issue.

Date of earliest closing of the issue.

(f) Name and address of auditors and lead managers.

(g) Name and address of trustee under debenture trust deed (in case of debenture issue).

(h) Whether rating from *CRISIL, ICRA, CARE* or any rating agency has been obtained for the proposed debenture/preference shares issue.

(i) *Underwriting of the issue:* Names and addresses of the underwriters and the amount underwritten by them. Declaration by board of directors that the underwriters have sufficient resources to discharge their respective obligations.

2. **Capital Structure of the Company**

(a) Authorised, issued, subscribed and paid-up capital.

(b) Size of present issue giving separately reservation for preferential allotment to promoters and others.

(c) Paid-up capital

(i) after the present issue.

(ii) after conversion of debentures (if applicable).

3. Terms of the Present Issue

(a) Terms of payments

(b) Rights of the instrument holders

(c) How to apply—availability of forms, prospectus and mode of payment.

(d) Any special tax benefits for company and its shareholders.

4. Particulars of the Issue

(a) Objects

(b) Project cost

(c) Means of Financing (including contribution of promoters).

5. Company, Management and Project

(a) History, main objects and present business of the company

(b) Subsidiary(ies) of the company, if any

(c) Promoters and their background

(d) Names, addresses and occupations of managers, managing directors and other directors including nominee directors, whole-time directors, (giving their directorship in other companies)

(e) Location of project

(f) Plant and machinery, technology, process, etc.

(g) Collaboration, any performance guarantee or assistance in marketing by the collaborators

(h) Infrastructure facilities for new materials and utilities like water, electricity, etc.

(i) Schedule of implementation of the project and progress so far, giving details of land acquisition, civil works, installation of plant and machinery, trial production, commercial production, etc.

(j) The products

(i) Nature of the product(s)–consumer/industrial and end-users

(ii) Approach to marketing and proposed marketing set up.

(iii) Export possibilities and export obligations, if any (in case of a company providing any 'service' particulars, as applicable, be furnished)

(k) Future prospects—expected capacity utilisation during the first three years from the date commencement of production, and the expected year when the company would be able to earn cash profits and net profits.

6. **Information regarding company and other listed companies under the same management:** The following particulars in regard to company and other listed companies under the same management which made any capital issue during the last 3 years has to be given:

(i) name of the company;

(ii) year of issue;

(iii) type of issue (Public, Rights or Composite)

(iv) amount of issue

(v) date of closure of issue

(vi) date of completion of delivery of shares/debenture certificates

(vii) date of completion of project where the object of the issue is financing of the project; and

(viii) rate of dividend paid.

7. **Outstanding Litigation Pertaining to:**

(i) matter likely to affect operation and finance of the company including disputed tax liabilities of any nature;

(ii) criminal prosecution launched against the company for alleged offences under various enactments given in part I of Schedule 13 to the Companies Act, Indian Stamp Act, Central Excise Act, Industrial Development Regulation Act, Essential Commodities Act, Companies Act, Foreign Exchange Management Act, etc.

8. **Management Perception of Risk Factors** (e.g., sensitivity to foreign exchange rate fluctuations, difficulty in availability of raw materials or in marketing of products, cost/time over-run, etc.).

Part II of Schedule II

A. General Information

1. Consent of Directors, Auditors, Solicitors/Advocates, Managers to Issue, Registrar of Issue, Bankers to the Company, Bankers to the Issue and Experts.

2. Expert opinion obtained, if any.

3. Change, if any, in directors and auditors during the last three years, and reasons thereof.
4. Authority for the issue and details of resolution passed for the issue.
5. Procedure and time schedule for allotment and issue of certificates.
6. Names and addresses of the Company Secretary, Legal Advisors, Lead Managers, Co-Managers, Auditors, Bankers to the Company, Bankers to the Issue and Brokers to the Issue.

B. Financial Information: Following Reports have to be given:

(i) A report by the auditors of the company with respect to the profits and losses for the five financial years preceding the issue of prospectus. The report should also show the rates of dividend paid on each class of shares for each of the said years. If the company has been carrying on business for less than five years, the figures are to be given for the actual period. If the five financial years immediately preceding the issue of the prospectus cover a period of less than five years, the report should cover as many financial years as may be necessary, so that the aggregate period covered is not less than 5 years.

The report should also give statement of assets and liabilities as at the last date of the latest financial year. The report should indicate the nature of any provision or adjustments made or yet to be made in respect of the figures of any profits or losses or assets and liabilities. Assets and liabilities of the subsidiaries as at the last date to which the accounts of the company were made up must also be shown in the like manner.

(ii) If the company proposes to acquire any business, a report by a Chartered Accountant, upon the profits and losses of the business for each of the five financial years preceding the issue of prospectus and the assets and liabilities of business.

C. Statutory and other Information

1. Minimum subscription.
2. Expenses of the issue giving separately fee payable to:
   (a) Advisors
   (b) Registrars to the issue
   (c) Managers to the issue
   (d) Trustees for the debentureholders
3. Underwriting commission and brokerage.
4. Previous issue for cash.

5. Previous public or rights issue, if any (during last five years):
   (a) Date of Allotment: Closing Date:
   Date of Refunds: Date of listing on the stock exchange:
   (b) If the issue (s) is at premium or discount and the amount thereof.
   (c) The amount paid or payable by way of premium, if any, on each share which had been issued within two years proceeding the date of the prospectus or is to be issued, stating the dates or proposed dates of issue and, where some shares have been or are to be issued at a premium and other shares of the same class at a lower premium, or at a discount, the reason for the differentiation and how any premiums received have been or are to be disposed of.
6. Commission or brokerage on previous issue.
7. Issue of shares otherwise than for cash.
8. Debentures and redeemable preference shares and other instruments issued by the company outstanding as on the date of prospectus and terms of issue.
9. Option to subscribe.
10. The details of option to subscribe for securities to be dealt within a depository.
11. Purchase of property.

   Where proceeds of the issue are to be used in payment (wholly or partly) of property purchased or proposed to be purchased or acquired, the following particulars are required to be given:
   (a) the names, address, descriptions and occupation of the vendors;
   (b) the amount paid or payable in cash, shares or debentures, to the vendor;
   (c) the nature of the title or interest in such property acquired or to be acquired by the company.
   (d) short particulars of every transaction relating to the property completed within the two preceding years, in which any vendor of the property to the company or any promoter, or a director or a proposed directors of the company had any interest.
12. (i) Details of directors, proposed directors, whole-time directors, their remuneration, appointment and remùneration of managing directors, interests of directors, their borrowing powers and qualification shares.
   (ii) The dates, parties to, and general nature of—

(a) every contract appointing or fixing the remuneration of a managing director or manager when entered into that is to say, whether within or more than, two years before the date of the prospectus;

(b) every other material contract, not being a contract entered into in the ordinary course of the business carried on or intended to be carried on by the company or a contract entered into more than two years before the date of the prospectus.

A reasonable time and place at which any such contract or a copy thereof may be inspected.

(iii) Full particulars of the nature and extent of the interest, if any, of every director or promoter—

(a) in the promotion of the company; or

(b) in any property acquired by the company within two years of the date of the prospectus or proposed to be acquired by it.

Where the interest of such a director or promoter consists in being a member of a firm or company, with a statement of all sums paid or agreed to be paid to him or to the firm or company in cash or shares or otherwise, by any person either to induce him to become, or to qualify him as, a director, or otherwise for service rendered by him or by the firm or company.

13. Rights of members regarding voting, dividend, lien on shares and the process for modification of such rights forfeiture of shares.

14. Restrictions, if any, on transfer and transmission on shares/debentures and on their consolidation/splitting.

15. Revaluation of assets, if any, (during last 5 years).

16. Material contracts and inspection of documents, e.g.:

(a) Material contracts

(b) Documents

(c) Time and place at which the contracts together with documents will be available for inspection from the date of prospectus until the date of closing of the subscription list.

Part III of Schedule II

The provisions of this part apply to Part I and Part II of schedule II, given above. These provisions are summarised below:

(i) In the case of a company which has been carrying on business for less than five financial years, the reference in Part H of the Schedule for 5 financial years will mean only for the years for which the company has been carrying on business.

(ii) Any report by accountant, required by Part H shall be made by accountant(s), qualified under the Companies Act for appointment as Auditor(s) of the company.

(iii) The time and place at which copies of all balance sheets and profit and loss accounts, material contracts and document, etc., can be inspected should also be specified under this part.

(iv) The prospectus must end with the declaration that all relevant provisions of the Companies Act, 1956, and the guidelines issued by the Government have been complied with and no statement made in the prospectus is contrary to the provisions of the Companies Act, 1956 and the rules thereunder.

SHELF-PROSPECTUS (SECTION 60-A)

Any public financial institution, public sector bank of scheduled bank whose main object is financing shall file a shelf-prospectus.

A company filing a shelf-prospectus with the registrar shall not be required to file prospectus afresh at every stage of offer of securities by it within a period of validity of such shelf-prospectus.

A company filing a shelf-prospectus shall be required to file an information memorandum on all material facts relating to new charges created, changes in the financial position as have occurred between the first offer of securities, previous offer of securities and the succeeding offer of securities within such time as may be prescribed by the Central Government, prior to making of a second or subsequent offer of securities under the shelf-prospectus.

An information memorandum shall be issued to the public along with shelf-prospectus filed at the stage of the first offer of securities and such prospectus shall be valid for a period of one year from the date of opening of the first issue of securities under that prospectus:

Provided that where an update of information memorandum is filed every time an offer of securities is made, such memorandum together with the shelf-prospectus shall constitute the prospectus.

Explanation — For the purpose of this section—

(a) "financing" means making loans to or subscribing in the capital of, a private industrial enterprise engaged in infrastructural financing or, such other company as the Central Government may notify in this behalf;

(b) "shelf-prospectus" means a prospectus issued by any financial institution or bank for one or more issues of the securities or class of securities specified in that prospectus.

INFORMATION MEMORANDUM (SECTION 60-B)

A public company making an issue of securities may circulate information memorandum public prior to filing of a prospectus.

A company inviting subscription by an information memorandum shall be bound to file a prospectus prior to the opening of the subscription lists and the offer as a *red-herring prospectus,* at least three days before the opening of the offer.

The information memorandum and red-herring prospectus shall carry same obligations as are applicable in the case of a prospectus.

Any variation between the information memorandum and the red-herring prospectus shall be highlighted as variations by the issuing company.

Explanation: For the purposes of Sub-Sections (2), (3) and (4). "red-herring prospectus" means a prospectus which does not have complete particulars on the price of the securities offered and the quantum of securities offered.

Every variation as made and highlighted in accordance with Sub-Section (4) above shall be individually intimated to the persons invited to subscribe to the issue of securities.

In the event of the issuing company or the underwriters to the issue have invited or received advance subscription by way of cash or post-dated cheques or stock-invest, the company or such underwriters or bankers to the issue shall not encash such subscription moneys or post-dated cheques or stock-invest before the date of opening of the issue, without having individually intimated the prospective subscribers of the variation and without having offered an opportunity to such prospective subscribers to withdraw their application and cancel their post-dated cheques or stock-invest or return of subscription paid.

The applicant or proposed subscriber shall exercise his right to withdraw from the application on any intimation of variation within seven days from the date of such intimation and shall indicate such withdrawal in writing to the company and the underwriters.

Any application for subscription which is acted upon by the company or underwriters or bankers to the issue without having given enough information of any variations, or the particulars of withdrawing of offer or opportunity for cancelling the post-dated cheques or stock-invest or stop payments for such payments shall be void and the applicants shall be entitled to receive a refund or return of its post-dated cheques or stock-invest or subscription moneys or cancellation of its application, as if the said application had never been made and the applicants are entitled to receive back their original application and interest at the rate of fifteen per cent from the date of encashment till payment of realisation.

Upon the closing of the offer of securities, a final prospectus stating therein the total capital raised, whether by way of debt or share capital and the closing price of the securities and any other details as were not complete in the red-herring prospectus shall be filed in a case of a listed public company with the securities and exchange board and registrar, and in any other case with the registrar only.

STATEMENT IN LIEU OFF PROSPECTUS (SECTION 70)

In some cases, companies are able to. raise the original capital without inviting the public to subscribe. In such cases, the company need not issue a prospectus. Where a public company which has a share capital does not issue a prospectus on its formation it cannot allot any shares without first filing with the registrar a document called '*Statement in lieu of Prospectus*': This document must be in the form set out in Schedule Ill and must contain practically the same information as is required in the prospectus.

The document shall be delivered to the registrar at least three days before the first allotment of shares. The statement must be signed by every director or proposed director or his agent. If a company fails to deliver a statement in lieu of prospectus, it cannot allot any shares or debentures. An allotment, if made is voidable if the allottee notifies the company within 2 months after the statutory meeting or in cases where there is no such meeting within two months after allotment.

If a company fails to fulfil the above conditions, the company and every director who has been knowingly a party to this contravention shall be liable for fine up to Rs. 1,000. If a statement in lieu of prospectus delivered to the registrar contains an untrue or a misleading statement, every person who authorised the delivery of the statement shall be liable to imprisonment for two years and fine of Rs. 5,000.

PROSPECTUS BY IMPLICATION (DEEMED PROSPECTUS) (SECTION 64)

The provisions relating to a prospectus (as regards legislation, contents and full disclosure) are very stringent and the duty of preparing and filing a prospectus in accordance with the law is extremely onerous. These requirements used to be evaded by companies in the past by allotting the whole of an issue of shares or debentures to an issuing house at a certain price. The issuing house then published an advertisement in the nature of an offer for sale inviting public to buy the shares or debentures from it at a higher price. Sec.64 now specifically provides that a document by which an *offer for sale* is made to the public is within the definition of prospectus.

When application are received by the issuing house, it renounces its interest in the shares or debentures to the extent of the number of shares or debentures allotted in favour of the applicant. When this is done, the applicant becomes an allottee of the company. By this method of allotment, stamp duty is saved.

The provisions of Sec.64 are summed up as under:

1. **Prospectus by Implications:** All documents containing offer of shares or debentures for sale are included within the definition of the term 'prospectus', and are deemed to be prospectus by implication of law. Where a company allots or agrees to allot any shares in, or debentures of, the company to an issuing house with a view to all or any of those shares or debentures being offered for sale to the public, any document by which the offer for sale to the public is made by the issuing house is, for all purposes, deemed to be prospectus issued by the company and all enactments and rules of law in regard to a prospectus are applicable thereto.
2. **Intention to Offer Shares or Debentures to the Public:** Unless the contrary is proved, an allotment of, or agreement to allot, shares or debentures to an issuing house is deemed to have been made with a view to the shares or debentures being offered for sale of the public if it is shown—
   (a) that the offer of shares or debentures for sale was made within 6 months after the allotment or agreement to allot or
   (b) that at the date when the offer was made, the whole consideration to be received by the company in respect of shares or debentures had not been received by it.
3. **Additional Information:** The following additional information is required to be given in the document deemed to be prospectus:
   (a) Consideration and Time and Place of Inspections of Contract: (i) The net amount of the consideration received or to be received by the company in respect of the shares or debentures to which the offer relates; and (ii) The place and time at which the contract under which the said shares or debentures have been or are to be allotted may be inspected.
   (b) Issuing House to be Deemed Director: The persons making the offer of sale to the public are to be deemed directors of the company for the purpose of registration of the prospectus.
   (c) Signing of Prospectus: Where the issuing house, *i.e.*, the person making the offer, is a company or a firm, it is sufficient that the prospectus is signed on behalf of the company by 2 directors of the company or by not

less than one-half of the partners in the firm, as the case may be. Any such director or partner may sign by his agent authorised in writing.

Circumstances under which a document containing an offer for sale of shares or debentures ***be not deemed to be a prospectus***

A document containing an offer for sale of shares or debentures is a prospectus or not depends upon whether it extends an invitation to the public to subscribe or not. The prima fade test 'public offer' or 'public invitation' is whether the terms of the offer or invitation are such that despite its limited circulation, it is open to any person who so chooses to bring his money and apply for shares in response to the invitation. If the offer or invitation is so open, then it constitutes a 'public offer'. If, on the other hand, an offer or invitation can be accepted only by the person to whom it is made and none other, then it will not be deemed to be an offer or invitation to the public.

The word 'public' includes any section of the public (Sec. 67). It may, thus, include all registered medical practitioners in Delhi, all advocates of High Court of Delhi, all Englishmen living in India.

However, in the following cases, the document inviting subscription to shares or debentures of a company shall not be deemed as invitation to the public and hence shall not be a prospectus:

1. A circular inviting existing shareholders or debentureholders of the company. Although Section 67(1) provides that such an offer shall be an offer to the public yet in view of the provisions of Sub-Sections (3) and (4) of Sec. 67 and that of Sub-Section (5) of Sec. 56, considered view of the authors on the subject is that it does not amount to a public offer.

   The circular containing offer of rights shares is, therefore, not a prospectus.

2. The offering of shares of the kith and kin of a director is not an invitation to the public to buy shares ***(Rattan Singh vs. Moga Transport Co. Ltd. (1959))***. Such an offer, therefore, shall not be deemed as prospectus.

3. Where an invitation is made by the management of a company to selected persons for subscription or purchase by the sons receiving the offer or invitation, the shares or debentures and such invitation or offer is not calculated directly or indirectly to be availed of by other persons, such invitation or offer shall not be deemed as prospectus (Sec. 67(3)).

In ***Nash vs. Lynde (1929)***, a document marked 'strictly confidential' containing particulars of a proposed issue of shares was sent by the managing director to a coordinator and through him passed on privately to a small circle of friends of the directors. The House of Lords held that it was not a prospectus, as there has been no issue to the public.

Similarly, in Govt. Stock and other Securities, new company offering to buy all the shares of two existing company offering to buy all the shares of two existing companies and issue own shares in exchange of those shares, it was held that the circular was not an offer to the public as it neither involved an offer for the purchase of shares for money, nor an invitation for subscription of shares.

ABRIDGED FORM OF PROSPECTUS

Section 56(3), as amended by the Amendment Act of 1988, states that no application form can be issued for shares or debentures of a company unless it is accompanied by an abridged prospectus which complies with the requirements of the Act. However, full prospectus is to be furnished on a request being made by any person before the closing of the subscription list.

The Central Government has prescribed on 13-10-91 the salient features of 'abridged prospectus. For the purpose, Rule 4CC has been inserted in the Companies (Central Government's) General Rules and Forms, 1956. As per the Rule 4CC, the salient features required to be included in the abridged prospectus' shall be in "Form 2A". The abridged prospectus contains information very much similar to a 'Prospectus' in a concise and compact manner so that cost of public issue of capital my be reduced.

The abridged prospectus (in Form 2A) and the share application form should bear the same printed number. The investors may detach the share application form along the perforated line after he has had an opportunity to study the contents of the abridged prospectus, before submitting the same to the company or its designated bankers. The same procedure may also be followed while making available copies of the prospectus under Section 56 of the Act.

When 'Abridged Prospectus' Not Necessary

In the following circumstances, an 'abridged prospectus' containing the prescribed particulars as per Form 2A need not accompany the application forms:

(i) In the case of bonafide invitation to a person to enter into an underwriting agreement with respect to the shares or debentures Sec. (56(3) (a)).

(ii) When shares or debentures are not offered to the public (Sec.56(3) (b)).

(iii) Where offer is made only to existing members/debentureholders of the company by way of rights, whether with or without the right of renunciation (Sec.56(5) (a)).

(iv) In the case of issue of shares or debentures which are in all respects similar to those previously issued and dealt in and quoted on a recognised stock exchange (Sec. 56(5) (b)).

Penalty: Non-compliance of the aforesaid provision by any person shall attract punishment in terms of fine which may extend to Rs. 5,000.

Besides, the omission from a prospectus of a matter required to be included by Section 56 may give rise to an action for damages at the instance of a subscriber for shares or debentures who has suffered loss thereby. It should be noted that the Act does not say that directors shall be liable, but this seems to be implied from Sec. 56(4).

SEBI Guideness, 2000 with respect to abridged prospectus provide that the Lead Merchant Banker shall ensure:

(i) Every application form distributed by the Issuer Company or anyone else is accompanied by a copy of the abridged prospectus.

(ii) The application form may be stapled to form part of the Abridged Prospectus. Alternatively, it may be a perforated part of the Abridged Prospectus.

(iii) The Abridged Prospectus shall not contain matters which are extraneous to the contents of the prospectus.

(iv) The Abridged Prospectus shall be printed at least in point 7 size with proper spacing:

(v) Enough space shall be provided in the application form to enable the investors to fill in various details like name, address, etc.

Prospectus in Terms of Newspaper Advertisement

Where a prospectus is issued as newspaper advertisement, under Section 66, it is not necessary to specify therein the contents of the memorandum or the signatories thereto, or the number of shares subscribed by them. It means this section says, excepting these matters, all other particulars referred to must be given even in a newspaper advertisement. But then, it will be a very costly exercise indeed. In order to solve this expensive process, the Company Law Department has laid down that such an advertisement must state at the top — "THIS IS AN ANNOUNCEMENT AND NOT A PROSPECTUS", and in addition it must contain information about the company and proposed issue under the following heads:

1. Name of the Company. .
2. Address of the Registered Office.
3. Existing and Proposed activities.
4. Location of the Industry.
5. Board of Directors.
6. Manager/Managing Director(s), if any.

7. (a) Authorised Capital
   (b) Subscribed Capital.
   (c) Proposed issue to the public (whether at par, premium or discount)
8. Dates of opening and closing of the Subscription List.
9. Application forms along with prospectus to be had from the Registered Office of the Company or from the Underwriters/Brokers/Bankers whose names and addresses are given below:

	Name	Address
Underwriters	...	...
Brokers	...	...
Bankers	...	...

Further, the Central Government should impose no bar on the terms of payment being included in announcement made in the press provided it does not contravene the provisions of Section 56.

The above provisions do not apply to a private company.

Initial offer of Securities to be in Dematerialised Form (Section 68(b)):

The section has been introduced by the Companies (Amendment) Act, 2000 (w.e.f. 13.12.2000). It provides that notwithstanding anything contained in any other provisions of this Act, every listed public company, making initial public offer of any securities for a sum or Rs. 10 crore or more shall issue the same only in dematerialised form by complying with the requisite provisions of the *Depositories* Act 1996 and the regulations made thereunder.

LIABILITY FOR MIS-STATEMENTS OR OMISSION IN A PROSPECTUS (SECTION 62-63)

A prospectus constitutes the basis of the contract between the company and the person who purchase shares or debentures. The persons who are behind the company have all the knowledge or means of knowledge as to the future prospectus and present situation of the enterprise and the investing public has none. It is but fair that the former should not only disclose all the matters within their knowledge relating to the enterprise, which might affect the investing mind but should state them accurately, correctly and unambiguously. The responsibility of those who issue a prospectus was discussed by ***Kinderslesy V.C. in New Bruncwick, etc., Co. vs. Muggeridge. (1860) 1. Dr.* and Sm. 363.**

"Those who issue a prospectus holding out to the public the great advantages which will accrue to persons who will take shares in a proposed undertaking and inviting them to take shares on the faith of the representations therein contained, are bound to state everything with strict and scrupulous accuracy and not only to abstain from stating as fact that which is not so, but to omit no one fact within their knowledge the existence of which might in any degree affect the nature, or extent or quality of the privileges and advantages which the prospectus holds out as in document to take shares".

What is an Untrue Statement?

According to Section 65(1) of the Companies Act, 1956:

(a) A statement included in a prospectus shall be deemed to be untrue, if the statement is misleading in the form and context in which it is included; and

(b) where the omission from a prospectus of any mailer is calculated to mislead the prospectus shall be deemed in respect of such omission, to be a prospectus in which an untrue statement is included.

The expression 'Included' with reference to a prospectus means, included in the prospectus itself or contained in any report or memorandum appearing on the face thereof by reference incorporated therein or issued therewith.

Example

A company issued a prospectus. All the statements included therein, were literally true. One of the statements disclosed the rates of dividends paid for a number of years. But dividends had been paid not out of trading profits but out of realized capital profits. This material fad was not disclosed. Held, that the prospectus was false in material particulars and the managing director and chairman, who knew that it was false, was held guilty of fraud ***(Rex vs. Kylsant, (1932) 1 KB. 442).***

However, a mere silence cannot be sufficient ground for setting aside the allotment of shares. The withholding of facts should be such that if not stated it makes that which is stated absolutely false — ***Peek vs. Gurney (1873) LR 6 (HL) 377.***

Again, claiming experience of the promoters as the experience of the company was held not a misrepresentation — ***Progressive Aluminium Ltd. vs. Registrar of Companies (1997) 26 CLA 227 AR.***

Manipulative Practices

SEBI guidelines define what constitutes fraud, unfair trade practices, misleading statements and market manipulation.

The guidelines, expected to have a far-reaching impact, will be applicable to all individuals directly and indirectly associated with the market, and not just the intermediaries.

A broker executing a transaction with a client at a price different than the price at which it was by him will be committing an unfair trade practice.

"To pay money to any person for inducing another person to purchase or sell any security in order to inflate, depress or cause fluctuations in the market price" has been included in the purview of market manipulation.

Misleading statements include statements made by a person who does not care whether the statement is true or false.

In addition, the norms state: "No person shall make any statement which he knows, or ought reasonably have known, to be misleading."

Moreover, no person can, on his own behalf, or on behalf of any other person, knowingly buy or sell securities pending the execution of any order of his client relating to the same security.

The norms have for the first time provided parameters for defining and investigating market malpractices. Although for long there has been a clamour for checking these practices a beginning was not possible because no parameters were available for defining the scope and purview.

According to the guidelines, 'fraud' is any act committed with an intent to deceive somebody. It includes the deliberate suggestion of an untrue fact by someone, the active concealment of a fact by one having knowledge of the fact, a promise made without any intention of performing it, or any other act fitted to deceive.

On market manipulation, the norms stipulate that no person can take part in a securities transaction to artificially raise or depress prices for inducing sale or purchase by any person. A person who has applied for shares in the company, and who has been allotted shares has certain remedies against the company and the persons authorising the issue the prospectus. But a buyer of shares in the open market or a subscriber to the memorandum has no such right. If, however, a prospectus is issued with the object of inducing persons to buy shares in the open market, any person who buys shares even in the open market on the basis of the statements made in it has a right of action if the statements are untrue or there is material omission from the prospectus.

A false statement or omission of material facts gives rise to civil as well as criminal liability.

Where an untrue statement occurs in a prospectus there may be–(a) civil liability; and (b) criminal liability. The liability for mis-statement in statement lieu of prospectus is the same as in the case of prospectus.

CIVIL LIABILITY

A person who has been induced to subscribe for shares in a company on the strength of misstatement or omission in the prospectus may have a remedy either against the company or against the promoters or directors or experts.

Remedies Against the Company

A person who has been, induced to subscribe for shares may (a) rescind the contract to take up the shares, (b) claim damages for deceit.

(a) Rescission of Contract

Where a person has purchased the shares of a company on the faith of a prospectus which contained an untrue or misleading, but not necessarily fraudulent statement, he can seek rescission of the contract, *i.e.*, return the shares allotted to him, get back his purchase money with interest and get his name removed from the register of members. This remedy is available only to those persons who subscribed for any shares on the faith of the prospectus. Persons who have become shareholders by subsequent purchase or to whom the company has allotted the shares cannot avail this remedy. The right to rescind the contract is available if he proves the following:

(i) That the prospectus included an untrue or misleading statement or misrepresentation.

***Green Wood vs. Leather Shod Wheel Co. (1990) 1.Ch.421*:** The prospectus of a company stated in large bold type, "Orders have already been received, from the House of Commons" and "Wheels for the trolleys in the House of Commons have been ordered and are now in use." In fact the person who supplied refreshment to the House of Commons had one trolley with these wheels but orders had not been placed by the House of Commons. It was held that the statement was misleading and untrue.

(ii) That the untrue or misreading statement or mis-representation was in respect of a material fact or matter and was one of the inducements to apply for shares or debentures. There should be misrepresentation of a material fact. A statement of fact must be distinguished from a statement of opinion or expectation. A statement that the property of the company is worth a certain sum of money or that the profits are expected to reach a certain figure is only opinion and will give no ground for an action.

***Rex. vs. Kylsant ((1932) I.K.B. 442)*:** A prospectus of a company said that a company had paid a dividend every year between 1921 and 1927 years of depression, thus, giving the impression of a financially stable company, However, the company had in each of those years incurred considerable financial losses on trading account and was only able to pay a dividend out of reserves accumulated in previous years.

This fact was suppressed. The court held that the prospectus was false in a material matter and conveyed a false impression.

If the statement contained in the prospectus is true at the time it was made and becomes untrue before allotment of the shares, it would be a good ground for rescission. But where a statement in the prospectus though untrue when it was issued was true when the plaintiff applied for the shares, he would not be entitled to any relief against the company.

***Ship vs. Crosskill, ((1870) 10 Eq.73)*:** There was a statement in the prospectus to the effect that more than half of the shares had already been subscribed for and that the list would remain open only for a few days. This statement at the time of the issue of the prospectus was untrue but before the plaintiff had applied for shares the whole issue had been applied for. Nobody could say that the plaintiff had been deceived.

(iii) That he has taken action promptly to rescind the contract. The shareholder must start proceedings for rescission within a reasonable time and before the company goes into liquidation. But the investor need not act on rumour. He is entitled to wait until he has sufficient knowledge.

If a shareholder after becoming aware of the misrepresentation or misstatement does any act inconsistent with his right to rescind, for example, by attending meetings, by paying a call money or accepting dividend, he will lose his right to rescind.

(b) Damages for Deceit

Any person induced by fraud to take shares is entitled to sue the company for damages provided he has rescinded his contract in time. He cannot both retain the shares and get damages against the company. The company is liable in damages where the misrepresentation is an innocent one, unless it proves that it had reasonable grounds to believe.

The allottee can claim damages for deceit if he can prove that the mis-statement or omission was:

(i) one of fact and not of law, nor an expression of opinion,

(ii) material, and

(iii) acted upon by him.

(iv) that those acting on behalf of the company acted fraudulently;

(v) that those purporting to act on behalf of the company were authorised to act in its behalf; and

(vi) that he suffered a loss or damage.

It is important to remember that the allottee cannot both retain the shares and get damages from the company. In actual practice, suit for damages against the company is rarely filed. The usual claim against the company is for rescission of the contract of allotment. Damages are generally claimed from the directors, promoters and other persons who had authorised the issue of the prospectus personally, or from experts who had signed reports referred to in the prospectus.

REMEDIES AGAINST THE DIRECTORS, PROMOTERS AND EXPERTS

Any person who has purchased shares or debentures on the faith of the prospectus containing the untrue statement may sue (a) every director; (b) every person whose name appeared in the prospectus as a proposed director; (c) every promoter; (d) every person who authorised the issue of the prospectus;

The aggrieved person may claim (a) Compensation under Section 62; (b) damages for non-compliance with the requirements of Section 56; (c) damages under the general law.

1. Compensation for Untrue Statement under Section 62

Directors, promoters and all others who authorised the issue of the prospectus are liable to compensate persons who subscribe for shares on the faith of the prospectus for damages sustained by reason of any untrue statement in it. A statement is deemed to be untrue if it is misleading in the form and context in which it is issued. The liability consists in paying damages by way of compensation to the aggrieved party. The compensation payable will be the difference between the price paid for the shares or debentures and their value at the date they were allotted to him.

Defences Available to a Director to Avoid Civil Liability (Sec. 62 (2))

A director may escape liability if he proves—

(i) that he withdrew his consent to act as director before the issue of the prospectus, or

(ii) that the prospectus was issued without his knowledge or consent and that on becoming aware of its issue, he gave *reasonable public notice* to that effect; or

(iii) that after the issue of prospectus and before allotment, he on becoming aware of the untrue statement in it, withdrew his consent and gave reasonable *public notice of the withdrawal* and the reasons for it; or

(iv) that he had *reasonable grounds to believe* and did believe up to the time of allotment of shares or debentures that the statement was true; or

(v) that he made the statement upon the authority and based of the *report of an expert* whom he had reasonable ground to believe that the statement was a correct and true copy of an official document.

Defences Available to an Expert: An expert will not be liable if he can prove:

(i) that he withdrew in writing his consent to the issue of the prospectus before it was delivered to the registrar for registration;

(ii) that after delivery but before allotment of shares he became aware of a false statement in the prospectus, he publicly withdrew his consent in writing and gave the reasons therefore;

(iii) that he was competent to make the statement and had reasonable grounds to believe and did up to the allotment of shares believe that the statement was true.

Right of Contribution: Where any shareholder recovers any damages from any director or officer of the company for untrue statements in the prospectus, the other director and officers who authorised the issue of such a prospectus shall contribute and pay their share of damages to the person who has made the payment.

2. Damages for Non-compliance with Section 56

The omission from a prospectus of a matter required to be included by Section 56, may give rise to an action for damages at the instance of a shareholder who has suffered the loss thereby, even if the commission does not make the prospectus false or misleading.

However, the person would not be liable if he proves that—

(a) he had no knowledge of the matter not disclosed in the prospectus;

(b) the non-compliance arose from a honest mistake of fact on his part; or

(c) the non-compliance was not material and the court thinks that he ought to be excused.

3. Damages for Fraudulent Misrepresentation under General Law:

The directors would be liable under the common law action of deceit for making statement which is false and which is known by them to be false, or is made by them recklessly or without care, whether it is true or false. But they would not be liable for damages for false statements in a prospectus if they honestly believed them to be true, even if there was no reasonable ground for such belief.

***Derry vs. Peek, (1889) 14 A.C. 337*:** The directors of a tramway company issued a prospectus condition a statement that the Special Act of Parliament gave the company the right to work its trams by the steam power instead of horses. In fact, the Act empowered the company to use horses and with the consent of the Board of Trade steam power. P took shares on the basis of this statement. The Board of Trade refused its consent to the use of steam power and the company was wound up. It was held by the House of Lords that the directors were not liable in fraud because they honestly believed what they said in the prospectus to be true.

Only persons who relied upon the false statement can recover damages in an action of deceit. A false statement in a prospectus will render the directors liable to the original allotees only and not to subsequent purchasers from them.

Thus, where a person purchased shares in the open market cannot rely for an action on the prospectus containing false statement ***[Peak vs. Gurney, (1873) 6 H.L. 377].***

CRIMINAL LIABILITY OF DIRECTORS

Every person who authorised the issue of a prospectus containing untrue statement shall be punishable with imprisonment which may extend to two years or with fine which may extend to Rs. 5,000 or with both. The accused person, however, may not be liable if he proves—

(a) that the statement was immaterial, or

(b) he had reasonable ground to believe and did believe up to the lime of the issue of the prospectus that the statement was true. *(Section 63).*

The punishment for issuing an application for shares or debentures which is not accompanied by a prospectus is a fine up to Rs. 5,000.

Penalty for Fraudulently Inducing Persons to Invest Money: *(Section 68)* Any person who makes an untrue, deceptive, or misleading statement in a prospectus with a view to inducing persons to invest money shall be liable fore imprisonment for a term which may extend to five years or a fine up to Rs. 10,000 or both. This section attempts at preventing fraud in connection with obtaining capital from public.

Issue and Allotment of Shares in Fictitious Names: *(Section 68-A)* Benami shareholding and shareholding in the names of fictitious or non-existing persons are common. The object is to avoid tax. Section 68 makes it an offence to make applications for shares in the name of, or to induce the allotment or transfer of shares to fictitious persons. The punishment in such cases is imprisonment which may extend to five years.

The company has to reproduce in every prospectus and application form the provisions of Section 68-A (i).

UNDERWRITING COMMISSION (SECTION 76)

When a company offers its shares to the public, it often wants that the whole issue should be taken up. Consequently, a company is usually willing to pay a small commission on all the shares offered to the public to anyone who undertakes to take all the shares, that the public do not take. This is known as *'underwriting'*. It consists of an undertaking by some person or persons that if the public fails to take up the issue, he or they will do so. In return for this undertaking, the company agrees to pay the underwriters a commission on all shares, whether taken by the public or by the underwriters. It is, thus, in the nature of an insurance against the possibility of inadequate subscription.

A company may pay a commission to any person in consideration of his subscribing or agreeing to subscribe for shares, or procuring or agreeing to procure subscriptions for any shares in the company. Underwriting commission may be paid only if the following conditions are satisfied;

1. The payment of the commission must be authorised by the Articles of Association.
2. The rate of commission must not exceed 5% of the price of the shares and 2½ % of the price of the debentures at which they are issued or the rate authorised by the Articles whichever is less.

The government has prescribed the following maximum ceiling rates for payment of underwriting commission by a company.

	On amount devolving on underwriters	On amount subscribed by public
(i) Equity shares	2.50%	2.50%
(ii) Preference shares/Debentres for amount up to Rs, 5 lakh	2.50%	1.50%
(iii) for amount in excess of Rs. 5 lakh	2.00%	1.00%

3. The amount paid or agreed to be paid must be—(a) disclosed in the prospectus if shares are offered to the public, or (b) in other cases, disclosed in the statement in lieu of prospectus delivered to the registrar.
4. The number of shares or debentures which persons have agreed for a commission to subscribe for absolutely or conditionally is *disclosed in the prospectus or statement in lieu of prospectus.*
5. A *copy of the contract* for the payment of the commission must be delivered to the registrar along with the prospectus or statement in lieu of prospectus.

Underwriting commission will not be payable for securities taken up by promoters group, employees, directors, their friends and business associates. Where shares or debentures are not offered to the public underwriting commission cannot be paid to a person for his subscribing or agreeing to subscribe for the same.

Amounts paid by way of underwriting commission shall be shown in the Balance Sheet under the head 'Miscellaneous Expenditure'. In case of non-compliance, the compliance, the company and every officer in default shall be liable to a fine up to Rs.500.

MINIMUM SUBSCRIPTION (SECTION 69)

Where the public company for the first time invites the public to subscribe for its shares, it cannot allot those shares until the minimum amount stated in the prospects has been subscribed. This, amount stated in the prospectus is known as the *minimum subscription*.

The minimum subscription is not a sum fixed by the Articles or calculated as a percentage of the shares issued under the prospectus. It is the minimum amount stated in the prospectus which in the opinion of the directors must be raised in order to provide for–

(a) the purchase price of any property purchased or to be purchased;

(b) the preliminary expenses and any underwriting commission payable by the company;

(c) repayment money borrowed by the company in respect of any of the foregoing manners.

(d) working capital; and

(e) any other expenditure stating the nature and purpose thereof and the estimated amount in each case.

The object of the 'minimum subscription' provision is to prevent the company getting underway until it has raised the capital needed to carryout the objects in which it has invited the public to participate. This also affords protection to the creditors by ensuring that a limited company is not able to incur commitments if it is grossly under-capitalised.

All moneys received from applicant shall be deposited and kept disposited in *scheduled bank* until minimum subscription has been received by the company. An allotment made in contravention of the restriction of the minimum subscription is not void but only *voidable* and the applicant may avoid the allotment within the time specified in Section 71(1).

Where such minimum subscription is not received by the company within 120 days from the first issue of prospectus, all moneys received from applicants shall be returned within 130 days of the issue of the prospectus. On failure to pay, the directors shall be jointly and severally liable to repay that money with interest at the rate of 6 per cent per annum. *[Section 69(5)]*

No specific limit regarding amount of minimum subscription had been prescribed in the Act or no guidelines had been issued by the government in this regard until the Central Government issued additional guidelines relating to public/right issues of shares and debentures and allotment thereof, which have come into effect from 9.4.1990 and will be applicable to issue of which prospectus or letter of offer has been filed or issued on or after 9.4.1990.

The first guidelines provides that a company making public rights issue of shares/ debentures shall not make allotment unless it received *minimum of 90% subscription against the entire issue within 90 days* from the date of closure of the issue. Thus, this guideline makes it obligatory to raise not less than 90% subscription against the total issue of shares or debentures before allotment.

As per the sixth guidelines the promoters should make their subscription in advance before the public issue opens and gives a certificate to this effect to the regional stock exchange concerned.

The ninth guideline provides in this regard that companies will undertake in the prospectus, letters of offer, advertisement or publicity literature, etc., to refund the amount at the end of 90 days from the date of from the closure of the issue, if not subscribed up to 90% and to *pay interest@ 15% per annum if refunds are delayed by more than 10 days after this period.*

The minimum subscription stated in the prospectus must be reckoned exclusively of any amount payable otherwise than in cash. The amount payable on application on each share must not be less than five per cent of the nominal amount of the shares. All moneys received from applicants for shares are required to be deposited in a scheduled bank until the certificate to commence business is obtained.

QUESTIONS

Objective Type Questions

I. Fill up the Blanks

1. A Prospectus under Companies Act is an ________ for the purpose of mobilising capital from the public.
2. A Statement in lieu of prospectus is issued by a public limited company when funds towards capital are arranged from ________ resources.
3. A Prospectus after the date of registration is valid for ________ days as per Section 60(4) of the Companies Act.

4. In order to market the unsubscribed shares as subscribed shares ________ are appointed.
5. Prospectus are to be issued by public limited companies according to the guidelines of ________.
6. A Prospectus issued by any financial institution or bank for one or more issues of the securities is known as __________.
7. Prospectus need not be issued in the case of ________ of shares.
8. A Prospectus containing ________ clause is said to be invalid.
9. Implied prospectus or deemed prospectus arises for penalising the advertisement inviting shares are published by ________ Houses.
10. Misstatcments in Prospectus may give rise for ________ and ________ liabilities.

[*Answers:* (1) Invitation ot Notice; (2) Private; (3) 90 days; (4) Underwriters; (5) Securities Exchange Board of India (SEBI); (6) Shelf Prospectus; (7) Further Issue; (8) Waiver; (9) Issuing; (10) Civil and Criminal]

II. Match the following

1. Shelf Prospectus	1. Information about the credit-worthiness of securities
2. Disclosure of Risk Factor	2. 5% on the price of issued shares
3. Invitation to an offer	3. Bargainable Commission
4. CRISIL/CARE/ICRA	4. Opening of the subscription list
5. Underwriter	5. SEBI Guidelines
6. Broker	6. Fraud
7. Information Memorandum	7. Invitation of Deposits from public
8. Misstatements in Prospectus	8. Red herring Prospectus
9. Prospectus	9. Prospectus
10. No Allotment to be made until the 5th day after the issue of Prospectus.	10. Financial Institutions.

[*Answers:* 1 (10); 2 (5); 3 (9); 4 (1); 5 (2); 6 (3); 7 (8); 8 (6); 9 (7); 10 (4)]

III. Multiple Choice Questions

1. Any person who induces a company to allot shares in a fictitious name is punishable with
   (a) a fine of Rs 5,000.
   (b) a fine of Rs. 10,000.
   (c) imprisonment upto 5 years.
   (d) a fine of Rs. 5,000 and imprisonment upto 5 years.
2. A shareholder purchased in the open market shares of a company whose prospectus contained some misstatements. He
   (a) can rescind the contract only but cannot claim damages.
   (b) can claim damages only but cannot rescind the contract.
   (c) has no remedy against the company.
   (d) has remedy against the directors responsible for the issue of the prospectus.
3. A Statement in lieu of prospectus is required to be issued
   (a) by all companies which issue shares or debentures.
   (b) by public companies when shares are issued among friends and relatives.
   (c) by private companies as they do not issue shares to the public.
   (d) none of the above.
4. Underwriting means
   (a) selling shares at a discount.
   (b) purchasing property at less than market price.
   (c) agreeing to purchase shortfall of shares in a company in case of undersubscription.
   (d) offering new shares to outsiders.
5. The underwriting commission paid or agreed to be paid must not exceed
   (a) 2 per cent of the issue price of the shares.
   (b) $2\frac{1}{2}$ per cent of the issue price of the shares.
   (c) 5 per cent of the issue price of the shares.
   (d) 10 per cent of the issue price of the shares.

[*Answers:* 1 (c); 2 (c); 3 (b); 4 (c); 5 (c)]

Review Questions

1. What is a prospectus?
2. Write a brief note on statement in lieu of prospectus.
3. Is the issue of prospectus necessary?
4. State the objectives of underwriting.
5. List out the objectives of issuing a prospectus.
6. Briefly explain the conditions to be fulfilled for issuing a prospectus.
7. Define shelf-prospectus.
8. Who do you mean by 'information memorandum'?
9. What is a "prospectus"? What are its requirements?
10. State the objectives of issuing a prospectus.
11. What are the remedies available for any mis-statement made in the prospectus?
12. What is meant by statement in lieu of prospectus?
13. What is underwriting? What are its objects?
14. What is a prospectus? Is the issue of a prospectus compulsory on the part of a company?
15. What is a prospectus? What amounts to a mis-statement in a prospectus? What are the remedies available to a subscriber who has taken shares on the basis of a mis-statement in a prospectus?
16. Discuss the liability of a company for untrue statements or omissions in its prospectus.
17. Discuss the civil as well as criminal liabilily of persons who authorise the issue of a false prospectus.
18. Explain the legal provisions relating to issue and registration of a prospectus.
19. What are the remedies open to an allottee of shares who have had applied for them on the faith of a false and misleading prospectus and what are the defences available to the directors of the company who have issued such a prospectus?
20. Discuss in detail the contents and the form of a prospectus.
21. Who is deemed to be an expert in relation to the prospectus of a company? What conditions must be satisfied before a report by an expert can be published therein?
22. Is there any remedy available to the allottee of the shares who has been induced to take shares on the faith of an untrue statement of an expert in the prospectus?

23. "Prospectus is the window through which the company is displaced without distortion" Comment. Distinguish a prospectus from a statement in lieu of prospectus.
24. Write short notes on: (a) Statement in lieu of prospectus. (b) Prospectus by implication, (c) Registration of a prospectus, (d) Minimum subscription.

◈◈◈

CHAPTER 7

Shares and Debentures

Members and Shareholders

The words *members* and *shareholders*, are interchangeable in the case of company having a share capital. The word 'shareholder' is used in relation to a company having a share capital and there can be no membership except through the medium of shareholding. But the term '*member*' is wider in scope and may be used in relation to all types of company. A person may become a member of a company without holding any shares. Companies limited by guarantee or unlimited companies which may not have share capital and can, therefore, have no shareholders but they do have members.

Distinction Between a Member and Shareholder

1. A registered member may not be a shareholder, since a company may not be having share capital.

   For example, a *company limited by guarantee* and not having a share capital, does have a member but not shareholder. But a registered shareholder is a member, since his name appears in the register of members maintained by the company.

2. A person who owns a share warrant (bearer), is not a member since his name does not appear in the register of members maintained by the company. He is a shareholder only. (Section 115 (1)).

3. A legal representative of a deceased member is a shareholder but not a member, till he applies for registration and his name is entered in the registrar of members.

Acquiring Membership

A person may become a member of the company in any of the following ways : (a) By subscribing to the memorandum of association. (b) By agreeing to take qualification shares, (c) By application and allotment, (d) By transfer of shares, (e) By transmission of shares, and (f) By estoppel or holding out as a member.

Termination of Membership

A person will cease to be a member of the company when his name is removed from the register of members. It may take place in any of the following ways: (i) When a person *transfers* his shares. In such a case, the transferor ceases to be a member as soon as the name of the transferee is registered but not before, (ii) When his shares are validly *forfeited* by the company, (iii) When a person makes a valid *surrender* of his shares to the company, (iv) When a company sells the shares in exercise of its *right of lien* over them, (v) When he *dies*, (vi) When he is declared *insolvent* and the Official Assignee either disclaims or transfers the shares, (vii) When he *repudiates* the contract on the ground of false or misleading statement in the prospectus of the company, (viii) When he is holding redeemable preference shares and such shares are *redeemed*, (ix) When share warrants are issued in exchange of fully paid-up shares and the articles do not recognise *holders of shares warrants* as members, and (x) When the company is *wound-up*, but he remains liable as a contributory.

Rights of a Member

(i) *To have the certificate of shares* held or the certificate of stock issued to him within the prescribed time (Section 113).

(ii) *To have his name* entered in the register of members as well as to have the register rectified, and in the case of refusal by the company, to apply to the court for necessary relief (Section 155).

(iii) *To transfer shares* subject to any restrictions imposed by the Articles (Section 82).

(iv) *To attend meetings* of shareholders, receive proper notice and to vote at the meetings.

(v) To associate in the declaration of *dividends* and to apply to the court for an injunction restraining the directors from paying dividends on an *ultra-vires* declaration or out of capital.

(vi) To *inspect the registers*, indexes, returns and copies of certificates, etc., kept by the company and to obtain extracts or copy thereof (Section 16).

(vii) *To obtain copies of Memorandum and Articles* on request and payment of the prescribed fees (Section 39).

(viii) To have the first option in case of issue of new shares or a further issue of shares (i.e., *the right of pre-emption*) by the company (Section 81).

(ix) To receive a copy of the *statutory report* (Sections 165(1) and (2)).

(x) *To apply to the court* to have any variation or abrogation to his rights set aside by the court (Section 107).

(xi) *To have notice of any resolution* requiring special notice (Section 196(2)).

(xii) *To obtain on request minutes of proceedings* at general meetings (Section 196(2)).

(xiii) *To remove directors* by joining with others (Section 284).

(xiv) *To obtain a copy of the Profit and Loss Account and the Balance Sheet* with the auditors' report (Sections 210, 219).

(xv) *To apply for the appointment* of one or more competent *inspectors by the government to investigate* into the affairs of the company as well as for reporting thereon (Sections 235, 237).

(xvi) *To participate in the appointment of an auditor* or auditors at the Annual General Meeting (Section 224).

(xvii) *To receive the auditors' report* at the Annual General Meeting of the company (Section 230).

(xviii) *To receive a share* in the capital of the company and in the *surplus assets*, if any, on the company's liquidation;

(xix) *To participate* in passing of the *special resolution* that the company may be wound up by the court or voluntarily (Sections 433, 484(1)(b)).

(xx) To participate in *appointment* and in fixation of remuneration of one or more *liquidators in the case of a Members' Voluntary* Winding up and to fill any vacancy in the office of a liquidator so appointed by him (Sections 490, 492).

Liabilities and Duties of a Member

(i) *To take up shares, when they are allotted* in due time and in compliance with provisions of the Act, unless the refusal to accept the shares has been sent on the ground of non-compliance with the provisions of the Act as regards the issue of the prospectus or as regards allotment.

(ii) *To pay for the shares allotted* to him when the allotment is made and when calls have been made validly and in conformity with the provisions of the Articles.

(iii) *To abide by the doing of the majority of members* unless the majority acts vindictively, oppressively, malafide or fraudulently.

(iv) *To contribute to the assets* of the company in the case of winding up when the shares held are partly paid-up.

(v) Members are *severally liable for debts of the company contracted*, where its business is carried on beyond the expiry of six months from the date at which its membership is reduced below the legal minimum, (i.e., seven members in the case of a public company and two members in the case of a private company). However, such members are not liable for debts contracted before the expiry of six months. No liability will accrue to those members who are not cognizant of the fact that the business of the company is being carried on with members fewer than the legal minimum (Section 45).

SHARE CAPITAL

The word '*Capital*' used in connection with a company has a different meanings. It may mean the *nominal, issued, called-up, paid-up*, or *reserve share capital* of the company. Section 86 provides that the share capital of a company limited by shares shall be of two kinds only; namely (a) Preference Share Capital, and (b) Equity Share Capital. Preference share capital is that part of paid-up share capital which carries a preferential rights as to the payment of dividend at a fixed rate and also a preferential right to the repayment of the paid-up capital. Equity share capital means all the share capital which is not preference share capital.

Alteration of Capital: Under Section 94, a company limited by shares may in general meeting, if so authorised by its Articles, alter the conditions of its memorandum relating to share capital in order to: (a) increase its share capital by issuing new shares, (b) consolidate and divide all or any of its share capital into shares of larger amount than its existing shares, (c) convert all or any of its fully paid-up shares into stock or reconvert that stock into fully paid-up shares of any denomination, (d) subdivide its shares into shares of smaller amount than is fixed by the memorandum, provided the paid-up amount will remain at the same proportion of its share capital, and (e) by cancelling shares which have not been taken up and diminishing the amount of its share capital by the amount of the shares so cancelled. The powers conferred by Section 94 shall be exercised by passing an ordinary resolution of the company in a general meeting and shall not require to be confirmed by the court.

Reduction of Capital: A company may wish to reduce its capital for a number of reasons; namely: 1. The capital of the company may be more than enough for its needs, and so, it may return the surplus capital to the shareholders, 2. The paid-up capital of the company is sufficient and it may refrain from calling up the unpaid portion of share money, and 3. Some of the capital may in fact have been lost or diminished e.g., Rs. 100 shares may represent assets worth Rs. 50. The company may wish to write off the lost capital. Reduction of share capital under item (3) affects the rights of different classes of shareholders as well as the interest of the members of the public who may be induced to take shares in the company.

The question of reducing the capital is a domestic affair to be decided by the majority, but this power must be exercised in a fair and equitable manner. Reduction of capital may be effected in several ways which maybe classified under two heads:

1. Reduction without the Consent of the National Company Law Tribunal (NCLT): There are a number of cases where a company may reduce its capital without the sanction of the NCLT:

(a) Where *redeemable preference shares* are redeemed in accordance with the provisions of Section 80.

(b) Where any shares are *forfeited* for non-payment of calls.

(c) Where there is a *surrender* of shares or a gift is made to the company of its own shares.

(d) Where *unissued shares are cancelled,* and

(e) Where '*buyback scheme*' of shares is in operation. In all these cases, the procedure laid down under Section 100 of the Companies Act is not required to be followed.

2. Reduction with the Consent of the Court: Section 100 gives a company limited by shares or a company limited by guarantee and having a share capital the power to reduce its share capital in any way. The Act has not prescribed the manner in which the reduction is to be carried out, nor has it prohibited any methods of effecting that object. A company, if so *authorised by its Articles*, may, by *special resolution*, reduce its share capital subject to the *confirmation of the NCLT* in any one of the following ways: (a) Extinguish or reduce the liability on any of its shares in respect of share capital not paid-up, (b) Cancel any paid-up share capital which is lost or is unrepresented by the unavailable assets, and (c) Pay-off any paid-up share capital which is in excess of the requirements of the company.

After having passed the special resolution for reducing the share capital, sanction of the NCLT shall be obtained by the company. The object of requiring this sanction is two-fold: (1) To protect persons dealing with the company so that the fund available for satisfying their claim shall not be diminished except by ordinary business risks, and (2) To ensure that the reduction is equitable as between the shareholders of the company.

Where the court is satisfied that the interests of the creditors have been secured, it may confirm the reduction on such terms and conditions as it may think fit. The court may, at the time of confirmation, *direct the company to add to its name the words "and reduced"* for a specified period and these words will be deemed to be part of the company's name for such specified time. The court may also make an order requiring the *company to publish the reasons for such reduction for the information of the public.* (Section 102).

The company shall *deliver to the registrar a certified copy of the court's order and a minute approved by the court showing* the following details for registration: (a) the amount of the share capital, (b) the number of shares into which it is to be divided; (c) the amount of each share, and (d) the amount, if any, at the date of registration deemed to be paid-up on each share.

The registrar will, thereupon register the order and the minute. On such registration, the resolution for reducing the share capital takes effect. *Notice of the registration shall be published* in such manner as may be directed by the NCLT.

Reduction of Capital and Diminution of Capital: (Section 94(1) (c) and Section 100). Reduction of capital involves writing off past losses against capital cancellation of the uncalled capital or repayment of surplus capital. It may involve reduction of issued capital, subscribed or paid-up share capital. Diminution of capital does not constitute a reduction of capital within the meaning of the Companies Act.

Distinction between Reduction of Capital and Diminution of Capital

1. ***Nature:*** Reduction may involve reduction *inter alia* of issued capital, whereas diminution may be in respect of authorised capital but not of issued capital.

2. ***Resolution:*** If the Articles authorise, diminution can be effected by an ordinary resolution, while reduction can be effected only by special resolution.

3. ***Confirmation by NCLT:*** Diminution needs no confirmation by the NCLT, but reduction needs such confirmation.

4. ***And Reduced:*** Where a company is ordered to add to its name the words '*And Reduced* 'these words shall until the expiry of the period specified in the order, be deemed to be part of the company's name; but such a provision does not exist in the case of diminution of share capital.

5. ***Time Limit:*** In the case of diminution, notice is to be given to the registrar within 30 days from the date of cancellation where upon the registrar shall record the notice and make the necessary alternation in the Memorandum of Association and Articles of Association. In case of reduction of capital, however, more detailed procedure has been prescribed, though there is no such time limit as aforesaid.

SHARES

A share is the interest of a shareholder in a definite portion of the capital. It expresses a proprietary relationship between the company and the shareholder. A share is a personal estate capable of being transferred in the manner laid down in the Articles of Association. *A certificate of shares issued by a company under its common seal specifies the shares held by any member. The share certificate is the prima facie evidence of the title of the member to such shares.* (Section 84(i)). The share certificate is not a negotiable instrument. According to Section 86 of the Companies Act, a company can issue only two types of shares — (a) preference shares, and (b) equity shares.

Preference Shares: A preference share must satisfy the following two conditions:

(i) It shall carry a preferential right as to the payment of dividend at a fixed rate; and (ii) In the event of winding up, there must be a preferential right to the repayment of the paid-up capital. These are two dominant characteristics of preference shares. A preference share may or may not carry such other rights as — (a) a preferential right to any arrears of dividend, (b) a right to share in surplus profits by way of additional dividend, (c) a right to be paid a fixed premium specified in the memorandum, and (d) a right to share in surplus assets in the event of a winding up, after all kinds of capital have been repaid.

Issue of preference shares: No company limited by shares shall, after the commencement of the Companies (Amendment) Act, 1996, issue any preference share which is irredeemable or is redeemable after the expiry of a period of 20 years from the date of its issue.

Equity Shares: All shares which are not preference shares are equity shares. Equity shareholders have the residual rights of the company. They may get higher dividend than preference shareholders if the company in prosperous or get nothing if the business of the company flops. In the winding up, the equity shares are entitled to the entire surplus assets remaining after the payment of the liabilities and the capital of the company, unless the articles confer right on the preference shares a right to participate in the distribution of surplus assets.

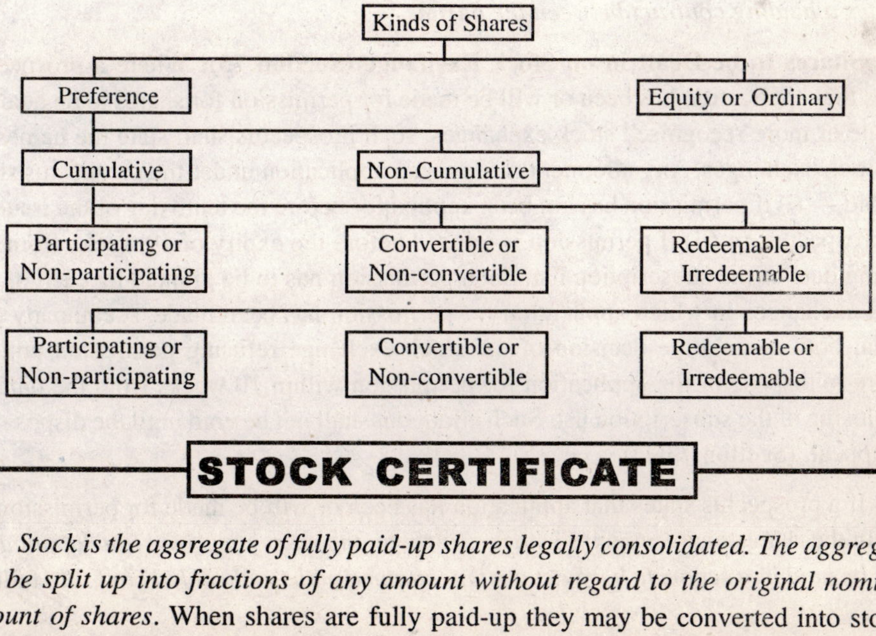

STOCK CERTIFICATE

Stock is the aggregate of fully paid-up shares legally consolidated. The aggregate can be split up into fractions of any amount without regard to the original nominal amount of shares. When shares are fully paid-up they may be converted into stock.

The issue of partly paid-up stock is invalid. The use of the term 'stock' merely denotes that a company has recognised the fact of the complete payment of the shares and that the time has come when these shares may be assigned in fragments, which, for obvious reasons, could not be permitted before.

A company limited by shares, may, if so *authorised by its Articles*, convert all or some of the fully paid-up shares into stock or reconvert its stock into fully paid-up shares of any denomination. The company shall *give notice to the Registrar* of such conversion within 30 days of its doing so. When shares are converted into stock, the register of members must show the amount of stock held by each member. Further, the annual return must state the amount of stock held by each member. Stock certificates, similar to share certificates must be issued.

Stock is transferable like share. The board may, however, fix the minimum amount of stock transferable. The holders of the stock have according to the amount of stock held by them the same rights, privilege and advantages as regards dividends, voting at the meetings of the company and other matters as if they held the shares from which the stocks arose. But no such privilege or advantage (except participation in the dividends and profits of the company and in the assets on winding up) shall be conferred by an amount of stock which would not, if existing in shares, have conferred that privilege or advantage.

Application and Allotment of Shares

A prospectus issued by a company inviting the public to subscribe to the shares of a company is a mere invitation. An application for shares is an offer by a prospective shareholder to take shares. *When an application is accepted it is an 'allotment'. Allotment creates a binding contract between the parties.*

Shares to be Dealt in on Stock Exchange (Section 73): Where a prospectus states that application has been or will be made for permission for shares to be dealt in on one or more recognised stock exchanges, such prospectus shall state the names of the stock exchanges. Any allotment made on an application under the prospectus shall be void — (i) if permission has not been applied for before the tenth day of the issue of the prospectus, or (ii) if permission is refused before the expiry of 10 weeks from the closing date of the subscription list. Such permission has to be granted by each of the stock exchanges in which application for permission has been made. A company can appeal both against the decision of the stock exchange refusing permission and its failure to dispose of the application for permission within 10 weeks from the date of the closing of the subscription list. Such allotment shall not be void until the disposal of the appeal. (Section 73(1)).

If a prospectus states that application has been or will be made for permission to deal in the shares on a recognised stock exchange, *the money received from applicants must be paid in a separate bank account maintained with a scheduled bank.* On failure to apply for permission or where permission has not been granted, the company has to *return all moneys received from the applicants within 8 days after the company becomes liable to pay.* If the application money is not repaid within 8 days, the directors are jointly and severally liable to repay the money with interest not less than 4% and not exceeding 15% per cent per annum from the expiry of the 8th day. A director will not be liable if he proves that the default was not due to any misconduct or negligence on his part (Section 72(2)). For failure to return the money within the time, the company and every officer who is in default shall be liable up to a fine to Rs. 5,000. (Section 73(5)).

Retention of Over-subscription: In case the issue is over-subscribed then shares etc., are alloted as per the scheme of allotment framed in consultation with the stock exchange(s) and passed by a board resolution.

As per the guidelines of SEBI, a company raising equity capital, (not being bonus shares) may retain over-subscribed equity to the extent of 15% of the amount sanctioned.

Essential of Valid Allotment

For an allotment to be called valid, some provisions of the Contract Act as well as Companies Act are to be complied with.

A. Provisions of Companies Act **say that Allotment must be made** by proper authority, within reasonable time, communicated, absolute and unconditional. The Companies Act does not prescribe any restrictions regarding the allotment of shares in case of private companies. But in case of public company:

(i) *When no public offer is made:* As per Section 70, company has to file a statement in lieu of prospectus with the registrar at least three days before the first allotment.

(ii) *When public offer is made:* In case of first allotment following statutory restrictions must be complied with:

1. A copy of the prospectus must be duly filed with the registrar for registration (Section 60).
2. The *minimum subscription* amount as disclosed in the prospectus must be received within 120 days of the issue of prospectus (Section 69).
3. The company must receive at least 5 per cent cash of nominal value of shares as application money (Section 69 (3)).
4. Application money must be deposited in a scheduled bank and it cannot be withdrawn till the company secures the '*Certificate to Commence Business*' or until the entire amount payable on applications for shares in respect of minimum subscription has been received by the company (Section 69(4)).

5. The company shall not proceed to allot shares until the beginning of the fifth day from the date of issue of prospectus or such a later date as may be specified in the prospectus.
6. Before the issue, the company must make an application to one or more recognised stock exchange for permission for the shares so offered to be dealt with in the stock exchange.

A *minor*, *lunatic*, being incompetent to enter into a contract, cannot be allotted shares of a company (***Mohri Bibi. vs. Dharamadas Chose (1930).*** If directors, in ignorance of the fact of minority, allot shares to a minor, and enter his name on the register of members, the company can repudiate the allotment and remove his name on the register of members, when the fact of applicant's minority comes to its knowledge. The minor can also repudiate the allotment at any time during his minority. In either case, the company must repay to minor all money received from his in respect of the allotted shares, and whether or not the minor should restore to the company the benefits he might have derived from the shares would be for the court to decide in view of the facts and circumstances of each case.

Irregular Allotment: An allotment made by a company before the minimum subscription is received or the filing of the statement in lieu of the prospectus is *voidable at the option of the applicant. Such an option must be exercised within two months of the statutory meeting* and where the company is not required to hold a statutory meeting or where the allotment is made after the statutory meeting, within two months after the date of allotment and not later. The allotment may be avoided although the company is being wound up. A member entitled to avoid an irregular allotment of shares will lose his right if, after becoming aware of the irregularity he exercises any rights of a member. Such an allotment though irregular, is nonetheless an allotment and the applicant may retain the shares notwithstanding the irregularities to allotment. Where the directors knowingly contravene the provisions as to allotment, they are liable to compensate the company and the allottee for any loss or damage suffered thereby. Proceeding against the directors must be commenced within two years of allotment.

Calls on Shares

When shares are issued, the full amount of each share is not generally payable at once. A part is payable on application, another part on allotment and the remainding by instalments when called for. A call may be defined as a *demand by the company on its shareholders to pay whole or part of the balance remaining unpaid on each share*. It is, thus, an intimation to the shareholder to discharge his obligation by paying the whole or part of the amount which remains unpaid on the shares. All money payable by any member to the company under the Memorandum or Articles is a debt due from him to the company. But he is not bound to pay unless a call has been made.

A call can be made by the directors during its lifetime and by the liquidator during its winding up.

Conditions of a Valid Call: The conditions of a valid call are as follows:

1 Resolution of the Board,

2 For the benefit of the company,

3 On uniform basis,

4 Amount, place and time of payment are clearly specified,

5. In accordance with Articles of Association

SHARE CERTIFICATE

Every person whose name is entered as a member in the register of members shall be entitled to receive one certificate for all his shares without payment. The share certificate must be issued under the common seal of the company and specify the shares to which it relates and the amount paid thereon. A share certificate under the common seal of the company, specifying any shares held by any member shall be *prima facie* evidence of the title of the member to such shares.

The issue of a share certificate by the company creates an estoppel as to title and also as to payment.

(a) *Estoppel as to title:* The company cannot deny the truth of the certificate as against a person who has relied upon it and who, in consequence, has changed his position. But if an officer of the company, who have no authority to issue certificates, issues a forged one; ***[South London Greyhound Resources Ltd. vs. . Wake 1931 Ch.496***]

(b) *Estoppel as to payment*: Where a company states that shares are fully paid-up, it cannot later contend that they were not, unless the person relying upon the certificate knew that the shares were not in fact fully paid-up [***Bloomenthal vs. Ford (1890) A.C., 156***]. It has also been held that the shares were not actually paid-up fully, could sell those shares away as fully paid to a person who knew that they were not fully paid so as to give the latter a good title to shares as fully paid because the latter derived title from the transferor who had a good title ***[Gulabdas's (1982) 17 Bom 672].***

A certificate, however, does not confirm the existence of an equitable interest in the share and as such, the company owes no obligation to a person who holds such an interest.

SHARE WARRANT

A share warrant is a document issued under the common seal of the company stating that the bearer is entitled to the shares specified therein. A share warrant is a bearer document and is transferable by mere delivery. Such *share warrants are negotiable instruments*. A public company limited by shares may issue share warrants. When shares are *fully paid*, the company may, if *authorised by its Articles* and subject to the *consent of the Central Government*, issue share warrants. Share warrants should contain the number of shares in respect of which they have been issued. Such a warrant must state that the bearer of it is entitled to the shares specified therein. The company may provide by coupons or otherwise, for the payment of future dividends on the shares specified in the warrant. (Section 114).

Difference between Share certificate and Share warrant

Basis of Difference	*Share Certificate*	*Share Warrant*
1. Issue	A share certificate can be issued at any stage,whether shares are fully paid-up or not	A share warrant can be issued only when shares are fully paid-up.
2. Membership	The holder of a share certificate is a member of the company	The holder of a share warrant will not be considered to be a member of the company, unless the Articles of Association of the company provide to the contrary.
3. Transfer	A share certificate is not a negotiable instrument. It cannot be transferred by mere delivery.	A share warrant is a negotiable instrument. it is transferable by mere delivery.
4. Profit Coupon	No profit coupon is attached with a share certificate	Profit coupon is attached with the share warrant.
5. Type of Company	A public company can issue share warrant	A private company cannot issue share warrant.
6. Qualifying shares for Director	The shares evidenced by a share certificate can be included in the qualification share of the director	The shares evidenced by a share warrant cannot be so included.
7. Rights	The holder of the share certificate has all the normal rights of membership.	The holder of a share warrant may or may not be given all the rights of membership by the Articles of Association
8. Application for winding up	The holder of share certificate has a right to give an application for the winding up of the company.	The holder of share warrant has no right to give an application for the winding up of the company.

Difference between Share and Stock

Basis of Difference	*Share*	*Stock*
1. Nominal Value	Share has nominal value	It has no nominal value
2. Fully paid-up	Share need not necessarily be fully paid-up	Stock is always fully paid
3. Transferability	It is transferable as a whole	It can be transferred in sums of any amount.
4. Distinctive Number	It has distinctive number by which it is distinguished from other shares	It does not have such a number but has a consolidated value.
5. Issue	It can be issued directly to the shareholders	It cannot be issued directly

TRANSFER OF SHARES

The shares in a company are movable property and they can be transferred in the manner provided by the articles of the company. (Section 82). Shares are the personal property of the shareholder and he has power to transfer his shares. It is an absolute right which cannot be taken away by any provision in the Articles. In the absence of any restriction in the Articles of Association, the shareholder can transfer his shares to any person even to a pauper or even if the transfer is made to escape liability provided that the transfer is real and bonafide in the sense that it is an out and out disposal of the property without retaining any interest in the shares.

Power to refuse registration of shares in the name of the transferee is covered under Section 111 of the Companies Act. It permits the company to empower itself through its Articles to refuse to register the transfer, or the transmission by operation of law, of the right to any shares or interest of a member in, or debentures of the company. Under this section, the company may empower the board of directors to refuse registration of a transfer even without assigning any reason besides providing for certain specific ground. Section 22-A if the Securities Contracts (Regulation) Act, 1956 provides that notwithstanding anything contained in its Articles or in Section 82 or Section 111 of the Companies Act, 1956, a company whose securities are listed on a recognised stock exchange, may refuse to register the transfer of any of its securities in the name of the transferee on any one or more of the following grounds, namely:

1. That the *instrument of transfer is not proper or has not been duly stamped and executed* or that the certificate relating to the security has not been delivered to the company or that any other requirement under the law relating to registration of such transfer has not been complied with.
2. That the transfer of security is *in contravention of any law.*

3. That the transfer of security is *likely to result in such change in the composition of board of directors* as would be *prejudicial to the interests of the company or to the public interest.*
4. That the *transfer of the security is prohibited by any order of any court*, tribunal or other authority under any law for the time-being in force.

Effect of a company's refusal to transfer: If the company refuses to register the transfer of shares for no fault or on default of the transferee, the transferor shall be treated as trustee for the transferee and would be bound to act in accordance with the directions of the transferee and for his benefit in respect of the shares unless the transferee has rescinded the contract. Until the transferee's name is placed on the register of members, the position is as follows:

1. The transferor continues to be the legal owner of the shares.
2. The transferee cannot exercise the rights of a shareholder *vis-a-vis* the company ***(Commissioner of I. Tax vs. M. Ramaswamy).***
3. The transferee has an equitable claim to the shares.
4. If calls are made, the transferor must pay them, but he can recover the amount from the transferee ***(Hardoon vs. Belilios).***
5. The transferor must vote as the transferee directs him, since the voting rights attached to the shares have passed to the transferee. ***(Musselwhite vs. Musselwhite and Sons).***

The company, after refusal to transfer the shares, whether in pursuance of any power under its Articles or otherwise, is required to send notice of refusal to the transferee and the transferor within two months from the date of receipt of request for the registration. The remedy against such refusal of the company is available under Section 111 of the Companies Act to the aggrieved parties to appeal to CLB.

Steps that investors can take in the case of delay or refusal of registration of transfers:

(i) The buyer or the seller can make an *appeal to the Company Law Board* against any refusal of the company to register the transfer. But the appeal has to be made *within two months* of the receipt of the notice by the company, or where no notice has been sent by the company for refusal of registration of transfer, *within four months* from the date on which the transfer form was delivered to the company. The appeal to the CLB has to be preferred in a form prescribed by the CLB bench rules.

(ii) For listed companies, if the shares are fully paid-up the investor can also avail of the remedy under Section 22-A of the Securities Contracts (Regulation) Act by *writing to the stock exchanges and the stock exchange division*, Ministry of Finance, Deptt. of Economic Affairs, New Delhi.

(iii) Under Section 62 of the Companies Act, the shareholder is authorised *to file criminal proceeding against the company and its officer in default.*

Powers of the Company Law Board

(i) The company and every officer in default of the company are liable to be punished with fine which may extend to Rs. 500 per day in case of non-compliance with Section 113.

The CLB has the powers under Section 111 of the Companies Act to —

(a) direct the company to register the transfers;

(b) direct rectification of the register;

(c) pass interim orders including orders as to injunction or stay;

Certification of transfer: Sometimes, a shareholder who is a holder of a large number of shares, desires to sell only a part of them. In such a case he hands over to the company the original share certificates for the whole amount thereof as he desires to sell. The company then stamps the transfer, (which is for desired lesser amount), with the original amount of the transferrer's holding. This is called "*certification of transfer*" and the transfer is called "*certified transfer*" e.g., 500 shares have been lodged in the company's office, the sale desired being 100 shares thereout. The company, prepares two new share certificates, one for 400 shares which is handed over to the transfer or and one for 100 shares which is handed over to the transferee, the original share certificate for 500 shares being kept by the company with itself for cancellation.

Section 112 of the Act makes the following provisions with regard to the subject: (i) the certificate of transfer by a company only amounts to a representation by the company to persons acting on the faith thereof, that documents have been produced before the company which on their face show a *prima facie* title to those shares (or debentures) in the transferred, (ii) It is not a representation that the transferee has any title to the shares (or debentures) in question, (iii) If such certificate is made by the company negligently, the company shall be liable to the person acting on the faith thereof as if it has been made fraudulently, (vi) "Certification" shall be deemed to be made by the Company if, (a) the person issuing the certificated instrument is authorised by the Company in that behalf, and (b) if the certification is "signed" by an officer or servant of the Company authorised in that behalf.

TRANSMISSION OF SHARES

The transmission of shares means transfer of title in shares by '*operation of law*'. In other words, the transmission of shares signifies involuntary assignment of shares because in this case the property in shares passes '*not by the act of the parties*', but by '*operation of law*'. For instance: (i) on the *insolvency* of a shareholder, property in shares passes to official receiver who shall become entitled to the shares owned by the insolvent, (ii) on the *death* of a shareholder, the property in shares passes to his legal representatives who shall become entitled to shares owned by the deceased, and (iii) on the *lunacy* of a shareholder, the property in shares passes to the administrator appointed by the court.

Distinction between Transfer and Transmission of Shares

Sr. No.	*Basis of Difference*	*Transfer of Shares*	*Transmission of Shares*
1.	Operation of the	Transfer of shares is the voluntarily act	Transmission of shares is the result of operation of law
2.	Base	Transfer is the method of transferring property	Transmission takes place only on the death, insolvency and lunacy of the owner of the shares.
3.	Consideration	There is adequate consideration in the case of transfer of shares	In the case of transmission of shares question of consideration does not arise.
4.	Lodgement	In the case of transfer of shares, lodgement of instrument of transfer is necessary.	In case of transmission of shares, lodgement of 'proof of title' is necessary.
5.	Stamp	In case of transfer of shares, stamp is not necessary	In case of transmission of shares, there need of stamp.

FORGED TRANSFER

A forged transfer is a nullity. It does not give the transferee concerned any title to the shares. If the company acts on a forged transfer and removes the name of the real owner from the Register of Members then the company is bound to restore the name of the real owner on the register as the holder of the shares and to pay him any dividends which he ought to have received (***Barton vs.North Straffordshire Railway Co. People Insurance Co.Ltd. vs.Wook & Co.Ltd., (1961***)).

Thus, if by forgery, A obtains a certificate of transfer of shares from a company and transfers the shares to a purchaser does not get a good title to the shares so transferred. But the company shall be liable to compensate the purchaser in sofaras the company had issued a certificate issued by the company could validly and reasonably assume that the person named in the certificate as the owner of shares was really the owner of the shares represented by the certificate (***Balkis Consolidated Co. vs. Tamkinson (1982) A.C. 1961***). If as a result of the forged transfer, the name of the true owner of shares is taken off the register of members he can *compel the company* *to restore his name to the register. He can also claim any dividend which may not have been paid to him during the intervening period* (**Barton vs.North Staffordhire Supra**}.

LIEN ON SHARES

A lien is the *right to retain possession of a thing until a claim is satisfied*. In the case of a company, lien on a share means that a member would not be permitted to transfer his shares unless he pays his debt to the company. The Articles generally provide that the company shall have a first and paramount lien on the shares of each member for the debts and liabilities to the company. The right of lien is not inherent but must be clearly provided for in the Articles. The Articles may give the right of lien over shares either for unpaid calls or for any other debt due by the member to the company. The company may have lien on fully paid-up shares. The lien also extends to the dividends payable on the shares.

SURRENDER OF SHARES

The Companies Act does not provide for surrender of shares. Shares are said to be surrendered when they are voluntarily given up. The Articles of a company may authorise the directors to accept surrender of shares. Surrender of shares is valid where it is done to relieve the company from going through the formality of forfeiture of shares and the shareholder is willing to surrender the shares. A surrender and a forfeiture have practically the same effect, the only difference being that the former is done with the assent of the shareholder, while the latter is done at the instance of the company.

FORFEITURE OF SHARES

A company has no inherent power to forfeit shares. *The power to forfeit shares must be contained in the Articles. Whereas the shareholder fails to pay the amount due on any call, the directors may, if so authorised by the Articles, forfeit his shares*. Shares can only be forfeited for non-payment of calls. An attempt to forfeit shares for any other reasons is illegal. Thus, where the shares are declared forfeited for the purpose of relieving a friend from liability, the forfeiture may be set aside.

Conditions to be Satisfied Before a Company may Forfeit Shares

A company may forfeit the shares of a shareholder if the following conditions are satisfied:

1. In Accordance with Articles: A forfeiture must be authorised by the Articles of the company. It must be strictly in accordance with the grounds specified in the

Articles, Any irregularity in the procedure or any departure from the rules laid down invalidate the forfeiture. Forfeiture is in the nature of penal proceedings. It is valid only if the provisions of Articles are strictly complied with (***Karachi Oil Products Ltd. vs. K.S.Narender Singhiji***).

2. Bonafide: Forfeiture must be bonafide and in the interest of the company. The right to forfeit shares, like the powers to make calls, is in the nature of a trust and must be exercised for the benefit of the company. For instance, if the shares are forfeited for the purpose of relieving a friend from liability, the forfeiture may be set aside (*Re Mirza Ahmed Nizami*).

3. Valid Call: When forfeiture is for non-payment of call, the call must have been properly made, i.e., by passing a proper resolution confirming to the provisions of articles on a uniform basis and bonafide in the interest of the company.

4. Notice Prior to Forfeiture: A proper notice must be served requiring a defaulting member to pay outstanding amount of call. The notice must give at least 14 days time from the date of its service for payment of the amount due and must inform the member that in the event of non-payment his share amount will be forfeited. Any defect in the notice, even though slight, invalidates it and is fatal to the forfeiture.

5. Resolution of the Board: If the defaulting shareholder does not pay the amount within the specified time as required by the notice, the directors must pass a resolution forfeiting the shares. If this resolution is not passed, the forfeiture as well, e.g., when it states that in the event of default, the shares shall be deemed to have been forfeited, no further resolution is necessary.

Legal Effects of Valid Forfeiture

1. The defaulting shareholder ceases to be a member of the company and his name is removed from the register of members.
2. He loses his claim to the paid-up amount on his shares.
3. He remains a contributory as a past member if liquidation commences within one year of forfeiture.
4. If the Articles provide so, he will remain liable for unpaid calls as an ordinary debtor for a period of 3 years from forfeiture.
5. Forfeited shares become property of the company which may reissue them or otherwise dispose of.
6. The title of the purchaser of reissued forfeited shares is not affected by any irregularity in the forfeiture.

Difference Between Forfeiture and Surrender of Shares

Both forfeiture and surrender of shares result in termination of membership of a person However, the two differ from each other in the following respects:

1. *Initiative*: In case of forfeiture, initiative is taken by the company, whereas in surrender of shares it is the member who takes the initiative.

2. *Reason*: Shares can be forfeited for non-payment of call only, but surrender of shares may be accepted for other reasons also, for example, for exchange of new shares.

3. *Object*: The object of forfeiture of shares is to penalise a member for non-payment of call, whereas the object of surrender of shares for the member is different. The member surrenders his shares either because he cannot make payments of calls due on it or because he wants to get it exchanged into new shares of the same nominal value.

4. *Legal Technicalities*: In case of forfeiture of share, the rules and regulations are to be followed exactly and carefully as a slight irregularity will invalidate the forfeiture made. However, it is not so in case of surrender of shares.

Issue of Sweat Equity Shares (Section 79-A)

Not withstanding anything contained in Section 79, a company may issue sweat equity shares of a class of shares already issued if the following conditions are fulfilled, namely:

(a) The issue of sweat equity shares is authorised by a *special resolution* passed by the company in the general meeting,

(b) The resolution specifies the number of shares, current market price, consideration, if any, and the class or classes of directors or employees to whom such equity shares are to be issued,

(c) Not less than one year has at the date of the issue elapsed since the date on which the company was entitled to commence business,

(d) The sweat equity shares of a company whose equity shares are listed on a recognised stock exchange are issued in accordance with the regulations made by the Securities and Exchange Board of India in this behalf (Sec. 79A(1)). However, in the case of a company whose equity shares are not listed, the same must be issued in accordance with the guidelines as may be prescribed.

Explanation I: For the purposes of this sub-section, the expression "*a company*" means a company incorporated, formed and registered under this Act and includes its subsidiary company incorporated in a country outside India.

Explanation II: For the purposes of this sub-seciton, the expression "*sweat equity shares*" means equity shares issued by the company to employees or directors at a discount or for consideration other than cash for providing know-how or making available rights in the nature of intellectual property rights, or value additions, by whatever name called.

All the limitations, restrictions and provisions relating to equity shares shall be applicable to such sweat equity shares issued under Sub-Section (1) (Sec. 79A(2)).

RIGHT SHARES

A company can at anytime by passing an *ordinary resolution* increase its capital by issuing new shares. If the directors could offer new shares to any person at their discretion, they would add to their own majority. According to Sectin 81, such shares must be offered to the existing equity shareholders of the company in proportion, as nearly as the circumstances admit, of the shares held by them. The restriction applies only when it is proposed to increase the subscribed capital of the company by allotment of further shares after the expiry of two years from the formation of the company or after the expiry of one year from first allotment of shres, whichever is earlier. Such shares are called '*rights shares*' and the right to receive them as the '*pre-emptive right*'.

The offer is made by giving each member a notice of shares offered to him. The notice must fix the time for payment which should not be less than fifteen days and should inform the shareholders that they have the right to renounce all or any of the shares offered to him in favour of their nominees. The shares which are not taken by the shareholders and which are left over after making proportional distribution may be allotted by the directors in such manner as they think most beneficial to the company. Subject to this restriction, the directors are at liberty to decide at what particular time the capital should be increased. Thus, in ***Nanalal Zavar vs. Bombay Life Assurance Co.,*** the Supreme Court approved a scheme for the increase of capital and its allotments to the existing shareholders even when the scheme was designed to prevent the domination of the company by a person who had purchased a majority of its shares in the open market. The directors had acted honestly in the interest of the company.

The new shares can however, be offered to outsiders to the exclusion of the existing shareholders in the following cases:

1. If the company has by passing a *special resolution* resolved to allot the new shares in a different manner than that provided in Section 81(2).
2. If an ordinary resolution to that effect has been passed and the Central Govtернment is satisfied that the proposal to offer the shares to outsiders is most beneficial to the company. The directors must not increase capital and allot it to themselves or their nominees solely for the prurpose of maintaining themselves in power.

Members of private companies do not have a right of pre-emption unless Articles so provide. Again, there is no right of pre-emption in case of convertible debentures and when Central Government converts its loan to a company into shares of the company.

The provision of Section 81 do not apply: (a) to a private company; or (b) to the increase of the subscribed capital of a public company caused by the exercise of an option attached to debentures issued or loans raised by the company — (i) to convert such debentures or loans into shares in the company; or (ii) to subscribe for shares in the company provided that the terms of issue of such debentures or loans, include a term providing for such option and such term (a) either has been approved by the Central Government before the issue of debentures or the raising of the loans, or is in conformity with any rules, made by that government in this behalf and (b) in case of debentures or loans other than debentures issued to, or loans obtained from the government or any institution specified by the Central Government in this behalf has been approved by a special resolution passed by the company in general meeting before the issue of the debentures or the raising of the loans.

Duty of Transferor to Transferee in Respect of Rights Shares

There may be pending transfers at the time when a rights issue takes place. This raises the question whether the transferor of an unregistered transfer is under any obligation towards his transferee to apply for the rights shares for the benefit of the transferee. The Bombay High Court in ***Dinge Venkataramana Reddy vs. Padampat Singhania AIR 1950 Bom. 76*** held that it was the duty of the transferor to apply for the new shares and to hold them in trust for the transferee. But, the Supreme Court in ***R. Mathalone vs. Bombay Life Assurance Co. Ltd. AIR 1953 SC 385*** has upheld a contrary view. The Supreme Court, in this case, observed that after the transfer form has been executed, the transferor cannot be held to undertake any additional financial burden in respect of the shares at the instance of the transferee where, after the transfer of shares, but before the company had registered the transfer, the company offered rights shares to its members. The transferor could not be compelled by the transferee to take up on his behalf the rights shares offered to the transferor and all that he could require the transferor to do was to renounce the rights issue in the transferee's favour.

SEBI Guidelines Regarding Rights Issues

Applicability: These guidelines apply to the rights issues made by existing listed companies, (i.e., companies whose equity capital is listed). Therefore, a company whose debentures/bonds are listed but not the equity, (i.e., shares) will not be governed by these guidelines.

These guidelines are not applicable where the size of the issue is up to Rs. 50 lakh.

Withdrawal of a rights issue: Rights issue cannot be withdrawn after the announcement of their record date. If done, then no security of the company shall be eligible for listing up to 12 months.

Underwriting: The underwriting of rights issued shall be optional.

Appointment of registrars: Appointment of registrars to issue shall be compulsory.

Appointment of merchant banker: Appointment of category-I merchant banker holding a valid certificate of registration issued by SEBI shall be compulsory.

Partly paid shares: Partly paid shares, if any, must either be made fully paid or forfeited.

Letter of offer : Letter of offer shall contain disclosures specified by SEBI as per Form 2-A. The lead merchant banker shall :

(i) ensure compliance of the requirements of SEBI guidelines with respect to the offer document relating to rights issues.

(ii) file with SEBI a copy of the offer document at least 21 days before filing of the same with the regional stock exchange.

Agreement with depository: The company shall enter into an agreement with the depository for dematerialisation:

(i) of securities already issued;

(ii) proposed to be issued;

(iii) the subscribers/shareholders must be given an option of holding the shares in a dematerialised mode or by way of share certificates.

Closure of rights issue: The rights issue must be kept open for a minimum period fo 30 days. It cannot remain open for more than 60 days.

Minimum subscription: SEBI requires the following clauses in respect of minimum subscription to be stated in the letter of offer.

"If the company does not receive the minimum subscription of 90% of the issue, the entire subscription will be refunded to the applicants within 42 days from the date of closure of the issue. If there is delay in the refund of the application money by more than 8 days after the company becomes liable to pay the amount, i.e., forty-two days after closure of the issue, the company will pay interest for the delayed period, @ 15% per annum as prescribed in Sub-Section (2) and (2A) of Section 73 of the Companies Act, 1956".

In case of composite issue, the Lead Merchant Banker shall ensure that the requirement of minimum subscription is satisfied both jointly and severally, i.e., independently for both rights and public issues.

No Reservations in rights issues: SEBI guidelines prohibit any preferential allotment in favour of the issuing companies' permanent employees and financial institutions. If a company desires to make any preferential allotment to the employees or any identified persons it may do so independent of rights issue by complying with the guidelines in that regard.

Promoter's contribution and lock-in period: The requirement of promoter's contribution shall not be applicable in case of rights issues.

Rights of FCD/PCD holders: No company shall, pending conversion of FCDs/PCDs, issue any shares by way of rights unless similar benefit is extended to the holders of such FCDs or PCDs. The benefits shall be extended by making a reservation of shares in proportion to the convertible part of FCDs/PCDs. The shares so reserved may be issued at the time of conversion of such debentures on the same terms on which the rights issue was made.

Restriction on further capital issues: No company shall make any further issue of capital in any manner whether by way of issue or otherwise, during the period commencing from the submission of offer documents to SEBI on behalf of the company for rights issues, till the securities referred to in the said offer document have been listed or application moneys refunded on account of non-listing or under subscription, etc.

Oversubscription not to be retained: Over-subscription shall not be retained under any circumstances.

Issue to be made fully paid-up: The issue shall have to be made fully paid-up within 12 months except where the issue size exceeds Rs. 500 crore.

Additional Facility for applying : The lead merchant banker shall ensure that an advertisement giving the date of completion of despatch of letters of offer, is released in at least one English National Daily with wide circulation, one Hindi National Paper and a regional language daily circulated at the place where registered office of the issuer company is situated. The advertisement must be published at least 7 days before the date of opening of the issue.

The advertisement must contain the following details.

(a) The centres other than registered office of the company where the shareholders or the persons entitled to rights may obtain duplicate copies of composite application forms in case they do not receive the original application form within a reasonable time even after opening of the rights issue.

(b) Where the shareholders have neither received the original composite application forms nor are they in a position to obtain the duplicate forms, they may make applications to subscribe to the rights on a plain paper.

(c) The advertisement shall also contain a format to enable the shareholders to make the application on a plain paper containing necessary particulars like name, address, ratio of rights issue, issue price, number of shares held, ledger folio numbers, number of shares entitled and applied for, additional shares if any, amount to be paid along with application, particulars of cheque, etc., to be drawn in favour of the company account rights issues.

(d) The advertisement shall further mention that application can be directly sent by the shareholders through registered post together with the application monies to the company's designated official at the address given in the advertisement.

(e) The advertisement may also invite attention of the shareholders to the fact that the shareholders making the applications otherwise than on the standard form shall not be entitled to renounce their rights and shall not utilise the standard form for any purpose including renunciation even if it is received subsequently.

(f) If the shareholder makes an application on plain paper and also in standard form, he may face the risk of rejection of both the applications.

Compliance Report: The post-issue lead merchant banker shall file :

(a) *3-day post-issue monitoring report* : The report shall be filed on the 3rd day from the date of closure of the subscription of the issue.

(b) *50 day post-issue monitoring report* : The report shall be filed on the 50th day from the date of closure of subscription of the issue.

BONUS SHARES

A company may, if the Articles so provide, capitalise profits by issuing fully paid-up shares to the members thereby transferring the sums capitalised from the Profit and Loss Account or Reserve Account to the Share Capital (Section 205(3)). Such shares are known as *bonus shares* and are issued to the existing members of the company free of charge.

Difference between Bonus Shares and Rights Shares

Sr. No.	*Basis of Difference*	*Bonus Shares*	*Rights Shares*
1.	Meaning	By bonus shares we mean the shares which are issued to the existing shareholders from the profits and reserves of the company without taking no extra payment.	The shares which are meant for the existing shareholders are known as rights shares.
2.	Objective	The issue of bonus shares implies the payment of dividend in the form of 'shares' instead of 'cash'	The object of the issue of right shares is to increase the subscribed capital of the company.

3.	Consideration	Bonus shares are issued to the existing shareholders without taking any extra payment	In case of issue of right shares, payment is made entirely by shareholders subscribing fresh capital
4.	Provision	Bonus shares are issued under the provisions of Secs. 78, 80 and 205.	Right shares are issued under the provisions of Sec. 81.

The issue of bonus shares is regulated not only by the Companies Act, 1956 but also by the guidelines issued by SEBI in this regard.

SEBI Guidelines, for Issue of Bouns Shares (w.e.f. 2000)

(a) The bonus issue shall only be made out of free reserves built out of the genuine profits or share premium collected in cash only.

(b) Reserves created by revaluation of fixed assets are not to be capitalised.

(c) The declaration of bonus issue, in lieu of dividend, is not made.

(d) The bonus issue is not made unless the party—paid shares, if any, existing, are made fully paid-up.

(e) The company (i) *has not defaulted in payment of interest or principal in respect of fixed deposits and interest* on existing debentures or principal on redemption thereof, and (ii) has sufficient reason to believe that it has *not defaulted in respect of the payment of statutory dues* of the employees such as contribution to provident fund, gratuity, bonus, etc.

(f) A company which announces its bonus after the approval of the board of directors must *implement the proposal within a period of 6 months* from the date of such approval and shall not have the option of changing the decision.

(g) There should be a provision in the Articles of Association of the company for capitalisation of reserves, etc., and, if not, the company shall pass a *special resolution* at its general body meeting making provisions in the Articles of Association for capitalisation.

(h) Consequent to the issue of bonus shares, if the subscribed and paid-up capital exceed the authorised share capital, resolution shall be passed by the company at its general body meeting for increasing the authorised capital.

(i) No company shal, pending conversion of FCSs/PCDs, issue any shares by way of bonus unless similar benefit is extended to the holders of such FCDs/PCDs through reservation of shares in proportion to the convertible part of FCDs/PCDs.

(j) The shares so reserved may be issued at the time of conversion of such debentures on the same terms on which the bonus issues were made.

Issue of Shares at a Premium (Section 78)

A company is free to sell its shares at a premium, i.e., at a price higher than their nominal value. The power to issue shares at premium need not be given in the Articles. The premium received on issue of shares, whether in cash or kind, must be transferred to a separate account called *Share Premium Account*. The provisions of the Act relating to the reduction of the share capital will apply as if the share premium account were paid-up share capital of the company.

The premium can, however, be used for the following purposes:

(a) for issuing to the members as fully paid *bonus shares*, the unissued shares of the company;

(b) for *writing-off preliminary expenses* of the company;

(c) for writing-off expenses, *commission or discount on the issue of shares* or debentures of the company;

(d) for providing for the *payment of premium payable on redemption* of redeemable preference shares or debentures. *Dividend cannot be paid out of share premium account* as it will amount to reduction of capital without the confirmation of the court, and hence, *ultra-vires* of the company.

Issue of Shares at a Discount

A company issues shares at a discount when shares are issued at a price less than their face value. Shares at a discount can be issued by the company if the following conditions are fulfilled :

(i) Shares to be issued must be of a class already issued.

(ii) Such issue is authorised by a resolution of shareholders.

(iii) Issue must be sanctioned by the Company Law Board.

(iv) The resolution must specify the rate of discount which must not exceed 10 per cent, unless the Company Law Board is of the opinion that a higher percentage of discount may be allowed in the special circumstances of the case.

(v) Not less than one year has elapsed since the date on which the company was entitled to commence business.

(vi) The shares must be issued within two months of the sanction by the Company Law Board or within such extended times as the Company Law Board may permit.

Purchase by a Company of its Own Shares (Section 77)

A company limited by shares or limited by guarantee having a share capital cannot buy its own shares except when the share capital of the company is reduced in pursuance of Sections 100-104 or where shares are to be purchased for prevention of oppression and mismangement under Section 402 of the Companies Act. Buying its own shares by a company will mean a permanent reduction of capital without sanction of the court which is *ultra-vires* of the Act.

DIVIDEND

Dividend is the portion of the profits of company which is allocated to the shareholders in proportion to their shares and in accordance with their rights as shareholders. *A dividend can be declared by the shareholders at the annual general meeting, but no dividend shall exceed the amount recommended by the board of directors.* If the directors feel that a dividend should not be declared, the shareholders in general meeting cannot themselves declare it. Apart from these, the Articles may empower the directors to declare interim dividend.

The Articles usually provide that the dividends shall be paid to the shareholders in proportion to the amounts paid on the shares held by them respectively. If not, dividends are paid on cash share in proportion to the nominal value of that share without reference to the amount paid upon it.

A company may declare and pay dividends out of current or previous years profit or out of both or out of money provided by the Central or state government for payment of the dividend in pursuance of a guarantee given by such Government. In the public interest the Central Government may allow a company to declare dividend out of profits of the current year without requiring the company to provide for depreciation. (Section 20(1)).

Interim dividend: The Articles of a company may empower the directors to declare interim dividend, i.e., *dividend in between its two annual general meetings.* The board may from time-to-time pay to the members such interim dividend as appears to it to be *justified by the profits of the company* (Articles 86 of Table A). But before declaring an interim dividend, the directors must satisfy themselves that the financial position of the company warrants the payment of such dividend out of profits available for distribution.

Dividend warrant: A dividend warrant is an instrument containing an order on a company's banker directing it to pay the stated amount to or to the order of the shareholder named therein who is entitled to claim the dividend. *It is in two parts*—one part is a notice of the dividend to the shareholder as well as the *certificate of deduction of income-tax*, and the other part is the dividend warrant.

(i) The board of directors can declare interim dividend and the amount of dividend or interim dividend shall be deposited in a separate bank account within 5 days from the date of declaration.

(ii) The amount so deposited shall only be used for payment of interim dividend.

(iii) The provisions of Sections 205, 205-A, 205-C, 206-A and 207 dealing with declaration and payment of dividend, treatment unclaimed dividend, establishment of *Investor Education and Protection Fund*, etc., shall apply to interim dividend also.

Since dividend include interim dividend, companies should provide depreciation as required by Section 205 and comply with *Companies (Transfer of Profits to Reserve) Rules, 1975* before declaring interim dividend. The company has to provide estimated depreciation for the full year before declaration of interim dividend. If the company does not transfer any profit to reserves, it has to be contended with declaring an interim dividend not exceeding 10% of the paid-up capital.

Section 205 (IB) provides that the amount of dividend including interim dividend so deposited shall be used for payment of interim dividend. It implies that even the amount deposited for payment of final dividend be used for payment of interim dividend.

Further, Section 205 has reduced the time from for payment of dividend from 42 days to 30 days from the date of declaration.

Penalty for Failure to Distribute Dividends

(i) This applies to dividend declared at AGM and also to interim dividend declared by board of directors.

(ii) Dividend shall be paid or dividend warrant shall be posted within 30 days. (It may be noted that the existing time limit of 42 days has been reduced to 30 days).

(iii) Every director who has knowingly made default in complying with the above requirement shall be punishable with simple imprisonment for a term which may extend up to 3 years and shall also be liable to fine of Rs. 1,000 for every day during which the default continues.

(iv) Simple interest at 18% p.a. shall also be payable by the director who has committed the default for the period of default.

(v) The existing provisions of Section 27 under which certain circumstances when the delay in payment is not considered as default have been retained.

Payment of Interest Out of Capital (Section 208)

When any shares are issued for the purpose of raising money to defray the expenses of the construction of any work or building or the provision of any plant, which cannot be made profitable for a lengthy period, the company may pay interest on paid-up share capital under certain conditions provided such payment is bonafide and in the interests of the company. The conditions are:

(i) Such payment is authorised by the Articles or a special resolution.

(ii) Previous approval of the Central Government is obtained.

(iii) Before sanctioning any such payment, the Central Government may, at the expense of the company, hold an inquiry and require the company to give security for the cost of the inquiry.

(iv) The interest shall be payable only for such periods as may be determined by the Central Government and such periods will, in no case, extend beyond the close of the half-year following the half-year during which the work or building has been actually completed, or the plant provided.

(v) The rate of interest shall not exceed 4 per cent or such other rates as may be sanctioned by the Central Government.

The payment of interest shall be charged to capital account and included in the cost of construction of the work or building or the provision of a plant. Such *payment of interest out of capital does not amount to a reduction of capital.*

DEBENTURES

The term '*debenture*' is defined in the Companies Act as, "*Debenture includes debenture stock, bonds, any other securities of a company whether constituting a charge on the assets of the company or not.*" A debenture is a document given by a company as evidence of a debt to the holder usually out of loan and most commonly secured by a charge.

Characteristics of Debentures

1. It is an instrument in writing.
2. It is an acknowledgement of the indebtedness of the company to its holders for the amount stated in it.
3. It is usually under the common seal of the company
4. It provides for the payment of a fixed sum with interest of a specified rate for a specified time.
5. It is generally secured by a charge, fixed or floating on any part of the company's property or undertaking.
6. Debentures can be issued on right basis to the existing shareholders of the company.
7. They are entitled to redemption of their capital as per the agreed terms.

8. They can enforce the sale of security in case of default.

9. They have no voting rights (Sec. 117 of the Companies Act, 1956).

Kinds of Debentures

Debentures are classified into four classes: (a) Debentures payable to a registered holder, and debentures payable to a bearer, (b) secured and unsecured debentures, (c) Redeemable and perpetual debentures, (d) fully or partly convertible and non-convertible debentures.

Fully Convertible Debentures (FCD): Fully convertible debentures are those debentures that are converted into equity shares of the company on the expiry of a specified period or periods where the conversion is to be made at or after 18 months from the date of allotment but before 36 months. The conversion is optional on the part of the debentureholders in terms of SEBI guidelines. Convertible debentures may or may not carry any interest.

Partly Convertible Debentures (PCD): PCD consist of two parts—*convertible* and *non-convertible*. The convertible portion(s), is/are convertible into equity shares at the expiry of specified period(s) whereas the non-convertible portion is redeemed at the expiry of a certain period(s). Where the conversion takes place at or after 18 months, the conversion is optional at the discretion of debentureholders.

Distinction Between the FCD and PCD

	FCD	*PCD*
1.Classification for debt equity ratio computation	Classified as equity for debt equity for computation	Convertible portion classified as 'equity' and non convertible portion as 'debt'
2. Flexibility in financing	Highly favourable debt equity ratio.	Favourable debt equity ratio.
3. Capital base	Highly equity capital on convertion of debentures.	Relatively lower equity capital on conversion of debentures.
4. Suitability	Better suited for companies with established record.	Better suited for companies without established track record.
5. Servicing of equity	Higher burden of servicing of equity	Relatively lesser burden of equity servicing.
6. Debenture redemp-tion reserve.	Not required	Required to be created for 50% of the face value of the non-convertible portion.
7. Buyback arrange-ment	Not required	Arrangements may be made for buy back of the non-convertible portion of the debentures.

8. Popularity	Highly popular with investors	Not so popular with investors.

Remedies of Debentureholders: In case of unsecured debentures, the holder is an *ordinary unsecured creditor*. If the company defaults in the payment of principal or interest he may—(i) sue for the principal or interest and after judgement, levy execution against the company; or (ii) petition for the winding up of the company by the court. If the company is already in the course of winding up, he may prove for the amount due to him. A secured debentureholder stands in a stronger position as compared to unsecured debentureholder.

CHARGES AND MORTGAGES ON THE ASSETS OF THE COMPANY

Where however the debenture is *secured* by a mortgage or a charge, the holder thereof who wishes to realise his security and recover the money due to him, may resort to all or any of the following remedies;

(i) He may sue on his behalf and on behalf of other debentureholders of the same class to obtain payment or *enforce his security by sale*;

(ii) He may *appoint a receiver* if the conditions of the issue of so permit;

(iii) He may *apply to the court* foreclosure of the company's right to redeem the debentures. But, in such an action, all debentureholders of the company, in contradiction to those of a class, as well as the company should be joined as parties;

(iv) He may, in the capacity of a creditor, *present an application for winding up* for the principal and interest thereon;

(v) He may *have the property sold by the trustee* if the debenture-trust-deed permits the sale;

FIXED CHARGES VS. FLOATING CHARGES

The charge on the assets of a company, given by a debenture or a trust deed, may be either (i) specific or fixed charge; or (2) floating charge.

Specific or Fixed Charge: A *fixed or specific charge* is created in respect of a definite and ascertained property and this prevents the company from dealing with that property without the consent of the debentureholders. In case of winding up of a company a debentureholder secured by a specific charge is in the highest ranking class of creditors. Where there are a number of specific charges on the same property, their priority is determined by the general rules relating to priority of charges.

Floating Charge: A '*floating charge*' is an equitable charge which does not fasten on any ascertained or definite property and as such the company can deal with any of its assets in the ordinary course of business. The consent of the debentureholders is not necessary for the company to deal with its assets. Whether a particular charge is a floating charge or not depends upon the construction of the words used in the document creating the charge. The nature of charge cannot be altered to become a floating charge merely because in spite of the charge, the business of the company continues to be carried on.

Difference Between Fixed Charge and Floating Charge

	Fixed Charge	*Floating Charge*
1.	It is a legal charge	It is an equitable charge
2.	It is a charge on specific, ascertained existing and future assets	It is a charge on present and no specific assets.
3.	Company cannot deal with the assets except with the consent of the chargeholder	Company is free to use or deal with the assets the way it likes until the charge crystalizes, i.e., becomes fixed.
4.	Registration of fixed charge on movable assets is not compulsory	Registration of all floating charge on all kinds of assets is compulsory by law
5.	Fixed charge has always priority over floating charge	Ambulatory and shifting in character.

Registration of Charges

Where a company creates a charge over its property, Section 125 requires that *charge to be registered with the registrar of companies*. The particulars of every charge and mortgage created on a movable or immovable property must be filed by the company with the registrar *within 30 days of their creation*. The registrar may extend the time for filing of the particulars and instrument creating the charge by seven days provided the company had sufficient cause for not filing the particulars within the specified period. *The charges which are required to be compulsorily registered are given below:*

1. A charge to secure any issue of debentures.
2. A charge on uncalled share capital.
3. A charge on any immovable property, wherever situated or any interest therein.
4. A charge on any book debts of the company.
5. A charge not being a pledge on any movable property of the company.
6. A floating charge on the undertaking or any property of the company including stock in trade.

7. A charge on calls made but not paid.
8. A charge on a ship or any share in a ship.
9. A charge on goodwill, or a patent or licence under a patent, on a trade mark or copy right.

Particulars to be filled with the registrar:

(a) If the charge is in connection with the secured debentures, then (i) total amount secured by the debentures, (ii) the date of resolution authorising the issue of debentures and the date of the instrument by which the security is created; (iii) general description of the property charged; (iv) name of the trustees for the debentureholders. If any commission has been paid to any person for subscribing to the debentures, the amount and the rate of commission so paid also to be indicated.

(b) In the case of anyother charge: (i) the date of creation of charge, (ii) the amount secured, (iii) short particulars of the property charged; (iv) the person entitled to the charge.

Consequences of Non-registration of Registrable Charge

(i) the charge will be *void as an against the liquidator* (if the company goes into liquidation) and against creditors, but an obligation to pay the debt remains.

(ii) the charge is good against the company and the *amount becomes payable immediately*;

(iii) until liquidation of the company, the person seeking to enforce such a charge, has available to him all remedies of a mortgage against the company, though not against other creditors;

(iv) the company may give a subsequent valid charge to secure the same debt. If that subsequent creditor even with the notice of the first charge takes a registered charge before the first said charge has been registered, the second creditor obtains priority;

(v) during liquidation the chargeholder (creditor) assumes the status of an unsecured creditor as the charge is void against the liquidator and creditors;

(vi) the holder of an equitable charge whose charge is void for failure to register has no lien on the title deeds or documents deposited with him.

(vii) although the security becomes void by non-registration, it does not affect the contract or obligation of the company to repay the money;

(viii) omission to register particulars of charge is punishable with fine; the company or every office of the company or other person who is in default shall be liable to be fined.

Crystrallisation of a Floating Charge: Floating charge crystallises or becomes fixed under any of the following circumstances:

* When the company goes into liquidation;
* When the company ceases to carry on business;
* When the debentureholders takes steps to enforce their security, e.g., by appointing a receiver, on defalult by the company to pay principal and interest.

DEBENTURE TRUST DEED

A trust deed for securing any issue of debentures shall be in such form and shall be executed within such period as may be prescribed. A copy of the trust deed shall be open to inspection to any member or debentureholder of the company and he shall also be entitled to obtain copies of such trust deed on payment of such sum as may be prescribed. If a copy of the trust deed is not made available for inspection or is not given to any member or debentureholder, the company and every officer of the company who is in a default, shall be punishable, for each offence, with fine which may extend to five hundred rupees for everyday during which of the offence continues.

Appointment of Debenture Trustees and Duties of Debenture Trustees

1. No company shall issue a prospectus or a letter of offer to the public for subscription of its debentures, unless the company has, before such issue, appointed one or more debenture trustees for such debentures and the company has, on the face of the prospectus or the letter of offer, state that the debenture trustee or trustees have given their consent to the company to be so appointed:

Provided that no person shall be appointed as a debenture trustee, if he — (a) beneficially holds shares in the company; (b) is beneficially entitled to monies which are to be paid by the company to the debenture trustee; (c) has entered into any guarantee is respect of principal debts secured by the debentures or interest thereon.

2. Subject to the provision of this Act, the functions of the debentures trustees shall generally be to protect the interest of holders of debentures (including the creation of securities within the stipulated time) and to redress the grievances of holders of debentures effectively.

3. In particular, and without prejudice to the generality of the foregoing functions, debenture trustee may take such other steps as he may deem fit—

(a) to ensure that the assets of the company issuing debentures and each of the guarantors are sufficient to discharge the principal amount at all times;

(b) to satisfy himself that the prospectus or the letter of offer does not contain any matter which is inconsistent with the terms of the debentures or with the trust deed;

(c) to ensure that the company does not commit any breach of convenants and provisions of the trust deed;

(d) to take such reasonable step to remedy any breach of the convenants of the trust deed or the terms of issue of debentures;

(e) to take steps to call a meeting of holders of debentures as and when such meeting is required to be held.

4. Where at anytime the debenture trustee comes to a conclusion that the assets of the company are insufficient or are likely to become insufficient to discharge the principal amount as and when it becomes due, the debenture trustee may *file a petition before the Company Law Board* and the Company Law Board may, after hearing the company and any other person interested in the matter, by an order, impose such restrictions on the incurring of any further liabilities as the Company Law Board thinks necessary in the interests of holders of the debentures.

QUESTIONS

Objective Type Questions

I. Fill up the Blanks

1. Authorised share capital is capital authorised to be raised according to the guidelines of _______.
2. The existing shareholders have a right to participate in the _______ issues of shares.
3. Uncalled capital according to Section 99 of the Companies Act could be converted into _______ capital by passing a _______ resolution.
4. Cancellation of unsubscribed capital is known as __________ capital.
5. Reduction of share capital takes place on account of __________ of assets and on account of _______ collection of capital.
6. When shares are allotted by passing a special resolution to persons providing know-how to the company, these shares are known as ___________.
7. According to Section 85 of the Companies Act, only two types of shares are to be issued namely __________ and ___________.
8. Fully paid-up shares can be converted into ___________.
9. Irregular allotment arises on account of not obtaining the permission of the ___________.
10. Shares can be forfeited only when there is ______ on the part of the shareholders.

[*Answers :* (1) SEBI; (2) Further; (3) Reserve capital; a Special; (4) Diminution of; (5) Depreciation; Excess or surplus; (6) Sweat equity shares; (7) Equity and Preference; (8) Stock; (9) Stock Exchange; (10) Calls-in-arrears]

II. State Whether the following statements are True or False

1. A public limited company cannot buy its own shares.
2. For alteration of Share capital, only ordinary resolution is enough.
3. Reduction of Share capital has to be sanctioned by the Company Law Board.
4. Members' liability may also be more than the reduced value on certain occasions.
5. Promoters of company are even now allotted deferred shares.
6. The ceiling on dividend in respect of issues of preference shares is fixed.
7. Issue of Bonus shares arises out of capitalisation of undistributed profits over a period of time.
8. Dividend may be paid at any time as the Board of Directors may decide.
9. A transfer deed relating to the shares of the public company must be registered with the company before the closure of the register or within 12 months from the date of the prescribed authority's seal.

[*Answers:* True: (2), (4), (8); False: (1), (3), (5), (6), (7), (9)]

III. Match the following

1. Further issue of Shares	(a) Sale of capital assets for profit
2. Capital Reserve	(b) Convertible as shares
3. Debenture deeds	(c) Not a reduction of share capital
4. Buy Back shares	(d) Innovative and creative project
5. Venture Capital	(e) Right Shares.
6. Blank transfer	(f) For issuing filly paid bonus shares
7. Transmission of shares	(g) Forfeiture of shares
8. Share premium	(h) Letter of Probate
9. Calls-in-arrears	(i) Board resolution
10. Valid calls	(j) Transferee's address not disclosed.

[*Answers:* 1. (f); 2. (a); 3. (b); 4. (c); 5. (d); 6. (j); 7. (h); 8. (f); 9. (g); 10. (i)]

IV. Multiple Choice Questions

1. A deemed public company must have at least
   (a) 1 director.
   (b) 2 directors.
   (c) 3 directors.
   (d) 5 directors.
2. The minimum number of directors in a public company is
   (a) 2. (c) 5.
   (b) 3. (d) 7.
3. Where the increase in the total number of directors of a company makes its directors more than 12, any such increase must be approved by
   (a) the Board of directors.
   (b) the Company in General Meeting.
   (c) the Company Law Board.
   (d) the Central Government.
4. An alternate director can hold office only
   (a) up to the commencement of the next annual general meeting.
   (b) during the absence of the original director for a period of not less than 3 months.
   (c) during the absence of the original director for a period of not less than 6 months
   (d) up to the date the original director would have held office.
5. The Central Government may remove any managerial personnel from office, after the necessary procedure has been complied with, on the recommendation of
   (a) shareholders.
   (b) creditors.
   (c) a High Court.
   (d) the Company Law Board.
6. The overall maximum managerial remuneration of a public limited company must not exceed
   (a) 5 per cent of its net profit.
   (b) 10 per cent of its net profit.

(c) 11 per cent of its net profit.

(d) 15 per cent of its net profit.

7. Which of the following powers of the Board of directors cannot be exercised except with the consent of the company in general meeting?

(a) Power to issue debentures.

(b) Power to invest the funds of the company.

(c) Power to sell the whole of the undertaking of the company.

(d) Power to make calls.

8. A director interested in a contract must disclose his interest in such contract at

(a) the Board meeting at which the contract is being first considered.

(b) the general meeting of the shareholders.

(c) the first Board meeting held after he becomes interested in the contract.

(d) any Board meeting after he becomes interested in the contract.

9. A company cannot appoint simultaneously a managing director and

(a) a manager.

(b) a secretary.

(c) general manager.

(d) any other wholetime director.

10. Share capital of a company means

(a) Equity share capital.

(b) Preference share capital.

(e) Equity and preference share capital.

11. Alteration of capital of a company must be authorised by

(a) the Articles and a resolution of the Board of directors.

(b) the Articles and a resolution passed in the general meeting of shareholders.

(c) a resolution passed in the general meeting of shareholders and also sanction of the Central Government.

12. A company which alters its share capital must give notice of alteration to the Register within

(a) 15 days of doing so.

(b) 21 days of doing so.

(c) 30 days of doing so.

13. Rights shares mean shares which are
    (a) issued by a newly formed company.
    (b) legally issued to the public.
    (c) offered to existing equity shareholders.

[*Answers:* 1 (b); 2 (b); 3 (d); 4 (b); 5 (d); 6 (c); 7 (c); 8 (c); 9 (a & c); 10 (c); 11 (b); 12 (c); 13 (c)]

Review Questions

1. In what ways may a person become and cease to be a member of the company?
2. Is every shareholder a member of the company?
3. Distinguish between a shareholder and a member of the company.
4. How can the share capital of a company be reduced?
5. What is the liability of the members in respect of reduction in share capital?
6. Define share. What are the different kinds of shares which a company may issue?
7. What is meant by allotment of shares?
8. Discuss the rules relating to the allotment of shares. Point out the consequences of irregular allotment.
9. Discuss the restriction on the allotment of shares under the Companies Act.
10. What is the effect of an irregular allotment?
11. How is the transfer of shares effected?
12. Can the board of directors refuse to register a transfer of shares? What is the remedy open to a transferee in such a case?
13. What do you understand by the forfeiture of shares? If so, when and under what conditions?
14. Has the company power to issue shares at a discount? If so, when and under what conditions?
15. Can a company purchase its own shares? If so, under what circumstances?
16. Define debenture. Discuss the different kinds of debentures.
17. Discuss the remedies available to debentureholders for the realisation of their security.
18. Enumerate the charges on properties of the company that require registration. Discuss the consequences of non-registration.

19. Write short notes on:
    (a) Share warrant
    (b) Surrender of shares
    (c) Floating charge
    (d) Interim dividend
    (e) Lien on shares
    (f) Calls on shares
    (g) Transmission of shares
    (h) Preference shares
    (i) Payment of interest out of capital
    (j) Stock certificate

CHAPTER 8

Company Administration: Directors

The company is not a natural person, though it is recognised as a legal person and a separate entity under the statute. Since it does not have physical existence it has to necessarily act through a human agency. The human agency primarily acting on its behalf are the directors, collectively called the board of directors.

Since the management of the entire affairs the company is entrusted upon the board of directors, the Companies Act provides for a number of checks and balances and restrictions on the authority of the directors. The Companies Act also provides for different circumstances under which directors can be appointed. It prescribes the boundaries within which the directors are allowed to act and also gives detailed prescriptions relating to the qualifications and disqualifications the directors and also they the manner in which they are appointed, the tenure of office and the manner in which they are removed.

Definition of Directors

The persons by whom the business of the company is carried on are termed directors. These are the persons elected by shareholders to manage and control the affairs of the company. It does not matter whether they are designated as directors, trustees or governors so long as they are charged with responsibility of management. " According to Section 2(13) of the Companies Act, 1956, "director" includes any person occupying the position of director by whatever name called. Only an individual can be appointed a director (Section 253). It means that a director is one who is performing the functions a director like controlling the affairs of the company.

Number of Directors: Minimum and Maximum

Section 252 provides that every public company (other than a public company which has become such by virtue of Section 43-A) must have *at least 3 directors* and every private company must have at least 2 directors. According to the *Amendment Act of 2000*, a public company with (a) paid-up capital of Rs. 5 crore or more, and (b) 1,000 or *more small shareholders* shall have at least *one director elected in the prescribed manner by small shareholders*. For this purpose *small shareholder* means a shareholder holding shares of the nominal value of Rs 20,000 or less in the company.

The Articles of a company may prescribe the maximum and the minimum number of directors for its board of directors. A company in a general meeting may be ordinary resolution increase or reduce the number of its directors within the limits fixed in that behalf by its Articles (Section 258). A public company or a private company which is a subsidiary of a public company cannot increase the number of directors beyond the permissible maximum under its Articles without the approval of the Central Government. However, no approval of the Central Government is required if such *permissible maximum is twelve* or less than twelve, and the increase in the number of its directors does not exceed twelve (Section 259).

ELIGIBILITY TO BECOME A DIRECTOR

Only an Individual be a Director

The Companies Act does not prescribe any specific qualifications for a person to become a director of a company. The only stipulation provided by the Act itself for a person to be eligible for appointment as a director of a company is that he should be an individual and not a body corporate, firm or association of persons. This stipulation is contained in Sec. 253 of the Companies Act, 1956.

The rationale behind the stipulation that only an individual can be appointed as a director not far to seek. As was discussed earlier, a director is the agent and trustee or a legal personality and a legal entity which itself is not a human being. If another entity like a body corporate or a firm or an association of person again who is also a legal fiction is allowed to be appointed as a director of a company fixing the responsibility for acts of omission and commission of a company would become difficult. To that extent the stipulation that only an individual can became a director of a company is understandable.

Competence to Contract

The statute itself does not prescribe any qualifications for a person to be eligible for appointment as a director of a company. One has to understand that since the director is a human agency through which a company enters into a contractual obligation, a person who is appointed as a director should naturally be competent to enter into contracts. In order to find out the competence of a person to enter into contract one has to fall back upon the provision of the Contract Act, 1872 where it has been specified as to who are the persons competent to enter into contracts. Section 11 of the Indian

Contract Act, 1872 specifies that every person, in order to be eligible to enter into a contract, should have attained the age of a majority and he should be of a sound mind and should not have been disqualified from contracting by any law to which he is subject. From the above provision of the Contract Act, one can deduce the qualifications required by law for a person to be appointed as a director are:

1. He should be a major;
2. He should be of sound mind; and
3. He should not have been disqualified from becoming a director.

Share Qualification

The Act does not make it obligatory on any director to hold shares in the company. The Articles of association generally require that the qualification of a director shall be the holding of a specified number of shares known as qualification shares. Unless he is already qualified, he must obtain the qualification shares within two months after his appointment as a director. Any provision in the Articles of a company insofar as it requires a person to hold the qualification shares before his appointment as a director or to obtain them within a shorter time than two months will be void. The nominal value of these shares must not exceed Rs. 5,000 or one share where the nominal value of one share exceeds Rs. 5,000. *The holding of share warrant shall not be deemed to be the holding of qualification shares.*

It is not essential for the director to buy his shares directly from the company. The director must also hold these shares in his own right. Shares held by a director jointly with any other persons may be a sufficient qualification. Again if a director holds the shares as a trustee, he is duly qualified provided that it does not appear on the register of members that he is a trustee. But if a director takes his qualification shares from a promoter, it amounts to a breach of trust.

If a person acts as, a director of a company without holding the qualification shares he will be punishable with fine which may extend to Rs. 500 for everyday between such expiry and the last day on which he acted as a director. Moreover, by virtue of Section 283, if a person fails to obtain the qualification shares as prescribed by the Articles within the period specified, he automatically vacates office and cannot act as a director after the expiry of that period. The above provisions do not apply to a private company unless, it is a subsidiary of a public company (Section 273); nor do they apply to directors appointed by the Central Government under Section 408.

Disqualifications of Directors

The circumstances in which a person cannot be appointed as a directors of a company are enumerated in Section 274. According to this section, a person cannot be appointed as a director of a company, if:

(i) he has been found to be of *unsound mind* by a competent court and the finding is in force;

(ii) he is an undischarged *insolvent*;

(iii) he has *applied to be adjudicated as an insolvent* and his application is pending;

(iv) he has been *convicted of an office* involving moral gratitude and sentenced to imprisonment for not less than 6 months and a period of 5 years had not elapsed since the expiry of his sentence;

(v) he has *not paid any call* in respect of shares of the company held by him for a period of six months from the last day fixed for the payment;

(vi) he has been *disqualified by an order of the court* under Section 203, of an offence in relation to promotion, formation or management of the company or fraud or misfeasance in relation to the company.

(vii) he has been disqualified, under Section 274(1) (g), for a *default in filing accounts and returns* for a continuous period of 3 years from 1-04-1999 or has *failed to repay its deposits* or *interest on due date or redeem its debentures on due date or pay dividend* and such failure continues for one year or more. Such disqualification will continue for a period of 5 years from such default.

The Central Government may by notification in the Official Gazette remove the disqualifications enumerated in clauses (iv) and (v) above. A private company which is not a subsidiary of a public company may be its Articles provide for additional grounds for disqualification.

Ceiling or Restriction on Number of Directorships

No person can be a director in more than fifteen companies. The following companies shall be excluded in calculating the number of companies of which a person may be a director:

(a) a private company which is neither a subsidiary nor a holding company of a public company;

(b) an unlimited company;

(c) an association not carrying on business for profit or which prohibits the payment of a dividend;

(d) a company in which such person in only an alternate director.

Where a person already holding the office of director in 15 companies is appointed as a director of any company, the appointment will not take effect unless such person has within fifteen days thereof, effectively vacated his office as a director in any of the companies in which he was already a director. His new appointment will become void if he does not *make a choice within fifteen days* as aforesaid. Any person who holds office or acts as a director of more than 15 companies in contravention of the above provisions shall be punishable with fine which may extend to Rs. 50,000 in respect of each of those companies after the first 15 companies. *[Section 279]*.

APPOINTMENT OF DIRECTORS

Directors may be appointed in the following ways:

First Directors

1. By the Articles of Association as regards first directors [Section 254]

Subsequent Directors

2. By the company in general meeting (Sections 255 to 257, 263, 264).
3. By the board of directors (Sections 260, 266, 313)
4. By third parties (Section 255)
5. By the principle of proportional representation (Section 265)
6. By the central government (Section 408)

1. First Directors

The first directors are usually named in the Articles. The Articles may also provide that both the number and the name of the first directors shall be determine in writing by the subscribers to the memorandum or a majority of them. Where the articles are silent regarding the appointment of directors, the subscribers of the memorandum who are individuals shall be deemed to be the first directors of the company. They shall hold office until the directors are appointed at the first annual general meeting. *(Section 254)*.

2. Appointment by Company

Appointment of subsequent directors is made at every general meeting of the company. Section 255 provides that *not less than two-thirds of the total number of directors of a public company must be subject to retirement* by rotation. The remaining directors of such a company must also be appcinted by the company in general meeting. In other words, *not more than one-third of the total number of directors can act as non-retiring directors, i.e.*, not subject to retirement by rotation.

At every subsequent annual general meeting one-third of the directors of a public company are liable to retire by rotation. If the number is not three or a multiple of three, then the number nearest to one-third must retire from office. The directors to retire by rotation at every Annual General Meeting must by those who have been longest in office since their last appointment. As between persons who becomes directors on the same day, those who are to retire will, subject to any agreement among themselves, be determined by lot.

At the Annual General Meeting at which a director retires, the company may fill up the vacancy by appointing the retiring director or some other person thereto. If the place of the retiring director is not so filled, and the meeting has not expressly resolved not to fill the vacancy, the meeting shall stand adjourned. If at the adjourned meeting also the vacancy is not filled, and the meeting has not expressly resolved not to fill the vacancy, the retiring director shall be deemed to have been reappointed at the adjourned meeting unless:

(i) at the meeting or at the previous meeting a resolution for the reappointment of such directors has been put to the meeting and lost;

(ii) he has, by a notice in writing, addressed to the company or its board, expressed his unwilling to be reappointed;

(iii) he is not qualified or disqualified for appointment;

(iv) a special or ordinary resolution is necessary for his appointment or reappointment. *(Section 256).*

A person other than a retiring director is also eligible for appointment to the office of director subject to his necessary qualification. A notice in writing signifying his candidature must be left at the office of the company at least fourteen days before the date of meeting. The notice may be given either by the candidate himself or by his proposer. This notice should be accompained by a deposit of Rs 500. The company in turn, shall inform the members at least seven days before the meeting about the candidature by individual notices upon the members or by an advertisement, in at least two newspapers. One of the newspapers must be in English language and the other in the regional language of the place where the registered office of the company is located. These provisions do not apply to a private company, unless it is a subsidiary of a public company.

A person who is being proposed as a candidate for the office of a *director must sign and file with the company his consent in writing to act as a director if appointed.* This requirement does not apply to a director retiring by rotation (Section 264).

3. Appointment by Board of Directors

The board of directors are empowered to appoint: (i) additional directors, (ii) directors filling casual vacancy, and (iii) alternate directors-

(i) Additional Directors: The board of directors may appoint additional directors from time-to-time. The number of directors and additional directors must not exceed the maximum strength fixed for the board by the Articles. The additional directors shall hold office only up to the date of the next annual general meeting *(Section 260).*

(ii) Casual Vacancy: Where the office of any director appointed by the company in general meeting is vacated before the expiry of his term (because of death, resignation or disqualification like bankruptcy), etc., the directors appointed will hold office till the end of the term of the director in whose place he is appointed. These provisions are applicable only to a public company and a private company which is a subsidiary of the public company *(Section 262).*

(iii) Alternate Director: The board of directors may appoint an alternate director if authorised by the Articles or by a resolution of the company in general meeting. Since the tenure of any director appointed by the board is essentially temporary and ultimately such directors will have to seek the confirmation of their appointment by the members in a general meeting. An alternate director acts in the place of a director who is absent for more than three months from the state in which the board meetings are held. He cannot hold office for a period longer than that permissible to the original director in whose place he has been appointed. He must vacate office on return of the original director *(Section 313).*

4. Appointment toy Third Parties

The Articles may give right to debentureholders, financial corporations IFCI, IDBI, etc., or banking companies who have advanced loans to the company may nominate director on the board of the company. The number of directors so nominated should not exceed one-third of the total strength of the board. *They are not liable to retire by rotation.*

Nominee Directors

Very often the companies raise their finance through loans and other borrowings. With the development of advanced financing techniques, usually the loan component of the projects is higher than the share capital of the company. When the financial institutions or banks provide loans to the company they often stipulate that one of their nominee or representative should be appointed as a director of the company, in order to safeguard the interest of the lenders. The loan agreement usually stipulates this condition. In order to facilitate the appointment of directors by such lenders, the Articles of Association usually allow the company to enter into an agreement with its lenders conferring the right on such lenders to nominate the directors in the board of the company. When such a right is conferred on the lenders, the appointment of these Nominee directors and their tenure is dependent upon the will and pleasure of the lenders.

Certain financial institutions, like, IDBI, State Financial Corporations, LIC, GIC and UTI are established by a separate Act of the Parliament. These legislations establishing these institutions have conferred the right on these institutions to appoint directors in the board of any company to which they advance financial assistance. These legislations are also specifically provide that such right can be exercised in spite of any contradictory or contrary provisions in the Companies Act. In other words, these legislations override the provisions of the Companies Act relating to the appointment and tenure of directors. When these institutions exercise their rights to nominate their directors, *such nominee directors are not subject to any restriction on either the appointment or the tenure as contained in the Companies Act, 1956.*

Special Directors Appointed by BIFR

In case of Sick Industrial Companies, it is necessary that a reference has to be made to the board for Industrial and Financial Reconstruction (BIFR) whenever the net worth of the company becomes negative and the entire share capital is eroded. This is a requirement of the Sick Industrial Companies (Special Provisions) Act, 1985. In such case the BIFR holds a hearing and if it finds that the company should be declared a sick industrial company it does so. BIFR also orders the preparation of rehabilitation scheme for such companies. Sec. 16 of the Sick Industrial Companies (Special Provisions) Act, 1985 empowers BIFR appoint one or more person to be Special directors of the company for safeguarding the financial and the other interests of the company. *The special directors was appointed by BIFR are also not subject to any of the restriction relating to either the number of directors or the tenure as contained the Companies Act, 1956 and they are immune from any prosecution for defaults in the provisions of the Companies Act.*

Persons Appointed to Replace the Board of Directors

There are certain statutes which provide for the replacement or supersession of the entire board of directors under certain exigencies. One such exigency is in the cases where there is a *complaint of mismanagement or oppression of minority*. In such cases amongst the powers conferred on the *National Company Law Tribunal*, is the power to order the regulation of the conduct of the company affairs in future. This power is so wide ranging in its scope that the National Company Law Tribunals order may also provide for supersession of the entire board of directors and appointment of a person or an agency to conduct the affairs of the company. In exercise of this power conferred by Sec. 402 of the Act, sometimes the person appointed by the National Company Law Tribunal shall become for all practical purposes of directors of the company.

In case of companies where the industrial undertaking have been closed for a period of three months or more and where there is management the *Industries (Development and Regulation) Act, 1951* also confers the right on the Central Government to supersede the board of directors and appoint a person or other agency to takeover the management of the industrial undertaking. In such cases the power of the board of directors is totally suspended and the authorised person is deemed to be the board of directors the company. However, the order taking over the management of affairs of the company is valid only for a period of 1 year and such order may be renewed or extended for further periods not exceeding 1 year at a time. The maximum period during which the order of taking over management can be in force is 8 years.

5. Appointment by Proportional Representation

The Articles of a company may provide that the appointment of not less than two-thirds of the total number of directors of a public company (or of a private company which is a subsidiary of a public company) shall be according to the principle of proportional representation, either by the single transferable vote or by a system of cumulative voting or otherwise. Such appointments shall be made once in three years and interim casual vacancies may be filled up according to Section 262.

Ordinary resolution, (i.e., simple majority) is enough for appointing or reappointing a director. According to Sec. 265, the minority may have an apportunity of having their representatives in the board by **"Proportionate Representative Principle"**.

This is subject to the provisions in the Articles. A maximum of two-thirds of the directors of a public company may be appointed either by single transferable vote system or by a system of cumulative voting or otherwise. A quota is fixed and the person who gets the quota votes is appointed as a director. For example, three directors are to be appointed, the first three candidates who get the maximum number of votes will be appointed. This can be explained with the help of the following example.

Suppose in an election 2,000 votes are cast and there are 3 seats. The quota is obtained by dividing the total number of votes cast by the total number of seats plus one and adding one to the result. Thus, the quota in this case will be:

$$\text{Quota} = \frac{2,000}{3+1} + 1 = 501 \text{ votes}$$

If candidate gets 501 first preference votes, he gets elected. The remaining candidates will be elected by eliminating one by one the candidates who get least first preference votes.

Under cumulative voting, a shareholder has for each share held by him as many votes as the number of directors to be elected. For example, if 5 directors are to be elected, each share will carry 5 votes. A shareholder holding 5 shares will have 25 votes. He may cast either all the 25 votes in favour of one candidate or he may distribute his votes over some candidates. The 5 candidates getting the highest number of votes will get elected. Under cumulative voting system, a shareholder holding a majority of the shares only may be able to elect majority of the directors. However, a minority group may also be able to obtain representation on the board.

The appointment shall be made once in three years and interim casual vacancies shall be filled in the manner as provided in the Articles.

6. Appointment by the Central Government

According to Section 408 of the Companies Act, the Central Government has the power to appoint director for the purpose of prevention of oppression and mismanagement. It provides that the Central Government may appoint such number of directors on the board of the company as it may think fit to effectively safeguard the interest of the company, its shareholders, or the public interest. Such an appointment shall be for a period not exceeding three years, and shall be made on the application of not less than 100 members or members holding not less than l/10th of the voting power of the company. *Such directors will not be required to hold any qualification shares, nor they shall be liable to retire by rotation.*

Deemed Director: According to Section 303 of the Act, any person in accordance with whose directions or instructions, the board of directors is accustomed to act is deemed to head director of the company.

LEGAL POSITION OF DIRECTORS

The exact position of directors with regard to the company is difficult to define. They are not servants of the company. Some describe the directors as trustees, agents or managing partners. **Jessel, M.R.** has observed, "it does not matter much what you call them so long as you understand what their true position is, which is that they are merely commercial men managing a trading concern for the benefit of themselves and all other shareholders in it. They stand in a fiduciary position towards the company in respect of their powers and capital under their control."

Directors not Employees

The directors are not servants of the company or members of its staff. They cannot be treated as the employees of the company. However, in addition to his directorship, he may hold a salaried employment in the company if there exists a special contract to that effect between the company and the directors. In such a condition he will enjoy all the rights available to an employee or servant of the company. Further, even in such a case his right as a directors will be separate from his rights as an employee or servant of the company.

Directors as Officers

For certain matters under Section 2(30) the Companies Act, the directors are treated as officers of the company. As such, they are liable to certain penalties if the provisions of the Act are not strictly complied with.

Directors as Trustees

The directors are persons selected to manage the affairs of the company for the benefit of the shareholders. It is an office of trust. It is their duty to perform fully and entirely. Directors are trustees of the company's money and property and the powers entrusted to them. They are trustees of the company's money and property in the sense that they must account for all the company's money over which they exercise control and must refund to the company any of its money which they have improperly paid away. Directors are trustees of their power and they must exercise their powers honestly and in good faith and in the interest of the company.

The director is a trustee as regards powers of the company such as powers of issuing and allotting shares in the company making calls and forfeiting shares, approving transfer of shares, etc., which he must exercise solely for the benefit of the company. As was held in *G.E. Railsay's case* the directors are trustees for the company and not for the shareholders or for the creditors of the company in their individual capacity.

However, it is to be noted that the directors are not trustees in the strict sense of the term. The distinction between a director and a trustee has been very clearly made by ***(James L.J.* in *Smith vs. Anderson)*** in these words:

The distinction between a director and a trustee is an essential distinction founded on the very nature of things. A trustee is a man who is the owner of property and deals with it as principal, as owner and as master, subject only to an equitable obligation to account to some persons to whom he stands in the relation of a trustee, who are his beneficiaries. The office of a director is that of a paid servant of the company. A director never enters into a contract for himself, but he enters into contract for his principal, that is, for the company of which he is a director, or for whom he is acting.

Directors as Agents

Company being an artificial person, is governed by human agency, Directors control the affairs of the company as its agents. Acts of the directors for and on behalf of the company exclude directors from personal liability, provided they are within the scope of their authority. To put another way, the acts of the directors within four-walls of their authority are acts of the company itself and the company is liable for them. The relationship between the company and directors is that of principal and agent. On this point, the observations made by ***(Lord Cairns in Ferguson vs. Wilson)*** case are self-explanatory, that is:

What is the position of the directors of a public company? They are merely agents of the company. The company itself cannot act in its own persons for it has not persons; it can only act through directors, and the case is, as regards those directors, merely the ordinary case of a principal and agent, for wherever an agent is liable those directors would be liable. Where the liability would attach to the principal, and the principal only, the liability is the liability of the company.

The general principles of agency regulate the relations of directors and the company and of persons dealing with the company. The importance functions of the directors as agents of the company are to enter into contracts, to create negotiable instruments and to borrow money on behalf of the company. The directors have also to disclose their interest, if any, in the transactions of the company. However, they cannot be declared only the agents of the company as they also exercise independent powers, they are the agents of the company, and not of individual shareholders. Directors are agents of the company and not agents of individual shareholders. Powers of the directors are something more than the powers of the agents. When directors act within the scope of the authority conferred upon them the company will be liable unless they contract in their own names. Where the directors exceed the powers given to them by the Memorandum and Articles, they will be liable for breach of warranty of authority.

Directors as Managing Partner

The directors are elected representatives of the shareholders and as such, they are in the position of managing partners. But they are not exactly partners in legal sense as the liability of directors is limited to the value of shares held by them and a director has no authority to bind the other directors and shareholders.

Directors as Organs of the Company

The company is an artificial person and it acts through the persons known as 'directors'. Therefore, they are known as organs of the company, the board of directors are the brain and the only brain of the company which is the body and the company can and does act only through them. When the brain functions, the corporation is said to function. The organic character of the company's life is well explained by *Lord Denning* in the following word:

A company may in many ways be compared to a human body. It has a brain and a nerve centre which controls what it does. It has also hands which hold the tools and act in accordance with directions from the Centre. Some of the people in the company are mere servants and agents who are nothing more than hands to do the work, and cannot be said to represent the mind or will. Others are directors and managers who represent the directing mind or will of the company and control what it does. The state of mind of these managers is the state of mind of the company and is treated by the law as such. This theory which treats certain official as organs of the company for whose action the company is to held liable just as a natural person is for the action of his limbs.

In a nutshell, we can say that the directors, are neither agents nor trustees, mere managing partner in full sense of the term. In fact, the director combine in themselves all these positions. Thus, the best way to sum up their position is to describe it as a fiduciary relationship to the company. Further, Section 2(30) of the Act demonstrated that the directors may be called as 'officers' of the company, hence, they may be held responsible for their faults and commissions.

How Does a Person Cease to be a Director

Having been appointed as a director of a company, a person can cease to be a director in any of the following manners or methods:

1. Resignation
2. Retirement
3. Acquiring a disqualification
4. Vacation of office
5. Removal
6. Withdrawal of nomination

Each of the methods of cessation of directorship are described briefly below:

Resignation of Director

The serving of a person as a director of a company is a voluntary act. In fact Sec.264 of the Companies Act, 1956 specifically provides that a person willing to act as a director of the company, if appointed, should first communicate his consent in writing for such appointment before the appointment is made. After the appointment is made, the communication of the concerned should also be filed with the registrar of companies in the form prescribed under the Companies (General Rules and Forms) 1956. Since no person can be forced to hold an office unless he is willing, it automatically follows that a director once appointed can always withdraw his consent to act as a director and resign from his post as a director.

A resignation once communicated to the company need not be accepted by the board in order to become effective. There is a misconception that any resignation has to be accepted by the appointing authority. The resignation of a director becomes effective on the date if any specified by him in his letter of resignation. If he does not specify any date, it becomes effective only from the time when the letter of resignation is received by the company.

The effect of the resignation is that the person ceases to be liable for any acts of the company after the date of the resignation and he cannot be held responsible for such acts of omission or commission after he had resigned.

It is also necessary to remember that the fact of the cessation of a person as a director of the company should be intimated to the Registrar of Companies, Sec.303 of the Companies Act, 1956 makes it incumbent upon the company to file a return relating to any changes in the board of directors. However, once a person resigns as a director he cannot file this return as a representative of the company. In order to ensure that the cessation of a directorship is taken note of by the registrar, a person has to either get the proof of filing of the details of the change in the constitution of the board by the company or he has to intimate by way of a letter to the registrar of companies or the fact of his cessation as a director. Unless this is done, if by chance the company fails to file the details of resignation with registrar of companies, the person who was the director would still receive notices for defaults if any of a company since the registrar has no intimation about his cessation as a director.

Provisions Relating to Resignation of Directors

There is no provisions in the Companies Act, 1956 relating to the resignation of office of a director.

Precedents to be followed: In the following case, the question relating to resignation of office by a director was thoroughly discussed. The facts of this case were as follows:

Murart(T) vs. State, (1976) 46 Comp. Cas. 613 (Mad.) The managing directors of a company had tendered their resignation in writing on January 17, 1968. The company failed to submit the balance sheet and annual return of the company for 1968 which should have been submitted before January 8, 1969, and February 7, 1969, respectively. Held, the resignation tendered by the managing director had taken effect on January 17, 1968; he ceased to hold office from that date and as such conviction passed on him by the lower court was set aside.

The position was further reviewed in ***S. Lakshmana Pillai vs. Registrar of Companies, (1977) 47 Comp. Cas. 652 (Mad)***. It was observed in this case that "as there is no express provision for vacancy by resignation of directors, we have to fall back upon the precedents and practices on the subject. "So far as the Indian Company Law is concerned, it has followed the English Law relating to resignation of directors. The position may be summed up as follows:

1. If there is any provisions in the Articles given right to director to resign at any time, the resignation will take effect without any need for its acceptance by the board or the company in the general meeting. Acceptance is also not necessary where the resignation says that it is to take effect immediately, unless the Articles or any provision of law make acceptance compulsory.

In ***State of Bihar vs. Sitaram Jhunjhunwala, A.I.R (1967) Pat. 433,*** it was held that the acceptance of resignation is unnecessary for the resignation to take effect when it is tendered in writing. In that case, the Articles of the company itself provided that the director will cases to hold office *ispo facto* upon giving the notice of resignation in writing.

2. Where the resignation states that it is to take effect on acceptance or where the Articles so requires, acceptance is necessary to end the tensure of office.
3. In the absence of any provision relating to resignation in the Articles, a director may by notice to the company resign ***(Municipal freehold Land Co. vs.***

Polington, (1980) 3 L.T. 238). It is well settled that a resignation once made takes effect immediately.

4. Resignation once made cannot be withdrawn except with the consent of the company or the board ***(Glossop vs. Glossop, (1907) 2C.370)***.
5. Even resignation orally tendered at a general meeting and accepted by the meeting is held to the effective ***(Latchford Premier Cinema Ltd. vs. Ermion, (1931)2 Ch. 409)***.
6. The net result of the above analysis is that a director, who has submitted his resignation, will be deemed to have resigned from the date of his resignation, without prejudice of course to his liability and obligations which had occurred up to that date and which he cannot evade by severing his connection with the company ***(Abdul Huq vs. Katpadi Industries Ltd., A.I.R.(1960) Mad. 482)***.

Retirement of Director

As discussed earlier every director is liable for retirement by rotation unless he is appointed as a non-rotational director by the General Meeting. The tenure of office of a director liable to retire by rotation is 3 years since l/3rd of all the retiring directors have to retire every year. If a person does not wish to continue as a director of a company, the simplest method of ceasing to be a director available to him is to intimate the company of his intention not to seek re-appointment as a director at the Annual General Meeting in which he is due to retire. Once such an intimation is given a resolution for his re-appointment at the Annual General Meeting naturally cannot be placed and he automatically ceases to be a director of a company from the date of the Annual General Meeting.

What happens if a resolution for re-appointment a Director is not passed at the Annual General Meeting: The answer to this question is found in Sec. 256 of Companies Act, 1956. Sub-Section (4) of this section states that if the place of retiring director is not filled-up, and the Annual General Meeting does not specifically and expressly resolve that the vacancy caused by this retirement shall not be filled, the meeting shall be adjourned till the same day in the next week at the same time and place. If the same day in the next week be a public holiday, the meeting is adjourned to the next succeeding day which is not a public holiday at the same time and place. If the place of the retiring director is not filled up, *he shall be deemed to have been reappointed at the adjourned meeting*.

However, such *deemed reappointment* is not applicable under the following circumstances:

1. If the meeting has specifically resolved not to fill up the vacancy caused by the retirement.

2. If the resolution proposing the re-appointment has been put to vote and lost either in that meeting or in the previous meeting.
3. The retiring director has expressed his unwillingness to the re-appointed.
4. He is disqualified for re-appointment for acquiring any of the disqualifications discussed earlier.
5. Where the Articles provide that a specific resolution need to be passed for appointment or reappointment of a director, and the provision relating to deemed re-appointment is not applicable.

Completion of Tenure

As discussed earlier, a director can also be appointed by the board and when such appointment is made, the tenure of the director is limited. He ceases to be in office automatically on completion of tenure unless a resolution by the General Meeting is passed appointing him again as a director. *The circumstances and dates on which the tenure is completed are listed below:*

1. In case of additional directors—on the date of the next Annual General Meeting
2. In case of directors appointed to fill the casual vacancy—on the date when the original director was due to retire
3. In case of alternate directors—on the returning of the original director to the State in which the board meetings are ordinarily held.

The tenure of office of a director may also expire on specific dates. In case of nominee directors, if the nominating authority specifies a tenure while nominating him to the board of directors of a company, such directors cease to hold office on the expiry of the date so specified.

Vacation of Office by Director (Section 283)

The office of a director shall become vacant if—

(a) he fails to obtain or ceases to hold the *share qualification* required of him by the Articles of the company;

(b) he is found to be of *unsound mind* by a competent court;

(c) he applies to be adjudicated an *insolvent*;

(d) he is *adjudged an insolvent*;

(e) he is *convicted by a court* of an offence involving moral turpitude and sentenced to imprisonment for not less than 6 months;

(f) he *fails to pay any calls* on the shares held by him within six months from the date fixed for payments; unless the Central Government has by notification in the Official Gazette removed his disqualification;

(g) he *absents himself from three consecutive meetings* of the board of directors or from all the meetings of board for a continuous period of 3 months whichever is longer without obtaining leave of absence from the board;

(h) he (whether by himself or by any person for his benefit or on his account) or any firm in which he is a partner or any private company of which is a director; accepts a loan or any guarantee or security for a loan from the company in contravention of Section 295;

(i) he *does not disclose to the board* of directors of his interest in any contract or proposed contract with the company.

(j) he is *restrained by courts from being a director* for committing fraud or misfeasance in relation to the company under Section 203;

(k) he is *removed by the company* in general meeting in pursuance of Section 284;

(l) having been appointed as a director by virtue of his holding any office or the other employment in the company, he ceases to hold such office or other employment in the company.

Of the above grounds the first six are similar to those which disqualify a director from holding the office under Section 274 of the Act. The grounds stated in (d), (e) and (f) above shall not disqualify a director from holding his office immediately until thirty days have elapsed from the date of the adjudication, sentence or order where no appeal is preferred. But in case of an appeal the specified disqualifications shall take effect on the expiry of the seven days from the date on which such appeal is finally disposed of.

A person who acts as a director knowing fully well of his disqualifications is subject to a penalty which may extend to Rs. 5,000 for each day on which he so acts as a director.

A private company which is not subsidiary of a public company may by its Articles provide for additional grounds for vacating the office of a director.

Removal of Director

A director of a company can be removed by (a) shareholders, (b) Central Governament, or (c) the court.

***Removal by Shareholder*:** Section 284 empowers the company to remove a director by ordinary resolution before the expiry of his period of office *except* in the following cases:

(a) A director appointed by the Central Government under Section 408.

(b) A director in case of a private company, holding office for life on the 1st day of April, 1952. (A director for life subsequent to that date may be removed).

(c) Directors appointed in accordance with the principle of proportional representation, under Section 265. This is to ensure that the directors appointed by the minority are not removed by a bare majority.

(d) Nominee directors appointed by financial institutions pursuant to stipulations under their loan agreements viz., IDBI, IFCI, etc., under their respective Acts.

(e) Directors appointed by board for industrial and financial reconstruction.

Special notice is required of any resolution to remove a director or to appoint somebody in his place at the meeting at which he is removed. On receipt of such notice, the company will immediately send a copy thereof to the directors concerned. He may make any representation in writing and the copy of such representation may be sent by the company to every member. Where the copy of the representation is not sent to the members because it is received too late or because of the company's default, in that case the director concerned may require the representation to be read at the meeting. The director has a right to make representation and speak at that general meeting. *The director so removed is entitled to claim compensation or damages for breach of contract. But the removed director cannot be re-appointed.*

Removal by the Central Government **(Sections 388-B to 388-E):** A director can also be removed at the initiative of the Central Government. The Companies Act enables the Central Government to remove managerial personnel (including a director) from office on the recommendation of the National Company Law Tribunal. The Central Government may refer to the Tribunal cases against managerial person on any of the grounds mentioned in Section 388-B.

1. the director or directors is or are guilty of fraud, misfeasance, negligence or default in carrying out his/their functions, or
2. the business is carried on against sound business principles or commercial practices, or
3. the company is carried on in a manner likely to cause injury to the interest of the trade, industry or business to which it belongs, or
4. the concerned director manages the company for defrauding the creditors or members or for a fraudulent or unlawful purpose.

Every such reference will be made in the form of an application which must contain a statement of material facts. The person against whom such reference is made must be join as a respondent to the application. The tribunal on such reference may inquire into the case and record a finding as to whether such person should hold office or not.

The person who is so removed cannot hold office of director for a term of five years unless the period is remitted. The person removed cannot claim any compensation for loss or termination of office.

Removal by the National Company Law Tribunal: On an application under Sec.402 to the Tribunal for prevention of oppression and mismanagement the tribunal may terminate, or set aside or modify an agreement between the company and the managing director, or any other director or manager. On such termination, the director can't serve the company in a managerial capacity for a period of five years from the date of the order of termination, without the permission of the court. *The director on removal cannot sue the company for damages or compensation for loss of office.*

Compensation for Loss of Office

Section 318 enables a company to pay compensation for loss of office or as consideration for retirement from office to a managing director or a director holding the office of manager or a director in the whole-time employment of the company. No such compensation shall be paid to any other director. Further no compensation is payable in the following cases:

(i) Where the director resigns his office because of the reconstruction or amalgamation of the company and is appointed as the managing director, manager or other officer of the reconstructed or amalgamated company;

(ii) where the director *resigns* his office otherwise;

(iii) Where the office of the director is *vacated* by virtue of Section 203 or Section 283;

(iv) where the company is being *wound up due to the negligence* or default of the director;

(v) where the director has been *guilty of fraud or breach* of trust or gross negligence or mismanagement in the affairs of the company;

(vi) where the director has *instigated or has taken part* in bringing about the termination of his office.

The amount of compensation shall not exceed the remuneration which he would have earned if he has been in office for the unexpired residue of his term or for three years, whichever is shorter.

Loans to Directors

Section 295 regulates the lending of money by the companies to its directors. Under this section a company shall not directly or indirectly make any loan or give guarantee or provide security for any loans to the following without the previous approval of the Central Government:

(a) a director of the company or of its holding company;

(b) a partner or relative of any such director;

(c) any firm in which any such director or relative is a partner;

(d) any private company of which any such director is a director or member;

(e) any body corporate in which such director or directors control 25% of voting power

(f) any company whose board or other managers are accustomed to act in accordance with the instructions of Board of director, any director or directors of the lending company.

These restrictions do not apply to (a) loans by a private company, (b) loans by a banking company, (c) loans by a holding company to its subsidiary.

Every persons who knowingly contravenes the above provisions including any person to whom the loan is made shall be punishable either with fine which may extend to Rs. 5,000, or with impose imprisonment up to six months.

Remuneration of Directors

The remuneration payable to directors is usually determined by the Articles of Association or a resolution passed by the company in its General Meeting, However, this will be subject to the subject to the provisions of Sections 198 and 309 of the Act.

According to Section 198, total managerial remuneration payable to directors, managing director(s), or manager and whole-time director, in respect of any financial year should not exceed 11% of the net profits of the company for the financial year. In years of inadequate profits, a sum not exceeding Rs.50,000 per annum may be paid to all managerial personnel with the prior approval of the Central Government. In this context, however, the Central Government has been empowered to sanction greater sum by way of minimum remuneration provided:

(i) It is satisfied about satisfied bonafides of the case, and

(ii) a monthly payments is being made or is proposed to be made to any managing or whole-time director or the manager or to anyone or more of them.

Note that, this provision with regard to managerial remuneration does not apply to an independent private company, (i.e., a private company not being a subsidiary of a public company).

The term 'remuneration' includes payment of any obligation of the director by the company, expenditure by the company or rent free accommodation, any expenditure on amenities provided free of cost or at concessional rate and payment of life insurance premium on the life of director by the company. *But, the term 'remuneration' shall not include:*

1. any amount paid to director for services, if (i) services are of a professional nature; and (ii) in the opinion of the Central Government, the director possesses the requisite qualification for the practise of the profession. (Sec. 309 (1))

2. Any fees payable to the director for attending each meeting of the board or a committee thereof. (Sec.198(2)).

As regards the part-time directors, ordinarily they should be paid only sitting fees and travelling and halting allowances. But where company wishes to pay more, it must satisfy the government that in specific cases such directors rendered some specific service to the company beyond merely attending board meetings.

Remuneration received by a director in any other capacity (for example, for service of professional nature for which the director had requisite qualifications) shall not be included in overall limit.

Section 637-AA inserted by Companies (Amendment) Act, 1974, provides that while fixing remuneration, the government is bound to take into account:

(a) the financial position of the company;

(b) the remuneration or commission drawn by him in any other company;

(c) professional qualifications and experience of the individual concerned;

(d) public policy relating to removal of disparities in income.

For determining the maximum remuneration of managerial personnel, net profits are to be calculated in the manner laid down in Sections 349 to 351. The overall limits may be shown in the following Table:

	Remuneration receivers	**Maximum of annual net profits**
1.	All directors, while they are assisted by managing director(s) or manager and/or whole-time director(s).	1%
2.	All directors, when not assisted by managing director(s), or manager and/or whole-time director(s).	3%
3.	Managing director (when there is one managing director).	5%
4.	Manager (there cannot be more than one manager.)	5%
5.	Whole-time director (when there is one such director.)	5%
6.	The managing director or whole-time director (when there are more than one of either category or of both categories.)	10%
7.	Total managerial remuneration to all directors, managing director(s), or manager and/or (in case of inadequate whole-time director(s). profit Rs. 50,000 per approval of the Central Govt.)	11%

MEETINGS OF BOARD

The directors of a company exercise most of their powers in a joint meeting called the meetings of the board. The directors elect chairperson from among them, who chairs the meetings of the board. In the case of every company, a meeting of the board of directors must be held at least once in every three months and at least four such meetings shall be held in every year. However, the Central Government is empowered to relax the rate with regard to any class of companies (Section 285).

The word *'every three months'* had caused certain confusion initially. Some people interpreted this provision as to a prescription of a time gap between two consecutive meetings and opined that there should not be a gap of more than three months between the two consecutive meetings of the board. However, another interpretation of this provision was that the word 'every three months' referred to a period of block of three months—and that even if the time gap between two meetings would more than 3 months it would not be a contravention of the Act, if a meeting is held in every block of three months.

Finally the department of company affairs had clarified the matter through its circular No. 103/72- CL. III dated 2.6.1973, that the intention of the law is that there should be a board meeting in every block of three months in a year. Even if the gap between two succeeding meeting exceeds three months it would be adequate compliance of the Act.

Stretching this interpretation to its extremity one can say that the provisions of the Section 285 would be satisfied if, for instance the dates of four meetings in a year are 30th June, 1st July, 30th September and 1st October of the year. The department seems to have given a very liberal interpretation of this provision, only with a view that companies are not necessarily put to hardships by a strict interpretation of this provision. However, most companies ensure that the time gap between two succeeding meeting is less than three months.

It is to be noted further that this prescription of Sec. 285 is the minimum requirement relating to the number of board meeting and the frequency of meetings. Managed companies ensure that the frequency of the board meeting is reasonable. It is not usual for many companies to hold meetings as frequently as once a month.

Notice of every meeting of the board of directors must be given in writing to every director for the time-being in India and at his usual address in India to every other director. Every officer of the company who is under a duty to give the notice as aforesaid and who fails to do so, shall be punishable with fine which may extend to Rs. 100 (Section 286).

The quorum for a meeting of the board shall be one-third of its total strength (any fraction contained in that one-third being rounded off as one) or two directors whichever is higher. Interested directors are not counted for the purpose of the quorum (Section 287).

When the meeting of the board could not be held for want of quorum, then unless otherwise provided by the Articles, the meeting shall automatically stand adjourned till the same day in the next week. (Section 288).

Powers of Board

As the company is an artificial person, it acts through its directors. The directors enjoy such powers as are given to them by the Act, Memorandum or Articles. Sections 29 to 293-A contain the powers of the board and the restrictions thereon. The powers of directors are discussed under the following heads:

General Powers: Section 291 empowers the board to exercise all such powers and do all such acts and things, as the company is authorised to exercise and do. But the board cannot do any Act which is to be done by the company in General Meeting. In exercising any power, the board will be subject to the provisions of this or any other Act, the Memorandum or the Articles.

While Section 291 of the Act specifies the general powers of the board, the Act itself prescribes certain restrictions on the powers of the board relating to specific matters. These restrictions can be generally divided into five categories:

1. Procedural restrictions;
2. Matters requiring proper approval of members in General Meeting;
3. Matters on which the board can decide but the decisions are subject to the approval of the members in a General Meeting;
4. Matters requiring the approval of the Central Government; and
5. Matters requiring the approval or confirmation of National Company Law Tribunal. These restrictions are discussed below:

Powers to be Exercised by Board only at Meeting

Under Section 292, the following powers can be exercised by the board, only by resolutions passed at the board meeting:

(i) the power to make calls;

(ii) the power to issue debentures;

(iii) the power to borrow money otherwise than on debentures;

(iv) the power to invest the funds of the company;

(v) the power to make loans.

Powers specified in points (iii), (iv), and (v) above can be delegated by the board, at a meeting by means of a resolution to a committee of directors, to the managing director, to the manager or to other principal officer of the company.

An examination of the above provisions would reveal that all the above powers are in respect of financial matters of the company involving either inflow or outflow of funds. The Companies Act recognises that the matter relating to inflow and outflow of funds cannot be dealt within a routine fashion without a discussion, and the board has to discuss the matter in a meeting before taking a decision.

However the compulsions for borrowing, lending or investing monies may arise from time-to-time. During the course of business, it may not be practical for the board of directors to have a meeting to approve proposals to borrow money, to invest money or to lend money every time such an occasion arises. Does the Law recognise this practical problem?

Penalty for Default: If a default is made in complying with the provisions of this section, the company, and every officer who is in default, shall be punishable with imprisonment for a term which may extend to one year, or with fine which may extend to fifty thousand rupees, or with both.

The proviso to Sec.292 of the Act clearly recognises the above reality. These provisos state that the powers in respect of borrowing, lending or investing can be delegated either to the managing director, a committee of directors or any other principal officer of the company. However, such delegation of powers can be made only through a resolution passed at a meeting. Further, these resolutions should also specify the ceilings and the limitations to the delegation of powers and explicitly slates the maximum amount that the delegate can borrow, invest or lend on behalf of the company.

Apart from Sec. 292, there are other sections in the Companies Act where a similar procedural requirement is prescribed and spells out the matter on which decisions could he taken only at a meeting of the board. These matters are:

1. The power of filling casual vacancy in the board under Sec. 262.
2. Sanctioning or giving consent to the contracts in which a director is interested under Sec. 297.
3. Receiving the notice of disclosure of interest by a director under Sec.299.
4. Appointment of a person as a managing director or manager of a company if he is already holding the post of the managing director or manager in another company. This particular item requires a unanimous consent of the Board and also a prior notice has to be given to all the directors that the item would be proposed at the meeting (Secs.316 and 386 of the Act).

5. Making of investments in companies in the same group (Sec. 372), This decision also further requires the unanimous consent of all the directors. The other mailers which requires the approval of the members in a general meeting are as follows:
6. Receipt of notice of disclosure of the shareholdings of directors in the company (Section 308).

AUDIT COMMITTEE (SECTION 292 A)

Composition of the Committee Members: Every public company having paid-up capital of not less than five crore of rupees shall constitute a committee of the board known as "*Audit Committee*" which shall consist of not less than three directors and such number of other directors as the board may determine of which two-thirds of the total number of members shall be directors other than managing or whole-time directors.

Every Audit Committee constituted under Sub-Section (1) shall act in accordance with terms of reference to be specified in writing by the board. The members of the Audit Committee shall elect a chairman from amongst themselves. The annual report of the company shall disclose the composition of the Audit Committee.

Meetings of the Committee: The auditors, the internal auditors, if any, and the director-in-charge of finance shall attend and participate at meetings of the Audit Committee but shall not have the right to vote. The Audit Committee should have discussions with the auditor periodically about internal control systems, the scope of audit including the observations of the auditors and review the half-yearly and annual financial statements before submission to the board and also ensure compliance of internal control systems.

Powers and Duties of the Committee: The Audit Committee shall have authority to investigate into any matter in relation to the items specified in this section or referred to it by the board and for this purpose, shall have full access to information contained in the records of the company and external professional advice, if necessary. The recommendations of the Audit Committee on any matter relating to financial management, including the audit report, shall be binding on the board. If the board does not accept the recommendations of the Audit Committee, it shall record the reasons therefore and communicate such reasons to the shareholders. The chairman of the Audit Committee shall attend the Annual General Meetings of the company to provide any clarification on matters relating to audit.

Restrictions on Powers (Section 293)

The Board of directors of a public company or of a private company which is a subsidiary of a public company shall not exercise the following powers except with the consent of the company in General Meeting.

(i) Power to sell, lease or otherwise dispose of the whole or substantially the whole of the undertaking of the company;

(ii) Power to remit or give time for repayment of any debt due to the company by a director. However, no such consent is required for renewal or continuance of an advance made by a banking company to its director in the ordinary course of its business;

(iii) Power to invest otherwise than in trust securities, the amount of compensation received by the company in respect of the compulsory acquisition of any undertaking or property of the company;

(iv) Power to borrow money, where the money to the borrowed together with the moneys already borrowed by the company will exceed the aggregate of the paid-up capital of the company and its free reserves;

(v) Power to contribute to charitable and other funds not directly relating to the business of the company or the welfare of its employees, any amount exceeding in any financial year Rs. 50,000, or five per cent of the average net profits of the three preceding financial years, whichever is greater.

Section 293-A puts a restriction on the powers of the board of directors to contribute any amount to any political party or for any political purpose to any individual or association. If the company contravenes this provision, it shall be punishable with fine which may extend to Rs. 5,000.

The matters which require the approval of members in general meeting are as follows:

1. Alteration of the Objects Clause of the Memorandum of Association (Sec. 17)
2. Change in the name of the company (Sec. 21)
3. Omitting the word "limited" or the words "private limited" for non-profit companies (Sec. 25)
4. Alteration of the Articles of Association of the company (Sec. 31)
5. Issue of shares at a discount (Sec. 79)
6. Issue of further shares to persons other than the existing shareholders after a period of one year of the commencement of business of the Ccmpany (Sec. 81)
7. Alteration of the share capital of the company by way of increase, consolidation or subdivision, etc. (Sec. 94)
8. Creation of reserve liability (Sec. 99)
9. Reduction of share capital (Sec. 100)
10. Alteration of the rights of the shareholders (Sec. 106)
11. Transfer of the registered office outside the municipal limits of the town or city in which the registered office is situate (Sec. 146)

12. Commencement of any business which is listed under the other objects clause of the Memorandum of Association (Sec. 149 2-A).
13. Decision to keep the statutory registers in a place other than the registered office of the company (Sec.163)
14. Payment of interest out of capital (Sec. 208)
15. Appointment of statutory auditors (Sec. 224)
16. Making incorporate loans beyond prescribed limits (Sec. 370)
17. Making incorporate investments beyond prescribed limits (Sec. 372)
18. An arrangement or compromise either by way of amalgamation, absorption or restriction (Sec. 391)

Powers which can be exercised by the board but they are subject to the approval of the General Meeting later

Certain powers may be exercised by the board but these decisions have to be ratified by the General Meeting at a future date. Some of the matters coming under this category are given below:

1. Appointment of the managing or whole-time director (Sec. 269)
2. Payment of remuneration to a managing or a whole-time director (Sec. 309)
3. Appointment of a director or his relative to an office or place of profit (Sec. 314)
4. Appointment of a sole selling agent (Secs.294-A, 294-AA)

Matters Requiring the Approval of the Central Government

Certain matters or transactions would require the approval of the Central Government in addition to a decision by the board of directors or a General Meeting.

These provisions also act as restrictions on the powers of the Board. Some of the matters which require the approval of the Central Government are listed below:

1. Change in the name of the company (This is an addition to the approval of the General Meeting) – Sec. 21
2. Dispensing with the word limited or private limited in the name of the company – Sec. 25
3. Conversion of a public company into a private company – Sec. 31
4. Appointment of cost auditors – Sec. 233-B
5. Appointment of sole selling Agents in respect of companies having a paid-up capital exceeding Rs.50 lakh – Sec. 294-AA
6. Making of loans to directors – Sec. 295

7. Appointment of managing or whole-time director if the appointments are not within the norms prescribed by Schedule-XIII to the Companies Act – Sec. 269
8. Payment of remuneration to directors exceeding the norms prescribed in Schedule-XIII to the Companies Act – Sec. 309
9. Approval of contracts in which directors are interested if the paid-up capital of the company exceeds Rs. I crore – Sec. 297
10. Appointment of relatives of directors to office or place of profit-at a remuneration exceeding prescribed limits – Sec. 314
11. Waiver of recovery of sums refundable to the company by the relatives of the directors who have been appointed for office or place of profit – Sec. 314(2)(b)
12. Appointment of a person as a managing director if he has already a Managing Director of more than two companies – Sec. 316
13. Making of incorporate loans to companies under the same management beyond the prescribed limits – Sec. 317.
14. Making of incorporate investments in excess of prescribed limits – Sec. 372

Powers that can be exercised only with the approval or confirmation of the National Company Law Tribunal

Certain powers can be exercised only with the confirmation or consent of the Company Law Board. These are:

1. Changing the objects clause of the Memorandum of Association (Section 17)
2. Shifting the registered office of the company from one state to another, (Section 17)
3. Issue of shares at a discount (Section 79)
4. Issue of further redeemable preference shares in lieu of irredeemable preference shares, or when the company is not in a position to redeem preference shares when they become due for redemption. (Section 80A)
5. Extension of time for delivery of share certificates (Section 113)

DUTIES OF DIRECTORS

As directors hold a key position, they are bound to comply with the provisions of the Companies Act. They shall carry out all duties placed upon them by either the Act or the Articles. The duties of the directors of a company have been laid down by Lord Justice Romer in *Re City Equitable Fire Insurance Company's case* and are summarised as under:

1. Duty of reasonable care: In discharging the duties of his position, a directors must exercise some degree of skill and diligence. A director need not exhibit in the performance of his duties a greater degree of skill than may reasonably be expected from a person of his knowledge and experience. The directors are not liable for mere error of judgement.

2. Duty to act honestly: A director must act honestly in the performance of his duties. He must not try to make personal gain out of a transaction in the name of the company.

3. Attend meetings: A director is not bound to give continuous attention to the affairs of his company. He is not bound to attend all board and committee meetings.

4. Inspect books of accounts: Though all books of account and other books and papers of the company are open to inspection by him, he is not bound to examine individual entries in the books.

5. Act personally: The directors must perform their duties personally. The maxim "*delegatus non-potest delegate*" (a delegate cannot delegate further) applies to them like all agents. Hence, unless permitted by the Articles specifically, the directors must not delegate any of their powers to some other person.

6. Director's duty of disclosures: Section 297 provides that except with the consent of the board of director, a director or his relative or any firm in which he or his relative has any interest or any private company of which he is a member or a director shall not enter into any contract with the company for the sale, purchase or supply of goods, materials or services or for underwriting the subscription of any shares or debentures.

In the case of a company having a paid-up share capital of rupees one crore or more, no such contract can be entered into except with the previous approval of the Central Government.

Consent of the board of directors is not necessary in the following cases:

1. Sale or purchase of goods for cash at prevailing market prices.
2. Contracts entered into in the regular course of business involving Rs. 5,000 in the aggregate in any year.
3. Any transaction in the ordinary course of business of a banking or insurance company.

In the case of urgent necessity contracts may be entered into but consent thereof must be obtained within 3 months from the date of contract. Such consent must be supported by a resolution passed at the board meeting. If consent is not given, acts done pursuant to the contract is voidable at the option of the board.

It is the duty of every director to disclose to the board the nature of his concern or interest in any contract or arrangement entered into by or on behalf of the company.

The disclosure must be made at the meeting of board of directors. An interested director cannot take part in the discussion of or vote on a such contract. His presence at the board's meeting shall not be taken into account for the purpose of forming a quorum nor will his vote be counted. In default of disclosure, the director is punishable with a fine of Rs. 5,000, besides vacating office.

LIABILITIES OF DIRECTORS

The liabilities of directors may be discussed under three heads: (a) Liability to outsiders, (b) Liability to company and (c) Criminal liability.

Liability to Outsiders

The directors are not personally liable to outsiders if they act within the scope of powers vested in them. The general rule in this regard is that wherever an agent is liable, those directors would be liable, but where the liability would attach to the principal only, the liability is the liability of the company.

The directors are personally liable to third parties of contract in the following cases:

(a) They contract with outsiders in their personal capacity

(b) They contract as agents of an undisclosed principal.

(c) They enter into a contract on behalf of a prospective company.

(d) When the contract is *ultra-vires* the company.

In default of statutory duties, the directors shall be personally liable to third parties in the following cases:

1. mis-statement in prospectus.
2. irregular allotment.
3. failure to repay application money if allotment of share and debentures is not dealt on the stock exchange as provided in the prospectus.

Liability to Company

The directors shall be liable to the company for the following:

(i) *Where they have acted ultra-vires the company*. It is not necessary to prove fraud in such cases or that they acted bonafide. For example, where they apply the funds of the company to objects not specified in the Memorandum of Association or when they pay dividends out of capital.

(ii) *When they have acted negligently*. Negligence may give rise to liability; there need not be fraud. But they will not be liable where they have acted bonafide and for the benefit of the company.

(iii) *Where there is a breach of trust.* Directors being the trustees of the company, they should discharge their duties in the best interest of the company. Where they commit a breach of trust resulting in a loss to the company, they are bound to make good the loss. For example, where the directors apply company's property for their own benefit they are guilty of breach of trust.

(iv) *Misfeasances* directors are liable to the company for misfeasance. The word *misfeasance* covers wilful misconduct or wilful negligence. Mere failure on the part of the director to take necessary steps for recovery of debts due to the company does not constitute misfeasance. If the company is in the course of winding up, the court may, on the application of the liquidator, creditor or contributory examine into the conduct of a director for any misfeasance or breach of trust in relation to the company.

Criminal Liabilities of Directors

So far we have dealt with the civil liability of directors. For acts of fraud, default in discharging their duties and misdemeanour, the Act provides penalties by way of fine or imprisonment. Sections 75, 95, 113, 115, 143, 162, 168, 303, etc., impose penalty upon the directors for omitting to comply with or contravening certain provisions of the Act.

Relief from the Liability

Very often in companies where a managing director or manager is existence, the other part time directors are not involved in the day-to-day affairs of the company. In the process, they may not be in a position to ensure the compliance of the various requirements of the Act since they are directors of the company only on a part-time basis. Section 633(1) of the Companies Act provides for a relief from the liability they may be incurred by the directors in certain cases.

In brief, the provisions of Sec. 633 state that if a director apprehends prosecution for non-compliance of any of the provisions of the Act and he applies to the court and proves to the court that he had acted honestly and reasonably and that he should be excused for the default of the company, the court may allow the relief against prosecution and default.

In conclusion, it may be stated that the cornerstone of most of the provisions of the Companies Act is in good faith. If a director can prove and satisfy the court that he had acted in good faith and the default had occurred in spite of his acting in good faith he would be excused by the court from the liability arising out of the default.

Directors with Unlimited Liability (Sections 322 and 323)

In a limited company, if so provided by the memorandum, the liability of the directors or of any director or managing director or manager director or manager may be unlimited. But before such a person accepts the office, notice in writing that his liability will be unlimited must be given to him by the promoters of the company or its directors or managers, if any.

In case the memorandum originally framed does not contain any such provision, a company may, if so allowed by its articles, alter its memorandum by a special resolution and made the liability of any of the above managerial personnel unlimited. But such an alteration shall not apply to existing managerial personnel unless they accord their consent to it.

DISABILITIES OF THE DIRECTORS

To protect the interests of shareholders and the company, the Companies Act has attached following disabilities to the office of a director:

1. Restriction on Number of Directorships (Sec. 275): A person cannot hold office of director at the same time in more than 15 companies.

2. Prohibition of Assignment of Office (Sec. 312): A director cannot assign his office to another person after the commencement of Companies Act, 1956. In this context, Section 312 lays down that any assignment of his office made after the commencement of this Act by any director of a company shall be void.

It may be pointed out that the word 'assignment' in Section 312 does not mean 'appointment' and this section intends to render a transfer of his office by a director void, and not the appointment by him of his successor. An appointment to an office can be made only if the office is vacant.

3. Restriction on Indemnity (Sec. 201): A director cannot claim any exemption from indemnity against any liability which, by virtue of any rule of law, would attach to him in respect of any negligence, default, misfeasance, breach of duty or breach of trust or which he may be guilty in relation to the company by reason of any provision contained in the articles or in any separate agreement with the company. Liability arising under the misfeasance proceedings is based on the principle that a person who has caused loss to the company by an act amounting to breach of trust, should make good the loss.

4. Restriction of Delegation: The director of a company cannot delegate his powers to any one else unless he is expressly authorised by the Articles to do so.

5. Undischarged Insolvent: An undischarged insolvent cannot be appointed to act as director of any company or in any way take part in the management of the company.

6. Restriction on Loans (Section. 295): A director cannot directly or indirectly receive any loan or guarantee of a loan or security for a loan without the previous approval of Central Government. The loan extended to director's partner or relative of a director, or to any firm of which a director is a partner or to private company of which a director is a director or a member.

7. Restriction on Entering into Contracts (Sec. 297): Without the consent of the Board, a director shall not enter into contract with the company;

(a) for the sale, purchase or supply of any goods; and

(b) after the commencement of this Act for underwriting of the subscription of any shares or debentures of the company.

A proviso added to Section 297 by the Amendment Act of 1974, states that in the case of a company having a paid-up share capital of not less than Rs. 1 crore no such contract shall be entered into except with the previous approval of the Central Government. The provision applies to contracts made by relative of a director or director's partner or by a firm of which such director or relative is a partner or any other partner in such a firm or a private company of which such director is a director or a member.

Further, by virtue of Section 297(2), no such consent of the board would be necessary if the company or the director, relative, firm, partner or private company regularly deals or does business in the subject matter of such contract so long as its cost does not exceed Rs. 5,000 in the aggregate in any year comprised in such contract.

Also, consent of the board is not necessary in the following cases:

(i) the purchase from (or sale to) a company of goods and materials by the directors for cash at the prevailing market rates; and

(ii) In the case of a banking company or insurance company, any transaction in the ordinary course of business of such company with any director, relative, firm, partner or private company as stated above.

8. Restriction on Holding Office of Profit (Sec. 314) : Except with the consent of the company accorded by a Special Resolution:

(a) a director of the company must not hold any office or place of profit; and

(b) no partner or relative of such director, no firm in which such director, or a relative of such director is a partner, no private company of which such director is a director or member, and no director or manager of such a private company, must hold any office or place of profit carrying total monthly remuneration of Rs. 5,000 or more.

These provisions do not apply to managing director, manager, legal, or technical adviser, banker or trustee for the holders of debentures of the company. But it shall be sufficient if the special resolution according the consent of the company is passed at the General Meeting of the company held for the first time after the holding of such office or place of profit.

9. Restrictions on Powers of the Board (Sec. 293): Section 293 imposes important restrictions on the powers of the board of directors of a public company or any subsidiary of a public company. Following powers can be exercised by the board only with the consent of the company in general meeting:

(a) sale or lease of the company's undertaking;

(b) extension of the time for payment of a debt due by a director;

(c) investment of compensation received on compulsory acquisition in securities other than trust securities;

(d) borrowing of money beyond the paid-up capital of the company. This, however, does not include temporary loans obtained from the company's bankers in the ordinary course of business;

(e) contribution to any charitable or other funds beyond Rs. 50,000 in one financial year or 5% of the average net profits during the preceding three financial years, whichever is greater.

10. Prohibition Regarding Political Contributions (Sec. 293-A): Neither a company in general meeting, nor its board of directors can make contributors to any political party, or to any individual or body for political purposes.

If a company contravenes these provisions, then:

(i) it is punishable with fine which may extend to Rs. 50,000, and

(ii) every officer of the company who is in default is punishable with imprisonment for a term which may extend to 3 years and is also liable to fine.

QUESTIONS

Objective Type Questions

I. Fill up the blanks

1. Every public company having a paid-up capital of five crores or more, may have a director elected by___________ shareholders in the manner prescribed.
2. Companies which were in existence on 21st July, 1961 call increase the directors within the permissible minimum of numbers
3. Generally directors in the first annual general body meeting are appointed according to __________.

4. A company shall have ________ number of directors out of its total numbers as retiring directors by rotation.
5. The maximum qualification in order to become eligible as a director must possess shares of nominal value or more which should be Rs. __________.
6. A director can be director in other companies which should not be more than __________.
7. The board of directors is entitled to appoint the following directors__________ and __________.
8. An Audit committee is said to be mandatory in every public company having a paid-up capital of not less than Rs. __________ crores.
9. The terms and conditions of appointment for the post of a director must be in accordance with Schedule __________.
10. No public company shall directly or indirectly make any loan or invest its funds in any other body corporate exceeding the limit of __________ % of its paid-up capital and free reserve.

[*Answers:* (1) Small; (2) 12; (3) Proportional representation; (4) 2/3; (5) Rs. 5000 and above; (6) 15 (Section 275); (7) additional directors and alternate directors; (8) 5; (9) (XIII); (10) 60%]

II. State whether the following statements are True or False

1. A director must be an individual.
2. A director may be considered as an agent, a trustee and a principal officer of a company.
3. The individual signatories or subscribers to the memorandum shall be considered as first directors.
4. Directors are always appointed in a general body meeting.
5. A person can be appointed as a managing director in not more than one company.
6. There can be a managing director and a manager to work together in a company.
7. The total remuneration of the managerial personnel in a public limited company should not exceed 11% of the net profit.
8. Director's remuneration includes also his sitting fees in a board meeting.
9. An alternate director must he appointed for a period of not less than three months.
10. An elected director can be terminated by the Central Government.

[*Answers:* True: (1), (3), (7), (9), (10); False: (2), (4), (5), (6), (8)]

III. Match the following

1.	Sole selling agent	(a)	cannot give time for repayment of debt by a director
2.	Political contributions	(b)	not to exceed 30% of the paid up capital and free reserves
3.	Board of directors	(c)	common directors
4.	Audit committee	(d)	twenty five years of age.
5.	Interested directors	(e)	not to exceed 5% of its average profit
6.	Director vacates	(f)	Scrutiny of financial statement
7.	A managing director	(g)	not to exceed five years
8.	Inter-company loan	(h)	failure to pay call money

[*Answers:* 1 (g); 2 (e); 3 (a); 4 (f); 5 (c); 6 (h); 7 (d); 8 (b)]

Review Questions

1. Define the term "*director*".
2. Who is eligible to become a director?
3. Who are first directors?
4. What do you mean by oligarchy in company management?
5. Is there any ceiling on the number of directorships?
6. Can directors appoint directors?
7. When is the office of a director deemed to be vacated?
8. What do you understand by Audit Committee?
9. Can there be directors with unlimited liability in a company?
10. Who are eligible to become directors?
11. What are the circumstances under which a director is automatically vacate from the office?
12. Who can remove a director?
13. What are the powers of directors?
14. What are the duties of directors?
15. Describe the scope and extent of liability of directors.
16. Define a director. What is the law relating to number of directors?
17. Enumerate the: provisions of the Companies Act, 1956 relating to appointment of a person other than a retiring director.

18. When does the resignation of a director become effective?
19. What is the procedure for removing a director (a) by the shareholders, (b) by the Central Government, (c) by the court?
20. Discuss the scope of the powers of the board of directors.
21. What powers are to be exercised by the directors at board meetings?
22. What powers can be exercised by the board of directors with the consent of members in General Meeting?
23. Enumerate the duties of directors.
24. Discuss the legal position of directors.
25. Discuss the liabilities of a director (i) to the company, and (ii) to outsiders for their acts.
26. How does a person cease to be a director?
27. State and explain the provisions relating to remuneration to directors.
28. What are the powers of the board of directors in a company?

CHAPTER 9

Managing Director, Manager and Secretary

MANAGING DIRECTOR (SEC. 2(26))

Meaning and definition: Managing director means a director who is entrusted with substantial powers of management which would not otherwise be exercisable by him. It includes a director occupying the position of a managing director by whatever name called. The *'substantial powers of management'* may be conferred upon him by virtue of an agreement with the company, or of a resolution passed by the company in its general meeting or by its board of directors, or by virtue of its Memorandum or Articles of Association.

On analysing the definition of a 'managing director' as given in Section 2(26) of the Act, it follows that the appointment of a managing director can be made by any one of the following modes:

1. By an agreement with the company; or
2. By a resolution passed by the company in its general meeting; or
3. By a resolution of the board of directors; or
4. By a clause in the Memorandum of Association or Articles of Association of the company.

However, the power to do administrative acts of a routine nature when so authorised by the board such as:

(a) the power to affix the common seal of the company to any document; or

(b) to draw and endorse any cheque on the account of the company in any bank; or

(c) to draw and endorse any negotiable instrument; or

(d) to sign any certificate to share or to direct registration of transfer of any share shall not be deemed to be included within the 'substantial powers of management'.

Remember that only an individual can be a managing director. He should be a director of the company. He should not be the one who is disqualified for directorship. The managing director of a company shall exercise his powers subject to superintendence, control and direction of its board of directors. Since the managing director must be a director, he has also the duties, responsibilities and liabilities of an ordinary director.

Articles of a company generally authorise the directors to appoint one of them as managing director. A public company or a private company being subsidiary of a public company must get the approval of the Central Government before appointing the Managing Director for the first time or within 3 months of doing so.

It is to be noted that the Government shall not grant approval unless it is satisfied that:

(i) it is in the interest of the company to have a managing director or Whole-time Director;

(ii) the proposed person is a fit and proper person and the appointment is not against public interest; and

(iii) the terms and conditions of appointment are fair and reasonable

The Central Government is empowered to reduce the period of appointment proposed by the company. Further, Section 269(5) provides that in case the appointment is not approved, then the proposed would vacate office from the date on which the decision of the Government is communicated to the company.

Disqualification of Managing Director (Sec. 267)

Following persons cannot be appointed as a managing director:

1. A person who is an undischarged insolvent or who has at anytime been adjudged an insolvent;
2. A person who suspends or has at any time suspended payment to his creditors or who makes or has at anytime made a composition with them.
3. A person who is or has at anytime been convicted by a court of an offence involving moral turpitude.
4. Further, a person cannot be a managing director of more than two companies at the same time.

Every public company, or a private company, which is a subsidiary of a public company having a paid-up share capital of Rs.5 crore or more shall have a managing or whole-time director or a manager.

Term of Office and Re-appointment of Managing Director (Sec. 269 and 317):

Approval of Central Government: The re-appointment of a person as managing director shall also be approved by Central Government. Note that, a company cannot appoint managing director for more than 5 years at a stretch but under the Act, the re-appointment is not forbidden and such re-appointment cannot be sanctioned earlier than 2 years from the date on which it is to come into force. Such provision does not apply to a private company unless it is a subsidiary of public company.

Approval of the Central Government is not required in the case of appointment of managerial personnel made on or after 15th day of June 1988 as per the conditions specified in Schedule XIII to the Act.

Provisions Relating to Appointment Where it Requires Approval of the Central Government

In the case of appointment, which requires approval of the Central Government, the following provisions are to be observed.

1. Every application seeking approval to the appointment of a managing or whole-time director or manager shall be made to the Central Government within a period of 90 days from the date of such appointment.
2. The Central Government shall not accord its approval to the application if it is satisfied that–
   - (i) The managing or whole-time director or the manager appointed is in its opinion, not a fit and proper person to be appointed as such or such appointment is not in the public interest; or
   - (ii) The terms and conditions of the appointment of the managing or whole-time director or the manager are not fair and reasonable.
   - (iii) The Central Government may accord approval for a period lesser than the period for which the appointment is proposed to be made.
   - (iv) If the appointment is not approved by the Central Government, the person appointed shall vacate his office on the date on which the decision of the Central Government is communicated to the company. If he fails to vacate his office, he shall be punishable with fine, which may extend to Rs.5,000 for everyday during which he fails to vacate such office.

An appointment without the approval of the Central Government may sometimes be made by a company, in contravention of the requirements of Schedule XIII. In such a case if the Central Government suo *moto* or on any information received by it is *prima facie* of the opinion that such an invalid appointment has been made, the Central Government may refer the matter to the National Company Law Tribunal. On receipt of such a reference, the National Company Law Tribunal shall issue a notice to:

(i) the company,

(ii) the managing or whole-time director or the manager, as the case may be, and

(iii) the director or other officer responsible for complying with the requirements of Schedule XIII, to show cause as to why such appointment shall not be terminated and the penalties provided under Sec. 269 shall not be imposed.

If the National Company Law Tribunal, after giving a reasonable opportunity to the company, the managing or whole-time director or the manager, or the officer who is in default, as the case may be, comes to the conclusion that the appointment has been made in contravention of the requirements of Schedule XIII, it shall make an order declaring that a contravention of the requirements of Schedule XIII has taken place. On the making of an order by the National Company Law Tribunal–

1. the company shall be liable to a fine, which may extend to Rs.50,000;
2. every officer of the company who is in default shall be liable to a fine of Rs.1,00,000; and
3. the appointment of the managing or whole-time director or the manager, as the case may be, shall be deemed to have come to an end and the person so appointed shall, in addition to being liable to pay a fine of Rs. 1,00,000, refund to the company the entire amount of salaries, commissions and perquisites received or enjoyed by him between the date of his appointment and the passing of such order.

If a company contravenes penalty provisions referred to above or any direction given by the National Company Law Tribunal, every officer of the company who is in default and the managing or whole-time director or the manager, as the case may be, shall be punishable with imprisonment for a term which may extend to 3 years and shall also be liable to a fine which may extend to Rs.500 for everyday of default. As per Sec. 269, *'Appointment'* includes re-appointment and *'whole-time director'* includes a director in the whole-time employment of the company.

Number of Managing Directorship: A person cannot be a Managing Director of more than 2 companies where one at least of the 2 companies is a public company. But the Central Government may allow a person to be managing director of more than 2 companies provided it is of the view that the companies should have for their proper working functions as a single unit and have a common managing director. A person can be appointed as the managing director of any number of private companies without any restrictions (Sec.316).

Two-fold Capacity of Director and Manager

The managing director works in a two-fold capacity. As a director he has a seat on the board and can take part in the board meeting proceedings. As a manager he is responsible for routine management of the company. He may be given a fixed salary and a certain rate of commission on the net profits of the company, so that he may have extra incentive to work hard and take more personal interest in securing efficiency and economy in the administrative machinery of the company. A managing director of a public company cannot vote in the matter of his appointment or of fixing his remuneration.

M.D. is Non-retiring Director: The managing director is exempted from the normal rule of retirement by rotation. So he need not retire at the end of every three years as long as he is acting as managing director. Thus, he may be termed as a *non-retiring director*. But if he ceases to act as a director on account of any disqualification, e.g. non-payment of call within six months thereof, his managing directorship is automatically terminated.

In addition to rights and duties of a director, the managing director has many other rights and duties as provided for in the Articles and delegated by the board. The idea of appointing a managing director is to place one of the directors in charge of the day-to-day administration of the affairs of the company and to relieve the board of going through all the details. Such duties may also be performed by the manager, but the manager cannot take that amount of interest which is expected of one who has the form of qualification shares. Secondly, managing director, being also a director, can common considerable influence in the board and his solving many problems of management; manager being a mere employee, cannot have such influence in the board and he cannot do such duties as can be performed by a director on behalf of the board.

Distinction between a Director and Managing Director

Director	*Managing Director*
1.Elected by shareholders.	1. Elected by directors.
2. Appointment is for 3 years.	2. Appointment is for 5 years.
3. Subject to retirement by rotation at the end of 3 years.	3. Exempted from the provisions of retirement by rotation.
4. Not a salaried office, but receiving only honorarium.	4. Regular office of profit or salary.
5. Cannot have individual powers of management. Powers exercised collectively through a body, i.e. board meeting directors work as a team.	5. Entrusted with substantial special powers of management as per board resolution or agreement. These are delegated to him by directors.
6. May or even may not be a shareholder	6. Must be a director first and then can act as managing director
7. Not in charge of routine management. Acts only as a guide, consultant or adviser.	7. In charge of routine management, Chief executive and head of the company.

8. Considered as agent of the shareholders or company	8. Considered as agent of the board of directors.
9. In absence of managing director, or manager all directors may have 3 p.c. of annual net profits as their remuneration. Otherwise they would have only 1 p.c.	9. For one managing director managerial remuneration is 5 p.c. and for two or more it is 10 p.c. of annual net profits.
10. Directors are in charge of overall supervision and control of company's business and act as the brain of the company policy and decision-making authority	10. Managing director is in charge of executive and administrative work and acts as the hands, eyes and ears of the company executive arm of the board of directors

WHOLE-TIME DIRECTOR

A 'whole-time director' includes 'a director in the whole-time employment of the company'. The provisions applicable to the appointment of a managing director are also applicable to the appointment of a whole-time director. He is an employee director. There is no restriction on his period of service. He has no discretionary power and cannot act like a managing director.

Disqualification of a Whole-time Director

No company (public or private) can appoint or employ or continue the appointment or employment of any person as its whole-time director:

(a) who is an undischarged insolvent or has, at any time been adjudged an insolvent;

(b) who suspends or has, at any time suspended payment to his creditors; or makes or has made composition with them; or

(c) who is or has been convicted by the court of an offence involving moral turpitude.

'Whole-time Director' and 'Managing Director'—A Comparison

Similarities: It is noteworthy that many salient features of Whole-time Director are similar to managing director, for instance:

1. Both whole-time director and managing director must be directors.
2. Section 267 of the Act applies to both, viz., whole-time director as well as managing director cannot be appointed or employed if they are undischarged insolvent, or if they are convicted by a court of an offence involving moral turpitude, etc.
3. Section 283 of the Act is applicable to whole-time director as well as managing director, namely: the office of a whole-time director and the managing director

shall become vacant if they are found to be of unsound mind; if they fail to obtain the share qualification (if any) required of them by the Articles of the company, if they fail to pay any call money in respect of shares held by them, etc.

4. Section 274 of the Act also applies to both the Whole-time Director and the managing director, i.e., laying down the circumstances under which a person cannot be appointed as whole-time director or managing director of a company.

Distinction between Whole-time Director and Managing Director

Yet, there are many points of differences between a whole-time director and a managing director, which are discussed hereunder:

1. Appointment: The appointment of whole-time director requires the consent of shareholders by a special resolution.

The appointment of a managing director need not necessarily be made with the consent of shareholders.

2. Term of Appointment: The term of appointment of a whole-time director is not fixed and as such the appointment can be for any number of years.

The managing director can be appointed for a maximum period of 5 years at a time.

3. Managerial Personnel: Whole-time director can be appointed along with a manager or a managing director. That is, whole-time director and managing director can work at the same time and thus, can co-exist.

A managing director cannot be appointed along with a manager. That is, managing director and a manager cannot work together and thus, cannot co-exist.

4. Number of Directorship: Whole-time director cannot be a whole-time director for more than one company, thus cannot have more than one whole-time directorship.

Managing director can be a managing director of more than one company. Thus, managing director can have more than one directorships.

5. Powers: Whole-time director is an employee director of the company and performs important administrative functions. He does not exercise 'substantial powers of management' such as introduction of new products, adoption of new techniques, trade discount structure, etc.

The managing director exercises 'substantial power of management'.

MANAGER

According to Section 2(24), 'Manager' means "an individual who subject to the superintendence, control and direction of the board of director, has the management of the whole, or substantially the whole, of the affairs of a company. It includes a director or any other person occupying the position of a manager, by whatever name called, and whether under a contract of service or not".

'Manager' is "a person who has management of the whole work of the affairs of the company, not an agent who is to do a particular thing, or a servant who is to obey order, but a person who is entrusted with power to transact the whole of the affairs of the company". (Gibson V. Bartain).

On a true construction of Section 2(24), it is clear that the word 'Manager' does not include 'Director'. In other words, a plain reading of the definition of 'Manager' as embodied in Section 2(24) of the Act clearly indicates that '*every manager cannot be a director and every director cannot be a manager*'. Also, the duties attached to the managers are quite different from those of directors. To put it in one sentence, a 'director' cannot be said to be a 'manager' unless he is appointed as such.

The status and position of a manager

1. He is the paid executive of the company.
2. He is subject to the control of the board of directors.
3. He has the management of the whole or substantially the whole of the affairs of the company.
4. A director may be appointed as a manager under a special contract of service.
5. He is not a mere head or foreman of a section or office.

It is to be noted that the provisions applicable to a managing director regarding his appointment, term of office and the number of companies which can be managed are also applicable to a 'manager'.

Disqualifications of a Manager

According to Section 384, only an individual can be appointed as a manager of the company. A firm, body corporate (company) or association cannot be appointed as a 'manager' of the company. Besides, the following persons cannot be appointed as manager of a company.

1. A person who is an undischarged insolvent or who has at any time within the preceding 5 years been adjudged an insolvent;
2. A person who suspends or who has at any time within the preceding 5 years suspended payment to his creditors or who has at any time within the preceding 5 years composition with them:

3. A person who is or who has at any time within the preceding 5 years been convicted by a court in India of an offence involving moral turpitude.

The Central Government may, by notification in the official gazettes, remove the above disqualifications, either generally or in relation to any company or companies specified in the notification.

Appointment of 'Manager' (Section 386)

Normally one cannot be manager of more than one public company at a time. No company can appoint any person as 'manager', if he is either the manager or managing director of any other company. Even then, if the company wants to employ him, then:

(a) it must be approved by a resolution passed at the meeting;

(b) specific notice of such appointment must be given to every director present in India;

(c) it is approved by Central Government who will approve only if a common manager is necessary for the proper working of more than 2 companies.

Remuneration

The manager of a company may, subject to the provisions of Section 198 as applicable to the managing director, receive remuneration either by way of a monthly payment, or by way of a specific percentage of the net profits of the company or partly by one way partly by the other. Except with the approval of the Central Government such remuneration shall not exceed in the aggregate 5% of the net profits (Sec. 387). Increase in remuneration of a manager shall require sanction of the Central Government. The above provision is not applicable to a private company.

Difference between a Manager and a Managing Director

1. Manager need not be a director of the company. He is just an employee. As a director he is the member of the board and right to vote in the board meeting like other directors.

Managing director must be a director of the company.

2. There can be only one manager in the company.

A company may have more than one managing director each incharge of a division or activity of the business.

3. Total remuneration of the manager cannot exceed 5% of the annual net profits of the company.

Managing director's remuneration cannot exceed 5% of net profits of the company, but where the managing directors are more than one the remuneration cannot exceed 10% of the net profits for all of them taken together.

4. Manager does not exercise 'substantial powers of the management'.

Managing director exercises 'substantial powers of the management' such as buying and selling policy, adoption of new techniques, fixation of price of products, etc.

5. Manager may be appointed under a contract of service.

Managing director can be appointed either—

- by agreement with the company,
- by resolution passed by the company in its general meeting,
- by the board of directors, or
- by the Memorandum of Association or Articles of Association of the company.

Managing Agents, Secretaries and Treasurers (Sec. 324-A)

By the Companies (Amendment) Act of 1969, the system of managing agency or of secretaries and treasurers has been abolished and the companies have been prohibited to employ managing agents, secretaries and treasurers after 3rd of April, 1970.

Prevention of Management by Undesirable Persons

Section 202 and 203 provide for the prevention of management by undesirable persons. They are as under:

1. Undischarged Insolvent not to Manage Company (Sec. 202): Such a person cannot act or discharge any of the function of a director or manager of any company, and is not entitled to take part in the promotion, formation or management of any company.

It may be added that the company for above purposes also means an unregistered company and a foreign company. If he does any of these things or discharges any of these functions, he shall be punishable with imprisonment for a term which may extend to 2 years or with fine to the extent of Rs. 5,000 or with both.

2. Power to Restrain Fraudulent Persons from Managing Companies (Sec. 203). Where:

(i) a person is convicted of any offence in connection with the promotion, formation or management of the company.

(ii) Where in the course of winding up of a company it appears that a person has been guilty under Section 542 of fraudulent conduct of business or has been guilty of any fraud or misfeasance in relation to the company or of any breach of his duty to the company, the court may make an order that such a person shall not, with the leave of the court, be a director of any company or take part in the promotion, formation or management of a company for a period not exceeding 5 years. A person who intends to apply for such an order shall to give 10 days' notice of his intention to the person against whom the order is sought. An application for such an order may be made by the liquidator of the company or by any person who is or has been a member or creditor of the company.

A person acting in contravention of such order shall be punishable with imprisonment for a term which may extend to 2 years or with fine which may extend to Rs. 50,000 or with both.

COMPANY SECRETARY

A company secretary means "a person who is a member of the Institute of Company Secretaries of India" (Sec.2(1) (c) of the Company Secretaries Act, 1980). According to Sec. 2(45) of the Companies Act as amended in 1988 'secretary' means a company secretary within the meaning of Sec.2(1) (c) of the Company Secretaries Act, 1980, and includes any individual possessing the prescribed qualifications appointed to perform the duties which may be performed by a secretary under this Act and any other ministerial or administrative duties.

Secretary in Whole-time Practice: 'Secretary in whole-time practice' means a secretary who shall be deemed to be in practice and who is not in full-time employment (Sec. 2 (45-A)). Now the small companies which cannot employ a whole-time company secretary will be in a position to avail of the services of the company secretaries in whole-time practice for complying with various statutory requirements.

Status of Company Secretary: The status of a company secretary has altered a great deal now. He is now the chief administrative officer of a company. Sec. 2 (30) also says that an 'officer' includes 'secretary'. The courts have also recognised the improvement in the status of the secretary. ***(Panorama Developments ((Guildford) Ltd. vs. Furnishing Fabrics Ltd. (1971)3 AII E.R. 16.B.)***

Thus, whereas the directors are the brain of a company as they lay down the general policy of the company and direct its affairs, the secretary is the company's eyes, ears and hands as he carries out the policies of the managements, follows directions and executes many a decision taken by the directors on the authority delegated to him.

Appointment: A company secretary is generally appointed by the directors at their meeting. He may also be appointed by the Articles in which case his appointment shall be confirmed by a resolution of the directors passed in their first meeting after his appointment. A copy of the resolution appointing a person as secretary shall be forwarded to the registrar of companies.

Qualifications: The qualifications of a person to be eligible for appointment as secretary are as follows:

1. Every company having a paid-up share capital of not less than Rs. 50 lakh shall have a whole-time secretary.
2. A company shall not appoint anyone as a whole-time secretary unless he is a member of the Institute of Company Secretaries of India constituted under the Company Secretaries Act, 1980.
3. A company having a paid-up share capital of less than Rs.50 lakh may appoint any individual as its whole-time secretary to perform the duties of a secretary under the Companies Act, 1956, and any other ministerial or administrative duties. But no individual shall be eligible to be so appointed unless he possesses one or more of the following qualifications, namely:
   - (i) Membership of the Institute of Company Secretaries of India:
   - (ii) Pass in the intermediate examination conducted by the Institute of Company Secretaries of India:
   - (iii) Postgraduate degree in commerce or corporate secretaryship granted by any university in India;
   - (iv) Degree in law granted by any university;
   - (v) Membership of the Institute of Chartered Accountants of India;
   - (vi) Membership of the Institute of Cost and Works Accountants of India;
   - (vii) Postgraduate degree or diploma in management sciences, granted by any University, or the Institutes of Management, Ahmedabad, Kolkata, Bangaluru or Lucknow;
   - (viii) Postgraduate diploma in company secretaryship granted by the Institute of Commercial Practice under the Delhi Administration or Diploma in Corporate Laws and Management granted by the Indian Law Institute, New Delhi;
   - (ix) Postgraduate diploma in Company Law and Secretarial Practice granted by the University of Udaipur; or
   - (x) Membership of the Association of Secretaries and Managers, Kolkata.

Where the paid-up share capital of a company is increased to Rs. 25 lakh or more, the company shall, within a period of 1 year from such increase, appoint a whole-time secretary, who is a member of the Institute of Company Secretaries of India.

Certain companies to have secretaries (Sec.383-A): Every company having paid-up share capital of Rs. 25 lakh or more shall have a whole-time secretary. Where the board of directors of any such company or companies have only 2 directors, neither of them shall be the secretary.

Penalty: If a company fails to comply with the provision of Sec. 383-A, the company and every officer of the company who is in default, shall be punishable with fine which may extend to Rs. 500 for everyday during which the default continues. When any proceedings against a person in respect of this offence are taken, he may defend himself by providing that all reasonable efforts to comply with the provision of Sec. 383-A were taken or that the financial position of the company was such that it was beyond its capacity to engage a whole-time secretary.

QUESTIONS

Objective Type Questions

I. Fill in the Blanks

1. A managing director means a person who is entrusted with __________.
2. No person shall be appointed a managing director who is __________ __________.
3. The maximum term of appointment of a managing director can be __________ years at a time.
4. A company __________ __________ employ a firm or body corporate as its manager.
5. A company shall not be liable to pay to its sole selling agent any compensation for the loss of his office where his appointment is not approved by the __________.
6. A qualified Wholetime Company Secretary is mandatory in a public limited company with capital of __________.
7. Every company not required to employ a wholetime Secretary and having a paid-up share capital of Rs. __________ shall file with the Registrar a certificate from __________.
8. As per Section 215, the Secretary is required to authenticate the __________ and __________.
9. A qualified full-time Secretary need not be appointed in companies with capital of __________.
10. The First Secretary is appointed by the __________ at the __________ stage.

[*Answers :* (1) administration; (2) an insolvent; (3) 7; (4) cannot; (5) government; (6) Rs. 50 lakhs (with effect from 13.12.2000); (7) Rs. 10 lakhs and above; Wholetime Practising Secretary; (8) Balance Sheet; Profit and Loss Account; (9) Less than Rs. 50 lakhs; (10) Promoters; Pre-incorporation]

II. State whether the following Statements are True or False

(a) A Director can be appointed as a Company Secretary.

(b) A Secretary is the agent of the company.

(c) A Secretary is only an employee of the company like others.

(d) The duties of a Company Secretary are of managerial nature.

(e) A Secretary appointed for the company must be an individual.

[*Answers:* True: (a), (c), (d), (e); False: (b)]

III. Multiple Choice Questions

State which of the alternatives is correct in the following cases:

1. The term of office of a managing director cannot exceed
   (a) 2 years at a time. (c) 5 years at a time.
   (b) 3 years at a time. (d) 7 years at a time.
2. The remuneration of a managing director cannot exceed
   (a) 1 per cent of the net profit. (c) 10 per cent of the net profit.
   (b) 5 per cent of the net profit. (d) Rs. 50,000.
3. Except with the approval of the Central Government, remuneration payable to the manager of a company cannot exceed
   (a) 2, (c) 4,
   (b) 3, (d) 5 per cent of the net profit of the company for any financial year.
4. The secretary of a company may be
   (a) any individual, firm or body corporate. (c) only a body corporate.
   (b) only an individual. (d) only a firm.
5. The appointment of a qualified secretary is compulsory in case of a company having
   (a) such authorised share capital as may be prescribed.
   (b) such issued share capital as may be prescribed.
   (c) such paid-up share capital as may be prescribed.
   (d) Rs. 20 lakhs or more as its paid-up capital.

6. A person who is already the manager of 2 companies can be appointed as the manager of a third company only if such company
   (a) passes a special resolution to that effect.
   (b) passes a unanimous Board resolution to that effect.
   (c) obtains the permission of the Central Government to that effect.
   (d) passes a special resolution to that effect and obtains the Central Government's permission.
7. The Companies Act permits an individual, at any given time, to act as managing director of
   (a) any number of private companies.
   (b) any number of public companies.
   (c) any number of companies with the Central Governmen'ts permission, if it is satisfied that the companies should function as a single unit and have a common managing director.
8. No company having a paid-up share capital of Rs. 50 lakhs or more shall appoint a sole selling agent except with the consent of members by
   (a) an ordinary resolution.
   (b) a special resolution.
   (c) a special resolution and approval of the Company Law Board.
   (d) a special resolution and approval of the Central Government.

[*Answers:* 1 (c); 2 (b); 3 (d); 4 (b); 5 (c and d); 6 (c); 7 (a); 8 (d)]

Review Questions

1. Who is a managing director? What are his qualifications?
2. Who can be a manager?
3. Distinguish between manager and managing director.
4. What are the disqualifications of a managing director?
5. Who can be a managing director of company? Distinguish between director and managing director.
6. State the legal, provisions regarding a managing director.
7. Explain the legal provisions regarding remuneration payable to managerial persons.
8. State the difference between whole-time director and managing director.
9. Who can be a managing director? Briefly explain the legal provisions regarding a managing director?

10. Who can be a manager? Distinguish between manager and managing director.
11. Write an essay on managerial remuneration in a company.
12. Discuss the law relating to the remuneration of the managing director of a public company.
13. Who is a company secretary? State the provisions relating to his qualification and appointment.

CHAPTER 10
Corporate Governance

Corporate governance is the system by which business corporations are directed and controlled. The corporate governance structure specifies the distribution of rights and responsibilities among different participants in the corporation, such as, the board, managers, shareholders and other stakeholders, and spells out the rules and procedures for making decisions on corporate affairs. By doing this, it also provides the structure through which the company objectives are set and the means of attaining those objectives and monitoring performance.

Corporate governance can be defined narrowly as the relationship of a company with its stakeholders or, more broadly, its relationship with society. Corporate governance is about promoting corporate fairness, transparency and accountability. It is a system and a process, consistent with principles and practices which are used by the corporate firms of a free and open society. It assigns final authority and full responsibility of managing the firm to the board of directors of the firm.

Corporate governance should therefore include *self-regulation* in terms of stopping of formations of price cartels as they vitiate healthy competition so important in free markets. In the free market the consumer usually gets the maximum benefit, as he the one getting a choice of products, at reasonable prices and on good terms of business. It also makes the consumer less inclined to become loyal to a brand as he finds new brands entering the market all the time.

Corporate Governance Concepts

The concept of corporate governance is defined in several ways because it potentially covers the entire gamut of activities having direct or indirect influence on the financial health of the corporate entities. As a result, different people have come up with different definitions, which basically reflect their special interests in the field. The best way to define the concept, perhaps, is to list a few of the different definitions.

It would be interesting to look at the earliest definition of corporate governance by the economist and the nobel laureate, *Milton Friedman*. According to him, 'Corporate governance is to conduct the business in accordance with owner or shareholders' desires, which generally will be to make as much money as possible, while conforming to the basic rules of the society embodied in law and local customs.' This definition is based on the economic concept of *market value maximisation through profit generation* that puts stress on shareholder-based capitalism.

Friedman's definition is narrow in scope, as can be seen from the existing business scenario. Over a period of time the definition of corporate governance has become broad-based, has been widened. It now encompasses the interests of not only the shareholders but also other stakeholders.

According to some economists, corporate governance is a field in economics that investigates how corporations can be made more efficient by the use of institutional structures such as contracts, organisational designs and legislation. This is often limited to the question of shareholder value, i.e., how the corporate owners can motivate and secure that the corporate managers will deliver a competitive rate of return on shareholder's investments.

According to **J. Wolfensohn**, President, World Bank 'Corporate governance is about promoting corporate fairness, transparency and accountability.'

According to some experts 'Corporate governance means doing everything better, to improve relations between companies and their shareholders; to improve the quality and usefulness of outside directors; to encourage people to think long-term; to ensure that information needs of all stakeholders are met and to ensure that executive management is monitored properly in the interest of shareholders.' This definition is an all encompassing one and it can be used in Indian context.

Corporate governance is a process or *a set of systems and process to ensure that the company is managed to suit the best interests of all*. The systems that can ensure this may include structural and organisational matters. The stakeholders may be internal stakeholders (promoters, employees, workmen and executives) and external stakeholders (shareholders, customers, suppliers, financial institutes, dealers, vendors, bankers, community, trade bodies, government, regulators and fauna and flora of the area).

Corporate governance can also be considered, as a *voluntary ethical code of corporate-business*. Corporate governance is the system by which companies are directed and controlled. The shareholders (the owners) role in the governance is to appoint the directors and the auditors and to satisfy themselves that an appropriate governance structure is in place.

The concept of corporate governance is on *transparency, integrity, and accountability of the management*, which includes non-executive directors. It is a system of making management accountable to the shareholders for the effective management of companies, in the interest of the company with its ethics and values.

Corporate governance has extended beyond the accountability of the corporate sector alone. There is need to evolve a voluntary code of conduct also for enforcement and regulatory agencies as well. The overall scenario calls for setting up of behavioural standards, supported and protected by structural system, under public accountability.

Corporate governance deals with laws, procedures, practices and implicit rules that determine a company's ability to take correct managerial decisions for its stakeholders, in particular, its shareholders, creditors, the government and employees. Global consensus about the objective was of good corporate governance for long-term shareholder value.

Unethical conduct by corporate management is not a new phenomenon. However, in the first half of the last century such a conduct was a rare occurrence, but today it has become commonplace. It is difficult to isolate ethical functioning groups from unethical ones as the latter can be found almost everywhere.

Traditionally, before elections, the politicians are looking out for getting donations for their election campaigns. In India when the candidate to whom the firm gave the donation won the election, the firm would not settle for anything less than twenty times the amount of donation, which they must earn an extra profit with the active connivance and support of their candidate. It really did not matter whether the candidate sat in the government benches or in the opposition, since even the opposition legislators have a lot of political clout and they can get favours from the government for the firm on a *quid pro quo* basis; they will agree to support any government legislation to return the favour. Those were the days of permit and license raj, where the politicians had the power to issue these to their fàvourites, which would enable them to make huge profits.

Businessmen seek favours from bureaucrats who in turn offer financial support. It could also be true that the bureaucrats beckon businessmen to their parlours, luring them to extra benefits, made possible because of the positions that bureaucrats hold. On the other hand, there are politicians in need of money for fighting elections. The financial support they get from business is with a collateral of protection from bureaucrats. Today, all the four pillars of human society — the legislature or politics, the bureaucracy, the judiciary and the media — have become polluted with the scourge of corruption. The malaise of corrupt practices has disseminated fast — crossing the national barriers at an alarming rate, and unless drastic measures are taken by all concerned there appears little hope of any redemption. Business is part of the entire social structure and, therefore, it only reflects the state of the country's societal degradation.

Need for Corporate Governance

The need for corporate leadership has been felt acutely in the 21st century for the following reasons:

1. **Market driven economy:** Market-driven economy deals with economic factors like interest rates, taxation norms, and entry of new competitors towards which the markets are moving. With lower interest rates and lower cash reserve ratios, the money supply position in the market has improved. This has led to the revival of markets, in as much that the market for second hand products is fast disappearing. Considering this phenomenon, the Maruti car company has started buying second hand Maruti cars, refurbishing them and then selling them in the market as true value cars.
2. **Globalisation:** Globalisation and liberalisation has led the Indian firms into a fast moving market situation, where competition is mounting at a rapid pace and unless the firms become responsive enough to the changing market needs, they are likely to be swamped out of the market. Firms have to quickly plan their strategies for gaining sustainable competitive advantage. The firm's brand equity, product portfolio and the reputation of their quality of service are the key success factors today.
3. **Severe and chaotic competition:** Efficiency and effectiveness are now the critical success factor. With severe and chaotic competition, only those firms are likely to survive who 'do the right things rightly', i.e., who are both effective and efficient in their operations, as the market being a cruel entity does not forgive defaulters at all.
4. **Liberalisation process:** Institutional investors have moved in the arena and domestic markets and therefore the risk has now been spread geographically. This has resulted in major firms seeking money from overseas. However, more efforts in the liberalisation process are needed from the side of the government to make India a favourite destination for international investors, who find China a better alternative for making investments despite their government's political philosophy.
5. **High and consistent standards for reporting:** High and consistent standards for reporting is a necessity in every area, for both financial and non-financial issues. These reports should reflect how the shareholder's interests are looked after by the CEOs.
6. **Changing ownership Structure:** The profile of corporate ownership has changed significantly. Public financial institutions are the single largest shareholder in most of the large corporations in the private sector. Institutional shareholders have reversed the trend of scattered shareholders. Institutional investors (foreign as well as Indian) and mutual funds have now become singly or jointly direct challenges to managements of companies. Due to threat of hostile takeover bids and the growth of institutional investors the big business houses started talking about corporate governance.

7. **Corporate oligarchy:** Shareholder activism and shareholder democracy continue to remain myths in India. Postal ballot system is still absent. Proxies are not allowed to speak at the meetings. Shareholders, associations, investors, education and awareness have not emerged as a countervailing force.

Parties (Actors and Factors) to Corporate Governance

Parties involved in corporate governance include the governing or regulatory body – the chief executive officer, the board of directors, management and shareholders. Other stakeholders who take part include suppliers, employees, creditors, customers and the community at large.

Firms must keep the interest of stakeholders along with commercial value and social causes. The success or failure of firms will depend on the fact whether they are stakeholder inclusive or stakeholder exclusive in their operations.

The following are the stakeholders of the firms:

Primary social stakeholders	Secondary social stakeholders
➢ Customers	➢ Government
➢ Suppliers	➢ Society
➢ Investors	➢ Unions
➢ Managers and employees	➢ Media and communicators
➢ Local communities	➢ Trade bodies
➢ Business partners	➢ Competitors
➢ Global citizens	
Primary non-social stakeholders	**Secondary non-social stakeholders**
➢ Natural environment	➢ Environmental pressure groups
➢ Non-human species	➢ Animal welfare pressure groups
➢ Future generations	

The major players in the area of corporate governance can also be classified into two groups – (i) external, and (ii) internal. Externally, the pace of corporate governance is set by the government, investors, financial institutions, suppliers and customers. Government as the regulator sets the legal, financial and business framework defines the scope and extent of corporate governance. Internally, corporate boards, shareholders and employers with the corporation decide how companies are directed and controlled.

In corporations, the principal (shareholder) delegated decision rights to the agent (manager) to act in the principal's best interests. This separation of ownership from control implies a loss of effective control by shareholders over managerial decisions.

Partly as a result of this separation between the main two parties, a system of corporate governance controls is implemented to assist in aligning the incentives of managers with those of shareholders, in order to limit the self-satisfying opportunities for managers.

A board of directors often plays a key role in corporate governance. It is their responsibility to endorse the organization's strategy, develop directional policy, appoint, supervise and remunerate senior executives and to ensure accountability of the organization to its owners and authorities.

All parties to corporate governance have an interest, whether direct or indirect, in the effective performance of the organization. Directors, workers and management receive salaries, benefits and reputation: whilst shareholders receive capital return. Customers receive goods and services; suppliers receive compensation for their goods or services. In return these individuals provide value in the form of natural, human, social and other forms of capital.

PRINCIPLES OF CORPORATE GOVERNANCE

Corporate governance principles and codes have been developed in different countries and issued from stock exchanges, corporations, institutional investors, or associations (institutes) of directors and managers with the support of governments and international organisations. As a rule, compliance with these governance recommendations is not mandated by law, although the codes linked to stock exchange listing requirements may have a coercive effect.

Key elements of good corporate governance principles include honesty, trust and integrity, openness, performance orientation, responsibility and accountability, mutual respect, and commitment to the organisation. Commonly accepted principles of corporate governance include:

1. **Rights and equitable treatment of shareholders:** Organisations should respect the rights of shareholders and help shareholders to exercise those rights. They can help shareholders exercise their rights by effectively communicating information that is understandable and accessible and encouraging shareholders to participate in general meetings.
2. **Accountability:** Corporate governance has to be a top down approach. Chairman, board of directors and chief executives must fulfil their responsibilities to make corporate governance a reality in Indian industry. In companies with good governance, accountability is not just bottom up but also follows the reverse order. A departmental head is, for example, responsible for every decision taken on behalf of his department. Accountability also favours the objective of creating shareholder value.

3. **Disclosure and transparency:** Organisations should clarify and make publicly known the roles and responsibilities of board and management to provide shareholders with a level of accountability. They should also implement procedures to verify and safeguard the integrity of the company's financial reporting. Disclosure of material matters concerning the organisation should be timely and balanced to ensure that all investors have access to clear, factual information.

4. **Integrity and ethical behaviour:** Organisations should develop a code of conduct for their directors and executives that promotes ethical and responsible decision-making. It is important to understand though, that systematic reliance on integrity and ethics is bound to eventual failure.

5. **Interest of other stakeholders:** Organisations should recognise that they have legal and other obligations to all legitimate stakeholders.

6. **Role and responsibilities of the board:** The board needs a range of skills and understanding to be able to deal with various business issues and have the ability to review and challenge management performance. It needs to be of sufficient size and have an appropriate level of commitment to fulfil its responsibilities and duties. There are issues about the appropriate mix of executive and non-executive directors. The key roles of chairperson and CEO should not be shared.

7. **Transparency:** Transparency means accurate, adequate and timely disclosure of relevant information to the stakeholders. Without transparency, it is impossible to make any progress towards good governance. Business heads should realise that transparency also creates immense shareholder value. But many a times information-sharing is hindered under the excuse of confidentiality. There is need to move towards international standard in terms of disclosure of information by the corporate sector and through all this to develop a high level of public confidence in business.

   Once a company has public shareholding it is imperative that its commitment to financial transparency must be total. The company is a trustee of the investors' money and this responsibility in turn demands full disclosure. Corporations in India must learn to work with transparency and impeccable integrity as these are the essential ingredients to maximise their wealth and the wealth of the nation. Transparency and disclosure are the key pillars of corporate governance because they provide all the stakeholders with the information necessary to judge whether their interests are being taken care of.

ISSUES INVOLVING CORPORATE GOVERNANCE PRINCIPLES

1. **Mechanisms and controls:** Corporate governance mechanisms and controls are designed to reduce the inefficiencies that arise from moral hazard and adverse selection. For example, to monitor managers' behavior, an independent third party (the auditor) attests the accuracy of information provided by management to investors. An ideal control system should regulate both motivation and ability.
2. **Internal corporate governance controls:** Internal corporate governance controls, monitoring activities and then take corrective action taken to accomplish organisational goals.
3. **Monitoring by the board of directors:** The board of directors, with its legal authority to hire, fire and compensate top management, safeguards invested capital. Regular board meetings allow potential problems to be identified, discussed and avoided. Whilst non-executive directors are thought to be more independent, they may not always result in more effective corporate governance. Different board structures are optimal for different firms. Moreover, the ability of the board to monitor the firm's executives is a function of its access to information. Executive directors possess superior knowledge of the decision-making process and therefore evaluate top management on the basis of the quality of its decisions that lead to financial performance outcomes.
4. **Remuneration:** Performance-based remuneration is designed to relate some proportion of salary to individual performance. It may be in the form of cash or non-cash payments such as shares and share options, superannuation or other benefits. Such incentive schemes, however, are reactive in the sense that they provide no mechanism for preventing mistakes or opportunistic behaviour, and can elicit myopic behaviour.

APPOINTMENT OF DIRECTORS

There are four types of directors in a limited company:

1. Working directors.
2. Non-working directors but from the entrepreneurs' family.
3. Outside directors inducted for their expertise in some area connected with the firm's business, like advocates, chartered accountants and technical consultants.
4. Directors nominated by the lending financial institutions and banks.

Corporate governance should ensure that the decision-making process in the board is participatory in nature with the directors talking active part in the proceedings leading to decision-making. External directors must have a role in decision-making otherwise there is no purpose in appointing them. Most of these directors are placed on the board because of their talent in some field or the other related to the functioning of the firm; or they could be the nominees of the financial institutions and the banks who have financed the firm.

STEPS TO BE TAKEN IN GOVERNING CORPORATIONS

It is important to consider what is needed in governing the corporations in the 21st century India. The following steps need to be taken in this regard:

1. **Forward looking reporting:** The CEO has to keep himself always updated regarding the firm's operations and for that purpose he needs the support of his team members. These teams have to act according to the strategic plan given to them by the board of directors and then report to the board about the jobs done and the results achieved. Reports emanating from different levels in an organisation should reflect the results achieved, along with a futuristic view of the subject of the report. The report should not only point out the problems but also provide the possible solutions to these problems to be of use to the directors. The report forms should be developed to convey the critical points at a glance, before going into details. Reports become the basis for the CEO's decisions and wrong or half-baked reports will lead to incorrect decisions, detrimental to the organisation.
2. **Score-card approach:** Information should be provided in proper sequence for easy understanding and to save time. The scoreboard gives the salient features of the report at a glance.
3. **Measurements and controls:** Measurements and controls are required for sustained business success and to steer the firm in the right direction. Areas which cannot be measured, like motivation and energy levels, need special attention. HR Department should develop forms with digital approach to make measurement possible so that readers like the CEO understand the overall picture at a glance.
4. **Responsibility and accountability:** Responsibility and accountability towards stakeholders can never be overemphasised, as the firm must consider their interest as foremost. Any neglect of the stakeholders can become fatal to the firm.
5. **Transparency of operations:** Transparency of operations, especially with the stakeholders, will make the functioning smooth and goals achievable with

team effort. The decision-making process should involve the relevant stakeholders to get their views. The problems faced by the CEO emerge from the secrecy maintained, which ultimately leads to distrust among employees as they get disillusioned and as a result demotivated too!

6. **Trust with teams:** The CEO has to create an aura of *trust within the team both intra- and inter-teams* and this can be easily achieved by setting examples of his own trustworthy conduct. The CEO has to be a good role model as the employees look up to him with respect to their own conduct in the organisation. As the CEO shows leadership qualities he will be creating more leaders from among his followers. In turn these leaders will be ready to become role models for their followers and thus the chain keeps moving.
7. **Fairness:** As the board of directors has to deal with a number of stakeholders, it must maintain fairness and a sense of justice in its dealings. This would encourage the stakeholders to take active interest in the firm for its betterment.

Corporate governance has succeeded in attracting a good deal of public interest because of its importance to the economic health of corporations and the welfare of society, in general. There is also an overbearing influence on the country's economy connected to the way firms are managed in the country. The GDP, per capita income, GNP and a succession of other economic parameters get a direct impact of the corporate governance in an overall coverage in the country. As can be seen, better corporate performance means bigger pay packets, increase in income tax, bonuses, overall economic sustained growth of the country.

ETHICAL BUSINESS

There is a need to adhere to ethical business practices. There is a need to have transparency in respect of board of directors' information system to shareholders and of distancing and yet a cooperative relationship between the owners and the managers. The managers are given the authority with accountability and yet the directors should have their control points to know about the operations of the firm.

The process of integration of India into the world economy would enable the Indian industry to act according to standard of international rules rather than continue with the present local practices. It would ensure that promoters of a company remain accountable and responsive to shareholders, and stakeholders. Corporate governance is a must as a part of strategic management for survival, consolidation and growth. Corporate governance helps to enhance board performance by the contributions of professionally qualified and experienced non-executive directors and board committees.

The following are the ideas behind corporate governance:

1. Adequate information to stakeholders
2. Focused approach

3. Streamlined delegation
4. Professional management

These would result in maximising the shareholder value and in protecting the interest of other stakeholders.

CODE OF BEST PRACTICE IN U.K.

The *Adrian Cadbury Report* in U.K. gave a Code of Best Practice, which was to serve as a guideline to those public companies, which wanted, on voluntary basis, higher standards of corporate governance. These are as follows:

- In every firm there should be a separate CEO and chairman of the board of directors. When the same person carries on with the two roles, that of the CEO and the chairperson of the board, it provides too much authority with little check on such power with the person. (The old saying that, '*power corrupts and absolute power corrupts absolutely*' holds good in corporate governance also.)
- It should be the function of the chairman to manage the affairs of the board, including the hiring and firing of the CEO of a company when necessary. The CEO on the other hand is responsible for the day-to-day management of the organisation.
- Day-to-day management consists of planning, organising and the implementation of the strategies approved by the board. The chairman should thus be responsible for setting the goals and objectives of the CEO and of monitoring the CEO's performance in the implementation of the organisation's strategy. If the chairman and the CEO are one and the same person, this level of supervision is lost, bringing with it higher risks to the organisation. Besides, the non-executive directors should be independent, unbound by the fetters of the board's hierarchy.
- It is in the interests of the organisation to have *non-executive directors* bringing to the board their experience and expertise and not be part of the board as only figureheads or rubber stamps for endorsing the chairman's decisions. The rationale is that these experienced *past-time directors* are already in senior executive positions with other companies, and they would supplement the efforts of the full-time executive directors on the board. Their involvement would provide a validity check in a manner in which the executive directors seek to influence strategic decisions at the board level.

Yet, if these non-executive directors are to fulfil their role then they must be able to act independently and in the best interests of the organisation on whose board they sit. This deals with two problems many boards face in the appointment of non-executive directors. On the one hand there is a situation, where a majority or significant shareholders appoint the non-executive director or directors and these individuals often perceive their role on the board merely as an added opportunity to protect the interests of their employer by becoming their mouthpiece or their 'yes men'. They are more concerned with what is in the best interests of their employer rather with the best interests of the organisation.

The other situation is where the chairman on the basis of personal acquaintance or reciprocal arrangements appoints the non-executive directors. Too often arrangements are made whereby one chairman appoints another firm's chairman on the board as a director, on the understanding that that chairman would reciprocate and have him or her appointed to their own board. This often leads to situations in which conflicts of interest arise, as the loyalties of such non-executive directors are not close enough to the interests of the organisation. The risk in getting only the '*yes persons*' on the board as non-executive directors is of loss of people with divergent and at times lateral thinking, the persons who can play the role of the devil's advocate to give the board a different facet of the problem, so that they take decisions with full comprehensive information base and such decision would not usually go wrong. Non-executive directors should have sufficient representation to carry weight at the board meetings.

The emphasis in the code is on creating a situation in which the chairman of the board cannot ignore the contributions of the non-executive directors even if these prove to be uncomfortable or inconvenient to him. To this effect the position of the non-executive directors must be strong enough to ensure that they do not end up as a powerless minority forced to rubber-stamp the board decisions. On the contrary, the scope is to ensure that they serve as a significant force on the board whose support is crucial to any major initiative, thereby acting as a check on the executive directors on the board who will generally support each other better on the basis their stronger working relationships rather on the rationale of the issues involved. The board meetings cover mainly the important strategic initiatives and unless a coordinated view is taken the CEO's tasks of a day-to-day operations could get lopsided where the CEO could start witch-hunting for throwing out people not falling in line with his personal view, ignoring the view of the board.

Board monitoring committees should be established to deal with specific areas such as the setting of director remuneration. These should consist primarily of non-executive directors who would act as monitors and independent judges of management.

CORPORATE GOVERNANCE IN INDIA

In India, corporate governance has assumed significance and urgency mainly due to the changing profile of corporate ownerships, preferential allotment of shares of promoters, increasing flow of foreign capital and dismantling of controls that hitherto provided protective cover to poorly managed corporates. The main issues in the area of corporate governance in India are as follows:

1. **Role of board of directors:** An independent and effective board is essential for good corporate governance. The overall responsibility of the board is to guide the management and to oversee the operations of the company to subserve the interests of stakeholders.The board is expected to ensure that the management complies with the legal and ethical standards. Board is also responsible for ensuring information and control systems which can guide the top management in meeting the corporate objectives.
2. **Composition of the board:** The Cadbury committee suggested that non-executive directors can play a crucial role in corporate governance. They can exercise independent judgement in matters of corporate practices, performance and resource management and monitoring. The committee suggested that the non-executive directors should be selected through a formal process and the board as a whole should decide their nomination. They should be appointed for a specific term and re-appointment should not be automatic.

   Directors nominated by the financial institutions in the boards of assisted companies have failed to exercise effective controls due to several reasons. *Kumar Mangalam Birla Committee* (appointed by SEBI) recommended that nominee directors should be done away with for fear of insider trading. But it would be better to streamline the system by removing its deficiencies rather than discarding the system altogether. The solution lies in tightening the insider trading regulations and creating an institution of independent directors from which financial institutions can nominate directors.
3. **Audit committee:** Section 292-A of the Companies Act in 1956 provided that all public limited companies with a paid-up capital of Rs. 5 crore and above must establish audit committees consisting of independent non-executive directors. Audit committee can improve the quality of financial reporting by reviewing the financial statements, creating a climate of discipline and control and reducing the opportunity for fraud. It can provide communication link with external auditor and strengthen the position of the internal audit function. There may be more than one audit committee with specified role in specific areas. An audit committee may include non-executive directors, auditors, the company secretary or any senior manager.

CORPORATE GOVERNANCE STRUCTURE AT ITC

- Strategic supervision by the board of directors.
- Strategic management by the corporate management committee.
- Executive management by the divisional management committee.

The three-tier structure ensures that strategic supervision on behalf of shareholders being free from the task of the strategic management, can be conducted by the board with objectivity thereby sharpening accounting of the management.

4. **Shareholders' committee:** SEBI's code of corporate governance provides for constitution of shareholders' committee under the chairmanship of a non-executive director to ensure that the grievances of shareholders are properly received and solved to the satisfaction of shareholders.

   In order to improve the quality of corporate governance, the Companies Act, enlarged the items to be transacted at board meetings, provisioned for constitution of Audit Committee and Directors' Responsibility Statement in the Directors, Report. In 1998, Confederation of Indian Industry (CII) appointed a committee on corporate governance under the chairmanship of *Shri Rahul Bajaj*.

J.J. Irani Panel for Allowing Investors to Approach Consumer Courts

- Says shares and securities are legally deemed to be good
- Favours letting investors file class action suits against wrong-doing promoters and managers
- Wants ombudsman for capital market set up by SEBI to be strengthened
- No cap on number of subsidiaries, directors
- Limited liability partnership to be allowed
- Companies can issue loans to directors
- Companies can issue perpetual/longer duration preference shares
- Nidhi companies to come under RBI regulation
- Financial statements to be signed by MD, CEO, CFO, company secretary
- New liquidation regime with test for insolvency

CII CODE OF CORPORATE GOVERNANCE

The Confederation of Indian Industry issued in 1997 a comprehensive code titled ***"Desirable Corporate Governance-A Code"***. The salient features of the code are given below:

1. The key to good corporate governance is a well-functioning board of directors. The board should have a core group of excellent, professionally acclaimed *non-executive directors* who understand their dual role of appreciating the

issues put forward by management and of honestly discharging their fiduciary responsibilities towards the company's shareholders as well as creditors.

2. A single-tier board can ensure desirable corporate governance. However, the *full board should meet a minimum of six times a year*, preferably at an interval of two months and each meeting should have agenda items that require at least half a day's discussion.

3. Any listed company with a turnover of Rs. 1 crore and above should have professionally competent and acclaimed non-executive directors. They should *constitute at least 50 per cent of the board* if the chairman and managing director is the same person and 30 per cent in other cases.

4. No single person should hold directorship in *more than 10 companies at a time.*

5. Non-executive directors must be active with clearly defined responsibilities and must have knowledge of various company laws and financial statements.

6. Non-executive directors should be paid *commission* and offered *stock options* for their professional inputs in addition to their *sitting fees.*

7. Directors who have *not been present for at least 50 per cent of the board meetings* should not be re-appointed,

8. All key Information must be placed before the board of directors.

9. An *audit committee* comprising at least *three non-executive directors* should be constituted and given access to all financial information.

10. Listed public companies should disclose *Additional Shareholders Information* in the annual report on the monthly average share prices, value added, financial performance of divisions and segments.

11. *Major Indian Stock Exchanges should gradually insist upon a compliance certificate*, signed by the CEO and CFO which clearly states that:

    (a) The management is responsible for the preparation, integrity and fair presentation of the financial statements and other information in the Annual report, and which also suggest that the company will continue in business in the course of the following year.

    (b) The accounting policies and principles conform to standard practice, and where they do not, full disclosure has been made of any material departure.

    (c) The board has overseen the company's system of internal accounting and administrative control systems either through its Audit Committee for companies with a turnover of Rs. 100 crore or paid-up capital of Rs. 20 crore, whichever is less or directly.

12. The quality and quantity of disclosure for any domestic issue should be the same as required for GDR issues.
13. The government must allow for greater funding to the corporate sector against the security of shares and other papers.
14. Financial institutions should *eliminate nominee directors* except in the event of serious and systematic debt default, and in case of the debtor company not providing six monthly or quarterly operational data to the financial institutions concerned.
15. In case a *company obtains multiple credit ratings*, all the ratings should be disclosed with companies explaining their significance.
16. *Companies that default on fixed deposits* should not be permitted to accept further deposits, make inter-corporate loans or investments and declare dividend until the default is made good.

At the best and the brightest multinationals in India, you've now got a hotline or toll-free number to report any irregularity direct to board. Take Johnson & Johnson, Heinz, GE, Bayer, Xerox, Castrol, Citibank, etc., Indian employees are now free to blow the whistle.

SEBI CODE OF CORPORATE GOVERNANCE

(Issued by the Securities and Exchanges Board of India (SEBI), Secondary Market Department dated 21.2.2000.)

SEBI had constituted a committee on corporate governance under the chairmanship of Kumar Mangalam Birla, member, SEBI board, to promote and raise the standard of Corporate Governance in respect of listed companies. The SEBI Board in its meeting held on January 25, 2000 considered the recommendations of the committee and decided to make the amendments to the listing agreement. Pursuance of the decision of the board, it is advised that a new clause, namely *Clause 49* be incorporated in the listing agreement as under:

I. Board of Directors

1. The company agrees that the board of directors of the company shall have an *optimum combination of executive and non-executive* directors with not less than fifty per cent of the board of directors comprising of non-executive directors. The number of independent directors would depend on whether the chairman is executive or non-executive. In case of a non-executive chairman, at least one-third of board should comprise of independent directors and in case of an executive chairman, at least half of board should comprise of independent directors.

Explanation: For the purpose of this clause of expression ***independent directors*** means directors who apart from receiving director's remuneration, do not have any other material pecuniary relationship or transactions with the company, its promoters, its management or its subsidiaries, which in judgement of the board may affect independence or judgement of the director.

2. The company agrees that all pecuniary relationship or transactions of the non-executive directors, *viz-a-viz*, the company should be disclosed in the Annual Report.

II. Audit Committee

1. The company agrees that a qualified and independent audit committee shall be set up and that:

   (a) The audit committee shall have minimum three members, all being non-executive directors, with the majority of them being independent, and with at least one director having financial and accounting knowledge;

   (b) The chairman of the committee shall be an independent director;

   (c) The chairman shall be present at Annual General Meeting to answer shareholders' queries.

   (d) The audit committee should invite such of the executives, as it considers appropriate (and particularly the head of the finance function) to be present at the meetings of the committee, but on occasions it may also meet without the presence of any executives of the company. The finance director, head of internal audit and when required, a representative of the external auditor shall be present as invitees for the meetings of the audit committee;

   (e) The company secretary shall act as the secretary to the committee.

2. The audit committee shall meet at least thrice a year. The meeting shall be held before finalisation of annual accounts and one every six months. The quorum shall be either two members or one-third of the members of the audit committee, whichever is higher and minimum of two independent directors.

3. The audit committee shall have *powers* which should include the following:

   (a) To investigate any activity within its terms of reference.

   (b) To seek information from any employee.

   (c) To obtain outside legal or other professional advice.

   (d) To secure attendance of outsiders with relevant expertise, if it considers necessary.

4. The company agrees that the *role of the audit committee* shall include the following:

   (a) Oversight of the company's financial reporting process and the disclosure of its financial information to ensure that the financial statement is correct, sufficient and credible.

   (b) Recommending the appointment and removal of external auditor, fixation of audit fee and also approval for payment for any other services.

   (c) Reviewing with management the annual financial statements before submission to the board, focusing primarily on:

   - Any changes on accounting policies and practices.
   - Major accounting entries based on exercise of judgement by management.
   - Qualifications in draft audit report.
   - Significant adjustments arising out of audit.
   - The going concern assumption.
   - Compliance with accounting standards.
   - Compliance with stock exchange and legal requirements concerning financial statements.
   - Any related party transactions, i.e., transactions of the company of material nature, with promoters or the management, their subsidiaries or relatives, etc., that may have potential conflict with the interests of company at large.

   (d) Reviewing with management, external and internal auditors, the adequacy of internal control systems.

   (e) Reviewing the adequacy of internal audit function, including the structure of the internal audit department, staffing and seniority of the official heading the department, reporting structure, coverage and frequency of internal audit.

   (f) Discussing with internal auditors any significant findings and follow-up thereon.

   (g) Reviewing the findings of any internal investigations by the internal auditors into matter where there is suspected fraud or irregularity or a failure of internal control systems of a material nature and reporting the matter to the board.

   (h) Discussing with external auditors before the audit commences, nature and scope of audit as well as have post-audit discussion to ascertain any area of concern.

(i) Reviewing the company's financial and risk management policies.

(j) To look into the reasons for substantial defaults in the payment to the depositors, debentureholders, shareholders (in case of non-payment of declared dividends) and creditors.

5. If the company has set up an audit committee pursuant to provision of the Company Act, the company agrees that the said audit committee shall have such additional functions/features as it contains in the listing agreement.

III. Remuneration of Directors

1. The company agrees that the remuneration of non-executive directors shall be decided by the board of directors.
2. The company further agrees that the following disclosures on the remuneration of directors shall be made in the section on the corporate governance of the Annual Report.
   - All elements of remuneration package of all the directors, i.e., salary, benefits, bonuses, stock options, pension, etc.
   - Details of fixed component and performance linked incentives, along with the performance criteria.
   - Service contracts, notice period, severance fees.
   - Stock option details, if any, and whether issued at a discount as well as the period over which accrued and over which exercisable.

IV. Board Procedure

1. The company agrees that the board meeting shall be held at least four times a year, with a maximum time gap of four months between any two meetings. The minimum information to be made available to the board is given in Annexure-I.
2. The company further agrees that a director shall not be a member in more than 10 committees or act as chairman of more than five committees across all companies in which he is a director. Furthermore, it should be a mandatory annual requirement for every director to inform the company about the committee positions he occupies in other companies and notify changes as and when they take place.

V. Management

1. The company agrees that as part of the directors' report or as an addition thereto, ***a Management Discussion and Analysis Report*** should form part of the annual report to the shareholders. This management discussion and analysis should include discussion on the following matters within the limits set by the company's competitive position:

(a) Industry structure and developments.

(b) Opportunities and threats.

(c) Segment-wise or product-wise performance.

(d) Outlook.

(e) Risks and concerns.

(f) Internal control systems and their adequacy.

(g) Discussion on financial performance with respect to operational performance.

(h) Material developments in Human Resource/Industrial Relations front, including number of people employed.

2. Disclosures must be made by the management to the board relating to all material, financial and commercial transactions, where they have personal interest, that may have a potential conflict with the interest of the company at large (e.g., dealing in company shares, commercial dealings with bodies, which have shareholding of management and their relatives, etc.).

VI. Shareholders

1. The company agrees that in case of the appointment of a new director or reappointment of a director the shareholders must be provided with the following information:

   (a) A brief resume of the director;

   (b) Nature of his expertise in specific functional areas; and

   (c) Names of companies in which the person also holds the directorship and the membership of committees of the board.

2. The company further agrees that information like quarterly results, presentation made by companies to analysts shall be put on company's website, or shall be sent in such a form so as to enable the stock exchange on which the company is listed to put in on its own website.

3. The company further agrees that a board committee under the chairmanship of a non-executive director shall be formed to specifically look into the redressing of shareholder and investors' complaints like transfer of shares, non-receipt of balance sheet, non-receipt of declared dividends, etc. This Committee shall be designated as ***shareholders/investors grievance committee***.

4. The company further agrees that to expedite the process of share transfer the board of the company shall delegate the power of share transfer to an officer or a committee or to the registrar and share transfer agents. The delegated authority shall attend to share transfer formalities at least once in a fortnight.

VII. Report on Corporate Governance

The company agrees that there shall be a separate section on corporate governance in the annual reports of company, with a detailed ***compliance report on corporate governance***. Non-compliance of any mandatory requirements, i.e., which is part of the listing agreement with reasons thereof and the extent to which the non-mandatory requirements have been adopted should be specifically highlighted.

VIII. Compliance

The company agrees that it shall obtain a ***certificate from the auditors of the company regarding compliance of conditions of corporate governance*** as stipulated in this clause and annex the certificate with the directors' report, which is sent annually to all the shareholders of the company. The same certificate shall also be sent to the stock exchanges along with the annual returns filed by the company.

Schedule of Implementation

The above amendments to the listing agreement have to be implemented as per schedule of implementation given below:

- By all entities seeking listing for the first time, at the time of listing.
- Within financial year 2000-01, but not later than March 31, 2001 by all entitles, which are included either in Group A of the BSE or in S&P CNX Nifty Index as on January 1, 2000. However, to comply with the recommendations, these companies may have to begin the process of implementation as early as possible.
- Within financial year 2001-02, but not later than March 31, 2002 by all the entities, which are presently listed, with paid-up share capital of Rs. 10 crore and above, or net worth of Rs. 25 crore or more any time in the history of the company.
- Within financial year 2002-03, but not later than March 31, 2003, by all the entities, which are presently listed, with paid-up share capital of Rs. 3 crore and above.
- As regards the non-mandatory requirements given in Annexure-3, they shall be implemented as per the discretion of the company. However, the disclosures of the adoption/non-adoption of the non-mandatory requirements shall be made in the section on corporate governance of the Annual Report.

Annual Reports of leading companies like Infosys, Bajaj Auto, Reliance, ICICI, HDFC, contain detailed information on corporate governance practices. But the overall picture of corporate sector in India in the area of corporate governance is quite dismal. According to Mr. Tarun Das, Director General of CII, nearly 70 per cent of Indian companies are not committed to the principles of corporate governance.

Corporate governance is a mindset and a cultural revolution is needed to develop this mindset in Indian companies. A strategic collaboration between industry, SEBI, government, credit rating agencies and stock exchanges is required to develop the required business culture. Laws and regulations can only facilitate and encourage shareholders to exercise their rights. Shareholders' activitism with the help of the media is necessary because all company boards are not likely to improve governance on their own. The scope of statutory audit is limited to reporting on whether the accounts have been properly prepared as at certain date. Institutional shareholders should play a more active role. Management education system should impart knowledge of ethics to encourage fair play on the part of managers. Thus, the system of corporate governance in India requires drastic reforms.

QUESTIONS

Objective Type Questions

I. Fill up the Blanks

1. SEBI issued code of Corporate Governance in year ________.
2. Confederation of Indian Industry (CII) appointed a committee on Corporate Governance under the chairmanship of ________.
3. The Cadbury committee suggested that ________ directors can play a crucial role in Corporate Governance.
4. Code of Best Practice U.K. is based on the ________ Report.

[*Answers:* (1) 2000; (2) Rahul Bajaj; (3) Non executive; (4) Adrian Cadbury]

II. State the following True or False

1. Milton Friedman's concept of Corporate Governance is based on the economic concept of market value maximisation through profit maximisation.
2. Corporate Governance is about promoting corporate fairness, transparency and accountability.
3. Shareholders' activism and shareholder democracy continue to remain myths in India.
4. Corporate governance is not a voluntary ethical code of corporate business.

[*Answers:* True: (1), (2), (3); False: (4)]

Review Questions

1. Define corporate governance.
2. Enumerate need for corporate governance.
3. What is code of corporate governance?
4. How does corporate governance help to discharge social responsibilities of business?
5. What is the role of board of directors in corporate governance?
6. What is an Audit Committee? Explain the role of non-executive directors in it.
7. What is corporate governance? Explain its need and importance in the Indian context.
8. Discuss the fundamental principles of corporate governance.
9. Define corporate governance. What are the principles of corporate governance?
10. Explain the present position corporate governance in India.
11. Describe the main provisions of CII code of corporate governance.
12. Explain the salient features of SEBI code on corporate governance.
13. What are the powers of Audit Committee?
14. Explain the role of audit committee in corporate goverance.

◈◈◈

CHAPTER 11

Whistle-blowing

No topic in corporate business ethics is more controversial than whistle-blowing. A host of issues are involved.

- When is whistle-blowing morally permissible?
- Is it ever morally obligatory?
- To what extent, if any, do corporate business have a right to whistle-blow, and when is doing so immoral and imprudent?
- When is whistle-blowing an act of disloyalty to an organization, and could it sometimes be consistent with company loyalty–even an expression of it?
- Should it sometimes be viewed as an act of moral heroism that goes beyond the call of duty?
- What procedures ought to be followed in blowing the whistle?

Before considering these questions we need to define "whistle-blowing."

DEFINITION OF WHISTLE-BLOWING

In a wide sense, whistle-blowing is alerting relevant persons to some moral or legal corruption, where "relevant persons" are those in a position to act in response, if only by registering protest. In this sense, an individual need not be a member of an organization in order to blow the whistle on it. Journalists, politicians, and consumer groups may learn of corruption in organizations they do not work for and blow the whistle on them by publishing articles or informing regulatory agencies. Our main interest in this section, however, will be in whistle-blowing by present and former employees.

In a narrower sense, whistle-blowing is sometimes defined as making public accusations about misconduct by one's organization. Yet not all whistle-blowing involves public statements outside the organization. Sometimes the whistle is blown within the organization, whether in bypassing approved organizational channels or by going against the desires of one's supervisor or others.

Features of Whistle-Blowing

As we shall define it, whistle-blowing occurs when an employee or former employee conveys information about a significant moral problem outside approved organizational channels (or against strong pressure) to someone in a position to take action on the problem. There are four main features of whistle-blowing that characterize the cases of interest here.

1. Act of Disclosure: Information is intentionally conveyed outside approved organizational channels or in situations where the person conveying it is under pressure from supervisors or others not to do so.

2. Topic: The information concerns what the person believes is a significant moral problem for the organization (or an organization with which the company does business). Examples of significant problems are criminal behaviour, unethical policies or practices, injustices to workers within the organization, and serious threats to public safety and well-being.

3. Agent: The person disclosing the information is an employee or former employee (or someone else closely associated with the organization).

4. Recipient: The information is conveyed to a person or organization in a position to act on the problem (as opposed, for example, to telling it to a relative or friend who is in no position to do anything). The "action" may consist in remedying or merely protesting the problem, and the recipient may in fact decide not to act on the information received. Typically, though not always, the information being revealed is new or not fully known to the person or group it is sent to.

Using this definition, we will speak of *external whistle-blowing* when the information is passed outside the organization. *Internal whistle-blowing* occurs when the information is conveyed to someone within the organization (but outside approved channels or against pressures to remain silent).

The definition also allows us to distinguish between open and anonymous whistle-blowing. In *open whistle-blowing* individuals openly reveal their identity as they convey the information. *Anonymous whistle-blowing,* by contrast, involves concealing one's identity. There are also overlapping cases that are partly open and partly anonymous, such as when individuals acknowledge their identities to a journalist but insist their names be withheld from anyone else.

Persuasive Definitions of Whistle-Blowing: Notice that the above definition does not mention the motives involved in the whistle-blowing, and hence, avoids assumptions about whether those motives are good or bad. Nor does it assume that the whistle-blower is correct in believing there is a serious moral problem. In general, it leaves open the question of whether whistle-blowing is justified. As we shall suggest in a moment, sometimes it is and sometimes it is not.

By contrast, some writers have packed into their definitions of whistle-blowing much of their own particular value perspectives concerning it. In doing so they have created persuasive or prescriptive definitions that sometimes blur the issues, consider, for example, the following two proposals:

> "Whistle-blowing"– the act of a man or woman who, believing that the public interest overrides the interest of the organization he (or she) serves, publicly "blows the whistle" if the organization is involved in corrupt, illegal, fraudulent, or harmful activity
>
> Some of the enemies of business now encourage an employee to be disloyal to the enterprise. They want to create suspicion and disharmony and pry into the proprietary interests of the business, However, this is labelled-industrial espionage, whistle-blowing or professional responsibility–it is another tactic for spreading disunity and creating conflict.

The first definition was set forth by Ralph Nader at the beginning of a book that evaluates whistle-blowing positively. Notice that the definition assumes that whistle-blowing springs from an admirable motive: the belief that one is acting on behalf of the higher of two duties. It also assumes that whistle-blowers hold accurate views about corporate wrongdoing. Thus, in two ways it automatically implies a favourable general attitude toward whistle-blowers.

The second passage was written by James M. Roche while he was chairman of the board of General Motors Corporation. It builds into whistle-blowing the motives of disloyalty and a malicious desire to harm the organization.

Whistle blowers often pay a high price for their acts of dissent. Retaliation is common and can take many forms:

- From poor evaluations and demotion to outright dismissal
- Blacklist whistle-blowers; they cannot obtain jobs in the same industry
- Suffer career disruption; financial hardship resulting from job dislocation and legal expenses
- Severe emotional strain on whistle-blowers and their families as co-workers, friends and neighbours turn against them.

The questions are:

(i) Should people really be encouraged to blow the whistle?

(ii) Is the exposure of corruption and mismanagement in government and industry by this method, the best way to correct these faults?

(iii) Are there more effective ways to deal with them without requiring individuals to make heroic personal sacrifices?

(iv) Should whistle-blowers be protected? How can this best be done?

- Whistle-blowing is an action that takes place within an organisation.
- Whistle-blowing can be done only by a member/ex-member of an organisation.

Not Whistle-blowing

- When a witness of a crime notifies the police and testifies in court
- For a reporter who uncovers some illegal practices in a corporation to expose it in print

In these cases, both the witness and the reporter have incrementing information. They are not under any obligation that prevents them from making it public.

Whistle-blowing occurs when an employee reports the organization to an outside agency for what the employee believes is an illegal or unethical practice. In the past, these employees were often subjected to severe punishment for doing what they believed was right. For instance, several years ago, an employee in General Electric's nuclear fuel facility operation complained that "radioactive spills in the work setting were not properly cleaned up." As the employee attempted to document her case, she was subjected to personnel actions by the company. The company believed that the employee, instead of leaving the "mess" for all to see, should have cleaned it up. This employee was ultimately terminated, and unfortunately no federal law protected her.

Although federal legislation is lacking, state laws may be available in some jurisdictions. However, the extent of these laws, and how much protection they afford, differ greatly. Nonetheless, many firms have voluntarily adopted policies to permit employees to identify problem areas. The thrust of these policies is to have an established procedure whereby employees can safely raise these concerns and the company can take correct action. A suggested whistle-blower policy is presented in below:

TEN STEPS TO AN EFFECTIVE WHISTLE-BLOWING POLICY

1. Develop the policy in written form.
2. Seek input from top management in developing the policy, and obtain their approval for the finished work.
3. Communicate the policy to employees using multiple media. Inclusion in the employee handbook is not sufficient. Active communication efforts such as ethics training, departmental meetings and employee seminars will increase awareness of the policy and highlight the company's commitment to ethical behaviour.

4. Provide a reporting procedure for employees that does not require them to go to their supervisor fits instead, designate a specific officer individual to hear initial employee complaints. Streamline the process and cut the red tape make an easy for the employees to use the procedure.
5. Make it possible for employees to report anonymously at least initially.
6. Guarantee employees who report suspected wrongdoing in good faith that they will be protected from retaliation from any member of the organization. Make this guarantee suck.
7. Develop a formal investigative process and communicate to employees exactly how their reports win be handled. Use this process to investigate all reported wrongdoings.
8. If the investigation reveals that the employees suspicions are accurate take prompt action to correct the wrongdoing. Employees will quickly lose confidence in the policy if disclosed wrongdoing is allowed to continue. Whatever the outcome of the investigation, communicate it quickly to the whistle-blowing employee.
9. Provide an appeals process for employees dissatisfied with the outcome of the initial investigation. Provide an advocate (probably from HRM) to assist the employee who wishes to appeal an unfavourable outcome.
10. Finally, a successful whistle-blowing policy requires more than a written procedure. It requires a commitment from the organization, from top management down. This commitment must be to create an ethical work environment.

Commonsense Procedures

It is clear that a decision to whistle-blow, whether within or outside an organization, is a serious matter that deserves careful reflection. And there are several rules of practical advice and common sense that should be heeded before taking this action.

1. Except for extremely rare emergencies, always try working first through normal organizational channels. Get to know both the formal and informal (unwritten) rules for making appeals within the organization.
2. Be prompt in expressing objections. Waiting too long may create the appearance of plotting for your advantage and seeking to embarrass a supervisor.
3. Proceed in a tactful, low-key manner. Be considerate of the feelings of others involved. Always keep focused on the issues themselves, avoiding any personal criticisms that might create antagonism and deflect attention from solving those issues.
4. As much as possible, keep supervisors informed of your actions, both through informal discussion and formal memorandums.

5. Be accurate in your observations and claims, and keep formal records documenting relevant events.
6. Consult colleagues for advice-avoid isolation.
7. Before going outside the organization, consult the ethics committee of your professional society.
8. Consult a lawyer concerning potential legal liabilities.

THE RIGHT TO WHISTLE-BLOW

Whistle-blowers who proceed responsibly and take special care to document their views are fulfilling their obligations to protect and serve the public. To this extent they have a professional moral right to whistle-blow. This important right is a restricted one, however, and its appropriate extent can vary depending on a number of factors.

Engineers working for the government have as public servants an especially strong charge to protect the public. It is appropriate that they have correspondingly strong rights to whistle-blow in the public interest. That right is limited by legitimate needs to keep some information confidential. But not all information stamped "classified" is legitimately confidential. There have been many instances where government corruption has been hidden under claims of confidentiality. The electronic surveillance involved in Watergate is but one example. Moreover, even where legitimate confidentiality is involved, the public interest served by whistle-blowing may be of even greater importance.

Engineers working in the private sector also have obligations to the public, especially those based on public's right to make informed decisions about the use of technological products. Thus, they also have a professional right to whistle-blow when such action is justified by the appropriate conditions. And we, along with the observers noted above, hope and believe that the courts and professional organizations will continue to expand the legal and institutional recognition and protection of this right.

QUESTIONS

Objective Type Questions

I. Fill up the Blanks

1. Whistle-blowing occurs when an employee makes ________ about the misconduct one's organisation.
2. When the information about misconduct or illegality is passed outside the organisation it is called ________ whistle-blowing.

3. ________ whistle-blowing occurs when the information is conveyed to someone within the organisation.

4. ________ whistle-blowing involves concealing one's identity.

[Answers: (1) Public accusations; (2) external; (3) internal; (4) Anonymous]

II. State the following True or False

1. Whistle-blowing occurs when a witness of a crime notifies the police and testifies in a count.
2. If the person disclosing the information about the organisational misconduct is former employee, he is not a whistle-blower.
3. Before whistle-blowing, consult a lawyer concerning potential legal formalities and consequences.
4. Organisation should develop the policy of whistle-blowing in written form.

[*Answers:* True: (3), (4); False: (1), (2)]

Review Questions

1. What is meant by whistle-blowing?
2. What are the different types of whistle-blowing?
3. What are the main features of whistle-blowing?
4. Explain the steps or procedures to an effective whistle-blowing policy.
5. Corporate India now wakes up to whistle-blowing insurance. Comment.

◈◈◈

CHAPTER 12

Accounts, Audit and Investigation

BOOKS OF ACCOUNT

Section 209 of the Companies Act requires every company to keep at its registered office proper books of account with or financial books respect to—(a) all sums of money received and expended by the company and the matter in respect of which the receipt and expenditure take place; (b) all sales and purchases of goods by the company; (c) the assets and liabilities of the company; and (d) in the case of a company engaged in production, processing, manufacturing or mining activities, such particulars relating to utilisation of material or labour or to other items of cost as may be prescribed, if such class of companies is required by the Central Government to include such particulars in the books of account.

Statutory Books

In addition to the books of account or financial books to be maintained by every company under Section 209, every limited company must maintain the following statutory books: (1) Register of members, (2) Index of members, (3) Annual Return to be made by a company having a share capital, (4) Minute books—directors meetings and of general meetings, (5) Register of directors and managers, (6) Register of contracts in which directors are interested, (7) Register of charges, (8) Register of debenture-holders with index, (9) Register of director's shareholdings, (10) Register of investments not held in company's name, (11) Director's attendance book, (12) Register of loans to companies under the same management, (13) Register of investments in the shares of other companies.

Statistical Books

In addition to statutory books, there are many other books which are required to be maintained for the proper and efficient running of a company. These books are not only found to be desirable but often indispensable in practice. Some of the important statistical or non-statutory books are as follows: 1. Share application and allotment book, 2. Share call book, 3. Register of share warrants, 4. Register of share certificates, 5. Register of share transfers, 6. Register of lost share certificates, 7. Register of balance tickets issued, 8. Register of transfers certified, 9. Agenda book, 10. Register of lists of dividends, 11. Dividend mandate register, 12. Register of debenture interest, 13. Register of documents sealed, 14. Register of powers of attorney, 15. Register of probates, 16. Register of directors' attendance.

Annual Accounts and Balance Sheet

The annual accounts of a company consist of two statements:, namely the profit and loss account and the balance sheet. In the case of a non-trading company, an income and expenditure account is prepared instead of a profit and loss account. A balance sheet is a formal arrangement of facts and figures showing the total value of assets owned and the total amount of liabilities owed by a business on a particular date or at the end of a particular period. It is also known as a statement of assets and Liabilities.

Authentication of Balance Sheet and Profit and Loss Account: Every balance sheet and profit and loss account of a company shall be signed on behalf of the board by the manager or secretary, if any, and not less than two directors of the company. One of the directors, who signs, must be a managing director where there is one. *(Section 215).*

Profit and Loss A/C and Auditors' Report to be attached to Balance Sheet: The profit and loss account shall be annexed to the balance sheet. The auditor's report including the auditors' separate, special or supplementary report, if any is also to be attached to the balance sheet. *(Section 216).*

Board's Report. (Section 217): There must be attached with every balance sheet a report by its board of directors. The report shall deal with the following:

(a) The state of the company's affairs.

(b) The amounts, if any, which it proposes to carry to any reserves in the balance sheet.

(c) The amount which it recommends for payment as dividend.

(d) Material changes and commitments, if any, affecting the financial position of the company which have occurred between the end of the financial year to which the balance sheet relates and the date of the report. (Section 217(1)).

The board's report shall also deal with any changes which have occurred during the financial year; (a) in the nature of the company's business; (b) in the company's subsidiaries or in the nature of the business carried on by them; and (c) generally in the classes of business in which the company has interest (Section 217(2)).

AUDITORS

A person shall not be qualified for appointment as auditor of a company unless he is a chartered accountant within the meaning of the Chartered Accountants Act, 1949. A firm of chartered accountants can also be appointed as an auditor of the company in its firm's name. In such a case any partner so practising may act in the name of the firm.

The following *persons shall not be qualified for appointment as the auditor* of a company: (1) A body corporate, (2) An officer or employee of company, (3) A person who is a partner or who is in the employment of an officer or employee of the company, (4) A person who is indebted to the company for an amount exceeding Rs. 1000, (5) A person who has given any guarantee or security in connection with the indebtedness of any third person to the company for an amount exceeding Rs. 1,000, (Section 226(3)).

Appointment of Auditors: The *first auditor(s)* of a company shall be appointed by the board of director within one month of the incorporation of the company. The auditors so appointed shall hold office until the conclusion of the first Annual General Meeting of the company. *Subsequent auditor(s)* must be appointed at each Annual General Meeting of the company, and the auditor so appointed shall hold office from the conclusion of that meeting until the conclusion of next Annual General Meeting. Every company shall, within seven days of the appointment of an auditor at its Annual General Meeting, give intimation thereof to the auditor so appointed. Every auditor so appointed shall inform the registrar within 30 days of the receipt of the intimation of his appointment, whether he has accepted the appointment or not.

Removal of an Auditor: The company may at a general meeting remove the first auditors appointed by the board by an ordinary resolution. The company may appoint in their place any other persons who have been nominated for appointment by any member of the company and of whose nominations notice has been given to the members of the company not less than 14 days before the date of the meeting. Subsequent auditors may be removed from office before expiry of their term by an ordinary resolution in the General Meeting and with the previous approval of the Central Government (Section 224(7)). A *special notice* is required for a resolution at an annual meeting to appoint a person other than the retiring auditor or to provide that the retiring auditor shall not be reappointed (Section 224(1)).

Special Audit: The Central Government under Section 23-A may direct a special audit of the company's accounts for a specified period. It may do so where it is of the opinion—

(a) that the affairs of the company are not being managed in accordance with sound business principles or prudent commercial practices; or

(b) that the company is being managed in a manner likely to cause serious injury or damage to the interests of the trade, industry or business to which it pertains; or

(c) that the financial position of the company is such as to endanger its solvency.

Audit of Cost Accounts: The Central Government may issue necessary direction under section 233-B for conducting cost audit of companies engaged in production, processing, manufacturing or mining activities. The companies shall maintain books according to rules framed by the Central Government and must include particulars relating to utilisation of material, labour or other items of cost.

The Central Government may, by order, direct that an audit of the cost accounts of these companies shall be conducted by an auditor who shall be a cost accountant within the meaning of the Cost and Works Accountants Act, 1959. But where the Central Government is of the opinion that sufficient number of cost accountants are not available for conducting the audit of cost accounts of companies, the Central Government may be, in notification in the Official Gazette, direct that for a specified period the chartered accountants possessing the prescribed qualifications may also conduct such audit of cost accounts. The cost auditor shall be appointed by the board of directors with the previous approval of the Central Government. An audit, conducted under this section, will be in addition to an audit conducted under Section 224.

Audit Committee

Every public company having paid-up capital of not less than Rs.5 crore shall constitute a committee of the board known as "*Audit Committee*" which shall consist of not less than three directors and such number of other directors as the board may determine of which two-thirds of the total number of members shall be directors, other than managing or whole-time directors.

Every Audit Committee constituted under Sub-Section (1) shall act in accordance with terms of reference to be specified in writing by the board. The members of the Audit Committee shall elect a chairman from amongst themselves. The Annual Report of the company shall disclose the composition of the Audit Committee. The auditors, the internal auditors, if any, and the director in-charge of finance shall attend and participate at meetings of the Audit Committee but shall not have the right to vote. The Audit Committee should have discussions with the auditor periodically about internal control systems, the scope of audit including the observations of the auditors and review the half-yearly and annual financial statements before submission to the board and also ensure compliance of internal control systems.

The Audit Committee shall have authority to investigate into any matter in relation to the items specified in this section or referred to it by the board and for this purpose, shall have full access to information contained in the records of the company and external professional advice, if necessary. The recommendations of the Audit Committee on any matter relating to financial management, including the audit report, shall be binding on the board. If the board does not accept the recommendations of the Audit Committee, it shall record the reasons therefore and communicate such reasons to the shareholders. The chairman of the Audit Committee shall attend the Annual General Meetings of the company to provide any clarification on matters relating to audit. If a default is made in complying with the provisions of this section, the company, and every officer who is in default, shall be punishable with imprisonment for a term which may extend to one year, or with fine which may extend to fifty thousand rupees, or with both.

INVESTIGATION

The Central Government has been vested with wide powers to investigate into the affairs of a company. The investigation may be done on the request of the members or the registrar or at the initiative of the government.

Investigation on application by members or report by register. (Section 235): According to Section 235, the Central Government may appoint one or more inspectors to investigate into the affairs of a company on an application made by—

(a) In the case of a company having a share capital, not less than 200 members or members holding not less than *one-tenth of the total voting power.*

(b) In the case of a company not having a share capital not less than *one-fifth of the members* of the company.

(c) In the case of any company *on the report of the registrar* under Section 234.

The application of members must be supported by evidence showing that the applicants have good reason for requiring the investigation. In addition, the applicants must furnish security for a sum not exceeding Rs. 1,000 for payment of cost of investigation (Section 236).

Further powers have been given to the Central Government under Section 237 to order investigation by competent inspectors and to report to the Central Government thereon. The Central Government is bound to appoint inspectors to investigate the affairs of a company if the company by special resolution or the court by order defaults that the affairs of the company ought to be investigated. (Section 237(a)).

Investigation at its own initiative: The Central Government under Section 237 (b) may on its own initiative appoint an inspector to investigate into the affairs of a company wherein its opinion there are circumstances suggesting the following—

(a) that the business of the company is being conducted with intent to defraud creditors, members or any other person, or for a fraudulent or unlawful purpose or in a manner oppressive to certain members or that the company was formed for any fraudulent or unlawful purpose.

(b) that the persons concerned with the formation of the company or management of its affairs have been guilty of fraud, misfeasance or other misconduct towards the company or any of its members.

(c) that the members of the company have not been given all the information which they might reasonably expect as to the company's affairs (Section 237(b)).

Inspector's Report: On the conclusion of his investigation, the inspector shall make a written or printed report to the Central Government. He may also make interim report if so directed by the Government. Copies of the final report shall be sent by the Central Government to the company and also to any body corporate to which the report relates. A copy of the report may also be made available to a member of the company or a creditor of the company on request and on payment of the prescribed fee.

Powers of the Government on the Basis of Inspectors Report: The Central Government on the reports of the inspectors takes any one or more of the following actions:

1. The Central Government may launch criminal prosecution against any person who is guilty of any criminal offence in relation to the company on the basis of the inspectors report.
2. The Central Government may, on the basis of the inspectors report apply to the court for winding up of the company or make an application to the court for prevention of oppression and mismanagement or may do both (Section 243).
3. The Central Government may institute proceedings (i) for the recovery of damages from any person guilty of fraud, misconduct or misfeasance in connection with the promotion or formation or management of the company, or (ii) for the recovery of any property of the company which has been misapplied or wrongfully retained. The Central Government shall exercise its power in the public interest.

In the first instance the expenses of investigation are borne by the Central Government. But in certain circumstances the government can recover the same from the person convicted.

Investigation of Ownership of Company: Sometimes it becomes necessary to determine the true persons who are financially interested in the success or failure of the company and who are controlling or influencing materially the policy of the company.

QUESTIONS

Objective Type Questions

I. Fill up the Blanks

1. Companies having share capital must file their annual return before the expiry of ________ days from the date of annual meeting.
2. It is mandatory that the Annual Accounts and balance sheet must be placed before the annual meeting within a period of ________ months from the date of closing of the financial accounts.
3. The Board of directors' report is nothing but a representation of ________.
4. A special auditor is directed to be appointed by ________.
5. A cost audit is recommended by the Central Government in companies engaged in ________ ________ etc.
6. An Auditor can do his audit work in not more than ________ companies out of which not more than ________ number of companies could have a paid-up share capital of rupees ________.
7. For removing an auditor appointed in a company before the tenure of his office ________ resolution should be passed with ________ notice.
8. First auditor of the company is appointed by ________.
9. An auditor appointed in a casual vacancy shall hold office until ________.
10. A person shall not be eligible to be appointed as an auditor of a company unless he is a ________.

[*Answers :* (1) 60 days; (2) 6 months; (3) Profit and Loss Appropriation Account; (4) Central government; (5) production, processing or manufacturing or mining; (6) Twenty, Ten, Twenty five lakhs or more; (7) Ordinary, special; (8) Board of directors; (9) The conclusion of the next Annual General Meeting [224(6)]; (10) Qualified chartered accountant.]

II. State whether the following Statements are True or False

1. The first auditor of the company is appointed by the Board of directors.
2. An auditor's remuneration is fixed by the board of directors.
3. In order to conduct cost audit, a person must be a cost accountant.
4. An auditor can be a partner in two firms and conduct the audit work in more than 20 companies.
5. An auditor is responsible to the shareholders to present a true picture of the state of affairs of the company.

6. Annual return must be filed with the registrar of companies whether meeting is held or not.
7. Audit of Branches of a company must be done only by branch auditor.
8. A retiring auditor cannot be reappointed.
9. An auditor as a matter of right is entitled for notice and bound to be heard at annual meeting.
10. A body corporate cannot be appointed as auditors.

[*Answers:* True: (1), (5), (6), (9), (10); False: (2), (3), (4), (7), (8)]

Review Questions

1. Name the books of account a company is bound to maintain.
2. State the provisions of the Companies Act relating to the preparation, authentication, circulation, adoption and filing of the annual accounts of a company.
3. How an auditor of a company is appointed? What are his qualifications?
4. Discuss briefly the provisions of the Act regarding the investigation of the affairs of the company by the Central Government.
5. Write short notes on: (a) Financial books; (b) Statutory books; (c) Statistical books; (d) Audit Committee.

CHAPTER 13

Meetings and Resolutions

Need for Meetings

Whenever a decision has to be taken by more than one person, it is necessary that the people concerned should meet. They should exchange their veiws, discuss the matter, debate on points of disagreements, and arrive at a decision which would be binding on all people concerned. In respect of business organisations where the process of decision-making is involved, and the decision have to be taken collectively by more than one person, the importance of meetings gains added significance. As has been discussed earlier chapter the hierarchy of a company form the organisation consists of:

1. a body of individuals who own the company, namely of shareholders;
2. a body of directors collectively called the board of directors who are the overall in charge of the management of the affairs of the company.
3. In many cases there is also a body of creditors in the form of debentureholders, who have lent money to the company, though generally have less to do with the affairs of the company, except when their rights are effected. If all these peoples have to participate in the decision-making process, the most convenient medium of making the decision is a meeting.

To facilitate proper conduct of the meettings and to arrive at and record the decisions of these bodies of individuals at the meetings, and to prepare and preserve the records of these meetings, a set of rules, regulations and conditions are absolutely essential. Recognising the importance of the meetings for a company, the Company Act has framed extensive rules governing the meetings. The law relating to the meetings, and the procedures are proposed to be discussed in this chapter.

It is at the meeting of the directors, members, creditors, etc., of a company express their will by passing resolutions. Such meetings are: (i) Board of Directors Meeting, (explained in the previous chapter), (ii) Statutory, (iii) Annual General Meeting,

(iv) Extraordinary Meeting, (v) Class of shareholders Meeting, and (vi) Creditors Meeting.

The meetings of the shareholders can also be broadly divided into three categories, namely:

1. Mandatory Meetings
2. Optional Meetings, and
3. Contingent Meetings

Mandatory meetings are those meetings of the shareholders, which must be compulsorily held by the companies according to the Act.

Statutory meetings required to be held under Section 165 of the Act, and the *Annual General Meeting* required to be held under Section 166 of the Act.

Optional meetings are such meetings, the convening of which is not mandatory under the law. These meetings are convened at the discretion the board of directors, should they feel the need for convening the meeting of the sharehloders.

The meetings falling under this category are *Extraordinary General Meetings*, voluntarily convenced by the board of directors

Contingent meetings are such meetings of the shareholders, the need for which arises only if certain contingencies and circumstances arises. These meetings become mandatory, as when the contingencies provided for in the Act take place.

Extraordinary General Meetings on requisition under Section 169 of the Act.

Meetings of a class of shareholders, called class meetings to approve the proposal for the variations of the rights of that class of shareholders,

Meetings of shareholders held under the orders of the High Court to approve the Schemes of Arrangements or Compromise under Section 391 of the Act, or the Scheme of Reconstruction of Amalgamation proposed by the Company, or the meetings of winding up of the company, ordered by the court.

STATUTORY MEETING (SECTION 165)

Every company limited by shares and every company limited by guarantee and having a share capital shall within a period of not less than one month and not more than six months from the date at which the company is entitled to commence business, hold a general meeting of the members of the company. Such a meeting shall be called the "*Statutory meeting*" (Section 165(1)).

This meeting is held once during the lifetime of the company. A private company, an unlimited company or a company limited by guarantee and not having a share capital are not required to hold a statutory meeting.

Notice of the Meeting: The notice for calling the meeting must be given at least 21 days before the meeting. The notice convening the statutory meeting must specifically state that the meeting is the statutory meeting.

Object of Holding the Statutory Meeting

1. The object of such a meeting is to ensure that at an early date, the *members may have an opportunity of ascertaining the precise position progress made by the company since its formation and prospect of the company.* According to Palmer, "The object of the statutory meeting is to put the shareholders of the company at as early a date as possible in possession of all the important facts relating to the new company".
2. To provide an *opportunity to the members to discuss the various matters connected with the formation of the company* and its working without any previous notice.
3. To approve or to effect any modification to contracts mentioned in the prospectus.

Statutory Report: In order to achieve this object, the directors, are required to send a report called the *'Statutory Report'* to every member of the company at least 21 days before the date of the meeting. Even if the report is sent later than is required, it shall be deemed to have been duly forwarded if it is so agreed to by all the members entitled to attend and vote at the meeting.

Contents of the Statutory Report (Section 165(3))

The statutory report shall contain the following particulars:

(a) The total number of *shares allotted* distinguishing those allotted as fully or partly paid-up otherwise than in cash, and stating in the case of shares partly paid-up the extent to which they are so paid-up and in either case the consideration for which they have been allotted.

(b) The total amount of *cash received* by the company in respect of all the shares allotted.

(c) An abstract of *receipts and payments made* there at up to a date within seven days of the date of the report.

(d) An account or estimate of the *preliminary expenses.*

(e) *Names, addresses and occupations of its directors and auditors* and also if its manager and secretary, if any, and the changes which have occurred since the date of the incorporation.

(f) The particulars of any *contract and the modification* or the proposed modification of any contract which is to be submitted for the approval of the members at the meeting.

(g) The extent to which the *underwriting contracts* have not been carried out and the reasons therefore.

(h) The arrears, if any, due on *calls from any director and the manager.*

(i) The particulars of any *commission or brokerage paid or to be paid* to any director or to the manager in connection with the issue or sale of shares or debentures of the company.

Certification of the Report: The statutory report must be certified as correct by not less than two directors, one of whom shall be the managing director if any. The auditors of the company then shall certify it as correct regarding the shares allotted, cash received in respect of such shares and the receipts and payments of the company.

Filing of the Report: A certified copy of the statutory report shall be delivered to the registrar for registration immediately after the same have been sent to the members of the company.

Procedure at the Meeting

At the commencement of the meeting, the board shall place a list showing the names, addresses and occupation of the members of the company and the number of the shares held by them. The list shall remain open for inspection by members during the continuance of the meeting. The members present at the meeting may discuss any matter relating to the formation of the company or arising out of statutory report, whether previous notice has been given or not. But the meeting cannot pass a resolution on any item or on a subject of which notice has not been given as required by the Act. The meeting, however, may adjourn from time-to-time and a resolution may be passed at any such adjourned meeting if due notice thereof has been given in the mean time. The adjourned meeting is treated as if it is an original meeting for the purpose of transacting business.

Consequences of default or effect of non-compliance

If any default is made either in delivering the statutory report to the registrar or in holding the statutory meeting, every director and officer of the company who is in default will be liable to a fine which may extend to Rs. 500. *Failure to comply with the provisions of Section 165 of the Act will be a ground for winding up of the company by the court* under Section 433 of the Act, the Court may, however, give directions for the statutory report to be filed or a meeting to be held, as the case may be and refuse to order the winding up of the company *(Section 433).*

ANNUAL GENERAL MEETING

Every company must in each year hold in addition to any other meeting, an Annual General Meeting. The notice convening the meeting must specify that it is a notice of the Annual General Meeting.

Time gap between two meetings: The first Annual General Meeting must be held within 18 months from the date of incorporation of the company. The year of incorporation or in the following year. Year means calendar year ***(Park vs. Lawton (1911) K.B. 588)***. The registrar has no power to extend the time limit to hold the first Annual General Meeting.***(Dalmia Cement (Bharat) Co Ltd. vs. Registrar of Companies)***

Example: A company incorporated on October 1, 2006 may hold its first Annual General Meeting by April 1, 2007 and then no other meeting will be necessary either for 2004 or 2005. Similarly, a company incorporated on January 1, 2007 may hold its first Annual General Meeting within 18 months, *i.e.,* up to July 1, 2008. If the meeting is held, say in June 2008, the company need not hold any other meeting in the years 2008 and 2009. There after

(i) it must be held in each and every calendar year;

(ii) there shall not be a gap of more than fifteen months between two annual general meetings. However, the registrar has the power to extend the time for holding the Annual General Meeting (except the first Annual General Meeting) by a period not exceeding three months.

In the case of *Sree Meenakshi Mills Co. Ltd. vs. Assistant Registrar of Companies, A.I.R. (1938) Mad. 640*, the Annual General Meeting of a company called in December 1934 was adjourned and held in March 1935. The next meeting was held in January 1936, no other meeting being held in1935. The company was prosecuted for failure to call the Annual General Meeting in1935. The company contended that it did hold a meeting in the year 1935, but the court held that the meeting of March 1935 was the adjourned meeting of 1934.

(iii) The Annual General Meeting must be held within six months of the close of the accounting year.

It should be noted that the all the above time limits should be adhered to for holding Annual General Meeting. This means that the earlier of the above dates will become the last date for holding the Annual General Meeting.

Illustrative Example

The following *example* will explain the provision clearly.

Let us assume that for company X Ltd.

The closure of the accounting year is 31st March

The date of the 4th Annual General Meeting was 28th August, 2007

The deadlines for holding the 5th Annual General Meetings as per the above points would be:

1. To be held every Calendar Year	31st December, 2008
2. Maximum gap of	15 months
from the previous AGM	28th November, 2008
3. Six months from the expiry of the financial year	30th September, 2008

The 5th Annual General Meeting must be held before the earliest of the above three dates, namely, 30th September, 2008.

In the above illustration, had the 4th Annual General Meeting been held on 29th May, 2007, the deadline as per Criterion 2 would have been 29th August, 2008.

In that case, the 5th Annual General Meeting will have to be held before 29th August, 2008, though the deadline as per Criterion 3 is 30th September, 2009.

First Annual General Meeting an Exception

Provisio to Sub-Section (1) provides the exception to the above rule relating to the time limit for the Annual General Meeting. According to this, the first Annual General Meeting of the company should be held within 18 months of the date of its incorporation. This proviso states that if first AGM is so held, there need not be an Annual General Meeting either in the year of incorporation, or the following year.

Correspondingly, Sub-Section (3) fo Section 210 also states that the closure of the first financial year should not precede the date of the first Annual General Meeting by a period of nine months (instead of six months as in case of subsequent AGMs).

The following illustration will clarify the point:

Let us assume that

The date of incorporation of the company is	10th November, 2006
The closure of the accounting year is	30th September, 2007

As per the criterion 1 in previous illustration, the company has hold the Annual General Meeting in the years 2003, as well as 2004.

However, the deadline for the first Annual General Meetings would be:

As per the proviso to Section 166(1) (18 months from the date of incorporation)	10th May, 2008
As per Section 210 (3) (Nine months from the closure of the first Accounting year), *i.e.*, 30th September, 2007	30th June, 2008

In this case, the first Annual General Meeting must be held before the earlier of the above two deadlines, namely 10th May, 2008.

Day, Time and Place of the Meeting

Every Annual General Meeting must be held on a working day and during business hours. It should be either held at the registered office of the company or at some other place within the city, town or the village in which the registered office of the company is situated. However, the Central Government may exempt any class of companies from these provisions subject to such conditions as it may impose. Public companies and private companies which are subordinates of public companies may fix the time of their Annual General Meeting. A private company may also in a like manner and by a resolution agreed to by all the members fix the time as well as the place for its Annual General Meeting.

With regard to the holding of the Annual General Meeting, no distinction is made between a public company and a private company. It was decided in the case of ***Registrar of Companies vs. Cabral & Co. Pvt. Ltd.***

Notice of the Meeting: According to Sec. 171(1) of the Act, a 21 clear days notice is necessary to hold an Annual General Meeting. However, a shorter notice is sufficient if all the members give their consent. The notice should specifically state that it is the notice of the Annual General Meeting.

Contents of the Notice : The notice of the meeting should contain the following:

1. The place where it is to be held.
2. The date and hour of the meeting.
3. A statement of the business to be transacted.
4. Any special business to be transacted.

Annual Accounts: The balance sheet and the profit and loss account and the report of the directors must accompany the notice of the Annual General Meeting. The annual accounts should be made for a period up to a date not more than six months before the date of the meeting and they should be laid before the meeting.

From the wordings of the Secs. 173 and 200, it is implied that the annual accounts must be laid only before the Annual General Meeting and not at any other meeting. In case the annual accounts are not ready, it is open to the company concerned to adjourn the said Annual General Meeting to a specific date when the annual accounts are expected to be ready for placing before it.

An adjourned meeting is the continuation of the original meeting. The statutory requirement as to laying of the accounts before the Annual General Meeting would be satisfied if the accounts are laid before the adjourned meeting. It was decided in the case of ***Sudhir Kumar Seal vs. Assistant Registrar of Companies.***

To whom the notice should be sent: Notice of the Annual General Meeting must be sent to:

1. Every member of the company.
2. Every person entitled to shares due to transmission.
3. Auditor or auditors of the company.

Business Transacted at the Annual General Meeting

Sec. 173 of the Act has classified the business to be transacted at an Annual General Meeting into two kinds namely:

1. Ordinary business, and
2. Special business.

The ordinary business to be transacted at an Annual General Meeting may relate to the following matters:

1. Consideration and adoption of the accounts and the reports of the directors and auditors.
2. Declaration of dividend.
3. Appointment of directors in the place of those retiring.
4. Appointment of auditors and fixing remuneration to them.

All other businesses transacted at this meting are called special business. Also every business transacted at any other general meeting other than the Annual General Meeting is also a special business. Some of the examples of special business are —

1. Removal of a director.
2. Issue of rights/bonus shares.
3. Election of a person (other than a retiring director) as director.

Drafting the Notice of the Annual General Meeting

The following points must be considered while drafting the notice of the Annual General Meeting of a company.

1. The meeting should be *held either at the registered office or at a place within the city, town or village* in which the registered office is situated.
2. The meeting should not be convened on a day which is a public holiday within the meaning of the Negotiable Instruments Act.
3. The meeting should be convened during the *usual business hours*.
4. The first item for consideration at an Annual General Meeting is adoption of the accounts. It must be ensured that the gap between the period up to which accounts are prepared and the date of the Annual General Meeting should not be more than six months.

5. If the provision of Sec. 224-A of the Act are applicable to the company, *the appointment of auditors will require approval by means of a special resolution.*

6. In case any special business is proposed to be transacted at an Annual General Meeting, then the resolution must be set out for each of the items proposed to be considered.

7. Notice should be under proper authority. Therefore, the words ***"By Order of the Board"*** should be added before the name of the secretary.

8. The gap between the date of the notice and the date of the meeting should not be less than 25 days so that after excluding 48 hours for effecting the notice as per Sec. 53 (2) (b), the date of service of notice and the date of holding the meeting, there is left a clear period of 21 days.

9. Section 176 provides that it must be indicated in the notice that a member entitled to attend and vote at a meeting is entitled to appoint a proxy to attend and vote instead of himself and such proxy need not be a member of the company. Therefore, it is necessary to include this by means of a note with the notice of the Annual General Meeting. Similarly, an additional note is to be given in the notice is that proxies to be valid should be lodged 48 hours before the time of the meeting though there is no statutory provision.

10. A note should be added to the notice indicating the period for which the *register of members* would be closed.

11. A note is to be added to the notice indicating the date by which the *dividend warrants* will be posted.

12. In case of special business, which is proposed to be transacted, the *explanatory statement* under Section 173 (2) of the Act must be attached to the notice.

Default in Holding the Annual General Meeting

If any company fails to hold an Annual General Meeting within the prescribed period, the Central Government on the application of any member, may either call or direct the calling of a general meeting of the company. It may give such directions as it thinks fit in regard to the calling, holding or conducting of such meetings. The Central Government may direct that one member of the company present in person or by proxy shall be deemed to constitute a meeting. A general meeting held at the directions of the Central Government shall be regarded as an Annual General Meeting.

It must be noted that the Company Law Board has not been given the powers to all, hold and conduct the Annual General Meetings of the companies beyond the period specified in Section 166. Section 186(1) excludes these meetings from its purview. Under Section 186(1) the Company Law Board is empowered to call, hold and conduct extraordinary meetings of the companies in certain circumstances.

If default is made in holding the meeting of the company in accordance with Section 166, or in complying with any directions of the Central Government, the company and every other officer of the company who is in default shall be punishable with fine which may extend to Rs. 5,000 and in the case of a continuing default with a further fine which the default continues (Section 168).

The company is liable for mere default but for the prosecution of a director or an officer of the company, it must be shown that he was knowingly a party to the default. Further, the company would not be liable for the default, if it is due to a cause beyond its control. In re *Bank of Deacon Ltd. AIR 1960. Kerala-15*, the books of the company had been seized by the police and produced in the criminal court, the Kerala High Court held that the company would not be punished because the default was beyond the control of the company.

EXTRAORDINARY GENERAL MEETING

Every general meeting of the company which is not statutory or the Annual General Meeting is an 'extraordinary general meeting.' This meeting is generally held for the purpose of dealing with any extraordinary matter which cannot be postponed till the next Annual General Meeting, e.g., issue of right *shares, increase in the remuneration of managing director, **persons authorised to convene the meeting.***

Meeting Convened by the Board: The extraordinary general meeting can be *convened either by the board of whole-time director, etc., directors whenever they think fit or on the requisition of the members of the company.* Where the directors think fit to convene a meeting, they do so by resolution passed at a duly convened and constituted meeting of the board. If at any time sufficient number of directors to form a quorum are not present in India, any director or any two members of the company may call an extraordinary general meeting.

On the Requisition of the Members: The directors are bound to call an extraordinary general meeting of the company if the requisition is made by members:

(i) holding not less than 1/10th or 10% of the paid-up share capital of the company and having a right to vote at the date of the deposit of the requisition; or

(ii) if the company has no share capital, members having not less than 1/10th or 10% of the voting powers of all the members having a right to vote at the date of the requisition.

(iii) 100 members can requisition a meeting even if their collective shareholding is less than 10%.

Contents of a Valid Requisition

1. The requisition should be in writing
2. It should state the business to be transacted at the requisitioned meeting.

3. It should be signed by all the requisitions.
4. It should be deposited in the registered office of the company.

While the Act does not specifically require proof of the fact that requisitionists hold sufficient number of shares or voting powers as required above, it is always a good practice for the requisitionists to spell out of the company rejecting the requisition on technical grounds.

On receipt of the requisition, the board shall proceed within 21 days to convene a meeting which must be held within 45 days from the date of the deposit. If the board does not, within 21 days from the date of the deposit of a valid requisition, proceed duly to call a meeting on a day not later than 45 days from the date of the deposit of the requisition, the meeting may be called –

(a) by the requisitionists themselves;

(b) in the case of a company having a share capital, by such of them as represent either a majority in value of the paid-up share capital held by all of them or not less than one-tenth paid-up share capital of the company, whichever is less; or

(c) in the case of a company not having share capital, by such of the requisitionists as represent not less than one-tenth of the voting power of the members of the company.

The extraordinary general meeting requisitioned by the members must be held within three months of the deposit of the requisition. Where a meeting is called by the requisitionists themselves and the registered office is not made available to them, for holding the meeting, they may hold the meeting elsewhere. The company is bound to repay all reasonable expenses incurred by the requisitionists in calling such a meeting and the company can recover the said sum from the directors at default.

Power of the National Company Law Tribunal to Call Meeting (Section 186): The National Tribunal has been vested with the power to call a meeting of the company other than the Annual General Meeting. This power which was earlier vested in the court, has after the passing of the Companies (Amendment) Act, 1974, been transferred to the National Tribunal. Where for some reason it is impracticable to call a meeting of the company, other than the Annual General Meeting, the National Tribunal Law may either on its own motion or on the application of any director or member of the company order a meeting to be called, held and conducted in such manner as it thinks fit. It can give such directions in regard to the calling, holding and conducting of the meeting. It can also direct that even one member of the company present in person or by proxy shall be deemed to constitute a meeting. The word 'impracticable' means impracticable from a reasonable point of view. The National Tribunal should take a common sense view of the matter and act as a prudent person of business.

Time and Place: Unlike in the case of Annual General Meetings, the Act does not contain any restrictions on the time and place of extraordinary general meeting. Hence, an extraordinary general meeting can be held on a public holiday. It is also not essential that the extraordinary general meeting must be held in the town or city where the registered office of the company is situated.

Business Transacted: The extraordinary general meeting can transact any business as may be contained in the notice excepting the items of business specifically reserved for the Annual General Meeting, viz, adoption of annual accounts, election of directors in place of those retiring by rotation. appointment of auditors, etc. All the items of business transacted in extraordinary general meeting are treated as special business. An explanatory statement should accompany the Notice for every item of business proposed in the extraordinary general meeting.

Meeting Convened by any Director or any two Members: Regulation 48(2) of Table A provides that if any time the directors capable of acting and forming sufficient quorum, may call for an extraordinary general meeting. Such meeting is also deemed as a meeting conducted by the board of directors

Drafting of the Notice of Extraordinary General Meeting

While drafting the notice of the extraordinary general meeting following guidelines may be noted:

1. There is no statutory restriction that extraordinary general meetings should not be called on date which is a public holiday. However, they are usually called on a date, which is not a public holiday during usual business hours either at the registered office or within the city, town or village in which the registered offices is situated.
2. As all business at extraordinary general meetings are special, it is not necessary to say so in the notice of the meeting.
3. All business must be given in the form of resolution indicating whether they are ordinary or special.
4. Proper authority must issue notice.
5. A note covering the right of a member to appoint a proxy must be indicated in the notice.
6. In terms of Section 173(2) of the Act, an explanatory statement must always be annexed to the notice covering an extraordinary general meeting since all business at such meeting will be special.

CLASS MEETINGS

Class meetings are generally held for obtaining the consent of a particular class of shareholders for altering their rights and privileges or for the conversion of one class into another. For instance, there may be a meeting of preference shareholders for paying their rate of dividend or investing them into equity shares.

Class Meeting for the Purpose of Compromise or Arrangements

When there is a proposal for the compromise of arrangement, or for the amalgamation or reconstruction of companies under Section 291 of the Act, the court normally orders that a meeting of each case of the shareholders has to be held separately.

These class meetings held on the orders of the court have to follow the procedureas directed by the board. Usually, the procedure is the same as the procedure for the other general meetings, but the Chairman of the Meeting is Companies (Court) Rules, 1959.

Thus, for effecting such changes it is necessary that a separate meeting of the holders of those shares is to be held and the matter is to be approved at the meeting by a special resolution. For example, for cancelling the arrears of dividends on cumulative preference shares, it is necessary to call for a meeting of such shareholders and pass a resolution as required by Sec. 106 of the Act. In case of such a class meeting, the holders of other class of shares have no right to attend and vote.

REQUISITES OF A VALID MEETING

1. Proper Authority to Call Meeting

A meeting to be valid must be called by a proper authority. It is the board who can normally convene a meeting. But under certain circumstances meetings can also be convened by the members, National Company Law Tribunal or the Central Government.

2. Notice of the Meeting

The second requirement of a valid meeting is that all those who are concerned with the business of the meeting and are entitled to attend it, are communicated of the date, time, place and business of the meeting. Such a communication is called '*Notice of the Meeting*, Not less than 21 clear days notice in writing should be given to the members to call a meeting of any kind. 'Not less than 21 clear days' means that both the date of the meeting and the date on which it is served are to be excluded, *i.e.*, 21 clear days notice. Where the notice is sent by post, it shall be deemed to have been received at the expiration of forty-eight hours after the posting.

Length of the Notice: The requirement of 21 days notice of the meeting overrides any provision in the Articles for a shorter period. But the Articles can validly provide for longer notice than the statutory minimum period.

Shorter Notice: The meeting can, however, be called by giving a shorter notice in the following cases.

(a) In the case of an Annual General Meeting, by the consent of all the members entitled to attend and vote.

(b) In the case of any other meeting, by the consent of the members holding not less than 95 per cent paid-up share capital of the company, or holding not less than 95 per cent of the total voting power of the company (when a company does not have a share capital).

Place, Day and Time: Every notice of a meeting of a company must specify the place, day and hour of the meeting and shall contain a statement of the business to be transacted there at.

To Whom Notice to be Given: Notice of every meeting must be given to the following person: (i) Every members of the company, (ii) Every person entitled to a share in consequence of the death or insolvency of a member, (iii) The auditor or auditors of the company. If notice of a meeting of the company is not given to every person entitle to receive notice, any resolution passed at the meeting will be of no effect.

Where notice of the meeting is given by advertisement in a newspaper circulating in the neighbourhood of the registered office of the company under Section 53(3) of the Act, explanatory statement need not one annexed to the notice under Section 173 of the Act. But it is necessary to mention in the advertisement that the explanation statement has been forwarded to the members of the company. The accidental omission to give notice to or non-receipt of the notice by any members, shall not invalidate the proceedings at the meeting.

Content of Notice/Business to be Transacted: Notice of meeting must contain a statement of nature of the business to be transacted in the meeting. Section 173 classifies the business into *ordinary business* and *special business*.

Ordinary Business: The following business which is transacted at every Annual General Meeting is considered as ordinary business:

(i) The consideration of accounts, balance sheet and the report of the board of directors and auditors.

(ii) The declaration of a dividend.

(iii) The appointment of directors in place of those retiring.

(iv) The appointment of and fixing the remuneration of auditors.

Special Business: Any business other than ordinary business transacted at an annual general meeting and all business transacted at the statutory meeting and at any extraordinary general meeting is deemed as *special business*.

Explanatory Statement: In case of any items of special business to be transacted in the general meeting, an explanatory statement shall be annexed to the notice of the meeting. The statement must set out all material facts concerning each such item of the business including in particular the nature of the concern or the interest if any, therein of any director and the manager. Where any item of such business relates to or affects any other company, the statement must set out the extent of shareholding interest in such other company, of every director and the manager if any, of the company, if such interest is not less than 20 per cent of the paid-up share capital of such other company. Where the item of such business relates to the according of approval to any document by the meeting, the statement annexed to the notice must specify the time and the place where the document can be inspected. The purpose of the statement is to enable the members to understand and appreciate the nature of the business or items of business proposed to be considered at the meeting and make up their mind whether to go to attend and vote at the meeting or abstain from voting.

Who Signs the Notice Convening the Meeting

The Annual General Meeting is convened by the board of directors of the company. The notice of the Annual General Meeting, and every other general meeting is usually signed by the secretary under the authority of the board. If a company does not have a secretary, the notice is signed either by a director or any other officer of the company duly authorised by the board.

3. Quorum (Section 174)

A quorum may be defined as the minimum number of members who must be present at a meeting in order that the business of the meeting may be validly transacted. Unless the Articles of the company provide for a larger number, *five members* personally present in the case of public companies (other than a public company which has become such by virtue of Section 43-A) and *two persons* personally present in the case of private company will be the quorum for a meeting of the company. It may be noted that the Articles cannot provide for a smaller quorum. *No proxy is counted in forming the quorum.*

Consequences of Incomplete Quorum: If *within half an hour from the time fixed for the meeting,* the quorum is not present, the meeting shall stand dissolved if it was called at the requisition of the members. In any other case, the meeting shall stand adjourned to the same day next week, at the same time and place. If at the adjourned meeting also, the quorum is not present within half an hour, the members present shall be the quorum.

In *Re Hartley Baird Ltd. (1954) 3 A.E.R. 695* the court held that the quorum required is the quorum to be present at the time of beginning to consider the business and it need not be present throughout or at the time of taking the vote on any resolution.

One Member Forming the Quorum: Where the total number of members of a company becomes reduced below the quorum fixed for a meeting, it would appear that the rule as to quorum would be satisfied, if all the members of the company, though less than the quorum are present. But, where only one person is present, he cannot form a quorum as a *single member cannot constitute a meeting*. However, the Company Law recognizes certain *exceptions* which are as follows:

(i) If all the shares of a particular class or all the debentures are held by only one person then he will constitute a valid quorum for the meeting.

(ii) One member may constitute a quorum for an Annual General Meeting when it is called by the Central Government under Section 167 of the Act.

(iii) One member of the company present in proxy or by person shall be deemed to constitute a meeting where the Company Law Board orders a meeting of the company to be held (Section 186).

4. Agenda for the Meeting

The term agenda means the "**things to be done**" or "**business to be transacted at a meeting.**" In order to transact the business of a meeting systematically and without omission of any important item, it is necessary to put down the items of business to be done on a paper called the "**Agenda Paper**" or "**Agenda**."

The agenda should be circulated amongst the members along with the notice of the meeting. No business should be transacted at a meeting unless it is specified in the agenda paper.

The preparation of the agenda is the work of the company secretary. He should do this job in consultation with the chairman of the company. In preparing the agenda, the secretary should take care to include therein all the business to be transacted. The matters should be presented clearly and in a summary form so that the members can grasp the matter in advance, and form some opinion.

The agenda should be so drafted as to help the quick disposal of the business. The usual practice is to put the routine items first and complicated matters later. So the routine matters can be disposed of first and the latter part of the meeting can be utilised for discussion of more important items. It is also considered advisable that matters of similar or related nature should be placed in continuous order.

There are generally two ways in which the agenda for a meeting can be prepared. They are as follows:

(i) By referring to the business very briefly by writing just one line about each item. For example:

(a) To read the minutes.

(b) To pass the transfers.

(c) To produce financial statement.

(ii) By giving more details about each item and even sometimes including suggested drafts of the resolutions for the consideration of the meeting. For example:

(a) To read and sign minutes of the previous meeting held on 25th March, 2007.

(b) To pass transfer of shares numbered 208 to 215.

The second method is found more suitable as it helps the secretary or his assistant to write the minutes easily.

5. Chairman (Section 175)

A meeting cannot proceed to transact any business without electing a chairman. The chairman is necessary element for the proper conduct by company meeting. He is the presiding officer of the company. Chairman is elected in every meeting before at it starts its business. He is neither a judicial officer nor an administrative head. The Articles of the company may provide who will be the chairman at a general meeting. Where the Articles are silent, the members present at the meeting may elect one of themselves to be the chairman thereof. Election may be by show of hands shall immediately take the poll. If some other person is elected as a result of the poll, he shall be the chairman for the rest of the meeting.

The chairman presides over the meetings of the company. His main function is to keep order and see that the business is properly conducted. He must decide questions arising at the meeting and must take care that the sense of the meeting is properly ascertained with regard to any question before it. He must give a reasonable chance to the members present to discuss any proposed resolutions. The chairman cannot arbitrarily adjourn the meeting or dispose it at his own choice without the consent of the shareholders unless the business for which it was convened has been concluded. The power of adjournment vests in the majority and they can appoint another chairman and conduct the business unfinished by the former chairman.

Powers and Duties of a Chairman

Powers:

(i) A chairman has *prima facie* authority or power to decide all the questions and points of order.

(ii) He can adjourn the meeting when it is not possible, by reason of disorder, etc., to conduct the meeting and complete business.

(iii) He has right to decide priority amongst the speakers to demand poll.

(iv) Power to exercise a casting vote.

(v) Power to expel unruly member behaving disorderly, and

(vi) He can, with the support of a majority, apply closure to the discussion after it has been reasonably debated.

Duties: He must act all times *bona fide* and in the interest of the company as a whole. A chairman who presides over a meeting of a company is neither wholly a ministerial officer nor wholly a judicial officer; his duties are of a mixed nature. He is not liable for damages, if acting *bona fide* according to the best of his judgement and without malice.

(i) It is his duty to see that the meeting is duly convened as to notice, quorum. etc.

(ii) It is his duty to preserve order, and to see that the business is properly conducted.

(iii) He must ensure that the sense of the meeting is properly ascertained in regard to any question before it.

(iv) He must ensure that the provisions of the Companies Act and the Articles of Association are observed, and that the business is taken in the order set out in the agenda, and that business is within the scope of the meeting.

(v) He must ensure that proper opportunity is given to the members to express their views that the voting is fair.

(vi) He must exercise his casting vote *bona fide* in the interests of the company.

(vii) He must decide questions arising for decision during the meeting, and must see to it that the majority do not refuse to bear the minority.

(viii) He must ensure that proceedings of the meeting are correctly and properly recorded in the minutes book.

6. Minutes of the Meeting (Sec. 195)

The term 'minutes' mean the official record of the meetings of a company. Minutes looks contain a summary of the business transacted, decisions and the resolutions arrived at the meeting. It is incumbent on the company to maintain minutes of proceedings of general meetings and of the board of directors and other meetings. Every company shall cause entries in the minutes of proceedings of every meeting within 30 days of the conclusion of every such meeting concerned. The minutes book shall be bound and its pages consecutively numbered. Each page of every minutes of proceedings shall be initialed or signed and the last page of the record of proceedings of each meeting in such book shall be dated and signed:

(a) in the case of minutes of the proceedings of a meeting of the board or of a committee thereof, by the chairman of the said meeting or the chairman of the next succeeding meeting.

(b) In the case of minutes of proceedings of a general meeting, by the chairman of the same meeting or in the event of the death or inability of the chairman by a director duly authorised by the board for the purpose.

Minutes of the proceedings of a meeting shall not be attached to any such book by pasting or otherwise. The minutes of each meeting shall contain: (a) a fair and correct summary of the proceedings; and (b) all appointments of officers made there at. In the case of a meeting of the board of directors or of a committee of the board, the minutes shall also contain: (a) the names of the directors who dissent from or do not concur in the resolution passed at the meeting. The minutes must not contain any matter which, in the opinion of the chairman of the meeting: (a) is or could reasonably be regarded as defamatory of any person; (b) is irrelevant or immaterial to the proceedings; or (c) is detrimental to the interests of the company. The discretion in regard to such inclusion or non-inclusion of any matter in the minutes lies with the chairman. If default is made in complying with the foregoing provisions, the company and every other officer of the company who is in default, shall be punishable with fine which may extend to Rs. 500 *(Section 193)*.

Minutes of the meetings kept in accordance of the provisions of Section 193 shall be evidence of the proceedings, recorded therein. *(Section 194)*. Until the contrary is provided, every general meeting of the company or meeting of the director or a committee of directors in respect of the proceeding thereof, minutes have been so made and signed, shall be deemed to have been duly called and held. The proceedings at these meetings shall be deemed to have duly taken place, and in particular, all appointments of directors or liquidators made at the meeting shall be deemed to be valid. *(Section 195)*.

Location and Inspection of Minutes Book: The minutes books of the general meetings of a company must be kept at the registered office of the company and be open during business hours for the inspection of any member without charge for at least two hours a day. A member is entitled to be furnished within 7 days, after he has made a request in that behalf to the company, with a copy of any minutes on payment of *thirty seven paise* for every one hundred words, or fractional part thereof, required to be copied. If inspection is refused or if any copy is not furnished within the specified time, the company and every other officer of the company who is in default shall be punishable with fine which may extend to Rs. 500 for each offence. Moreover, the court may, by order, compel an immediate inspection of the books or direct that the copy required shall forthwith be sent to the person requiring it *(Section 196)*.

Publication of Reports: No document purporting to be a report of the proceedings of a general meeting of a company can be circulated or advertised at the expense of the company, unless it includes the matters required by Section 193, to be contained in the minutes of the proceedings of such meeting. Contravention is punishable with fine which may extend to Rs. 5,000 *(Section 197)*.

7. Voting or Poll (Sense of Meeting)

Every person whose name appears on the register of members, has a right to vote. A shareholder's right to vote is a right of property which he may use in any manner he likes. In other words, he can exercise his right to vote for his own interest and even against the interest of the company. In the case of a company which has no share capital, each member is entitled to one vote only. But, where a company has a share capital, if the Articles are silent every shareholder has one vote is respect of each share.

A company is authorised to make provisions in its Articles restricting the voting rights of a member on the ground that (i) calls on his shares or any other sum presently payable have not been paid, or (ii) the company has exercised right of lien in respect of those shares. Where the Articles of a company do not contain such provisions, a member cannot be prevented from voting even though calls payable by him have not been paid (Section 181). A public company shall not put any restrictions put on the right of voting will be void even though such provisions are contained in the Articles *(Section 182)*. A member entitled to more than one vote is free to split his votes in favour of and against the same resolution. Such use of votes is possible only on a vote by poll, or on a show of hands no member can register more than one *(Section 183)*.

METHODS OF VOTING

In order to ascertain the sense of a meeting, voting may be only (i) show of hands, or (b) by poll.

Voting by a Show of Hands: Questions arising at a general meeting are to be decided in the first instance by a show of hands. But, where a poll is demanded it is not necessary that the resolution should be put to vote by show of hands. On a show of hands each member has one vote and a proxy cannot vote unless the Articles otherwise provide. The declaration by the chairman that a resolution on a show of hands has or has not been carried and an entry to that effect in the minutes book shall be conclusive evidence of that fact *(Section 178)*.

Voting by Poll: A vote by a show of hands is only a rough and ready method of taking the sense of a meeting. It is not an accurate method of ascertaining the wishes of the members of a company because the votes of those voting by proxy are not counted. Again it does not pay due regard to the wishes of a member holding a large number of shares since he has only one vote on a show of hands. A poll is more proper and effective means of arriving at the wishes of all the members. A poll may be demanded before or on the declaration of the result of the voting on any resolution on a show of hands. Such a poll cannot be demanded after the declaration of result and after the chairman has taken up any other item from the agenda for consideration of the meeting.

A poll may be ordered either by the chairman of his own motion or on a demand of the members. The chairman is bound to order a poll if demand is made by the following persons:

(a) In the case of a public company at *least by five members* having the right to vote on the resolution and present in person or by proxy.

(b) By any number of members present and having *not less than one-tenth of total voting right* of all the members entitled to vote at the meeting.

(c) By any member or members present and holding shares paid-up to the extent of not less than *10 per cent of the total sum paid-up on all the shares* having a voting right.

In the case of a private company, the number of members demanding for a poll depends on the number of members present at the meeting. Where the number of members present personally at the meeting does not exceed seven, one member can demand a poll if he has a right to vote on the resolution and is present in person or by proxy. But if the number of the members present personally at the meeting exceeds seven, two members can demand poll who have the right to vote on the resolution and are present in person or by proxy.

The demand for poll may be withdrawn at anytime by the person or persons who made the demand *(Section 179)*. If a poll is demanded on the election of chairman, it must be taken forthwith. Similarly, a poll demanded on the question of adjournment must be taken forthwith. But a poll demanded on any other question must be taken at such time, not being later than 48 hours from the time when the demand was made. *(Section 180)*.

The chairman of the company shall appoint two scrutineers to scrutinise the votes given on the poll and to report thereon to him. A scrutineer may be removed at any time by the chairman before the result of the poll is declared. The chairman in such case will fill the vacancy in the office of the scrutineer. He is also empowered to fill the vacancy in the office of scrutineer arising from any other cause. One of the scrutineers shall always be a member (not being an officer or employee of the company) present at the meeting provided that such a member is available and willing to be appointed. *(Section 184)*.

The chairman of the meeting shall have the power to regulate the manner in which a poll shall be taken. The result of poll shall be deemed to be a decision of the meeting on the resolution on which the poll was taken. *(Section 185)*.

8. Proxies

Any member of a company entitled to attend and vote may do so either in person or by a proxy. A proxy may be defined as a person authorised to attend and vote for another at a meeting. According to *Lord Hanworth M.R.*, Proxy is a personal representative of the shareholder who may be described as his agent to carry out a course which the shareholder himself has decided upon. It also refers to the instrument by which the appointment is made. A proxy need not be a member of the company. The proxy has no right to speak at a meeting, but he can demand a poll.

Cases Where a Proxy Cannot be Appointed: A member of a private company cannot appoint more than one proxy to attend on the same occasion and a member of a company without a share capital cannot appoint a proxy.

Form of Proxies: Two forms have been provided under Schedule IX of the Act. The instrument of proxy, however, need not necessarily be in either forms. The company can make its own form. The only advantage of these two forms is that the appointment of proxy made in any of such forms cannot be questioned on the ground that it has not complied with any special requirements contained in the Articles of the company.

Procedure for Appointing a Proxy: The instrument appointing a proxy must be in writing in the form prescribed and signed by the appointed or by his attorney duly authorised in writing. If the appointer is a corporate body, it must be under its seal or signed by an officer or attorney duly authorised. Every notice calling a meeting of the company having a share capital or the Articles of which provide for voting by proxy at a meeting, must mention with reasonable prominence a statement that a member entitled to attend and vote, is entitled to appoint a proxy and a proxy need not be a member. Every officer of the company who is in default in complying with this provision is punishable with fine which may extend up to Rs. 500.

Lodging of Proxies: The instrument appointing a proxy must be deposited with the company 48 hours before the meeting. Any provision in the Articles which requires the instrument appointing a proxy to be received by the company more than 48 hours before the meeting shall have effect as if a period of 48 hours had been specified in such provision. There is, however, nothing in the Act to prevent the lodging of such instruments less than 48 hours before the meeting, subject to this the instrument must be deposited within the time specified by the Articles.

Revocation of Proxy: A proxy is always revocable unless made irrevocable for valuable consideration. A proxy can be revoked at any time before the proxy has voted. A latter proxy revokes one of earlier date. Death of a member revokes the proxy but if the company has no notice of such death, then the vote given by the proxy will be valid. Where a shareholder who having given a proxy personally attends and votes at the meeting, the proxy is revoked thereby.

Inspection: Every member entitled to vote at the meeting is authorised to inspect the proxies during the 24 hours preceding the meeting till the conclusion of the meeting. For such inspection the member must give at least three days notice in writing to the company. Such inspection cannot be taken by a proxy.

Invitation to Appoint a Person as Proxy: Where a company issues invitations at its expense to members, giving names of persons to be appointed as proxies for the purpose of any meeting, then every office of the company who knowingly issued the invitation or permitted the same shall be liable to a fine which may extend to Rs. 10,000 *(Section 176)*.

Representation of Corporations in Meetings: A body corporate can be a member or creditor of another company. It may authorise a person not necessarily an employee to attend and vote at any meeting of the company. The representative thus appointed is a member personally present for the purposes of quorum and voting by the show of hands and is not merely in the position of a proxy. A representative can appoint a proxy to attend and vote at the meeting instead of himself *(Section 187)*.

Representatives of the President and Governors: Where the President of India or the Governor of a State is a member of a company, he may appoint such person as he thinks fit to act as the representative to attend and vote at any meeting of the company. Such a representative shall be deemed to be a member of such a company and shall be entitled to exercise the same rights and powers (including the right to vote by proxy) as the President or Governor could exercise as a member of the company *(Section 187-A)*.

9. Adjournment of the Meeting

The term *adjournment* literally means an act of putting off or breaking off for a later resumption. In relation to meetings, it denotes an act of dissolving or suspending a duly convened meeting after it has been duly commenced, to be reconstituted at a later time or date. The date or time of the meeting can be decided in the same meeting at the time of adjournment or to be decided later on if the meeting is adjourned *sine die*. It should also be noted that the discussion on a particular business or motion can also be adjourned without adjourning the meeting itself.

Distinction Between Adjournment and Postponement

The terms adjournment and postponement are different in their scope and meaning. The following are the points of distinction between the two:

- Adjournment refers to the suspension of a meeting to a future date after it commences its deliberations. In other words, a meeting can be adjourned only after it is convened, whereas a meeting can be postponed only before the meeting is convened.
- A meeting can be adjourned only by the meeting itself, whereas a meeting can be postponed by the person who convenes the meeting. In other words, postponement is the act of the convening authority, whereas adjournment is the act of the meeting itself.
- It is generally said that the power to convene a meeting also imply the power to postpone the meeting. But this proposition is not followed in many cases.

From the decisions of the courts, it appears that a meeting properly convened cannot be postponed unless there is some irregularity. But a meeting can be adjourned to a later date.

Reasons for Adjournment

A meeting can be adjourned due to the following reasons —

- If no quorum is present.
- If it is not possible to obtain the required information within the date of the meeting and the same is to be placed before it.
- If the meeting passes a resolution to this effect.
- If the chairman by virtue of the powers conferred upon him does so.

Statutory Provisions Regarding Adjournment

The statutory provisions relating to adjournment can be summed up as follows:

Right to Adjourn: The power of adjournment generally vests in the majority of those present at the meeting. If the majority of the members present at a meeting decides so, the chairman has no other alternative other than to adjourn the meeting. A resolution is to be passed to this effect.

Adjournment by the Chairman: For the proper conduct of the meeting, the right of adjournment is generally conferred upon the chairman. Therefore, the chairman should exercise this power only for the proper conduct of the meeting and not for his own willing and discretion. If the chairman acts *bona fide*, the meeting stands adjourned and hence the dissenting members have no right to continue the proceedings and the proceedings thereat shall be null and void.

Malafide Adjournment by the Chairman: If the chairman adjourns a meeting on his own accord ignoring the views of the majority, the following consequences shall follow:

- The remaining members can appoint another chairman and transact the business left unfinished.
- The proceedings of the meeting shall be valid and binding on the company.

Adjournment for Want of Quorum: If a meeting is adjourned due to want of sufficient quorum, the adjourned meeting is to be held on the same day and some time in the next week. If the quorum is not present within half an hour even in the adjourned meeting, the members present shall constitute the quorum and the proceedings thereat will be valid.

Notice for the Adjourned Meeting: An adjourned meeting is merely the continuation of the original meeting and so no fresh notice is necessary for the adjourned meeting. However, it is usual to serve a fresh notice if the time gap between the original and adjourned meeting exceeds 30 days, and if the original meeting is adjourned *sine die*.

Business at the Adjourned Meeting: Only those businesses, not completed in the original meeting should be transacted in the adjourned meeting. Therefore, no fresh business can be transacted in the adjourned meeting. However, in case of an adjourned statutory meeting, a new business, after proper notice, can be brought up for discussion in the meeting.

MOTIONS AND RESOLUTIONS

Decisions of the company are made by motions and resolutions of its members, passed at meeting of members. A proposal when passed and accepted by the members become resolution. Three kinds of resolutions are recognised by Companies Act.

- Ordinary Resolution,
- Special Resolution,
- Resolutions requiring a Special Notice.

Ordinary Resolution

An ordinary resolution is one which is passed at a general meeting by a simple majority of members entitled to vote therein. Simple majority means that the votes cast either by show of hands or on a poll in favour of a particular proposal including the casting vote of the chairman exceeds the votes cast against it. The votes may be cast by the members either in person or by proxy, if allowed. An ordinary resolution is sufficient to affect any transaction which is within the powers of the company and is not required either by the Articles or the Companies Act to be effected in some other manner. All resolutions which are not special or which do not require special notice are ordinary resolutions.

Business Transacted with Ordinary Resolution: The important items usually transacted with ordinary resolutions are the following:

1. Adoption of the Statutory Report.
2. Adoption of the Balance Sheet and Profit and Loss Account at the Annual General Meeting (Sec. 210).
3. Election of Directors.
4. Appointment of auditors and fixing their remuneration (Sec. 224).
5. Issue of shares at a discount.
6. Declaration of dividends and sanction of the sums to be transferred to the reserves.

7. Authorising the board to sell or dispose of the undertaking of the company.
8. Rectification of name or adoption of new name by a company where it resembles the name of an existing company with the previous approval of the Central Government (Sec. 22 (1)(a)).
9. Alteration of share capital (Sec. 94 (2)).
10. Re-issue of redeemed debentures who are liable to retire by rotation (Sec. 255 (1)).
11. Appointment of first directors who are liable to retire by rotation (Sec. 255 (1)).
12. Increase or reduction in the number of directors within the limit fixed by the Articles (Sec. 258).
13. Appointment of managing/whole-time director (Sec. 269).
14. Removal of a director and appointment of a director in his place (Sec. 284 (1)).
15. Approval of appointment of sole-selling agents (Sec.294).
16. Appointment and fixation of remuneration of liquidators in a members' voluntary winding up (Sec. 490 (1)).
17. Nomination of a liquidator in a creditors' voluntary winding up (Sec. 502 (1)).

Meaning and Essentials of Special Resolution

A resolution shall be a special resolution when:

(a) the intention to propose the resolution as a special resolution has been duly specified in the notice;

(b) the notice required under the Act (21 clear days) has been duly given, and

(c) the votes casted in favour of the resolution by member entitled to vote either in person or by proxy are not less than three times the number of votes, if any, cast against the resolution. The votes may be cast either on a show of hands or by poll. There is no question of a casting vote in case of a special resolution.

(d) An explanatory statement setting out all material facts concerning the subject-matter and the interest of the directors and the manager if any should be set out in the notice calling the meeting.

(e) A copy of each special resolution together with the copy of an explanatory statement should be filed with the registrar within 30 days from the date of passing the resolution.

A special resolution is a most useful part of the mechanism of a company. It is by and through the instrument of a special resolution that the companies carries important executive or administrative acts which are, or may be necessary for the company's benefit. The aim of passing a special resolution is to ensure that every important change shall be made only after due deliberation and with the sanction of the greater body of shareholders of the company.

Circumstances in Which a Special Resolution is Necessary

The Articles of Association may provide that certain types of business shall be approved by a special resolution. The Act also provides that in certain specified cases, a company must pass a special resolution. A special resolution is required for the following purposes:

1. To alter the provisions of the memorandum for changing the place of registered office from one state to another or objects of the company (Section 17).
2. To change the name of the company (Section 21).
3. To alter the Articles of the company (Section 31).
4. To offer further issue of subscribed capital when shares are offered to outsiders, (Section 81).
5. To create reserve capital (Section 99).
6. To reduce the share capital of the company (Section 100).
7. Commencement of a new line of business (Section 149).
8. To authorise payment of interest out of capital (Section 208).
9. To request the Central Government to appoint inspectors for investigation of the affairs of the company (Section 237).
10. To authorise payment of remuneration to directors who are not in the whole-time employment of the company (Section 309).
11. To make the liability of directors unlimited (Section 323).
12. Authorisation of inter-company loans (Section 370).
13. To have the company wound up by the court (Section 433).
14. To wind up the company voluntarily (Section 484).
15. Permission to liquidator to accept shares as a consideration for the sale of the property of the company (Section 484).
16. Omission or addition of the word *"Private"* from, or to, the name of a company (Section 21).
17. Change of name of a charitable or other non-profit company by omitting the word or words *"Limited"* or *"Private Limited"* (Section 25 (3)).
18. Variation of shareholders' rights (Section 106).
19. Keeping registers and returns at a place other than the registered office (Section 163 (1)).

20. Appointment of sole selling or buying agent in the case of companies having paid-up share capital of Rs. 50 lakh or more (Section 294-AA (3)).
21. Allowing a director to hold an office of profit under a company (Section 314 (1) and (1-B)).
22. Applying to the National Company Law Tribunal to wind up a company (Section 433 (a)).
23. Disposal of books and papers of a company in voluntary winding up when its affairs have been completely wound up (Section 550 (1)(b)).

Resolutions Requiring Special Notice (Section 190)

In addition to the above two types of resolutions, there is another class of resolutions provided under the Companies Act which require a special notice to be given in respect of them.

Circumstances in Which a Special Notice is Required: Special notice is required in the following cases:

1. For the appointment of an auditor other than the retiring auditor *(Section 225).*
2. For express resolution that the retiring auditor shall not be reappointed *(Section 225).*
3. For removing a director before before the expiry of his term *(Section 284).*
4. For appointing another person as director in place of the director removed *(Section 284).*

In the above cases, the proposer should give a special notice, of his intention to move the resolution to the company not less than 14 days before the meeting. In computing 14 days, the day on which the notice is served and the day of the meeting are excluded.

The company must, immediately after receiving the notice, give its members notice of the proposed resolution in the same manner as it gives notice of any meeting. If that is not practicable, the company must give notice either by advertisement in a local newspaper or in any other mode allowed by the Articles at least 7 days before the meeting *(Section 190).*

CIRCULATION OF MEMBERS RESOLUTIONS (SEC. 188)

Section 188 provides a method by which members desirous of moving a resolution at the Annual General Meeting can give notice and explanation in advance to the other members of what they intend to do.

Notice to the Members of the Company: A company is bound on requisition in writing by a specified number of members (a) to give notice to the members of any resolution which is intended to be moved at the next Annual General Meeting; (b) to circulate to the members any statement of not more than one thousand words with respect to the proposed resolution or any business to be dealtwith at the meeting. The expenses of any such notice and circulation will be borne by the requisitionists.

Requisition to Company: The requisition for circulating resolution shall be deposited with the company at its registered office not less than six weeks and any other requisition not less than two weeks before the next Annual General Meeting. The requisition must be signed by the required for requisition must either be (i) one hundred or more members having the right to vote on the resolution and holding shares on which a total amount of not less one lakh of rupees has been paid-up, or (ii) members representing not less than l/20th of the total voting power of all the members having the right to vote on the resolution.

On receipt of the requisition the company shall give notice of the proposal resolution to all members of the company entitled to receive notice of the next Annual General Meeting. The company shall also circulate the statement among its members entitled to notice of the general meeting. The company is not bound to circulate the resolution or statement if the court finds, on application by the company or an aggrieved person, the same to be defamatory or abuse of the provisions of the section. The cost of such application may be recovered from the requisitionists.

Passing of Resolution by Postal Ballot (Section 192- A)

1. Notwithstanding anything contained in the provisions of this Act, a listed public company may, and in this case of resolutions relating to such business as the Central Government may, by notification, declare to be conducted only by postal ballot, shall get any resolution passed by means of a postal ballot, instead of transacting the business in general meeting of the company.
2. Where a company decides to pass any resolution by resorting to postal ballot, it shall send a notice to all the shareholders, along with a draft resolution explaining the reasons therefore, and requesting them to send their assent or dissent in writing on a postal ballot within a period of thirty days from the date of posting the letter.
3. The notice shall be sent by registered post acknowledgement due, or by any other method as may be prescribed by the Central government in this behalf, and shall include with the notice, a postage pre-paid envelope for facilitating the communication of the assent or dissent of the shareholder to the resolution within the said period.
4. If a resolution is assented to by a requisite majority of the shareholders by means of postal ballot, it shall be deemed to have been duly passed at a general meeting convened in that behalf.

5. If a shareholder sends under Sub-Section (2) his assent or dissent in writing on a postal ballot and thereafter any person fraudulently defaces or destroys the ballot paper or declaration of identity of the shareholder, such person shall be punishable with imprisonment for a term which may extend to six months or with fine or with both.

6. If a default is made in complying with Sub-Sections (1) to (4), the company and every officer of the company, who is in default shall be punishable with fine which may extend to fifty thousand rupees in respect of each such default.

   Expalnation:- For the purposes of this section, "postal ballot" includes voting by electronic mode."

DIRECTORS RESOLUTIONS

Just like the shareholders, the directors give effect to their decisions by passing resolutions in the meeting of the board. Questions that come up for discussion are generally decided by a simple majority of votes. The following points are to be noted in this connection.

1. No Voting by Poll: No provision is made for voting by poll at the board meeting. This is because, each director has only one vote. Hence, voting by show of hands is generally followed.

2. Proxies are not Allowed: Proxies are not allowed in the board meetings as in the case of general meetings. However, if alternate director is appointed to act for an absentee director he can cast his vote.

3. Cases Where Unanimous Consent is Necessary: It is already noted that a simple majority is sufficient to decide the questions in the board meeting. But, as an exception to the above rule, there are three instances in which an unanimous decision is necessary. They are the following:

1. To appoint or employ a person as its managing director under Sec. 316.
2. To appoint or employ a person as its Manager if he is already a managing director or manager of another company.
3. To invest the funds of the company in any shares or debentures of any other body corporate under Sec. 372.

REGISTRATION OF RESOLUTIONS AND AGREEMENTS

Section 192 provides that certain resolutions and agreements shall be registered with the registrar so that he can maintain a complete record of the important transactions of the company. It affords an opportunity to the members of the public to ascertain the position of the company in certain respects.

The following are the resolutions of agreements which are to be registered:

1. Special resolutions.
2. Resolutions which have been agreed to by all members on a subject, which otherwise required a special resolution.
3. Any resolution of the board of directors of a company or agreement executed by a company relating to the appointment or variation of the terms of appointment of a managing director.
4. Resolutions or agreements which have been agreed to by all the members of any class of shareholders on a subject which required to be passed by a resolution of a particular majority in a particular manner.
5. All resolutions and agreements which effectively bind members of any class of shareholders even though not agreed upon by those members.
6. Resolutions authorising the directors of a company to: (i) sell, lease or otherwise dispose of the whole or any part of the company's undertaking; (ii) borrow money beyond the limits of the paid-up-capital and free reserves; (iii) contribute to charitable or other funds exceeding Rs. 50,000 or 5 per cent of the average of the net profits of the last three years, whichever is greater.
7. Resolutions approving the appointment of sole-selling agents.
8. Resolutions requiring a company to be wound up voluntarily.

Resolutions and agreements to be printed or typewritten and certified by an officer of the company shall be filed within 30 days of the passing of the resolution or the making of the agreement. In case of non-compliance the company and every officer of the company who is default shall be fined up to Rs. 20 for everyday during which the default continues.

QUESTIONS

Objective Type Questions

I. Fill up the blanks

1. In an annual general body meeting, when a special business has to be transacted __________ statement has to be annexed with the general notice.
2. When a notice has been issued less than twenty one clear day's notice in meetings other than annual general body meeting, it must be approved by members holding not less than __________ per cent of total voting powers.
3. In the case of an extraordinary general body meeting convened by the requisitions, if quorum is not present the meeting has to be __________.

4. Casting vote can be exercised only by Chairman when there is __________ which must be authorised by __________.
5. In the case of a public company having share capital poll can be demanded by any members having the right to vote on resolution holding at least __________ of the total paid-up capital or holding shares of the paid-up values of at least __________.
6. Minimum number of members to constitute a quorum for a public limited company is __________.
7. A special resolution must be passed supported by the votes of the members present in the meeting which should not be less than __________ of the majority.
8. Requisitions in the case of a company having share capital must be persons holding not less than of the paid-up capital of the company.
9. Board of directors' report is nothing but __________ account.
10. For altering the share capital which being a special business requires __________ resolution.

[*Answers:* (1) Explanatory; (2) 95%; (3) Dissolved; (4) Chairman, A tie, articles; (5) 1/10th, 50,000; (6) Five; (7) 3/4th or 75%; (8) 1/10th; (9) Profit and loss appropriation; (10) Ordinary (Section 94)]

II. State whether the following statements are True or False

1. A board meeting need not be held frequently in a year.
2. It is enough if quorum is present initially at the time when the business is taken for discussion.
3. A proxy can demand for a poll.
4. Every public company having paid up capital of not less than Rs. 5 crores shall constitute committee known as audit committee.
5. One member can constitute a quorum under special circumstances.
6. Chairman has no discretionary power to adjourn the meeting.
7. Minutes containing the resolution must be filed with the registrar within 30 days after passing the resolution.
8. Postponement and adjournment of the meeting are one and the same.
9. A point of order can be raised only by the chairman.
10. A privileged occasion is one in respect of which no legal action could be taken against any person making the statement.

[*Answers:* True: (3), (4), (5), (6), (7), (10); False: (1), (2), (8), (9)]

Review Questions

1. What are the essentials of a company meeting?
2. Define meetings. State the different kinds of meetings.
3. What is the significance of a statutory meeting?
4. What is an ordinary business?
5. What is a requisitioned meeting?
6. What you understand by a class meeting?
7. What are the objects of holding a statutory meeting?
8. What is a special resolution?
9. Which of the resolutions have special notice?
10. What is company meeting? What are its essentials?
11. What are the different kinds of meeting in a company?
12. What is statutory meeting? State its objects.
13. Describe the procedure for holding statutory meeting.
14. What is extraordinary general meeting? Who are authorized to convene it?
15. What is meant by board meeting?
16. What are the items of business require special resolution in a company meeting?
17. What business can be transacted with ordinary resolution in a company meeting?
18. Explain the various kinds of company meetings.
19. Indicate clearly the law relating to holding of a statutory meeting.
20. What should be the contents of statutory report?
21. Explain the provisions of the Companies Act, 1956, relating to Annual General Meeting.
22. Write an essay on extraordinary general meeting.
23. Enumerate the legal provisions regarding the board meeting.
24. Write shorts on
    - (a) Director's Resolutions
    - (b) Registration of Resolutions and Agreements
    - (c) Adjournment of a meeting

CHAPTER 14

Winding Up

A company is a legal person. In other words, a company is created through a legal process. As such, it can be put to an end only through a legal process known as *liquidation*. The Companies Act envisages *three specific methods* to bring an end to a joint stock company. They are:

1. *By winding up* under Part VII of the Act. This is the common method of putting an end to a joint stock company.
2. By transferring its undertaking to another company under a *scheme of reconstruction* or amalgamation. The procedure for this purpose is laid down in Sec. 394 of the Act.
3. *By removing the name of the company from the register of companies by the registrar*. For this purpose, the procedure laid down in Sec. 560 of the Act should be followed. This method of dissolution is cheap and easy.

Meaning and Definition of Winding Up

Winding up refers to the last stage in the life of a company. It refers to a legal process through which a company is put to an end. In the words of **Prof. Gower,** "Winding up is a process whereby the life of a company is ended as its property is administered for the benefit of its creditors and members. An administrator, called *liquidator* is appointed and he takes the control of the company, collects its assets, profits and debts and finally distributes any surplus among the members in accordance with their rights".

This definition clearly enumerates the procedure for winding up and its impact on the company.

To have a clear understanding, the steps involved in the process of winding up are given below:

1. Appointment of Liquidator: As soon as the proceedings are started, the board of directors ceased to act as such, and administrator called *Liquidator* is appointed. In a winding up by the National Company Law Tribunal the Liquidator is known as Official Liquidator and in a voluntary winding up, the Liquidator is known as Voluntary Liquidator or simply Liquidator.

2. Payment of Debts and Liabilities: The business of the company is then closed. Its assets and liabilities are ascertained. Its assets are sold and converted into liquid cash. The money is then applied to pay off the debts and liabilities of the company.

3. Distribution of Surplus: After satisfying the claims of the creditors if any surplus is left, it is distributed amongst the members in proportion to their rights or interests in the company.

4. Removal of the Name from the Register: When all these are done and the company has complied with certain formalities, the company is dissolved. The name of the company in the register of companies shall be struck off by the registrar of joint stock companies.

To sum up, winding up of a company is a process of putting an end to the life of a company. It is a proceeding by means of which a company is dissolved and in the course of such a dissolution its assets are collected, its debts are paid off out of the assets of the company or from contributions by its members, if necessary. If any surplus is left, it is distributed among the members in accordance with their rights.

MODES OF WINDING UP

There are two modes of winding up of a company. These are: (a) Compulsory winding up by the NCLT, (b) Voluntary winding up , which is itself of two kinds: (i) Member's voluntary winding up, (ii) Creditor's voluntary winding up.

Modes of Winding Up of Companies

- Compulsory Winding up By the NCLT (S. 433)
- Voluntary Winding up (Sec. 484)
  - 1. by Members
  - 2 . by Creditors

Note: Sections 522 to 557 relating to the winding up under the supervision or intervention of the court have been repealed by the companies (Second Amendment) Act, 2002. Hence, these provisions are not relavent at present.

COMPULSORY WINDING UP

Compulsory Winding up by National Company Law Tribunal (Sections 433-483)

A company may be wound up by an order of the tribunal. This is called *Compulsory Winding up*. Section 433 lays down the following grounds for the winding up of a company by the tribunal.

1. Special Resolution of the Company (Sec. 433 (a))

If the company has by a special resolution resolved that it may be wound up by the tribunal. The power of the tribunal in such a case is discretionary. The Tribunal may refuse to order winding up where it is opposed to public or company's interest.

2. Default in Holding Statutory Meeting (Sec. 433 (b))

If a company makes a default in delivering the statuary report to the registrar or in holding the statutory meeting, the court may order winding up of the company either on the petition of the registrar or on the petition of the contributory. The petition for winding up must not be filed before the expiration of 14 days after the last day on which the statutory meeting ought to have been held. However, the tribunal may instead of making a winding up order, direct that the statutory report shall be delivered or that a meeting shall be held.

3. Failure to Commence or Suspension of Business (Sec. 433 (c))

Where a company does not commence its business within a year from its incorporation, or suspends its business for a whole year, the tribunal may order for its winding up. The power of the tribunal is discretionary and will be exercised only where there is a fair indication that the company has no intention to carry on the business. Where the suspension of the business is temporary or can be satisfactorily accounted for, the tribunal will refuse to make an order. A company will not be wound up if it abandons one of its several business, unless that business is the main object of the company.

4. Reduction of Members Below Minimum (Sec. 433 (d))

Where the number of members is reduced below 7 in the case of a public company and below 2 in case of a private company, the tribunal may order the winding up of the company.

5. Inability to Pay Debts (Sec. 433 (e))

The tribunal may order for the winding up of a company if it is unable to pay its debts. The basis of an order for winding up under this clause is that the company has ceased to be *commercially solvent,* i.e., it is unable to meet its current demands, although the assets when realised may exceed its liabilities. According to Section 434 of the Act a company shall be deemed to be unable to pay its debts in the following cases:

Demand for Payment Neglected

(a) If a creditor to whom the company owes a sum of Rs. 1,00,000 or more has served on the company a notice for payment and the company has for three weeks neglected to pay or otherwise satisfy him. But where the company bonafidely disputes the debt, and the tribunal is satisfied with the defence of the company, the tribunal will not order for its winding up.

(b) Failure to pay public deposits on their due dates amounts to inability to pay debts. It is to be noted that a notice of demand giving less than three weeks does not vitiate the demand but merely postpones the right of action to a date after the expiry of three weeks. ***[Babu Ram vs. Krishan Bhardwaj Cold Stores Mills Ltd. (1965) 2 Comp. L.J.251]***

(c) A *dividend when declared becomes a debt due by the company* and the shareholder can also apply for company liquidtion if the company is uable to pay his dividend.

Decreed Debt Unsatisfied: If execution or other process issued on a decree or order of any court or tribunal in favour of a creditor is returned unsatisfied in whole or in part.

Commercial Insolvency: If proved to the satisfaction of the tribunal that the company is unable to pay its debts and in determining whether a company is unable to pay it debts, the tribunal will take into account the contingent and the prospective liabilities of the company. What has to be proved under this clause is not whether the company's assets exceed its liabilities, but whether it is unable to meet its current demands. If a company is unable to meet its current liabilities, it is commercially insolvent and liable to be wound up.

A company is said to be commercialy insolvent if "its assets are such and its existing liabilities are such, as to make it reasonably certain — as to make the court feel satisfied — that the existing and probable assets would be insufficient to meet the existing liabilities." ***Sir William vs. C. in Re. Europe Life Insurance Society (1869) 9 Eq. 122.***

6. Just and Equitable (Sec. 433 (f))

The last ground on which the tribunal can order the winding up of a company is when the tribunal is of the opinion that is just and equitable that the company should be wound up. This clause gives the tribunal a very wide power to order winding up wherever the tribunal considers it just and equitable to do. The tribunal will consider such grounds to wind up a company for just and equitable reasons as are not covered by the preceding five clauses.

The following are the *instances where the courts or tribunals have exercised their discretion* under this clause:

(i) Where there is a deadlock in the management.

(ii) Where it is impossible to carry on the business of the company except at a loss.

(iii) Where the company has ceased to carry on its authorised business and is engaged in an illegal business.

(iv) Where the object for which the company is formed is impossible of further pursuit.

(v) Where the minority is being disregarded or oppressed.

(vi) Where there is lack of confidence in directors.

(vii) Where a company has been conceived and brought forth in fraud.

(viii) Where the main object of the company has failed substantially or becomes impraticable.

(ix) Where the company is a more bubble and it does not carry on any business or does not have any property.

(x) Where the interest of the public is likely to be affected.

Failure to File Returns with Registrar (Sec. 433 (g)): If the company has made a default in filing with the registrar its balance sheet and profit and loss account or annaul return for any five consecutive financial years.

If the Company Acted Against the Interest of India (Sec. 433 (h)): If the company has acted against the interests of the sovereignty and integrity of India, the security of the state, friendly relations with foreign states, public order, decency or morality, etc., the National Company Law Tribunal shall make an order for winding up of a company under this Clause (h) on application made by the Central Government or a state government.

Who may Petition for Winding Up to the National Company Law Tribunal

Section 439 of the Companies Act enumerates the persons who can file a petition to the court for the winding up of a company. The following persons can file a petition.

1. The company.
2. Any creditor or creditors including any contingent prospective creditor or creditors.
3. Any contributory or contributors.

4. All or any of the aforesaid parties, together or separately.
5. The Registrar.
6. Workers.
7. Any person authorised by the Central Government under Section 243, like the official liquidator, etc.

Company's Petition: A company may itself file a petition for winding up. But it can do so only when the company has passed a *special resolution* to that effect. The directors have no power to present a petition for winding up (Sec 439 (1) (a)).

Statement of Affairs to be filed with winding up petition: Section 439(A) added by The Companies (Second Amendment) Act, 2002 provides as under:

1. Every company shall file with the tribunal a statement of its affairs along with the petition for winding up.
2. Where a company opposes a petition for its winding up, it shall file with the tribunal a statement of its affairs.
3. The statement of affairs referred to in Sub-Section (1) or Sub-Section (2) shall be accompanied by:
   (a) the last known addresses of all directors and company, secretary of such company;
   (b) the details of location of assets of the company and their value;
   (c) the details of all debtors and creditors with their complete addresses;
   (d) the details or workmen and other employees and any amount outstanding to them;
   (e) such other details as the tribunal may direct.

Creditor's Petition (Sec. (1) (b)): A creditor can also apply for the winding up of a company. The word 'creditor' includes a secured creditor, debentureholder and the trustee for debentureholders. The tribunal will not order the winding up of the company where the debt is bonafidely disputed. Where the creditors's petition is opposed by other creditors, the tribunal may ascertain the wishes of the majority of the creditors before making any order for winding up.

Where a petition is brought by a contingent or prospective creditor or creditors, it shall not be admitted before the leave of the tribunal is obtained. Such leave shall be granted only when the tribunal is satisfied that there is a *prima facie* case for winding up the company and reasonable security for costs has been given (Sec 439 (3)).

Contributory's Petition: The term 'contributory' means every person liable to contribute to the assets of a company in the event of its being wound up. It includes the holder of any shares which are fully paid-up and includes any person alleged to be a contributory.

A contributory shall be entitled to present a petition for winding up only: (a) When the number of members is reduced below 7 in the case of a public company and below 2 in the case of a private company; or (b) when he holds shares which were originally allotted to him or has held shares for six out of the eighteen months prior to the commencement of winding up or the shares have devolved in him through the death of a former holder. A contributory who is a holder of fully paid-up shares is also entitled to present a petition for the winding up. He shall be entitled to present a petition for winding up though the company may have no assets at all or have no surplus assets left for distribution after the satisfaction of its liabilities (Sec. 439 (4)).

Registrar's Petition (Sec. 439 (5)): The registrar is empowered to file petition to the tribunal for the winding up of a company only in the following grounds:

(a) when default has been made by the company in the filing of the statutory report or in the holding of the statutory meeting; or

(b) when the company has failed to commence business within one year from its incorporation or suspends its business for more than a year; or

(c) when it comes to know either from the accounts of the company or from the report of the inspectors that the company is unable to pay its debts within the meaning of Section 434 of the Act; or

(d) when the number of members in a company has fallen below the statutory minimum, viz., below 7 in the case of a public company and below 2 in the case of a private company; or

(e) where the court is of the opinion that it is just and equitable that the company be wound up; or

(f) when the Central Government authorises the registrar to make a petition vide Section 243 of the Companies Act.

(g) in a case falling under Section 433 (b), by the Central Government or a state government.

The registrar is not entitled to make a petition on the ground that the company is unable to pay its debts unless it so appears to him from the report of a special auditor appointed under Section 233-a or an inspector appointed under Sections 235 or 237. In all the above cases the registrar must obtain the previous sanction of the Central Government before making the petition for winding up. The Central Government shall not give such permission unless opportunity has been given to the company to make its representations.

Central Government's Petition: The Central Government can also file a petition for winding up in certain cases. The petition can be filed by the Central Government on the report of inspector to apply for winding up the company. The Central Government can authorise any person including the registrar to act on its behalf for the purpose.

Withdrawal of Petition

A petitioner may withdraw the petition for winding up with the permission of the tribunal. The tribunal may allow any other person who is entitled to present a petition and who is desirous of prosecuting the petition, to be substituted in place of the original petition provided the petition is otherwise sustainable (Vide Rule of Companies (court) Rules).

Commencement of Winding Up

The winding up of a company by the tribunal is deemed to commence at the time of the presentation of the petition for winding up. But where, before the presentation of the petition, a resolution has been passed by the company, the winding up shall be deemed to have commenced at the time of the passing of the resolution. If a winding up order has been made on more than one petition, the winding up shall commence from the data of presentation of the earliest petition (*Section 441*).

Power of Tribunal on Hearing Petition: After a winding up petition is filled, a notice is issued on the company to appear and state its case if any.

On hearing a winding up petition, the tribunal may:

1. dismiss it with or without cost; or
2. adjourn the hearing conditionally or unconditionally; or
3. make any interim order as it thinks fit; or
4. make an order for the winding up of the company with or without costs or any other orders as it thinks fit.

The tribunal, however, must not refuse to make a winding up order on the ground that the company's assets are mortgaged to an amount equal to or in excess of the assets or that it has no assets. Further, where a petition is presented on the ground that it is just and equitable that the company should be wound up, the tribunal may refuse to make a winding up order if in its opinion some other remedy is available to the petitioners and that they are acting unreasonably in asking for a winding up instead of pursuing that remedy. If a petition is presented on the ground of default in delivering the statutory report or in holding the statutory meeting, the tribunal may direct that the report be delivered or the meeting be held and may also make proper order as to costs (*Section 433*).

OFFICIAL LIQUIDATOR

Under the present Act, the only individual person is competent to act as the liquidator in a winding up is the *official liquidator*. For the purpose of winding up, there shall be attached to each High Court an official liquidator appointed by the Central

Government, who may be either a whole-time or part-time officer. In district courts the official receiver will be the official liquidator. The Central Government may appoint one or more deputy or assistant official liquidators to assist the official liquidator. On a winding up order being made the official liquidator, by virtue of his office, becomes the liquidator of the company.

The tribunal may appoint the official liquidator to be the liquidator provisionally at any time after the presentation of the petition for winding up and before the making of the winding up order. Before making such an appointment notice must be given to the company and a reasonable opportunity must be given to it to make representation. The court or tribunal may dispense with such notice where there are special reasons. Such reasons must be recorded in writing. On a winding up order being made, the official liquidator shall cease to be provisional liquidator and shall become liquidator of the company.

Statement of Affairs (Sec. 454)

After a winding up order is made or the official liquidator is appointed as *provisional liquidator*, a statement as to the affairs of the company must be made out and submitted to the official liquidator. It must be in the prescribed form and verified by an affidavit. The statement must contain the following particulars:

(a) The assets of the company stating separately the cash balance in hand and at the bank, if any, and the negotiable securities, if any, held by the company.

(b) Debts and liabilities of the company.

(c) The names, residences and occupations of its creditors, stating separately the amount of secured and unsecured debts.

(d) The debts due to the company and the names, residences and occupations of the persons from whom they are due and the amount likely to be realised on account thereof.

(e) Such further or other information as may be prescribed, or as the official liquidator may require.

The statement must be submitted within 21 days from the date of appointment of the provisional liquidator and in the absence of such an appointment within 21 days of the winding up order. The period may be extended for special reasons by the official liquidator or the tribunal to not more than 3 months. Failure without reasonable cause to company with the above requirements is punishable with fine. A person claiming to be a creditor or contributory of the company is entitled to inspect the statement and to a copy thereof non-payment of prescribed fees. Falsely claiming to be a creditor or contributory is an offence.

Duties of the Liquidator

The liquidator of a company is compulsory for winding up must perform such duties in reference thereto as the court may impose. These are asunder:

1. To Submit Preliminary Report: As soon as practicable after the receipt of the statement of affairs of the company, the offcial liquidator must submit a preliminary report to the tribunal not later than six months of the order or such extended period as may be allowed by the tribunal. The report shall contain the following information:

(a) The amount of capital issued, subscribed and paid-up and the estimated amount of assets and liabilities.

(b) Where the company has failed, the cause of such failure.

(c) Whether in his opinion further inquiry is desirable as to promotion, formation or failure of the company , or the conduct of the business thereof.

The official liquidator may also submit report or reports bringing to the notice of the tribunal the frauds and other improper conduct on the part of the directors and other officers (*Section 455*).

2. To Take-over Company's Assets: On a winding up order being made the liquidator must take into custody all the property, effects and actionable claims to which the company is or appears to be entitled. On the passing of an order of winding up, the company's assets are to be treated as being in the custody of the court or tribunal (*Section 456*).

3. Meeting of Creditors and Contributors: The liquidator is bound to follow the directions given by the creditors, or contributors or by the ***committee of inspection***. Any directions given by creditors or contributories at general meeting shall be deemed to override any directions given by the committee of inspection in case of conflict. The liquidator must summon meetings of creditors or contributories whenever required by not less than one-tenth in value of such creditors or contributories. He may apply to the tribunal for directions in relation to many matter arising in the winding up (*Section 460*).

4. To Maintain Proper Books: The liquidator must maintain proper books and cause entries or minutes to be made of all proceedings at the meeting and of such other matters as may be prescribed *(Section 461)*.

5. To Submit Accounts: The liquidator shall at least twice in any year present to the court an account of his receipts and payments as liquidator. The tribunal must cause the accounts to be audited. When the accounts have been audited, one copy thereof shall be filed and kept by the tribunal and the other copy shall be delivered to the registrar. Each copy shall be open to inspection of any creditor, contributory or person interested (*Section 462*).

6. To Submit Information in Pending Liquidation : Where the winding up of a company is not concluded within one year of its commencement, the liquidator shall, unless exempted by the Central Government within two months after the expiry of such year, and thereafter until the winding up is concluded, at intervals of not more than one year or at such intervals as may be prescribed file a statement duly audited with respect to the position of the liquidation. Such report shall be filed in the tribunal in the case of winding up subject to the supervision of the tribunal and with the registrar in case of voluntary winding up. The statement is open to inspection by a creditor or contributory. Failure to comply with the above provision makes the liquidator liable for a fine of Rs. 5,000 for everyday during which the failure continues.

Powers of Official Liquidator

The powers of the liquidator can be divided into two classes: (a) those which can be exercised with the sanction of the tribunal; and (b) those which do not require such sanction.

(a) Power to be exercised with the sanction of the tribunal.

(i) To institute or defend suits, prosecutions or other legal proceedings in the name and on behalf of the company.

(ii) To carry out on business of the company so far as it may be necessary for the beneficial winding up of the company.

(iii) To do all other acts as may be necessary to wind up the company and to distribute its assets.

(iv) to raise money on the security of any asset of the company.

(v) To do all other acts as may be necessary to wind up the company and to distribute its assets.

(b) Power to be exercised without the sanction of the tribunal

The following powers do not require sanction of the tribunal for their exercise:

(i) To do all acts and execute in the name of the company all deeds, receipts, documents, etc., and to use the company's seal for that purpose, wherever necessary.

(ii) To inspect the records an returns of the company on the files of the Registrar without payment of any fees.

(iii) To prove, rank and claim in the insolvency of any contributory and to receive dividend out of his estate.

(iv) to draw, accept, make and endorse bill of exchange, hundi or promote in the name of and on behalf of the company.

(v) To take out in his official name, letters of administration to any deceased contributory and in his official name to do all things necessary for obtaining any money from a contributory or his estate.

(vi) To appoint agents where necessary.

CONTRIBUTORY

In a going company, that is, before liquidation a member is liable to uncalled share capital portion of his subscribed shares or reserved capital and bound to pay full amount on the shares held by him. This liability continues even after the company passes into liquidation. The liquidator may make a formal call asking the members to pay the call money. The shareholder then becomes a contributory and certain changes occur in his status, rights and liabilities.

The liquidator shall prepare a list of all such contributories who may be made liable to contribute towards the assets of the company on account of deficiency in the assets of the company. In case there is a surplus in assets, the liquidator shall prepare a list of those members who are entitled to share this surplus. The term 'contributory' includes members of both the above categories.

Definition of Contributory

Section 428 defines the term 'contributory'. It means every person who is liable to contribute to the assets of the company in the event of its being wound up and includes the holders of fully paid-up shares. A debtor to the company is not a contributory nor a person who guarantees such debts. When a company goes into liquidation every member whether past or present has to contribute to the assets of the company.

List of Contributories

The list of contributories is made out in two parts A and B in accordance with Section 426. The A list comprises the present members and the B list those of past members, who have ceased to be members within one year preceding the winding up. The 'A' contributories, *i.e.*, those in the list of present members are primarily liable for everything and must be first individually exhausted before any 'B' contributory, whose liability is only secondary can be called upon.

When does the liability of the contributory arise: A contributory shall be required to contribute towards the asssets of the company in the following circumstances:

1. If the assets fall short for the payment of company's debts, liabilities and the cost of liquidation; or

2. In case money is required for the adjustment of the rights of contributories as between themselves. Holders of partly paid shares may be required to contribute in order to bring them at par with those shareholders who have paid in full.

Extent of Liability of a Contributory

The liability of a contributory extends only to the amount, if any, remaining unpaid on the shares held by him. There is no liability in the case of a contributory who holds fully paid-up shares. According to Section 429, the liability of a contributory is a debt but this liability to pay the debt arises only if and when calls are made. In other words, the liability of contributory, though commencing at the date when he entered into the contract with the company under which he became a member, is only contingent upon the company being wound up, in as much as until a call is made by the liquidator, it is only a liability to contribute to the assets of the company, if necessary for the payment of the debts due to its creditors and expenses of the winding up.

1. Before winding up, the member can avoid payment to a call made by the company on various grounds. The debt can also become time barred, under Article 112 of the Limitation Act. But if the winding up proceedings are commenced, the liquidator can ask him to pay the unpaid calls even if they had become time barred. Thus, winding up creates a new liability on the shareholder.
2. If the liability of any director or manager, whether present or past, is unlimited under the provisions of the Act, he has to contribute to an unlimited extent over and above his ordinary liability to contribute as an ordinary member.
3. If a person is both a contributory as well as a creditor of the company, he cannot set off his debts against his liability for calls. However, if the company is fully solvent, the contributory can do so.

Death and Insolvency of a Contributory

Section 430 provides that if a contributory dies either before or after he is placed on the list of contributories, his legal representatives shall be liable to contribute to the assets of the company to discharge of his liability. The liability of the legal representative is only a liability to pay out of the estate of the deceased and extends only to the value of the estate coming into his hands.

Where a contributory becomes insolvent his assignee in insolvency represents him for all purpose and is deemed to be a contributory (*Section 432*).

Where a contributory is a company and is itself in liquidation, the liquidators of a company represents it is a contributory for all the purposes of the winding up of the company (*Section 431*).

VOLUNTARY WINDING UP

The object of a voluntary winding up is that the company and its creditors are left to settle their affairs without going to the tribunal, but they may apply to the tribunal for any directions or orders if and when necessary. This form of winding up is by far the most common and the most popular form.

Circumstances for Voluntary Winding Up

A company may be wound up voluntarily when —

(a) the *period fixed* by the Articles for the duration of the company has expired or an *event* upon which the company is to be wound up has happened and the company in general meeting has passed a special resolution;

(b) The company has for any cause whatever passed a *special resolution* to wind up voluntarily (*Section 484*).

The company may be wound up by special resolution even if it is prosperous.

Procedure after Passing the Resolution

1. A resolution for voluntary winding up must be advertised in the official gazette and also in some newspapers, circulating in the district where the registered office of the company is situated, within 14 days of the passing of the resolution.

2. If default is made in complying with this provision, the company and every defaulting officer shall be punishable with fine which may extend to Rs. 500 per day for everyday during which default continues (*Section 485*). officer herein includes the liquidator also.

3. A voluntary winding up commences from the date of the passing of the resolution (*Section 486*).

4. From the commencement of the winding up the company cease to carry on its business except sofaras may be required for the beneficial winding up of such business. But the corporate status and powers continue until it is dissolved (*Section 484*)

Types of Voluntary Winding Up

A voluntary winding up is of two types. They are:

(a) Members' Voluntary Winding Up

(b) Creditors' Voluntary Winding Up.

The distinction between the two types of winding up is based upon whether a declaration of solvency has been made by the directors or not. Where a declaration is made by the directors, the winding up of the company is referred to as a members' voluntary winding up and where no such declaration is made, it is referred to as a creditors' voluntary winding up.

MEMBERS' VOLUNTARY WINDING UP (SECTIONS 489-498)

It is already stated that a members' voluntary winding up is possible only when the company is solvent and is able to pay its debts in full. In this case, it is not necessary for the members to consult the creditors or to call their meeting. A declaration of solvency should be made by the directors.

Declaration of Solvency: *Section 488* provides that where it is proposed to wind up a company voluntarily.

1. The directors or a majority of them, may, at a meeting of the board, make a declaration verified and certified by an affidavit that the company has no debts or that it will be able to pay its debts in full within a period not exceeding 3 years from the commencement of winding up as may be specified in the declaration.

2. The declaration must be accompanied by a statement of assets and liabilities up to the date of declaration.

3. A copy of the Auditors' Report on the profit and the loss account and on the balance sheet from the last accounting date to a date ending with the latest practicable date immediately before the date of making the declaration.

4. Such declaration shall be made and filed with the registrar within five weeks immediately preceding the date of the passing of the resolution for winding up and shall be delivered, the winding up following shall be called members voluntary winding up. Where the same is not duly made, it shall be called creditors voluntary winding up.

PROCEDURE FOR MEMBERS' VOLUNTARY WINDING UP

Sections 490-498 of the Act deal with provisions applicable to members, voluntary winding up. They are as follow:

1. Holding of the General Meeting: After filing the declaration of solvency, the directors should arrange to convene a meeting of the company and a resolution should be passed to this effect.

2. Appointment of Liquidator (Section 490): The company in general meeting shall appoint one or more liquidators for winding up the affairs of a company and for distributing the assets. The company shall also fix his remuneration and unless his remuneration is not fixed, he will not take charge of his office.

3. Notice of Appointment of Liquidator to Registrar (Section 493): The company shall give notice to the registrar of the appointment of a liquidator within 10 days of such appointment.

4. Board's Powers to Cease (Section 491) : On the appointment of a liquidator all the powers of the board of directors and other managerial personal shall come to an end, except in sofaras the company in general meeting or the liquidator sanctions the continuance thereof.

5. Power to Fill Vacancy in the Office of Liquidator (Section 492): Where a vacancy for what ever cause occurs death, registration or otherwise in the office of the liquidator the company in general meeting, subject to any arrangement with the creditors fill the vacancy. The general meeting may be called by any contributory or by any continuing liquidator.

6. Holding of the General Meeting at the end of the First Year (Section 496): Where the winding up continues for more than one year, the liquidator must call a general meeting of the company at the end of the first year and at the end of each subsequent year. He should lay before the meeting an account of his acts and dealings and the progress of the winding up during the year.

7. Final Meeting and Dissolution (Section 497): When the affairs of the company are fully wound up, the liquidator shall make up an account of the winding up, showing how the same has been conducted and how the property has been disposed of.

He shall call a general meeting of the company for laying before it the said accounts. The meeting shall be called by advertisement specifying the time, place and object thereof. The advertisement shall be made not less than one month before the meeting in the official gazette and also in some local newspapers where the registered office of the company is situated. Failure to call meeting is punishable with fine up to Rs. 500.

8. Notice to the Registrar and Official Liquidator: Within one week after the meeting, the liquidator shall sends a copy of the account to the registrar and the official liquidator attached to the concerned High Court and also a return of the holding of the meeting and the date thereof. The registrar on receiving the account and either of the returns shall forthwith register the same. The official liquidator on receipt of the account and the return is required to make a scrutiny of the books and papers of the company. The liquidator of the company, its past and present officers shall afford an opportunity to the official liquidator for this purpose. The offcial liquidator shall send a report, the court may order either further investigation of the affairs of the company or dissolution of the company with effect from the date specified in the order.

9. Report of the Official Liquidator to the National Company Law Tribunal: On receipt of the account and the return of the meeting, the official liquidator should make a scrutiny of the books and papers of the company. After scrutiny, the official liquidator should submit a report to the National Company Law Tribunal. If the report reveals that the affairs of the company were not conducted in a manner prejudicial to the interests of the members or public, the company is deemd to be dissolved from the date of submission of the report.

If the report, on the other hand, contains any adverse remarks, the National Company Law Tribunal must direct the official liquidator to make further investigation into the affairs of the company (Sec. 497 (6A)). On the receipt of the report of the official liquidator on such further investigation the National Company Law Tribunal may either make an order that the company shall stand dissolved with effect from the date to be specified by the National Company Law Tribunal therein or make such other order as the circumstances of the case brought out in the report permit (Sec. 497 (6-B)).

10. Duty to Call Creditors Meeting (Section 495): Where the liquidator is, at any time, of the opinion that the company will not be able to pay its debts in full within the specified period, he shall immediately call a meeting of the creditors and shall place before it a statement of the company's assets and liabilities. On default the penalty is a fine which may extend to Rs. 5,000. Where a liquidator has called a creditors meeting under Section 495, the winding up, then would proceed as if it was creditors voluntary winding up (Section 498).

11. Provisions as to Annual and Final Meeting in Case of Insolvency (Sec. 498): If in the case of a members' voluntary widing up, the liquidator finds that the company is insolvent, Secs. 508 and 509 shall apply as if the winding up were a creditors' voluntary winding up and not a members' voluntary winding up. It should be noted that in such a case Secs. 508 and 509 shall apply to the exclusion of Secs. 496 and 497. Sec. 508 deals with the duty of the liquidator to call a meeting of the company and of creditors at the end of each year and Sec. 509 deals with the final meeting and dissolution in case of creditors' voluntary winding up.

CREDITORS' VOLUNTARY WINDING UP (SECTIONS 500-509)

Where the declaration of solvency is not made the winding up is referred to as creditors' voluntary winding up. That is, creditors' voluntary winding up takes place only when the company is an insolvent condition and so it is unable to discharge its liabilities in full. The provisions for creditors' voluntary winding up are similar to those applicable to the members' voluntary winding up except that in the former, it is the creditors who appoint the liquidator, fix his remuneration and generally conduct the winding up. Sections 500 to 509 deal with creditors' voluntary winding up. They are discussed as under:

1. Meeting of the Members and Creditors (Section 500): When a declaration of solvency is not made by the directors, the company shall cause a meeting of the creditors of the company to be called for the day or for next following day on which the special resolution general meeting for voluntary winding up is to be proposed. Notice of the meeting of creditors shall be posted to each creditors simultaneously with notice of the general meeting of the company. The notice calling the meeting of the creditors shall be advertised once at least in the official gazette and once at least in two newspapers circulating in the district where the registered office of the company is situated. The board of directors shall lay before the meeting of the creditors a full statement of the position of the company's affairs together with the list of its creditors and the estimated amount of their claims. One of the directors must preside at the meeting.

2. Notice to Register (Section 501): The company shall give notice of resolution passed at the creditors meeting to the registrar within 10 days of its passing.

3. Appointment of Liquidator (Section 502): The creditors and the company shall appoint a person to be the liquidator. If different persons were nominated, the person nominated by the creditor of the company may, within 7 days of the nomination made by the creditors, apply to the court for an order that the person appointed by the company shall be the liquidator. Where no person is nominated by the creditors, the person nominated by the company shall be liquidator. On the other hand if no person is nominated by the company, the person nominated by the creditors shall be the liquidator.

4. Appointment of Committee of Inspection (Section 503): The creditors at their meeting may appoint a committee of inspection consisting of not more than six persons. Where such a committee is appointed, the members of the company may also appoint at a meeting such number of persons not exceeding five to act as the members of the committee. The creditors may resolve that any of the persons appointed by the company ought not to be the members of the committee of inspection. In such cases, unless the court otherwise directs, they cannot act on the committee. The court may appoint other persons in place of persons objected to.

5. Liquidators' Remuneration (Section 504): Remuneration of the liquidator may be fixed by the committee of inspection or by the creditors if there is no committee of inspection. Otherwise the National Company Law Tribunal may fix his remuneration. Remuneration fixed as above cannot be increased in any circumstances without the permission of the tribunal.

6. Power of Board of Directors to Cease (Section 505): The board of directors usually ceases to function on appointment of the liquidator. The Board of directors may act in sofaras the committee of inspection (if any) or the creditors in general meeting may sanction the continuance thereof.

7. Vacancy in Office of Liquidator (Section 506): The creditors in general meeting may fill up any vacancy caused by death, resignation or otherwise, in the office of the liquidator other than a liquidator appointed by or by direction of the National Company Law Tribunal.

8. Meeting at the end of Each Year (Section 508): Where the winding up continues for more than a year the liquidator shall call a general meeting of the company and a meeting of the creditors at the end of the first year from the commencement of the winding up and at the end of each succeeding year or within three months from the end of the year or such longer period as the tribunal may allow. The liquidator shall lay before the meeting an account of his acts and dealings and of the conduct of the winding up during the preceding year.

9. Final Meeting of the Members and also the Creditors and Dissolution (Section 509): As soon as the affairs of the company are wound up, the liquidator shall make up the account of the winding up showing how the winding up has been conducted and property of the company has been disposed of. He shall call a general meeting of the company and a meeting of the creditors for the purpose of laying the accounts of his debts and dealings before the meetings.

Each such meeting shall be advertised in the official gazette and also in some newspapers circulating in the district where the registered office of the company is situated.

The liquidator should submit the statement of affairs in each of the meetings. Within a week after the meeting the liquidator shall send to the registrar a copy of the account and a return to each of the meeting to the registrar and official liquidator.

The registrar, on receipt of the same (accounts, statement of affairs as well as return) shall register them immediately.

A similar copy should be sent to the official liquidator and the official liquidator should submit a report thereon to the National Company Law Tribunal. The follow-up proceedings are similar to the members' voluntary winding up.

Difference between Members' Voluntary winding up and Creditors' voluntary winding up

1. Declaration of Solvenvy: Declaration of solvency is a must in a members' voluntary winding up, whereas it is not necessary in a creditors' voluntary winding up.

2. Creditors' Meeting: It is not necessary to have a creditors' meeting in the case of members' voluntary winding up, whereas in the case of creditors' voluntary winding up, it is a statutory duty of the company to call a meeting of the creditors.

3. Appointing Authority of a Liquidator: The liquidator is appointed by the members in case of members' voluntary winding up, whereas both members and creditors' appoint liquidator in case of creditors' voluntary winding up.

4. Committee of Inspection: There is no committee of inspection in case of members' voluntary winding up, but in case of latter there is one.

5. Remuneration to Liquidator: In a members' voluntary winding up the remuneration can be fixed only by the members. In a creditors' voluntary winding up, it is generally fixed by the committee of inspection or by the creditors. If either of them does not fix the remuneration, the National Company Law Tribunal shall fix the remuneration.

6. Powers of Liquidators: In a members' voluntary winding up, certain powers can be exercised by the liquidator only with the sanction of members. While in a creditors' voluntary winding up, he can do so with the approval of the committee of inspection or the creditors of the National Company Law Tribunal.

7. Payment of Creditors: In a members' voluntary winding up, the company is solvent and hence the creditors are paid in full, whereas in a creditors' voluntary winding up, the company is not solvent and hence preferential payments are made first and the claims of other creditors are satisfied *pari passu* (i.e., ratably).

8. Control of Winding Up : In a members' voluntary winding up, the members control the winding up of the company and the creditors do not participate directly as the company makes a declaration of solvency. In a creditors' voluntary winding up, the creditors control the winding up of the company as the company is deemed to be insolvent.

CONSEQUENCES OF WINDING UP

1. Consequences as to Shareholders

When the company is a going concern, he is termed as a shareholder or member. In winding up he becomes a contributory. As a contributory, a shareholder is liable to pay the full amount up to the face value of the shares held by him. Not only the present members but past members are also liable in the event of winding up of the company. The liabilities of present member is the amount remaining unpaid on the shares held by him while a past member can be called upon to pay if the contributions made by the present members are not adequate.

Payment to the Shareholders: If there is any surplus (as it may happen in the case of a solvent company), capital is returned to preference shareholders first and then to equity shareholders. If there is still more surplus, it depends on the Articles as to whether preference shares are participating or not. If there is an agreement to pay interest, interest can also be claimed provided the company is solvent.

2. Consequences as to Creditors

A company, whether solvent or insolvent, can be wound up under the Act. In case of solvent company, all claims of its creditors when proved are fully met. But in case of insolvent company, the rules under the law of insolvency shall apply.

As regards the secured creditor, he need not prove his claim against the company. He may realise his security and satisfy the debts. For deficiency (if any), he may put up his claim before the liquidator. The secured creditor has also the option to relinquish his security and to prove the amount as if he were an unsecured creditor.

Proof of Debts: Persons who claim to be creditors must prove their debt within the time fixed by the National Company Law Tribunal or the liquidator (in case of a voluntary winding up). Even if a creditor fails to prove his debt within the specified time, he can prove his claim and get money until the assets are remianing with the liquidator. However, he cannot get any money if the assets are already utilised for payment. The liquidator should also trace out the creditor even if no claim is made and settle his dues if he is satisfied that the debt is actually due to the creditor and assets are still remaining with him. The liquidator is also empowered to pay off even statute barred debts, if the shareholders do not object.

3. Consequences as to the Employees and Officers

It is already stated that a winding up order operates as a notice of discharge to the employees and officers of the company. The following are the provisions of the Act.

(a) The winding up order operates as a notice of discharge except when the company is allowed to do business after passing of the order.

(b) In a voluntary winding up, the officers so discharged can claim damages if there is an express agreement of employment for a fixed period.

ORDER OF PAYMENT

As soon as the assets are realised and the list of claimants is finalised the liquidator has to commence making payment. From the provisions of Sections 511, 520, 529 and 530 it appears that:

(i) Costs, charges and expense of the winding up including liquidator's remuneration;

(ii) Workmen's dues and claims of secured creditors (as mentioned in Section 529-A).

(iii) Preferential creditors:

(iv) The creditors secured by floating charges:

(v) Unsecured or ordinary creditors; and

(vi) Members or contributories.

Regarding members, if any of them has paid in *excess of the amount of call made on him, that will be returned to him first* and then the preference shareholders are given their capital and thereafter, if any, surplus is left that will be distributed among the equity shareholders if the Articles of the company so provide.

As surplus still left, will also go to the equity shareholders unless the preference shares are the participating preference shares as per terms of the issue.

PREFERENTIAL PAYMENTS (SEC. 530)

'*Preferential Payments*' are the payments made to certain unsecured creditors in priority to all other debts on winding up of the company, the preferential payments are:

(a) All revenues, taxes, cesses and rates due from the company to the Central or State Government or to a local authority which have become due and payable within 12 months before:

(i) the date of appointment of provisional liquidator, or

(ii) the date of winding up order in case of compulsory winding up, and

(iii) the date of the passing of the resolution for winding up on the case of voluntary winding up.

(b) **All wages or salary of an employee** in respect of services rendered to the company and due for a period not exceeding 4 months within 12 months before the above relevant date and any compensation payable to any workman under any of the provisions of Chapter V-A of the Industrial Disputes Act, 1947. The total amount must not exceed Rs. 1,000 in the case of any one claimant.

(c) **All accured holiday remuneration** becoming payable to any or in the case of his death to any other person in his right, on the termination of his employment before or by the effect of, the winding up order or resolution.

(d) All amounts due in respect of contributions payable during 12 months next before the relevant date, by the company as the employer of any persons under the **Employee's State Insurance Act, 1948,** or any other law for the time in force. But this is not payable if the company is being wound up voluntarily for the purpose of reconstruction and amalgamation.

(e) All amount due in respect of death or disablement of any employee under the **Workmen's Compensation Act, 1923,** but this is not payable if the company is being wound up voluntarily for reconstruction or amalgamation.

(f) All sums due to any employee from a **provident fund, a pension fund, a gratuity fund** or any other fund for the welfare of the employees maintained by the company.

(g) The **expenses of any investigation** held in pursuance of Section 235 or 237, in sofaras they are payable by the company.

It is to be noted that the above *preferential creditors will rank equally amongst themselves.* They have to be paid in full, unless the assets are insufficient in which case they shall abate in proportion to their total amount. *They shall have preference even over those creditors who are secured by a floating charge on the assets.*

4. As to Proceedings Against the Company

As soon as winding up order is passed:

(a) No suit or other legal proceeding against the company can be commenced,

(b) pending suit at the date of the winding up order cannot be proceeded with against the company except by leave of the court and subject to such terms as the court may impose,

(c) Even in voluntary winding up, the court may restrain proceeding against the company if it thinks fit. The winding up order will operate in favour of all creditors and all the contributories of the company, and they can avail themselves of it as if the order was passed on a pêtition field by all of them jointly.

Effect of Winding up on Antecedent and other Transactions

Fraudulent Preference (Sec. 531)

Any transfer of property, movable or immovable, delivery of goods, payment, execution of other act relating to property made by or against a company within 6 months before the commencement of its winding up which had it been made, be deemed a fraudulent preference of its creditors and be invalid accordingly.

Fraudulent preference here relates similarly to fraudulent preference under insolvency law, where any individual transfers any property or makes any payment within 3 months before the presentation of an insolvency petition, shall be deemed a fraudulent preference in his insolvency. Under Companies Act, 1956, the period is 6 months instead of 3 months.

Avoidance of Voluntary Transfer

Section 531-A lays down that any transfer of property, movable or immovable, or any delivery of goods made by the company within a period of one year before the presentation of a petition for winding up by or subject to the supervision of the court or the passing of a resolution for voluntary winding up of the company, shall be void against the liquidator unless such transfer or delivery is made in the ordinary course of business or in favour of a purchase or encumbrances in good faith and for valuable consideration. Further, any transfer or assignment by a company of all its property to trustees for the benefit of all its creditors shall be void *(Sec. 532).*

Effect of Floating Charge (Sec. 534) : A floating charge on the property of the company shall be invalid if the company goes into liquidation within 12 months from the date of such charge. However, a floating charge will be valid in the following cases:

(a) if the company immediately after the creation of charge was solvent, or

(b) if the company had received any cash in consideration thereof at the time of or after the creation of such charge.

Disclaimer of Onerous Property (Sec. 535): 'Disclaimer' means abandoning. Where any part of the property of a company which is being wound up consists of:

(a) *land of any tenure, burdened with onerous covenants:*

(b) *Shares or stock in other companies;*

(c) *any other property which is un-salable* by reason of its binding the possessor thereof either to the performance of any onerous act or to the payment of any sum or money; or

(d) *unprofitable contracts;*

The liquidator of the company may, by writing signed by him, disclaim the properly with the leave of the court. It has to be made within 12 months after the commencement of the winding up. The court before granting leave to disclaim, may require such notice to be given to the persons interested. Where any such propert has not come to the knowledge of the liquidator within one month after the commencement of the winding up, the power of disclaiming the property may be exercised at anytime within 12 months after he has become aware thereof or such extended period as may be allowed by the court.

The disclaimer shall operate to determine the rights, interest and liabilities of the company but shall not affect the rights or liabilities of any other person, except sofaras is necessary for the purpose of releasing the company and the property of the company from liability.

The liquidator shall not be entitled to disclaim any property in any case where an application in writing has been made to him by any person interested in the property requiring him to decide whether he will or will not disclaim, and the liquidator has not within 28 days after the receipt of the application given notice to the applicant that he intends to apply to the court for leave to disclaim.

Further, any person injured by the operation of a disclaimant shall be deemed to be a creditor of the company to the amount of the compensation or damages payable in respect of the injury, and may accordingly prove the amount as a debt in the winding up.

OFFENCES BY OFFICERS OF COMPANIES IN LIQUIDATION (SEC. 538)

Any officer of the company, whether past or present, in the winding up the company is punishable with fine and imprisonment in connection with certain offences. To quote for instance, he is punishable:

(i) if he does not to the best of his knowledge and belief, **fully and truly disclose** to the liquidator all the property of the company.

(ii) if he does not deliver up to the liquidator, or as he directs, all such **part of the property** of the company as is in his custody or under his control and which he is required by law to deliver up.

(iii) if he does not deliver up to the liquidator, or as he directs, all such **books and papers** of the company as are in his custody or under his control and which he is required by law to deliver up.

(iv) if he **conceals any part of the property** to the value of Rs.100 or more within 12 months next before the commencement of the winding up or at anytime thereafter.

(v) if he **fraudulently removes any part of the property** to the value of Rs. 100 or more within 12 months next before the commencement of the winding up or at anytime thereafter.

(vi) if he **makes any material omission in any statement** relating to the affairs of the company.

(vii) if he knowingly or believing that a **false debt has been proved**, by any person under the winding up, fails for a period of one month to inform the liquidator thereof.

(viii) if he, after the commencement of the winding up, **prevents the proportion of any book or paper affecting or relating to the property or affairs of the company**.

(ix) if he **conceals, destroys, mutilates or falsifies, or is privy to the concealment**, destruction, mutilation or falsification of any book or paper affecting or relating to the property or the affairs of the company.

(x) if he makes, or is privy to the making if any **false entry in any book or paper** affecting or relating to the property or the affairs of the company.

(xi) if he, by **false representation or other fraud, obtains on credit** for or on behalf of the company any property which the company does not subsequently pay for.

(xii) if he attempts to account for any part of the company by **fictitious losses or expenses**.

(xiii) if he **pledges or disposes of any property** of the company which has been obtained on credit and has not been paid for, unless such pledge or disposal is in the ordinary course of the business of the company.

(xiv) if he is **guilty of any false representation or other fraud** for the purpose of obtaining the consent of the creditors of the company or any of them, to an agreement with reference to the affairs of the company or to the winding up.

In the case of any of the offences mentioned in (xi) and (xiii) the defaulting officer shall be punishable with imprisonment for a term which may extend to 5 years, or with fine, or with both and in the case of any other offence with imprisonment for a term which may extend to 2 years or with fine, or with both.

Falsification and Maintenance of Improper Books (Sections 539 and 541)

If with intent to defraud or deceive any person, any officer or contributory of a company which is being wound up (a) destroys, mutilates, alters, falsifies or secretes any books or papers or securities; or (b) makes any false or fraudulent entry in any register, books of account or documents belonging to the company, he shall be punishable with imprisonment for a term which may extend to 7 years and shall also be liable to fine.

Where proper books of account are not kept for a period of 2 years immediately preceding the commencement of the winding up, every officer of the company who is in default shall be punishable with imprisonment for a term which may extend to one year.

Fraud by Officers (Sec. 540)

If any of the below mentioned offence is committed by an officer of a company which subsequently goes into liquidation, he shall be punishable with both imprisonment and fine:

(a) if he has by false pretences or by means of any other fraud induced any person to give credit to the company, or

(b) if he, with intent to defraud creditors of the company, has made any gift or transfer of any of the company or has created a charge on any property of the company, or

(c) if he, with intent to defraud creditors of the company, has concealed or removed any part of the property of the company since the date of any unsatisfied judgement for or order for payment of money obtained against the company or within 2 months of such date.

Fraudulent Conduct of Business (Sec. 542): By virtue of Section 542 of the Act, if in the course of the winding of a company it appears that any business of the company has been carried on with intent to defraud creditors of the company, the Court may declare that any persons who were knowingly parties to such carrying on of the business shall be personally liable for all or any of the debts or other liabilities of the company. The application for this purpose may be made to the court by the liquidator, any creditor or contributory of the company.

Court to Assess Damages Against Delinquent Directors etc. (Sec. 543)

If in the course of winding up of a company, it appears that any person who has taken part in the promotion or formation of the company or any past or present director, manager, liquidator or officer of the company:

(a) has misapplied or retained or become liable for any money or property of the company, or

(b) has been guilty of any misfeasance or breach of trust in relation to the company, the tribunal may (on the application of the liquidator or creditor or contributory) examine into the conduct of such person and compel him to repay or restore the money or property or compensate the company for any loss suffered by it on account of his delinquent conduct.

In this context, it is to be noted that an application to the tribunal should be made within 5 years from the date of the winding up order or of the first appointment of the liquidator in the winding up or of commitment of above offence, whichever is longer. The tribunal has also the power under Section 545 to prosecute the offender, (i.e., delinquent officers/members of the company) or to refer the matter to the register.

It is important to note that Section 543 of the Act does not in fact create any new liability. It only provides for a summary remedy for determining the amount payable by such person on proof of the necessary ingredients. This section authorises the court to direct such persons chargeable under it to pay a sum of money to a company by way of compensation. This is not a provision intended to punish a person who has been found guilty of misfeasance but for compensating the company in respect of the loss occasioned by his misfeasance. In the case of ***Official Liquidator vs. Parthasarathi Sinha***, the Supreme Court observed that the proceedings initiated against a director of the company in liquidation under Section 543 can be continued after his death against his legal representatives and the amount declared to be due in such misfeasance proceedings and be realised from the estate of the deceased in the hands of his legal representative. Of course, the legal representative would not be liable for any sum beyond the value of the estate of the deceased in his hands.

Remember, the liability arising under the misfeasance proceeding, is based on the principle that a person who has caused loss to the company by an act tantamounting to breach of trust should make good the loss.

Final Disposal of Books and Papers of Company (Sec. 550)

When the affairs of a company have been completely wound up and it is about to be dissolved, its books and papers and those of the liquidator may be disposed of as follows:

(a) in the case of a winding up by or subject to the supervision of the court, in such manner as the court directs;

(b) in the case of a member's voluntary winding up, in such manner as the company by special resolution directs; and

(c) in the case of a creditor's voluntary winding up, in such manner as the committee of inspection or, if there is no such committee, as the creditors of the company may direct.

After the expiry of 5 years from the dissolution of the company, no responsibility shall rest on the company, the liquidator, or any person to whom the custody of the books and papers has been committed, if any book or paper could not be produced to any person interested therein.

Dissolution of a Company (Sec. 481)

The tribunal makes an order for the dissolution of a company on any of the grounds stated below:

(i) when the affairs of a company have been completely wound up, or

(ii) when the tribunal is of the opinion that the liquidator cannot proceed with the winding up of a company for want of funds or assets; or

(iii) when it is just and reasonable in the circumstances of the case that an order of dissolution of the company should be made, or

(iv) for any other reason whatsoever.

The company is dissolved from the date of the order of the court. Within 30 days of the order of the tribunal, the liquidator must send a copy of the order to the registrar, failing which he is punishable with fine which may extend to Rs. 50 for every day of default.

Where a company has been dissolved by process of winding up, or by order of tribunal under Section 481 or for facilitating reconstruction and amalgamation or otherwise, the tribunal may at anytime within 2 years of the date of dissolution make an order declaring the dissolution to have been void. A certified copy of such an order shall be filed with the registrar within 30 days after the making of such order.

DEFUNCT COMPANY (SECTION 560)

A 'defunct company' means a company which has never commenced business or which has ceased to carry to business.

Procedure of Registrar to Strike Defunct Company of the Register

Under Section 560, the registrar of companies can strike the name of such company from the companies register and for striking off the name, he is supposed to adhere to the following steps:

1. *Enquiry Letter:* He has to send to the company by post a *letter* enquiring whether the company is carrying on business or is in operation.
2. *Second Letter (Reminder):* If no reply is received within one month, then he must send within the next 14 days a registered letter referring to the first letter and stating that no answer thereto has been received and that if an answer is not received to the second letter within one month from the date thereof, a notice will be published in the official gazette with a view to striking of company's name from the register.
3. *Final Notice to the Company Publication in the Official Gazette:* If no satisfactory reply is received within one month from the date thereof, he must send to the company by post and publish in the official gazette a notice stating that unless cause is shown to contrary, the name of the company will be struck off from the register after 3 months and the company will be dissolved.

In any case where a company is being wound up, the registrar has reasonable cause to believe either: (a) that no liquidator is acting, or (b) that the affairs of the company have been completely 'wound up' and any return required to be made by the liquidator have not been made for a period of six consecutive months, the registrar shall publish in the official gazette and send to the company or the liquidator, if any, a notice by registered post stating that unless cause is shown to the contrary, the name of the company will be struck off from the register after three months and the company will be dissolved.

The dissolution of the company in the above stated manner shall not, however, affect: (i) the liability, if any of every director, manager or other officer who was exercising any power of management and of every member of the company. In other words, such persons shall be liable as if the company had not been dissolved; and (ii) the power of the court to wind up a company the name of which has been struck off from the register.

Restoration of the Name of Such Company: If a company or any member or creditor thereof feels aggrieved by the company having been struck off from the register, the company, or any member or creditor may make an application to the National Company Law Tribunal before the expiry of 20 years from the publication of the notice in the official gazette. The National Company Law Tribunal, if satisfied that the company was at the time of the striking off:

(a) carrying on business or was in operation, or

(b) otherwise that it is just that the company be restored to the register, order the name of the company to be restored to the register. The power of the tribunal to grant restoration is discretionary.

Effect of Restoration: For registration, a certified copy of the order shall be delivered to the registrar. The company shall then be deemed to have continued in existence as if its name had not been struck off.

It is, thus, clear that on the restoration of a company back to the register after its being struck off the consequence is as though it had never been struck off from the register. The company will be deemed to have had existence all through. Another consequence is that the rights of all parties would be as though there had been no cessation or interruption in the existence of the company on account of the striking off and the subsequent restoration.

WINDING UP OF UNREGISTERED COMPANIES (SECTIONS 583-588)

The term **'unregistered company'** includes any partnership, association or company consisting of more than seven members at the time when the petition for winding up is presented before the court. By virtue of Section 582 of the Act, an "unregistered company" does not include: (a) a railway company incorporated by any Act of Parliament or other Indian Law or any Act of Parliament of U.K.; (b) a company registered under the Companies Act, 1956; or (c) a company registered under any previous Companies Act and whose registered office is in India.

Generally, the 'unregistered company' has the following **characteristics**:

1. perpetual existence.
2. vesting of management in a selected body of directors appointed by the members.
3. unlimited liability of members.
4. transferability of shares.

An unregistered company may be wound up under the provision of this Act and with some exceptions all the provisions relating to winding up are applicable to it. However, such a company can only be wound up by the National Company Law

Tribunal. An 'unregistered company', therefore, cannot be wound up voluntarily or subject to the supervision of the court. Such a company may be wound up if:

(a) the company is dissolved or has ceased to carry on business or is carrying on business only to wind up its affairs:

(b) the company is unable to pay its debts; and

(c) the National Company Law Tribunal is of the opinion that it is just and equitable that the company should be wound up.

'Unable to Pay its Debts' [Sec. 582(5)]

An unregistered company shall be deemed to be unable to pay its debts if any of the following conditions is satisfied:

(i) if a creditor to whom the company is indebted a sum exceeding Rs. 500 has several demands on the company and the company has for three weeks thereafter failed to pay the sum or otherwise satisfy him;

(ii) if any suit or legal proceeding has been instituted against any member for any debt due from the company and notice in writing of the institution has been served on the company and the company has within 10 days thereafter, failed to pay any debt or get the proceedings stayed or satisfy the claimant;

(iii) if execution or other process issued or any decree or order of any court of the National Company Law Tribunal in favour of a creditor against the company is returned unsatisfied;

(iv) if it is otherwise proved to the satisfaction of the National Company Law Tribunal that the company is unable to pay its debts.

Contributions in Winding of Unregistered Company (Sec. 585)

In the event of an unregistered company being wound up, every person shall be deemed to be a contributory, who is liable to pay, or contribute to the payment of:

(a) any debt or liability of the company: or

(b) any sum for the adjustment of the rights of the members among themselves; or

(c) the costs, charges and expenses of winding up of the company.

Note that, every contributory is liable to contribute to the assets of the company all sums due from him in respect of any liability to pay or contribute as stated above.

Further, in the event of the death or insolvency of any contributory, his legal representative or assignee is liable to make the above payments.

Power to stay or restrain proceedings under the Act extends to suits and legal proceedings against any contributory of the company or NCLT (Section 586)

Suits, etc., Stayed on Winding up: Where an order has been made for winding up an unregistered company, no suit or other legal proceeding shall be proceeded with or commenced against any contributory of the company in respect of any debt of the company except by leave of the National Company Law Tribunal and except on such terms as the court may impose (*Section 587*).

If an unregistered company has no power to sue and be sued in a common name or if for any reason it appears expedient, the National Company Law Tribunal may by the winding up order direct that all or any of the party belonging to the company shall vest in the official liquidator. The National Company Law Tribunal or official liquidator may exercise any powers or do any act in the case of unregistered companies which might be exercised by the National Company Law Tribunal or official liquidator in winding up companies formed and registered under this Act.

WINDING UP OF FOREIGN COMPANIES (SEC. 584)

A foreign company may be wound up like an unregistered company under Part X of this Act. Section 584 clearly states that "where a body corporate incorporated outside, which has been carrying on business in India, ceases to carry on business in India, it may be wound up as an unregistered company under this Part, (*i.e.,* Part X), notwithstanding that the body corporate has been dissolved or otherwise ceased to exist as such under or by virtue of the laws of the country under which it was incorporated".

The law regarding winding up a foreign company has been well summarised by **Megarry J. in Re Companion Merabello san Nicholas (1972)** in the following ways:

1. For the court to have jurisdiction to wind up a foreign company, it is not necessary to establish either that the company had a place of business within the jurisdiction or that it had carried on business there, unless the petition is based on the circumstance that the company had ceased to carry on business or was carrying on business only to wind up its affairs;
2. It is sufficient to found jurisdiction to show that the company has some asset or assets within the jurisdiction and that there are one or more persons concerned in the proper distribution of such assets;
3. Such assets need not be of a commercial nature or assets which indicated that the company had carried on business within the jurisdiction, they can be of any nature; and

4. They need not be assets which would be distributable to creditors by the liquidator in the winding up; it is sufficient if by the making of the winding up order, they would be of benefit to a creditor or creditors in some other way.

The company is dissolved from the date of the order of the court. Within 30 days of the order of the court, the liquidator must send a copy of the order to the Registrar, failing which he is punishable with fine which may extend to Rs. 500 for every day of default.

Where a company has been dissolved by process of winding up, or by order of court under Section 481 or for facilitating reconstruction and amalgamation or otherwise, the court may at anytime within 2 years of the date of dissolution make an order declaring the dissolution to have been void. A certified copy of such an order shall be filed with the Registrar within 30 days after the making of such order.

Distinction Between Insolvency and Winding Up

The process of winding up closely resembles insolvency proceeding and follows the rules of insolvency. But a company can never be adjudicated as an insolvent, even if the company is in an insolvent condition, i.e., if it is unable to pay its debts and to meet its liabilities. There is a marked distinction between the insolvency of a firm or individual and winding up of a company. The points of distinction between them are given below:

1. A person can file an insolvency petition only when he is actually in an insolvent condition. A company which is in liquidation need not be in an insolvent condition. Even a flourishing company may voluntarily wound up if the members think so.
2. In case of insolvency, the whole of the property of the insolvent is taken out of his hands and vests in the court or the official assignee, whereas in case of winding up, the property remains with the company and not assigned to the liquidator. Only the administration of the property is vested in the hands of the liquidators.
3. In case of insolvency, the insolvent can get discharge of his debts and live freely without the burden of debts. The creditors cannot claim anything from the insolvent. The position is different in case of companies. The company in liquidation cannot obtain a discharge of its debts. It shall not be allowed to continue his business freely without the burden of its debts.
4. Insolvency proceedings can be taken up only by the court. However, liquidation proceedings can be taken up by the National Company Law Tribunal. Further, it can be wound up voluntarily without the intervention of the National Company Law Tribunal.

Though the rules of insolvency are applied in case of the assets of a company in liquidation, such rules are not identical with those of insolvency. There are many insolvency rules which shall not apply to a company in liquidation.

Distinction Between Winding Up and Dissolution

The words "**Windings Up**" and "**Dissolution**" are used to explain the same thing but legally there is difference between the two term. The legal entity of a company remains even after the issue of winding up order and before its dissolution. The important points of distinction between the two are as follows:

1. Winding up precedes dissolution. It is the first step and dissolution is the final step in dropping the curtain over a company.
2. Winding up involves the collection and realisation of the company's assets and the distribution of the proceeds among the creditors and if there be a surplus, among the contributories. Dissolution announces that all these formalities are over at the date of the dissolution or end of the company.
3. The liquidator can represent the company in the process of winding up. The winding proceedings are carried out by the liquidator. On the dissolution he can no longer represent the company as it ceases to exist.
4. Creditors can prove their debts in the winding up but never on the dissolution of the company.
5. Order of the court is not essential in winding up, while for dissolution the order of the court is essential.

QUESTIONS

Objective Type Questions

I. Fill up the blanks

1. A company is said to be wound up voluntarily when there is ________.
2. Declaration of solvency means ________.
3. The declaration of solvency has to be prepared and duly signed by ________.
4. A committee of inspection is constituted in ________ meeting .
5. Disclaimer of onerous property means ________.
6. Provisional liquidator is appointed ________.
7. A defunct company is one ________.
8. A Committee of Inspection shall consist ________ members.

9. Contributories in the B list are persons ________.

10. The registrar shall restore even a defunct company on application by members if it is proved ________.

[*Answers:* (1) no interference or interruption from Court in the process of winding up; (2) the company is solvent and that it will be able to discharge all its liabilities within 3 years from the commencement of winding up; (3) Directors; (4) Creditors; (5) Liquidator waiving his claim over a property over which there are lot of encumbrance created by other creditors; (6) after receiving the winding up petition; (7) Which has ceased to do business or function as a company. It has no assets or liabilities; (8) Five; (9) Past members who although transferred their shares yet continue to be liable because they ceased to be members within one year preceding the winding up; (10) that the company was in existence doing business within twenty years from the publication in the Official Gazette that its name has been removed.]

II. State whether the following statements are True or False

1. A company may be voluntarily wound up if a special resolution is passed.
2. A company has to be wound up only when it is insolvent.
3. Mere declaration of solvency by directors is enough for winding up the company voluntarily.
4. The liquidator has independent right to prove rank and claim in the insolvency of any contributory.
5. The liquidator appointed by the members could be removed by the creditors in their meeting for voluntary winding up.
6. When a liquidator is appointed, the board of directors ceases to function.
7. The debts due to secured creditors supersede the claims of the government dues.
8. Disclaimer of onerous property should be done by the liquidator only with the consent of the court.
9. Whenever there is conflict between creditors and members in their winding up meetings, it becomes a winding up subject to the supervision of court.
10. Once a company is made defunct company, it cannot be revived.

[*Answers:* True: (1), (4), (5), (6), (8), (9); False: (2), (3), (7), (10)]

Review Questions

1. Define the expression "*Winding Up*".
2. *What is a just and equitable clause for winding of a company?*
3. Who may petition to the National Company Law Tribunal for winding up?

4. Define declaration of solvency.
5. What are the various circumstances in which a company may wound up voluntarily?
6. What is creditors' voluntary winding up?
7. Define a contributory.
8. Describe the nature and extent of liability of a contributory.
9. What is meant by winding up of a company? Distinguish it from dissolution.
10. What are the different methods of winding up?
11. What is compulsory winding up? State the grounds for compulsory winding up?
12. What is just and equitable clause winding up of a company?
13. Who may petition to the National Company Law Tribunal for order of winding up?
14. What do you mean by voluntary winding up? Explain its kinds briefly.
15. What do you mean by dissolution of a company?
16. What are the kinds of voluntary winding up? State the points of distinction between the kinds.
17. What are defunct companies?
18. Who is a contributory ? Explain the nature and extent of liability of a contributory.
19. Explain the consequences of winding up as to shareholders.
20. Who is an official liquidator? What are his powers?
21. State the functions and duties of the official liquidator.
22. What are the liabilities of liquidator?
23. What are the duties of the voluntary liquidators?
24. Explain the various kinds of winding up under the Companies Act, 1956.
25. Enumerate the various grounds for compulsory winding up of a company.
26. Discuss the procedure for members' voluntary winding up.
27. Enumerate the procedure for creditors' voluntary winding up.
28. Write the points of distinction between members' and creditors' voluntary winding up of a company?
29. Write short notes on:
    (a) Defunct companies.
    (b) Winding up of unregistered companies.
    (c) Contributory.
30. Enumerate the consequences of winding up regarding various parties.
31. Who is an official liquidator? What are his powers and duties?
32. Discuss the powers and duties of voluntary liquidator.

◈◈◈